ARIZONA

LANDLORD'S

DESKBOOK

(Third Edition)

CONSUMER LAW BOOKS PUBLISHING HOUSE

ACKNOWLEDGMENTS

For her assistance with editing, my gratitude to:

Tami Lynn Casler

DEDICATED to the memory of James E. Casler, Jr.

Casler, Carlton C., 1958

Arizona Landlord's Deskbook / Carlton C. Casler -- 3rd ed.
p. cm.
Includes bibliographical references and index.
ISBN 1-881436-05-5

1. Landlord and tenant -- Arizona.   I. Title.

KFA2517.Z9C37 1998   346.791'043'4
                                      QBI98-11612

P-CIP

C.C. Casler, *ARIZONA LANDLORD'S DESKBOOK* (3rd ed. 1998)
COPYRIGHT © 1998 by Carlton C. Casler
All rights reserved.
Printed in the United States of America.
ISBN 1-881436-05-5

CONSUMER LAW BOOKS PUBLISHING HOUSE
c/o Golden West Publishers
4113 North Longview
Phoenix, Arizona 85014

Mailing address:
CONSUMER LAW BOOKS PUBLISHING HOUSE
P.O. Box 16146
Phoenix, Arizona 85011
(602) 255-0101
1-800-229-7686 (24 hour order line)

CONTENTS AT A GLANCE

TABLE OF CONTENTS

CHAPTER

2. (continued)

QUICK REFERENCE SECTION   215

I. QUESTIONS AND ANSWERS

APPENDICES

Foreword

My sincerest thanks to the many loyal readers of the first and second editions of the Arizona Landlord's Deskbook. Without your support, a third edition would not be possible or necessary.

Arizona law clearly favors tenants, not landlords. I am a landlord – just like you. You and I, as landlords, have a common bond; our interests are in complete alignment. I have written the Arizona Landlord's Deskbook from a landlord's point of view. What that means to you is that the recommendations contained herein are intended to (and do) protect and benefit the landlord, not the tenant. After all, it's **us** against **them**. Knowledge of the information revealed in this book and implementation of the practices and procedures recommended in this book will give you, the landlord, a distinct advantage. Most important, however, the Arizona Landlord's Deskbook will help you own and/or manage rental property profitably, with a minimum of problems, yet remain well within the bounds of the law.

This book will tell you the law in Arizona as it applies to landlords and tenants. It will tell you what you can do under the law and, more importantly, what you *cannot* do under the law. But the Arizona Landlord's Deskbook goes far beyond a mindless narration of Arizona law. I recognize, as do you, that being a landlord is a business. As a businessman, I understand that the law is only one element that a businessman will consider when making a business decision. Therefore, in addition to the law, this book will discuss some vitally important practical considerations that yield desirable results. By way of illustration, consider the practical approach to a "Real World" dilemma (Prologue).

This is the Third Edition of the Arizona Landlord's Deskbook. Changes in the law and, especially, comments and requests from readers have prompted a new and revised edition of the Arizona Landlord's Deskbook. For the first time, this Third Edition of the Arizona Landlord's Deskbook includes a chapter dedicated exclusively to commercial landlord/tenant law.

My goal, when writing this book, was to provide practical and useful answers for the day-to-day problems that confront landlords. Toward that end, this edition includes step-by-step instructions on how to evict a tenant, what notices to send and when, how to fill out the forms, how to appeal if you lose, how to collect your judgment, and, most important, how to avoid litigation in the first place. Your continued comments, suggestions, requests, etc., are appreciated and encouraged – they let me know you are using this book and help me to make subsequent editions more useful for you and others. *See* Chapter 1, Section F, for information about submitting comments, suggestions, etc.

PROLOGUE

Practical Approach to a "Real World" Dilemma

Most books and legal guides tell you what you can/cannot do under the law. That is all well and good, but a mere recitation of the law does not explain how to apply the law to the facts of the problem <u>you</u> have <u>right now</u>. What most landlords want is a quick, inexpensive and practical answer to their immediate problem. This book was written with those landlords in mind and with an eye toward "real world" problems that *actually happen* every day.

Consider this "hypothetical" situation. Your residential tenant tells you that he has just lost his job, his car has broken down and he has one dollar to his name. Assume that his rent is paid through the end of the month (one week away). The only thing hypothetical about this situation is the part about him voluntarily telling you this information <u>before</u> his rent is overdue. As we both know, tenants never volunteer any information. In truth, this is a very common "real world" scenario. Question - How do you handle this all too common occurrence? Answer - There are two possible solutions: (1) *the legal solution* and (2) *the practical solution*.

- **<u>The Legal Solution</u>:**   Give the appropriate notices and evict him when he fails to pay next month's rent.

How long will this really take? You can't give him a notice to vacate until his rent is overdue; rent is not yet overdue. Rent will again be due on the first of the month, but, let's face it, most rental agreements provide that rent is not delinquent until after the fifth of the month (what does your rental agreement say?). And most landlords won't do anything until rent is delinquent. In truth, even if your rental agreement provides rent is delinquent after the fifth of the month, rent is overdue (i.e., "unpaid and due")[1] on the second day of the month, and you may begin the eviction process on that day. As a practical matter, however, most landlords won't start the process until the sixth day of the month. Early on the day of the sixth, you give him a ***Five-Day Notice to Pay or Quit***. Five days later (<u>calendar days</u>),[2] not counting the day you served him with the Five-Day Notice, is the eleventh day of the month. On the twelfth day of the month you file your forcible detainer action (actually called a "Special Detainer" action). The justice court (most Special Detainer actions are filed in justice court) gives you a court date not less than three days nor more than six days away (not including the day you file the action), which will inevitably include a weekend and possibly a holiday, which also are not counted. That gives you a court date on approximately the eighteenth day of the month. You go to court on the eighteenth and receive a judgment for possession and past due rent. The ***Writ of***

---

1 ARIZ. REV. STAT. ANN. § 33-1368(B) (West Supp. 1998). Arizona Revised Statutes Annotated is properly cited as: ARIZ. REV. STAT. ANN. § ##-#### (West 19xx), where "##-####" is the specific statute title and section number, but for brevity is cited herein as ***A.R.S.*** § ##-#### (§ is a symbol that means Section); *see* Chapter 1, Section D, regarding other conventions used throughout this book.

2 A.R.S. § 33-1368(E) (West Supp. 1998).

Restitution, which grants you the right of possession of the premises, however, will not be issued until (you guessed it) another five calendar days has elapsed.[3] You get your Writ of Restitution on the twenty-fourth. You immediately pay the necessary fee to the Sheriff or constable to go out and "forcibly" evict him. It is your lucky day and the constable gets around to serving him with the Writ the very next day (if you haven't already guessed, this is an unlikely occurrence). It is now the twenty-fifth. But wait, the constable has learned through experience that once a tenant sees him at the door, s/he will pack-up and leave. So the constable goes to the door, the tenant sees him and "swears" that he will be out tonight. The constable will probably give the tenant twenty-four hours to get out before actually executing the Writ. The next day the tenant is either gone or the constable forcibly removes him. It is now the twenty-sixth day of the month. You are out nearly a month's rent, plus whatever time it takes to make repairs and get the unit ready for the next tenant. In addition, you are out the cost of filing the Special Detainer action, the fee paid to the constable and any administrative and legal fees. Incidentally, you have made the last thirty days very unpleasant for this tenant; in return, you may anticipate that the amount of repairs that have become necessary during the last thirty days will probably exceed "normal wear and tear."

> ● **The Practical Solution**:　　　Pay him to leave.

Remember, he is paid up through the end of the month. Tell the tenant that if he is out at the end of <u>this</u> month and the unit is reasonably clean, you will refund all his deposits (or, if he has no deposits, that you will give him some amount of money, i.e., $100, $200, etc.). "Heresy," you exclaim! You are offended by the mere notion of paying this deadbeat to get out. Remember, this is business. Take the course of least resistance and the one that is most economical in terms of <u>your time</u> (which I presume is worth something) and your <u>money</u> (don't forget the court costs, process server, constable's fee, etc.). Compare the two solutions:

- The legal solution gives you possession of the premises twenty-six days later (maybe), a judgment against a deadbeat, the wonderful opportunity to spend <u>lots</u> of time with those incredibly *fast, efficient and courteous* people down at the courthouse and a month of headaches.

- The practical solution, on the other hand, gives you possession of the premises on the first day of the month; with luck, the unit is even clean. In any event, the deadbeat is gone and you can immediately put in a paying tenant.

The decision is yours, <u>as it should be</u>. I will endeavor to give you guidance as to what you may or must do under the law. But, I will also tell you about other options available to you (which are also in accordance with the law) that I have learned through time, practice and experience, that usually produce the best result. Nevertheless, you, as the landlord, must make the ultimate decision.

---

3 A.R.S. § 12-1178(C) (West 1994).

CHAPTER 1

PRELIMINARY MATTERS

> **Summary of Chapter**
>
> - How to get the most benefit from this book
> - What this book covers
> - What this book does not cover
> - Conventions
> - Caveat from the author and publisher
> - Comments and Suggestions; Errors

A. HOW TO GET THE MOST BENEFIT FROM THIS BOOK.

First, go back and briefly scan the table of contents. Get a feel for the topics covered and the general layout of the book. Next, peruse the Quick Reference Section, in the back part of the book. The Quick Reference Section is divided into two parts: (I) Questions and (short) Answers and (II) Procedures. Part I is specifically designed to concisely answer the most frequently asked questions. In the event the answer given in this Section is insufficient (i.e., not clear, not exactly applicable to your situation), the Quick Reference Section directs you to the section of the book that deals with that subject in more depth. Part II provides step-by-step instructions for the most frequently encountered legal procedures. After reviewing the Quick Reference Section, return to the front of the book. Chapters Two through Six provide information about how to prepare your business and rental units, how to attract and manage tenants, and how to terminate tenants. Pay particular attention to Chapter 2, Section D, which will help you to review your rental agreement form. The rental agreement form is the single most important document that you will use as a landlord. Chapter 7 is exclusively for commercial landlords.

An extensive index is included in the back of the book which will refer you to both the Quick Reference Section and the section of the book that addresses the topic you are looking for. For example, say you want information on what to include in the Five-Day Notice to Pay or Quit. You may look under Pay or Quit, Five-Day Notice, 5-Day Notice, or Notice. In the event you run into a word or phrase that is unfamiliar, a glossary of terms is included at the back of the book. Important words are **_highlighted_** (like this -- bold and italics) the first time they are used and the first time the word is discussed at length. All highlighted words, plus others, are found in the glossary.

Consult Checklist Number 2, in Appendix A. This Checklist encourages you to review your existing rental agreement and other forms (or create them). This Checklist prompts you to take other action which is absolutely vital -- READ IT ! Finally, but most important, implement what you have learned and keep the Arizona Landlord's Deskbook handy.

B. WHAT THIS BOOK COVERS.

The Table of Contents reveals the precise areas covered by the Arizona Landlord's Deskbook. The main focus, however, in addition to informing you of the various laws that you must know, is to provide you with sound, _practical_ suggestions. After all, being a landlord is a business and, in business, the law is only one factor to be considered when making a decision. Toward that end, I will endeavor to provide you with practical suggestions in the areas of: screening applicants, preparing your forms, conducting your business, managing tenants, and perhaps most important: dealing with problem tenants, handling an eviction, getting a **_judgment_** and collecting on your judgment.

C. WHAT THIS BOOK _DOES NOT_ COVER.

"**Valuation of rental property**" and "**How to purchase rental property**." I have not included sections on how to value or purchase rental property for several reasons. First, this book assumes that you already own or manage rental units and are now concerned with managing the property to its fullest financial potential, but with a minimum of problems. Second, the space required to adequately cover valuation and/or purchase of rental property is sufficient to fill an entire separate volume. Which brings me to the third and last reason: a proliferation of books have already been written in those areas and are readily available.

Asset protection. **_Asset protection_** prevents creditors, including **_judgment creditors_** (a judgment creditor is someone who has taken you to court and been awarded a judgment against you by a court of law), from taking your property (i.e., real estate, bank accounts, personal property). *I consider asset protection to be vitally important* (*see* Chapter 2, Section B, for a graphic example). Nevertheless, I did not include a section on asset protection in the <u>Arizona Landlord's Deskbook</u> because the best way to protect *your* assets will depend on *your* circumstances. Asset protection is actually a plan or a strategy, if you will, that protects some, most or all of your assets from creditors. Consequently, nothing I say and nothing contained in any other book or publication will apply to everyone. The only way to design an asset protection plan is by consulting <u>personally</u> with an attorney. Moreover, the only way to implement an asset protection plan properly is with the assistance of an attorney who is skilled in asset protection. Therefore, rather than attempt to include a section about asset protection, that would have absolutely no practical value, I have opted instead to convey to you these messages: (1) asset protection is vitally important; and (2) consult an attorney immediately so that s/he can discuss a plan that is best for you.

D. <u>CONVENTIONS.</u>

The <u>Arizona Landlord's Deskbook</u> has been divided into two main sections: the Quick Reference Section, at the back of the book, and the main body of the book, consisting of seven chapters. Both sections employ the following conventions and type styles.

> - Footnotes[4]
> - Citations to statutes and cases
> - **Bold lettering**
> - <u>Underlined text</u>
> - *Italics*
> - ***Bold and italicized words***
> - Indented text (indented from left and right margin)
> - [bracketed text]
> - Ellipses (...)

● <u>Footnotes</u> and <u>citations to statutes and cases</u>. Footnotes are comments made at the bottom of the page.[4] The <u>Arizona Landlord's Deskbook</u> employs the use of footnotes to provide **citations**. Citations direct "lawyer types" to specific statutes and cases. For example, suppose the text says:

> The landlord must give the tenant five (5) days notice to pay or quit, prior to filing a Special Detainer action.[5]

---

4 This is a footnote.

5 *See* A.R.S. § 33-1368(B) (West Supp. 1998).

The superscript (raised) number 5, at the end of the above printed sentence, refers to the footnote at the bottom of page three. The footnote provides the legal authority (i.e., source) for the proposition that is cited. In this instance, the requirement that the landlord must give the tenant five days notice to pay or quit comes from Section 33-1368, subparagraph B, of the Arizona Revised Statutes Annotated.[6] A citation may also refer to the name of a specific case. For example, suppose the text says:

> The filing of a civil action against a tenant does not satisfy the statutory requirement that the landlord must give the tenant written notice of the amounts withheld from his security deposit within fourteen (14) days after termination of tenancy.[7]

In this instance, the requirement that the landlord must give the tenant written notice of the amounts withheld from his deposit within fourteen days after termination of tenancy comes from a *statute*,[8] but the principle that the filing of a civil lawsuit against the tenant does not satisfy the "written notice" requirement of the statute, comes from an actual lawsuit (or *case*) named Schaefer v. Murphey (the "v." stands for versus). A case is actually the written decision of a court of law about a particular lawsuit which sets forth the facts of that particular case and then (normally) gives the reasons why the judge ruled the way that s/he did. Assuming the case is well reasoned, judges hearing subsequent cases, that have similar facts, may regard the previous case as setting a *precedent* and may rule the same way. In footnote seven, the numbers - 131 Ariz. 295 - are called a *cite* or *citation*. This cite tells us that the judge's written opinion of this case may be found on page 295, of volume 131, of the *Arizona Reports*. Arizona Reports is a legal publication that contains written opinions of the Arizona courts. The other cite - 640 P.2d 857 - indicates that this opinion may also be found on page 857, of volume 640, of the *Pacific Reporter, Second Series*. The Pacific Reporter is a legal publication that contains written opinions of courts from Alaska, Arizona, California, Colorado, Hawaii, Idaho, Kansas, Montana, Nevada, New Mexico, Oklahoma, Oregon, Utah, Washington and Wyoming. The number in parenthesis - (1982) - denotes the year that the case was decided. The Arizona Reports and the Pacific Reporter may be found at a library that carries legal reference material.

It is not necessary that you seek out and read these other publications or the cases. The citations are provided merely so that those individuals who wish

---

6 Arizona Revised Statutes Annotated is properly cited as: Ariz. Rev. Stat. Ann. § ##-####, where "##-####" is the specific statute title and section number, but for brevity is cited herein as *A.R.S.* § ##-#### (§ is a symbol that means Section).

7 Schaefer v. Murphey, 131 Ariz. 295, 297, 640 P.2d 857, 859 (1982).

8 *See* A.R.S. § 33-1321(C) (West Supp. 1998).

additional information will know where to look. If you <u>do</u> wish to look-up these other publications, then take this book to a law library and ask the librarian to assist you in locating the cited publications.

- **Bold lettering**, <u>underlined text</u> and *italics*.

All three of these type styles are used to emphasize a particular word, phrase or sentence. Case names in the footnotes are also underlined (see footnote 7).

- ***Bold and italicized words***.

Words or phrases that are defined in the Glossary (in the back of this book) appear in bold and italicized print the first time they are used and the first time the word is discussed. Thereafter, they appear in normal print.

- Indented text, [bracketed text] and ellipses (...).

Occasionally, the exact text of a statute or case will be quoted. Text indented from both the left and right margin, as seen below, alerts you that this language is reprinted <u>exactly</u> (i.e., word-for-word) as it appears in the statute or case cited. The citation for the material reprinted in this manner may be found in the footnote at the end of the quote. For example:

> **D.** Upon termination of the tenancy, property or money held by the landlord as prepaid rent and security may be applied to the payment of all rent subject to a landlord's duty to mitigate, all charges as specified in the signed lease agreement, or as provided in this chapter, including the amount of damages which the landlord has suffered by reason of the tenant's noncompliance with § 33-1341 [tenant's obligations for maintaining the dwelling unit]. Within fourteen [business] days, excluding Saturdays, Sundays or other legal holidays, after termination of the tenancy and delivery of possession and demand by the tenant the landlord shall provide the tenant with an itemized list of all deductions together with the amount due and payable to the tenant, if any. Unless other arrangements are made in writing by the tenant, the landlord shall mail, by regular mail, to the tenant's last known place of residence.

E. If the landlord fails to comply with subsection D of this section the tenant may recover the property and money due the tenant together with damages in the amount equal to twice the amount wrongfully withheld.

. . . .

G. The holder of the landlord's interest in the premises at the time of the termination of the tenancy is bound by this section.[9]

You will note in the material quoted above that some text appears in brackets (i.e., [ ]). This means that the text inside the brackets <u>does not</u> actually appear in the material cited, but is included in this book for your benefit. For example, the caption for § 33-1341 is "Tenant to maintain dwelling unit." Therefore, although this information is <u>not</u> included in the text of the statute, it is included in the <u>Arizona Landlord's Deskbook</u> in brackets so that you will have a general idea what topic § 33-1341 addresses. Similarly, Section 33-1321, quoted above, later states that you have fourteen days to deliver a notice to the tenant. Although the statute states that Saturdays, Sundays and legal holidays are to be excluded, the word "business" is included in brackets (i.e., [business]) to clarify that the landlord has fourteen *business* days to provide an itemized statement to the tenant, but the phrase "business days" does not actually appear in the language of the statute.

The appearance of three periods, called an ellipsis (i.e., ...), mean that some words in a sentence have been omitted. Normally this is done to make the text easier to read by filtering out portions of the sentence that do not apply. For example, if a particular discussion assumes that the landlord <u>never</u> accepts property as security, the statute (previously quoted) would then appear as:

Upon termination of the tenancy, ... money held by the landlord ... may be applied ....[10]

This example demonstrates that an ellipsis may also indicate that the sentence continues. Similarly, the appearance of four periods, standing alone (i.e., ...), tell you that there are sentences or paragraphs to this statute that have not been reprinted here. For instance, in the example (above) Section 33-1321 also contains subparagraphs E and F, but those two paragraphs were not reprinted above.

---

9   A.R.S. § 33-1321(C), (D), (F) (West Supp. 1998).

10   A.R.S. § 33-1321(C) (West Supp. 1998).

E.   CAVEAT FROM THE AUTHOR AND PUBLISHER.

The Arizona Landlord's Deskbook covers a wide range of laws and rules affecting the residential landlord and tenant relationship in Arizona, but it is not an exhaustive synopsis of all laws, rules and regulations that impact upon such matters. Moreover, because a plethora of differing factual scenarios are possible for each individual landlord, the author and publisher cannot and do not assume any responsibility for conclusions drawn by the reader or for the conduct, acts or omissions of the reader or others taken in reliance hereon.

The author and publisher recommend that you consult with your attorney to obtain competent legal advice with regard to your own particular circumstances. In any instance where you have some doubt regarding application of the law to your specific circumstances, consult your attorney. If you don't have an attorney – get one! If you are at a loss as to how to find an attorney, talk to other landlords or call the Arizona State Bar; the phone number for lawyer referral is (602) 257-4434.

The author, Carlton C. Casler, is a practicing Arizona attorney and represents landlords. For preparation (creating or revising) of rental agreements and other forms and general advice, Mr. Casler can represent landlords who own and rent property anywhere in the state of Arizona, even if they live in another state or country. For other legal services, Mr. Casler may be able to provide you with full or limited representation, depending on your location and the nature of the services required. Mr. Casler's business and home phone number may be obtained from directory assistance (Mr. Casler lives and works in Phoenix).

F.   COMMENTS AND SUGGESTIONS; ERRORS.

Every effort has been made to ensure that the Arizona Landlord's Deskbook provides useful, practical and accurate information. Any comments and suggestions you care to make that will improve the usefulness of the Arizona Landlord's Deskbook will be appreciated. Specific examples include: suggestions regarding the layout of the book that may be more logical and/or would make particular topics easier to find, or suggestions regarding sections and/or particular situations that you feel would be of benefit to most readers. In short, any comment and suggestion that you care to make that you believe will improve future editions of the Arizona Landlord's Deskbook will be appreciated. Likewise, in the event that you detect an error in the substantive law provided herein, application of the law to the facts given in one of the hypothetical situations, or even a clerical error (grammatical or typographical), please notify me directly so that I may correct the problem immediately or in the next edition, as the urgency of the correction warrants. Please send comments, suggestions and notice of error(s) to:

Consumer Law Books Publishing House
Post Office Box 16146
Phoenix, Arizona 85011-6146

CHAPTER 2

PREPARATION

Summary of Chapter

- General guidelines for doing business
- Legal advice to landlords
- Applicability/scope of the Arizona Residential
  Landlord and Tenant Act
- Review/create your rental agreement
    - Rental Agreement MUST's
    - Rental Agreement SHOULD's
    - Rental Agreement CANNOT's
    - Deposits
- Prepare your other forms
    - Tenant Application
    - Tenant Information Sheet
    - Property Inspection Checklist
    - Personal Property Inspection Checklist
    - Notice to Terminate Tenancy
    - Disposition of Deposits
    - Five-Day Notice to Pay or Quit
    - Complaint Form
    - Parking Violation
    - Miscellaneous Notices
    - Federal Debt Collection Practices Act Notices

A.   GENERAL GUIDELINES FOR DOING BUSINESS.

The following guidelines do not apply exclusively to being a landlord. They are equally applicable to all types of businesses and, in fact, life in general. In any event, adherence to these guidelines will prevent most landlord/tenant problems from occurring in the first place. *Preventing a problem is always better than the cleverest of solutions to a problem.*

1. Be honest. It is vitally important that your audience (i.e., applicants and tenants) believe you. I am not cautioning you against outright falsehoods (which goes without saying), I am warning you against the hazards of "hedging." People tend to hedge when they do not know the answer or when the answer is something they do not think the listener wants to hear. Consequently, when the truth is finally revealed and it turns out to be something other than what you have stated, you lose credibility. The solution is simple. If you don't know – say so. If you are not sure – find out the correct answer and get back to them. If the answer is something you think they do not want to hear -- tell them anyway. In short, say what you mean; mean what you say.

2. Be straightforward. In reality, this is just another way of saying "be honest." This guideline lends itself better to illustration than to definition. For example, many landlords will give prospective tenants an opportunity to take the rental agreement form home with them so that they may read it at their leisure. I prefer to sit down with the applicants and read it to them. Yes, read it to them. I do not want them to be surprised by any term or condition contained in the rental agreement after they have already moved in. You may think that reading the rental agreement to them takes too much time. I assure you that you will be able to read any rental agreement to them in a shorter period of time than it will take to evict them or to defend the terms of your rental agreement in court. I have never had tenants tell me that they did not have time for me to go over the entire rental agreement with them.

3. Keep it simple. By this, I mean keep everything simple. Naturally, I am not suggesting that you sacrifice any of your rights for the sake of simplicity, merely that you should avoid using "too many" forms and/or forms that are "too long." Keep the number of forms that they must fill out (and that you have to keep track of) to a minimum. Keep the sentences used in your rental agreement and other forms, short and simple to understand. Clearly define your tenants' obligations in the rental agreement and in any supplementary ***rules and regulations*** that you have established for your tenants. Similarly, clearly define your obligations and policies. Tell them what you will do, tell them when you will do it, and do it.

4. Be businesslike. Organize your business. Most tenants find an unorganized landlord very unsettling because it makes them wonder if their rent is being properly credited to their account and/or whether the premises are properly and safely maintained. As a landlord, you must be reliable and methodical. When repairs are necessary -- make them. When rents are due – collect them. When payments arrive late – assess and collect late charges. Inconsistency in assessing and collecting late charges will encourage the tenant to be late again next month and when word gets out (and it will), it will encourage others to be late. Furthermore, if your inconsistent enforcement of policies, rules and regulations is revealed in court, said policy, rule or regulation is likely to be declared unenforceable because you have established a habit of "selective enforcement."[11]

5. Be authoritative. Know your policies and enforce them rigidly and uniformly. Know your rights under the Arizona Residential Landlord and Tenant Act (or at least act like you do) and, perhaps even more important, know your tenants' rights. The entire Arizona Residential Landlord and Tenant Act[12] is reprinted in the back of this book at Appendix C -- READ IT. You should also be familiar with the Landlord and Tenant statutes[13] and Forcible Entry and Detainer statutes,[14] which are also reprinted in the back of this book at Appendix C.

6. Stay up-to-date. The face of the law is ever changing. You've heard it before, "Ignorance of the law is no excuse." This is quite true and may also be stated as, "Ignorance of changes in the law is no excuse." In few places will this be more applicable than in the context of landlord (i.e., Goliath) versus tenant (i.e., David). Of course, I am not suggesting that judges favor tenants over landlords -- that would not be "fair." And we all know that our judicial system is a model of fairness. The moral -- you are a landlord; make a point of keeping abreast of changes in the law that impact on your position as a landlord.

7. Err conservatively. This will probably be the hardest guideline for many people to follow, but it is certainly one of the most important. What do I mean by "err conservatively?" In the case of evaluating tenant applications, it means rejecting "borderline" applications. Toward that end, I submit that screening out borderline applicants as being unacceptable is the cheapest eviction you will ever do.

Enough general guidelines. Let's get down to the nuts and bolts of being an effective landlord.

Summary of Guidelines for Doing Business
- Be honest
- Be straightforward
- Keep it simple
- Be businesslike
- Be authoritative
- Stay up-to-date
- Err conservatively

---

11   *See, e.g.,* Unif. Residential Landlord And Tenant Act § 3.102, 7B U.L.A. 475 (1985).

12   A.R.S. §§ 33-1301 to -1381 (West 1990 & Supp. 1998).

13   A.R.S. §§ 33-301 to -381 (West 1990).

14   A.R.S. §§ 12-1171 to -1183 (West 1994 & Supp. 1998).

B.   LEGAL ADVICE TO LANDLORDS.

At the beginning of this book I told you that this book does not and is not intended to take the place of individualized legal counsel with an attorney. Nevertheless, right here and right now, I am going to give you the best legal advice you will ever receive as a landlord. *The most valuable legal advice that you will ever receive is that advice which helps you prevent and/or avoid legal problems and **litigation*** (actual court proceedings). Litigation is expensive, stressful, and no one ever truly "wins." No one, except, of course, the lawyers. I know this -- I am a lawyer. I see the same scenario repeated day after day: plaintiffs (i.e., landlords) with valid claims, spend time and money in pursuit of a judgment that is usually uncollectible or they are forced to accept pennies on the dollar for their claim (i.e., bankruptcy of a tenant). When I tell you to avoid litigation at all costs, I mean it. Granted, I may be doing a horrible disservice to my fellow members of the Bar, who may be quick to accept your retainer and champion your cause, but your fellow landlords, who have already traveled the path of litigation, will tell you that I speak the truth. Therefore, I will give you several pieces of legal advice that will help you avoid legal problems and litigation; the first three are the most important.

The first piece of legal advice is -- **Get a lawyer**. You need not retain him/her on a continual basis. Just make sure that you have someone to call when you run into trouble or, better yet, *before* you get into trouble.

The second piece of legal advice is -- **Get the right lawyer**. For residential landlords, make sure your lawyer is conversant with the Arizona Residential Landlord and Tenant Act.[15] For commercial landlords, make sure your lawyer is conversant with the landlord and tenant statutes.[16] The attorney who got you a zillion dollars for that personal injury lawsuit and who is otherwise a very competent attorney, may not know the first thing about landlord/tenant law. The same goes for tax attorneys, estate planners, etc.

The third piece of legal advice is -- **Have your lawyer prepare (or revise) your rental agreement and other forms**. Money spent in advance on your rental agreement is money *very* well spent. An ineffective rental agreement (or other necessary form) can cause more problems than you can imagine. Moreover, the cost to resolve these problems may cost you many times the attorney's fee that you "saved" by drafting your own rental agreement or using the standard form from the stationery store. I have seen a great number of "standard forms" from various office supply and stationery stores. Because of the 1995 changes to the Arizona

---

15   A.R.S. §§ 33-1301 to -1381 (West 1990 & Supp. 1998).

16   A.R.S. §§ 33-301 to -381 (West 1990).

Residential Landlord and Tenant Act, none of the forms I have seen are in compliance with the law. A word to the wise — have your attorney review your rental agreement form.

Let me anticipate the next rebuke. "I've been using this rental agreement for the past millennia, and I have never had any problem." My response, "Has your rental agreement ever been challenged in a court of law?" The answer is usually no. Remember, a rental agreement is only important if there is a disagreement. If there is no disagreement, then, of course, there is no problem. In such a case, an oral rental agreement would suffice. Back in the real world, however, disagreements are common-place. Consequently, I never, never, never recommend an oral rental agreement.

I can hear you already, "Big deal, some legal advice, get a lawyer, hire a lawyer, pay a lawyer, etc." *You have not been listening.* The best legal advice that you will ever receive as a landlord is that advice which <u>prevents</u> legal problems and litigation. Sound business advice and skillfully drafted documents will prevent most legal problems and litigation from ever occurring -- they are worth their weight in gold. If you put this book down right now and never read another page, but adhere to these three pieces of advice, you will save yourself many times the cost of this book, not to mention the time and aggravation of defending (or prosecuting) a lawsuit.

Incidently, you may be interested to know that loan companies and mortgage companies go crazy when they discover that a lawsuit has been filed against you. Remember that "dream house" or fancy car that you have been lusting after and that you have just decided to buy? Well forget it; at least until the lawsuit against you has been finally resolved. Oh sure, you will tell the loan or mortgage company that the lawsuit filed against you is completely baseless, was filed by a vindictive tenant merely to get back at you for evicting him, that he has no chance of winning and that even if he does win it will be for a nominal amount. With regard to this lawsuit, the law may even be on your side. No matter. The loan or mortgage company can only see a lawsuit. And more times than not, the tenant won't even specify the exact amount for which he is suing you. The loan or mortgage company translates this into "unlimited" liability. Sound silly? It is silly. But that is not an argument that will bring the loan or mortgage company around to your point of view. The good news is that you *probably* will be able to get the loan anyway, but not without a few headaches and a mountain of additional paperwork. And it is possible that your loan will be rejected merely because of this lawsuit. This is the wrong time to realize that preventing litigation is far better than winning litigation.

The next piece of legal advice that I must give you is to tell you that you probably need an **asset protection** plan. Asset protection prevents creditors, including **judgment creditors** (a judgment creditor is someone who has taken you to court and been awarded a judgment against you by a court of law) from taking your property (i.e., real estate, bank accounts, personal property, etc.). An asset protection plan, to be effective, must be constructed <u>and</u> implemented by an attorney who is skilled in asset protection.

As previously stated (*see* Chapter 1, Section C), I do not attempt to cover asset protection in the <u>Arizona Landlord's Deskbook</u>. Nevertheless, I would be remiss if I did not briefly discuss its significance. Do not think, however, that because I do not devote an entire chapter to this subject that it is unimportant. Nothing could be farther from the truth. I intentionally do not deal with the subject at length because asset protection must be done one-on-one between you and an attorney. Nothing I say and nothing contained in any other book or publication will apply to everyone. Therefore, the advice I wish to convey about asset protection is: (1) it is vitally important, (2) you probably need it, and (3) consult an attorney immediately so that s/he can discuss a plan that is best for you.

There are two levels of asset protection: the first you may be able to do yourself, the second must be done by a lawyer competent in constructing an effective asset protection plan. A simple hypothetical scenario best demonstrates why I think you probably need an asset protection plan and will help to illustrate the two levels of asset protection.

Assume that someday you will be sued for "big bucks" and that you will lose. You may be asking, "How would this occur?" This type of problem is not going to arise out of any lawsuit for past rent. It will probably arise, if at all, from some type of personal injury incurred by one of your tenants or someone else while on your property. Assume it is one of your tenants and that he gets a judgment against you.

The first level of asset protection is insurance. <u>Now</u>, not then, would be a good time to ask yourself, "Do I carry enough liability insurance?"

"What if the tenant gets a judgment against me in excess of my insurance coverage?" Answer - the tenant now gets to satisfy the rest of his judgment by taking <u>your personal assets</u> (actually, he gets a Writ of Execution, whereby the Sheriff seizes your assets and then sells them at a Sheriff's sale; in any event, you lose your ASSets). Your next question, no doubt, is, "Will insurance guarantee that this will never happen to me?" No. Insurance will probably prevent this from happening, but there are no guarantees. Why? Because all policies of insurance have specific maximum loss limitations. If the judgment is for an amount in excess of your coverage, your personal assets are at risk.

"How much coverage should I have?" Only your insurance agent (one you can trust – if you are that fortunate) or your attorney can adequately counsel you on the amount of insurance coverage you need. Make a phone call today, right now, to find out if you have enough coverage.

"Will a zillion dollar insurance liability policy guarantee that this will never happen to me?" No. All policies of insurance exclude certain things from coverage; insurance companies call them **exclusions**. Look at your insurance policy. It will tell you what is covered and what is excluded. You will probably be surprised by the exclusions in *your* policy.

"Are there any other risks that I should be aware of?" Yes; too many to list. For one thing, you might think you are covered for a particular event, but the insurance company may find some way to "weasel" out of covering you (insurance companies don't do that – do they?). Or, through some incredible blunder, your insurance lapses, during which time, of course (never underestimate Murphy's law), the event occurs that is the basis for the lawsuit; a policy with no exclusions and unlimited coverage won't help you if you forget to pay the premium. Or, your premium could get lost in the mail (that never happens, does it?), or your insurance agent might abscond with your premium without issuing you a policy (actually, you might still be covered in that case, but maybe not). Get the point? Lots of things can happen that may leave you "insurance naked."

"So, what am I supposed to do?" I believe in contingency plans; so should you. Enter the second level of asset protection. The second level, to be effective, must be accomplished by an attorney. Asset protection is accomplished by structuring your business practices in such a manner that creditors and judgment creditors (this includes your tenant with the humongous judgment against you) cannot reach all your personal assets. This is accomplished with the use of corporations, limited partnerships, trusts, etc. "Is all this really necessary?" Read on, then you tell me.

Just by way of example, suppose a tenant gets a "large" judgment against you. For purposes of this example, assume that you are a single person with a duplex. You live in one side (owner occupant) and rent out the other side. Your only other major asset is a car and a minimal savings account. You might think that, under these facts, you would not need to spend much time or money on asset protection. Let's see.

Can the judgment creditor (i.e., the tenant) take your duplex? Probably not. In this case, the duplex is also your home and the homestead exemption will protect up to $100,000 of equity.[17] If you have more than $100,000 equity, however, the judgment creditor can force the sale of your home. Granted, you will still get the first $100,000, but you may have had some sentimental attachment to the place. In any event, you are out on the street.

Can he take your car? Maybe. The equity in your car is protected up to a statutory amount of $1,500.00.[18] If you have more equity in the car than that, he can force its sale. You will get the first $1,500; he will get the rest.

Can he get your bank account? Yes. The first $150.00 ($300 for joint accounts) of your bank account is statutorily exempted.[19] He gets everything over $150 (or $300). Sound grim? It gets worse.

Can he get to your wages? Yes. The statutes protect a portion of your wages, but he will get a percentage of your nonexempt wages.[20]

Can he get your rental income? Yes.

You are now faced with filing bankruptcy or working at your job until you pay off the judgment creditor (the tenant). No doubt you are shaking your head and mumbling, "What a disaster." You are right. And remember, this is a very simple example; using a minimum of assets. Now think about your own situation. Have I scared you? I hope so. I would prefer that you send me a mountain of "hate mail" because I scared you into running down and paying your attorney to structure your holdings to provide you with maximum protection and after twenty years as a landlord, you never needed it, rather than have you write a letter to me and tell me that my delivery on this point was not forceful enough, that you ignored my warnings, have just lost your property and may have to file bankruptcy. I also hope that this simple example illustrates just how complex the law is and why you need to consult an attorney to protect your assets.

Without question, the only way to know how to best protect your personal assets is by personally consulting with an attorney who is competent in this field. Okay, now you tell me, "Is all this really necessary?"

---

17 *See* A.R.S. § 33-1101(A) (West 1990).

18 A.R.S. § 33-1125(8) (West 1990).

19 A.R.S. § 33-1126(A)(7) (West Supp. 1998).

20 *See* A.R.S. § 33-1131 (West 1990).

> ### Summary of Legal Advice
>
> - Get a lawyer
> - Get the right lawyer
> - Have your lawyer prepare (or revise)
>   your rental agreement and other forms
> - Be sure you have enough insurance
> - Discuss asset protection with your lawyer

NOTE: The Arizona Landlord's Deskbook does not take the place of individualized legal counsel. You should consult your own attorney for legal advice (*see* Chapter 1, Section E, "Caveat from the author and publisher"). The Arizona Landlord's Deskbook, however, should help you to form your questions and focus them toward specific areas, thereby cutting down on the time you need to spend with your lawyer (God knows how expensive they are). In addition, the Arizona Landlord's Deskbook will help you to **avoid** legal problems, which, as stated, *is the single most valuable advice that a landlord can get anywhere, at any price.* Also, in the event legal action becomes necessary, this book will walk you through the routine procedures and steps, thereby reducing or eliminating your legal expenses. Nevertheless, you should have an attorney that you can call if you run into a problem.

C.   APPLICABILITY/SCOPE OF THE ARIZONA RESIDENTIAL LANDLORD AND TENANT ACT and THE LANDLORD AND TENANT STATUTES.

Before you do anything else, you must first determine what law applies to your situation. Arizona law will *probably* apply, but it may not. On federal land (i.e., Indian reservations), for example, Arizona state law may be **preempted** by federal law. Which means that where state and federal law conflict, federal law will apply. This is one of those instances where, if federal law applied, you would probably know it. The bottom line, however, is that you, as the landlord, should know whether or not your property is subject to the state law or to federal law. If you don't know, ask your attorney. For the vast majority of landlords, however, federal preemption is not a concern, and state law will apply.

Which state law applies? After determining whether state or federal law applies to your rental unit(s), the next thing to do is determine if the *Act* applies to you. Arizona has two separate sets of statutes (i.e., laws) that address landlord/tenant law. As a general rule, if you rent residential dwelling units, the *Act* applies. The Act refers to the Arizona Residential Landlord and Tenant Act. The Act is contained in Chapter 10 of Title 33 of the Arizona Revised Statutes.[21] The Act has been

---

21   A.R.S. §§ 33-1301 to -1381 (West 1990 & Supp. 1998).

reprinted *in its entirety* in Appendix C. If you do not fall within the scope of the Act, the second set of statutes apply.[22] This second set of statutes, known as the Landlord and Tenant Statutes (so as to cause as much confusion as possible), is contained in Chapter 3 of Title 33 of the Arizona Revised Statutes and applies when the Act does not, which is normally (but not exclusively) in the case of commercial rental property. This second set of statutes is also reprinted in Appendix C.

Where does the Act apply? The Act is state law. Consequently, if the Act applies, unless preempted by federal law, it is applicable statewide.[23]

Does application of the Act vary depending on the number of units? No. When the Act does apply, it applies equally to all residential rental property, regardless of size. For example, it applies equally to a duplex and to a 400-unit apartment complex. The apartment complex landlord doesn't have bigger or more complex problems than the duplex landlord, s/he merely has more of them.

Does the Act apply to you? The Act applies to "the rental of dwelling units."[24] To reiterate and to clarify any misunderstanding, there are two separate sets of statutes that address the landlord/tenant relationship in Arizona. The Act applies to almost all residential units (*see **exclusions***, following this discussion). The second set of statutes apply only when the Act does not.[25]

Generally speaking, if you rent a residential dwelling, the Act applies; and generally, the second set of statutes applies to commercial rental property.[26]

"Why," you may ask, "is the issue of whether or not the Act applies important?" I'm so glad you asked. The courts (i.e., judges) tend to favor residential tenants. As if that were not enough, the Act gives residential tenants certain rights they would not otherwise have (i.e., limitation on the amount of security deposit that a landlord may compel a tenant to pay)[27] and takes rights away from the landlord that would otherwise be available (i.e., the Act precludes ***distraint for rent***).[28] In short, the Act is clearly more favorable to tenants than to landlords. This is not news to veteran landlords.

---

22 A.R.S. §§ 33-301 to -381 (West 1990).

23 A.R.S. § 33-1307 (West 1990).

24 A.R.S. § 33-1304 (West 1990).

25 A.R.S. §§ 33-1303, -1304 (West 1990).

26 *See* A.R.S. §§ 33-301 to -381 (West 1990).

27 *See* A.R.S. § 33-1321(A) (West Supp. 1998).

28 A.R.S. § 33-1372(B) (West 1990).

There is another interesting and important distinction between the two sets of statutes. You may elect (by written agreement) to make the Act applicable to rental of nonresidential (i.e., commercial) real property (although I can think of no sane reason for doing such a thing). You <u>cannot</u>, however, elect, by written agreement or otherwise, to make the Act not applicable to the rental of residential property. While you may not agree with this policy, it does make sense. The Act is basically a set of consumer protection laws, designed to protect residential tenants.[29] The legislative intent would be easily frustrated if landlords could merely "elect" for the Act not to apply to them. <u>Bottom line</u> – if you rent residential property, unless you fall within one of the exclusions, the Act applies. The exceptions are best repeated word-for-word from the statute:

Exclusions from application of chapter

Unless created to avoid the application of this chapter [Chapter 10, the Arizona Residential Landlord and Tenant Act], the following arrangements are not covered by this chapter:

1. Residence at an institution, public or private, if incidental to detention or the provision of medical, educational, counseling or religious services.

2. Occupancy under a contract of sale of a dwelling unit or the property of which it is a part, if the occupant is the purchaser or a person who succeeds to his interest.

3. Occupancy by a member of a fraternal or social organization in the portion of a structure operated for the benefit of the organization.

4. Transient occupancy in a hotel, motel or recreational lodging.

5. Occupancy by an employee of a landlord as a manager or custodian whose right to occupancy is conditional upon employment in and about the premises.

---

29 *See, e.g.,* <u>Corrigan v. Janney</u>, 626 P.2d 838 (Mont. 1981) (common law doctrine of caveat emptor (buyer beware) does not apply to rental of residence).

6. Occupancy by an owner of a condominium unit or a holder of a proprietary lease in a cooperative.

7. Occupancy in or operation of public housing as authorized, provided, or conducted under or pursuant to title 36, chapter 12, or under or pursuant to any federal law or regulation.[30]

As you can see (above), other than paragraphs 5 and 7 (discussed next), the exceptions have fairly narrow application.

1.   Exclusion #5 and the case of the on-site manager.

Practically all apartment owners and/or landlords employ an on-site manager whose tenancy in the complex is contingent upon his/her continued employment. An on-site manager, however, should not be confused with a tenant who you pay (or allow to pay a reduced amount of rent) to perform various duties (i.e., maintenance). The distinction is that the on-site manager's tenancy is absolutely contingent upon his/her employment: no employment – no apartment. Whereas, in the second case, if the tenant discontinues to render services, s/he is entitled to continue tenancy, but gives up the right to receive payment (or reduction of rent).

Tenancy for the latter is subject to the Act – you cannot "elect" to have the Act not apply. Tenancy for the former (the on-site manager) need not be controlled by the Act. Nevertheless, most landlords have the manager sign the same rental agreement that the other tenants sign. And, typically, the rental agreement states that it is controlled by the Act, thereby "electing" to have the Act apply to a landlord/tenant relationship that otherwise need not be controlled by the Act. The point being, if for some reason you want the Act to apply to your on-site manager -- fine. But if not, don't "march blindly into the propeller" by using your standard rental agreement.

One last point, the language in the statute (previously quoted), "Unless created to avoid the application of this chapter ... ," means that you cannot have 400 "on-site managers" in your 400-unit complex. Scams engineered to circumvent application of the Act will be looked upon unfavorably by the courts and the courts have the means to punish you for such conduct.

---

30   A.R.S. § 33-1308 (West 1990) (footnote omitted).

Prohibited provisions in rental agreements

A. A rental agreement shall not provide that the tenant does any of the following:

1. Agrees to waive or to forego rights or remedies under this chapter.

. . . .

B. . . . If a landlord deliberately uses a rental agreement containing provisions known by him to be prohibited, the tenant may recover actual damages sustained by him and not more than two months' periodic rent.[31]

2. Exclusion #7 - Public Housing.

Similarly, the Act does not apply to **public housing**,[32] as that term is defined in Chapter 12 of Title 36 of the Arizona Revised Statutes Annotated.

You are probably familiar with a public housing program commonly referred to as **Section 8 Housing**. The Section 8 program is the federal housing assistance program.[33] In addition to the fact that public housing (i.e., the Section 8 program) is specifically exempted from the Act,[34] the Section 8 program is federal law and, therefore, preempts state law. That is not to say, however, that the law applicable to public housing and the Act are *completely* different, but you must be familiar with the distinctions. In short, if you are renting property under some type of public housing program, you must comply with the rules promulgated by that particular agency. Keep in mind that participation in the Section 8 program or other public housing programs is voluntary; you are not required to accept Section 8 or public housing tenants. As a practical matter, at the time you apply to make your property available under a public housing program, the public housing authority (i.e. HUD) will typically give you a copy of the applicable rules. Review them. If they are not acceptable, don't participate in the program.

---

31 A.R.S. § 33-1315 (West 1990).

32 A.R.S. §§ 36-1401 to -1501 (West 1993 & Supp. 1998).

33 *See* Tax Exemption of Obligations of Public Housing Agencies and Related Amendments, 24 C.F.R. §§ 811.101 to -.110 (1997).

34 A.R.S. § 33-1308(7) (West 1990).

D. REVIEW/CREATE YOUR RESIDENTIAL RENTAL AGREEMENT.

Summary of this Section

- Rental Agreement MUST's
- Rental Agreement SHOULD's
- Rental Agreement CANNOT's
- Deposits

A properly drawn rental agreement serves two purposes. First, it prevents litigation by clearly setting forth all the terms and conditions of tenancy. Normally, when a tenant has a grievance and then sees that the rental agreement *that s/he signed* clearly supports the position that the landlord is taking, s/he will mumble a few obscenities and then go away. Second, in the event the tenant does not go away, a well-drafted rental agreement ensures that a court of law will support the position that the landlord has taken. In which case, the tenant will pay court costs, mumble a few obscenities and then go away. In short, a well-drafted rental agreement prevents litigation and ensures success if litigation is inevitable. Few things the landlord does will be this rewarding. CAVEAT: success in litigation will only occur if the rental agreement says what you want it to say. If the rental agreement says "pets are allowed" and you don't want pets, you will lose.

I had originally intended to put a sample rental agreement in this book, but as soon as I contemplated the task of drafting one rental agreement that would suit all, or even most, landlords, the obvious became apparent -- no single rental agreement will work for everyone. Sure, you can buy a dozen different residential lease and/or rental agreement forms from various stationery stores, but the truth is, none of them will fit your circumstances perfectly. A rental agreement is much like an asset protection plan: your lawyer should prepare one *specifically for you*. Consequently, instead of trying to devise a "universal" form, I decided to provide you with a list of rental agreement **must**'s, **should**'s and **cannot**'s. That way, you will be able to start with whatever agreement you presently have and modify it so that it has all of the legally required provisions, does not contain prohibited provisions, and contains all or some of the provisions that I recommend you, as a landlord, include in your rental agreement.

Finally, although perhaps redundant, I have also consolidated and summarized everything you need to know about deposits from the various chapters at the end of this section.

1. Rental Agreement MUST's.

(a) Disclosure of manager and owner or owner's agent.

As discussed below, the Act does not require that the rental agreement be written. Nevertheless, even in the absence of a written rental agreement, the landlord must disclose to the tenant, in writing, at or before the commencement of the tenancy, the name and address of (1) the property manager and (2) the owner or the owner's agent (such agent must be authorized to accept notices, demands, and service of process).[35] Moreover, this information must be kept current and refurnished to the tenant upon request.[36]

(b) Deliver a signed copy of the written rental agreement.

The Act does not require a written rental agreement, but where the rental agreement is written, the landlord must deliver a signed copy of the rental agreement to the tenant within a reasonable time after the agreement is executed or, at the latest, upon move-in.[37]

(c) The written rental agreement must be complete.

All blank spaces on a written rental agreement must be completed. Failure to complete all blank spaces is a material noncompliance by the landlord.[38] This is particularly important when using the generic forms from the local stationery store because they contain a plethora of blank spaces in an attempt to accommodate everyone and to suit every situation. Again, spending some time and money to have your lawyer prepare your rental agreement to your specifications and to suit your particular needs will greatly reduce the number of blank spaces on the form, thereby reducing the chance of leaving one or more spaces blank. The consequence of inadvertently leaving a space blank may be no consequence at all or may mean a completely unenforceable rental agreement, depending on the judge.[39] Bottom line - fill in all the blank spaces.

---

[35] A.R.S. § 33-1322(A) (West Supp. 1998).

[36] A.R.S. § 33-1322(B) (West Supp. 1998).

[37] A.R.S. §§ 33-1322(D), -1321(C) (West Supp. 1998).

[38] A.R.S. § 33-1322(D) (West Supp. 1998).

[39] Section 33-1322(D) of the Arizona Revised Statutes Annotated provides in part: "A written rental agreement shall have all blank spaces completed. Noncompliance with this subsection shall be deemed a material noncompliance by the landlord or the tenant, as the case may be, of the rental agreement."

(d) The purpose of nonrefundable fees/charges must be stated in writing.

The purpose of all nonrefundable fees and charges must be stated in writing.[40] Usually, the logical place to put this information is in the rental agreement. The exception being a nonrefundable application fee, which should be disclosed on the Application Form.

Prior to July 1995, it was sufficient to identify whether a cleaning and/or redecorating deposit was nonrefundable.[41] That will no longer suffice. The exact language of the statute is as follows:

> The *purpose* of all nonrefundable fees or deposits shall be stated in writing by the landlord. Any fee or deposit not designated as nonrefundable shall be refundable.[42]

This language is clear: you must designate nonrefundable fees and deposits as nonrefundable <u>and</u> you must state the *purpose* of the nonrefundable fee or deposit. So what is the purpose of the a nonrefundable cleaning and/or redecorating fee? The answer will vary from property to property. By way of example, consider the following rental agreement provisions, which I have included in my own rental agreement.

> The nonrefundable cleaning fee is for additional cleaning performed by Landlord after Tenant vacates the rental unit, including sanitizing the kitchen and bathrooms, cleaning of window and floor coverings and cleaning/replacement of air-conditioning filters.

> The nonrefundable redecorating fee is for periodic replacement and/or repair of floor and window coverings, decorative items and periodic painting.

> The nonrefundable pet fee is to compensate Landlord for the additional wear and tear on the carpet, floor, drapes, etc., and the additional cleaning required thereto.

> The nonrefundable application fee is used to defray the administrative expense of processing and screening prospective applications.

---

40   A.R.S. § 33-1321(B) (West Supp. 1998).

41   A.R.S. § 33-1321(B) (West 1990) (before 1995 amendment).

42   A.R.S. § 33-1321(B) (West Supp. 1998) (emphasis added).

The nonrefundable re-keying fee is for installing new locks on the rental unit, just prior to the new tenant moving in, and providing the keys to the new tenant, which is intended to prevent entry into the rental unit by unauthorized personnel and for the new tenant's peace of mind.

Naturally, the foregoing are just examples. The language that you include in your rental agreement must accurately reflect the purpose of the nonrefundable fees or deposits that *you* collect.

Two additional points. First, the statute talks about "nonrefundable fees or deposits."[43] Which means that you may refer to a nonrefundable item as a "deposit" or a "fee." For clarity, however, I recommend referring to any nonrefundable item as a "fee" or "charge," rather than a deposit. The word "deposit" normally denotes an amount of money that the tenant is entitled to receive back, if certain conditions are met. A "fee" or "charge" puts the tenant on notice that this amount will not be refunded, under any conditions.

Second, the language of the statute addressing deposits was changed in 1995. Prior to 1995, it referred to "cleaning and redecorating deposits."[44] Now it refers to "all nonrefundable fees or deposits."[45] The change in the language means that the legislature recognizes that there are more nonrefundable fees and deposits than just cleaning and redecorating. For example, you may have a mail box or pool key deposit or a pet owner's fee. Again, the use of the word "fee" or "charge" will alert the tenant that this amount is nonrefundable, whereas the word "deposit" will inform the tenant that s/he must meet certain obligations before this amount will be refunded.

One last item. Remember to tally up all the "deposits" that you collect. The maximum you may collect as "security," however denominated, is an amount equal to one and one-half months rent (in addition to the first month's rent).[46] The Act defines "security" as "money or property given to assure payment or performance under a rental agreement."[47] This will include pet owner deposits (but not nonrefundable pet owner fees), key deposits, cleaning and redecorating deposits (but not nonrefundable cleaning or redecorating fees).

---

43   A.R.S. § 33-1321 (West Supp. 1998).

44   A.R.S. § 33-1321(B) (West 1990) (before 1995 amendment).

45   A.R.S. § 33-1321 (West Supp. 1998).

46   A.R.S. § 33-1321(A) (West Supp. 1998).

47   A.R.S. § 33-1310(14) (West Supp. 1998).

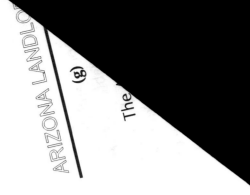

An example may be helpful. Assume rent i$ collect a $1,500 security deposit. You may also cc any reasonable amount, but you may not collect ε amount, because you are already at the one and on Similarly, you may also collect a nonrefundable clea any reasonable amount, but you may not collect a cle of any amount, for the same reason as stated above.

(e)   <u>Rental agreements longer than one</u>

The Act does not require that the rental agreeme   υιner sections of the law, however, provide that contracts that ca   ρerformed within one year must be in writing to be enforceable.[49] Therefore, rental agreements that provide for specific lease periods in excess of one year <u>must</u> be in writing. For example, a lease from January 1, 1998 to December 31, 1998 need not be in writing, but a lease from January 1, 1998, to January 1, 1999 must be in writing to be enforceable. Nevertheless, a month-to-month tenancy need not be in writing even though the tenancy continues for more than one year. For example, you rent an apartment to a tenant on January 1, 1998 on a month-to-month basis. The tenant continues to rent the apartment beyond January 1, 1999. The rental agreement need not be in writing and is enforceable. The reason is because a month-to-month tenancy terminates at the end of each month and is renewed each month, thereby complying with the requirement that the contract *may* be performed within one year.

(f)   <u>Give notice that the Act is available fee</u>.

The Act now requires the landlord to:

> [I]nform the tenant in writing that a free copy of the Arizona Residential Landlord and Tenant Act is available from the Arizona Secretary of State's Office.[50]

The logical place to do this is in the rental agreement. If you do not use a written rental agreement, however, then you must nevertheless provide this notice to the tenant, in writing, at or before commencement of the tenancy.

---

48   *See, e.g.*, A.R.S. § 33-1322(D) (West Supp. 1998).

49   A.R.S. § 44-101(5) (West 1994).

50   A.R.S. § 33-1322(B) (West Supp. 1998).

Give the tenant a move-in inspection form.

Act now requires:

> [W]ith respect to tenants who first occupy the premises or enter into a new written rental agreement after January 1, 1996, upon move-in a landlord shall furnish the tenant with a ... move-in form for specifying any existing damages to the dwelling unit ... .[51]

I recommended the use of a Property Inspection Checklist (Form 3 or 3A, Appendix B) long before it was required by law. Now it is required. Use of a Property Inspection Checklist is simply good business. Landlords *and tenants* often forget that there was a hole in the carpet in the living room, that the kitchen counter already had scratches, and/or that the interior of the unit was completely repainted just before the tenant took possession. A Property Inspection Checklist, or any similar form, ensures that tenants are financially responsible for damage that they cause and *not responsible* for damage that was pre-existing.

(h) Give notice that tenant may be present during the move-out inspection.

The Act now requires:

> [W]ith respect to tenants who first occupy the premises or enter into a new written rental agreement after January 1, 1996, upon move-in a landlord shall furnish the tenant with ... written notification ... that the tenant may be present at the move-out inspection. Upon request by the tenant, the landlord shall notify the tenant when the landlord's move-out inspection will occur.[52]

This does not mean that you must schedule a date/time that is convenient for the tenant; but you may, if you wish. On the other hand, you should not schedule a date/time that is intentionally inconvenient for the tenant. Schedule a date/time that is convenient for you and that is consistent with your prior business practices (i.e., only in the morning, only in the afternoon, only on particular days, etc.), and then provide a notice to your tenant of the date and time.

---

51 A.R.S. § 33-1321(C) (West Supp. 1998).

52 A.R.S. § 33-1321(C) (West Supp. 1998).

As an exception to the rule (above), you are not required to notify and/or conduct a move-out inspection with the tenant present if you are evicting this tenant for a material and irreparable breach *and* you have reasonable cause to fear violence or intimidation on the part of the tenant.[53]

(i) <u>Give the tenant a pool safety notice</u>.

The law now requires landlords of pool properties to give their tenant a state approved pool safety notice.

> A person on entering into an agreement to build a swimming pool or contained body of water or sell, rent or lease a dwelling with a swimming pool or contained body of water shall give the buyer, lessee or renter a notice explaining safety education and responsibilities of pool ownership as approved by the department of health services.[54]

Failure to give this notice is a petty offense. More importantly, it may cause the loss of child's life, which will then result in civil liability for the landlord.

When do you need to give the pool safety notice? Whenever you rent a property with a pool or "contained body of water" to a tenant. What is a "contained body of water"? A body of water eighteen inches or more in depth at any point and that is wider than eight feet at any point and is intended for swimming.[55]

Do I need to use this notice if I rent a property that has access to a community pool (i.e., a condominium or townhouse)? Yes, because you are renting a "dwelling unit with a swimming pool or contained body of water," which falls squarely within the language of the statute quoted above. Moreover, with so much at stake (i.e., children's lives), there is no excuse for not doing everything in your power to help prevent a child from drowning. Besides (have you forgotten already?), you are suppose to err conservatively (*see* Chapter 2(A)(7), "Err Conservatively") and avoid litigation (*see* Chapter 2(B) ("Legal Advice to Landlords").

Where do I get this form? Right here. A copy has been provided for you in the Appendix. (*See* Appendix B, Form 20).

---

53   A.R.S. § 33-1321(C) (West Supp. 1998).

54   A.R.S. § 36-1681 (E) (West 1993).

55   A.R.S. § 36-1681(A) (West 1993).

(j)   <u>Give the tenant notice about lead based paint.</u>

Federal law now requires landlords to make disclosure about the presence of lead-based paint and lead-based paint hazards.[56] This section will make compliance with this law easy.

Disclosure is required for "target housing." Target housing includes residential properties built before 1978.[57] If your rental units were built after 1978, no disclosure is necessary. Stop; you are done. Nothing further is required of you (*unless* your property was built after 1978 *and* you **know** that lead-based paint and/or lead-based paint hazards exist on the rental property; if this applies to you, read on). Nevertheless, when I draft a rental agreement, to eliminate any argument that I failed to address this point, I note that the property was built after 1978 and that no lead-based paint and/or lead-based paint hazards exist on the property. The following provision in the rental agreement will suffice.

> The leased premises were built after 1978. No known lead-based paint and/or lead-based hazards exist on the premises.

Of course, this must be true. If the property was built after 1978, but you have knowledge of lead-based paint in the leased premises and/or any lead-based paint hazards existing in or on the leased premises, then you cannot lawfully include this provision in your rental agreement and you must make a different disclosure (see below).

If your property was built before 1978, then you must:

● Disclose the presence of known lead-based paint and/or lead-based paint hazards (a lead-based paint hazard includes lead-based paint that is chipping, cracking or peeling; it also includes dust caused at friction points, such as doors, windows and stairs). The key is that you must disclose your *actual knowledge* of lead-based paint and/or lead-based paint hazards. You are not required to conduct any type of testing. If you know that lead-based paint exists in the property and/or you have had tests conducted by a company competent to perform lead-based paint and lead-based paint hazard testing, then you must disclose this information. Disclosure must occur before the

---

[56]   42 U.S.C. § 4852d (1994); 40 C.F.R. 745 (1997).

[57]   The federal law applies to the sale or lease of residential properties, except: (1) zero-bedroom dwellings, (2) housing for the elderly or disabled (unless occupied by a child under six years of age), (3) property sold at foreclosure, (4) rental property that has no lead-based paint, (5) property leased for 100 days or less, and (6) leased properties for which disclosure has already occurred and no new facts are known.

tenant is obligated under the rental agreement. This requirement can be met if the disclosure is made a part of rental agreement.

● For multiple units, the landlord must disclose unit specific information (i.e., specific to the unit/apartment being rented) and common area information.

● Provide the tenant with a copy of the tests results and/or report.

● Provide the tenant with a federally approved lead-based paint hazard information pamphlet. This pamphlet is available from the Government Printing Office (GPO). You may order copies by calling (202) 512-1800. The GPO stock number for this pamphlet is 055-000-00507-9. Alternatively, the pamphlet has been reproduced in Appendix B. You may make copies and provide your tenant with a copy, thereby satisfying this requirement (but you must provide the tenant with a *complete* copy of the pamphlet, not just part of it; follow the instructions accompanying the pamphlet in Appendix B, immediately following Form 21, the lead-paint disclosure form).

● The rental agreement must include certain specified disclosure language.[58]

So, if disclosure is required, how do I comply with the law? If your property was built before 1978 or you know that lead-based paint and/or lead-based paint hazards exist on the property, then include the following provision in the rental agreement and use Form 21 in Appendix B. This will satisfy the legal requirements.

> The leased premises were built before 1978 and/or known lead-based paint and/or lead-based hazards exist on the premises. See the attached Lead-Based Paint Addendum.

Don't omit these provisions. The civil penalty is up to $10,000 for each violation. Knowingly and willfully violating this law is punishable by up to one year of imprisonment. These penalties are in addition to the penalties under state law.[59]

If you own rental property in certain areas in Phoenix, Arizona, you may be eligible for free lead testing and/or removal. To find out more, call the City of Phoenix, Lead Hazard Control Program, (602) 534-3757.

On the next two pages is the EPA/HUD Fact Sheet, "EPA and HUD Move to Protect Children from Lead-Based Paint Poisoning; Disclosure of Lead-Based Paint Hazards in Housing," EPA-747-F-96-002, March 1996. This Fact Sheet summarizes the governmental concern, the requirements, and the types of properties affected.

---

58 When selling residential property, the seller must provide the buyer with a ten day period during which time the tenant may conduct a risk assessment or inspection for the presence of lead-based paint and/or lead-based paint hazards. The ten day testing period does not apply to lease transactions.

59 *See* A.R.S. §§ 36-1671 to 36-1676 (West 1993).

United States Environmental Protection Agency	Prevention, Pesticides, and Toxic Substances (7404)	EPA-747-F-96-002 March 1996

FACT SHEET

EPA and HUD Move to Protect Children from Lead-Based Paint Poisoning; Disclosure of Lead-Based Paint Hazards in Housing

SUMMARY
The Environmental Protection Agency (EPA) and the Department of Housing and Urban Development (HUD) are announcing efforts to ensure that the public receives the information necessary to prevent lead poisoning in homes that may contain lead-based paint hazards. Beginning this fall, most home buyers and renters will receive known information on lead-based paint and lead-based paint hazards during sales and rentals of housing built before 1978. Buyers and renters will receive specific information on lead-based paint in the housing as well as a Federal pamphlet with practical, low-cost tips on identifying and controlling lead-based paint hazards. Sellers, landlords, and their agents will be responsible for providing this information to the buyer or renter before sale or lease.

LEAD-BASED PAINT IN HOUSING
Approximately three-quarters of the nation's housing stock built before 1978 (approximately 64 million dwellings) contains some lead-based paint. When properly maintained and managed, this paint poses little risk. However, 1.7 million children have blood-lead levels above safe limits, mostly due to exposure to lead-based paint hazards.

EFFECTS OF LEAD POISONING
Lead poisoning can cause permanent damage to the brain and many other organs and causes reduced intelligence and behavioral problems. Lead can also cause abnormal fetal development in pregnant women.

BACKGROUND
To protect families from exposure to lead from paint, dust, and soil, Congress passed the Residential Lead-Based Paint Hazard Reduction Act

of 1992, also known as Title X. Section 1018 of this law directed HUD and EPA to require the disclosure of known information on lead-based paint and lead-based paint hazards before the sale or lease of most housing built before 1978.

WHAT IS REQUIRED
Before ratification of a contract for housing sale or lease:

- Sellers and landlords must disclose known lead-based paint and lead-based paint hazards and provide available reports to buyers or renters.

- Sellers and landlords must give buyers and renters the pamphlet, developed by EPA, HUD, and the Consumer Product Safety Commission (CPSC), titled *Protect Your Family from Lead in Your Home.*

- Home buyers will get a 10-day period to conduct a lead-based paint inspection or risk assessment at their own expense. The rule gives the two parties flexibility to negotiate key terms of the evaluation.

- Sales contracts and leasing agreements must include certain notification and disclosure language.

- Sellers, lessors, and real estate agents share responsibility for ensuring compliance.

WHAT IS NOT REQUIRED

- This rule does not require any testing or removal of lead-based paint by sellers or landlords.

- This rule does not invalidate leasing and sales contracts.

TYPE OF HOUSING COVERED

Most private housing, public housing, Federally owned housing, and housing receiving Federal assistance are affected by this rule.

TYPE OF HOUSING NOT COVERED

- Housing built after 1977 (Congress chose not to cover post-1977 housing because the CPSC banned the use of lead-based paint for residential use in 1978).

- Zero-bedroom units, such as efficiencies, lofts, and dormitories.

- Leases for less than 100 days, such as vacation houses or short-term rentals.

- Housing for the elderly (unless children live there).

- Housing for the handicapped (unless children live there).

- Rental housing that has been inspected by a certified inspector and found to be free of lead-based paint.

- Foreclosure sales.

EFFECTIVE DATES

- For owners of more than 4 dwelling units, the effective date is September 6, 1996.

- For owners of 4 or fewer dwelling units, the effective date is December 6, 1996.

THOSE AFFECTED

The rule will help inform about 9 million renters and 3 million home buyers each year. The estimated cost associated with learning about the requirements, obtaining the pamphlet and other materials, and conducting disclosure activities is about $6 per transaction.

EFFECT ON STATES AND LOCAL GOVERNMENTS

This rule should not impose additional burdens on states since it is a Federally administered and enforced requirement. Some state laws and regulations require the disclosure of lead hazards in housing. The Federal regulations will act as a complement to existing state requirements.

FOR MORE INFORMATION

- For a copy of *Protect Your Family from Lead in Your Home*, the sample disclosure forms, or the rule, call the National Lead Information Clearinghouse (NLIC) at (800) 424–LEAD, or TDD (800) 526–5456 for the hearing impaired. You may also send your request by fax to (202) 659-1192 or by Internet E-mail to ehc@cais.com. Visit the NLIC on the Internet at http://www.nsc.org/nsc/ehc/ehc.html.

- Bulk copies of the pamphlet are available from the Government Printing Office (GPO) at (202) 512-1800. Refer to the complete title or GPO stock number 055-000-00507-9. The price is $26.00 for a pack of 50 copies. Alternatively, persons may reproduce the pamphlet, for use or distribution, if the text and graphics are reproduced in full. Camera-ready copies of the pamphlet are available from the National Lead Information Clearinghouse.

- For specific questions about lead-based paint and lead-based paint hazards, call the National Lead Information Clearinghouse at (800) 424–LEAD, or TDD (800) 526–5456 for the hearing impaired.

- The EPA pamphlet and rule are available electronically and may be accessed through the Internet.
  Electronic Access:
  Gopher: gopher.epa.gov:70/11/Offices/PestPreventToxic/Toxic/lead_pm
  WWW: http://www.epa.gov/docs/lead_pm
  http://www.hud.gov
  Dial up: (919) 558-0335
  FTP: ftp.epa.gov (*To login, type "anonymous." Your password is your Internet E-mail address.*)

2. Rental Agreement SHOULD's.

(a) The rental agreement should be written.

Even if you intend to rent a piece of real estate for one week, the rental agreement should be in writing. Why? I have spoken with many landlords and even some real estate agents who are convinced that doing away with a written document simplifies and uncomplicates their lives. Pardon me if I have my doubts.

It is certainly true that an oral rental agreement is as enforceable as a written rental agreement drafted by the best attorney in the state, if not challenged. If challenged in a court of law, however, an oral rental agreement normally equates to no rental agreement because the tenant's version of "the agreement" will vary greatly from your version of the agreement. In such a case, the judge is forced to decide whether one of the parties is lying or whether both are telling the truth, which, in the latter case, means that there never really was an "agreement" (i.e., a meeting of the minds) and, therefore, the "agreement" cannot be enforced.

Nevertheless, if you insist upon having an oral agreement (an attitude you are likely to change the first time you are forced to go to court) and you and your tenant disagree about something, you do not automatically lose. If the landlord and tenant agree upon the precise language of the particular term in issue, but disagree as to the meaning of the term, then the court will decide the matter because questions regarding the interpretation of contract terms are questions of law, and courts are free to decide questions of law.[60] For example, assume the landlord and the tenant agree that the landlord agreed at the commencement of tenancy to pay for "utilities," but disagree whether Cable TV is included within the definition of "utilities." This is a question of law for the Court to decide. In reaching its decision, the Court may consider the intent of the parties, the custom in the area, and various other factors that will assist the Court in determining whether or not Cable TV should be included within the definition of "utilities" and, therefore, must be provided by the landlord. Absent unusual facts, the Court will probably conclude that Cable TV is not within the definition of "utilities."

If, on the other hand, the landlord and tenant disagree on what a particular provision was, the judge is in the unenviable position of having to decide who is telling the truth. For example, assume the landlord says the agreed rent was $500, but the tenant contends the agreed rent was $400. In this case, the judge is forced to decide whether one of the parties is lying or whether both are telling the truth. If the Court concludes that both are telling the truth, then the Court will find that

---

60   Hadley v. Southwest Properties, Inc., 116 Ariz. 503, 570 P.2d 190 (1977) (interpretation of contract is question of law for the court). *See also* LeBaron v. Crismon, 100 Ariz. 206, 208, 412 P.2d 705, 706 (1966); Stika v. Albion, 150 Ariz. 521, 523, 724 P.2d 607, 609 (App.1986).

there never really was an "agreement" (i.e., a meeting of the minds) and, therefore, the "agreement" cannot be enforced.

(b)   The written rental agreement should be comprehensive.

While a thirty-page rental agreement may be too much, a few notes scribbled on a napkin may be too little. Where there are "gaps" in an oral or written rental agreement, the provisions of the Act apply.[61] For example, assume you have an oral or written agreement with a tenant, specifying $500 rent for a particular rental unit, but do not discuss when rent is due. The Act fills in this "gap." The Act provides, "rent is payable at the beginning"[62] of the specified term, which in the case of a month-to-month tenancy, would be at the beginning of the month. The Act, however, is not comprehensive and not all contingencies are accounted for. Moreover, the Act favors the tenant – is that what you want? Your rental agreement should be as comprehensive as possible without being too long. And, naturally, **it should favor the landlord** – after all, whose side are you on?

(c)   The rental agreement should provide for abandonment.

Cross Reference:
● Procedural steps for reclaiming an abandoned rental unit, Quick Reference Section, Section II (Procedures)

From time to time, you may have the unfortunate experience of dealing with the situation where the tenant, for whatever reason, has simply disappeared and **abandoned** the rental unit. Typically, in such a case, you will be left with the dilemma of what to do with the tenant's personal property. Your first impulse may be to grind the personal property into dust – therapeutic, perhaps, but not wise. The Act requires you to store the tenant's property for at least ten (10) days after the declaration of abandonment. [63] If, however, you have had the foresight to include a provision in your rental agreement, you may be in luck. The Act provides:

> If provided by a written rental agreement, the landlord may destroy or otherwise dispose of some or all of the property if the landlord reasonably determines that the value of the property is so low that the cost of moving, storage and conducting a public sale would exceed the amount that would be realized from the sale.[64]

---

61 *See* A.R.S. § 33-1304 (West 1990). *See, e.g.,* New Hampshire Ins. Co. v. Hewins, 627 P.2d 1159 (Kan.App. 1981) (in absence of a valid rental agreement to the contrary, basic terms of landlord tenant relationship are provided by Uniform Residential Landlord and Tenant Act).

62 A.R.S. § 33-1314(C) (West Supp. 1998).

63 A.R.S. § 33-1370(E) (West Supp. 1998).

64 A.R.S. § 33-1370(E) (West Supp. 1998) (emphasis added).

There you have it – express permission from the Arizona legislature to grind the tenant's abandoned property into sawdust, provided, of course, the value of said property is less than the cost to move and store it. But the key is that you must include certain language in your rental agreement or else you have no alternative (i.e., you must move and store the tenant's property) no matter what the value. I use the following language in my rental agreement:

> Tenant expressly authorizes landlord to dispose of abandoned property and property left on the premises by tenant after tenancy has terminated, in any manner landlord deems fit, where the landlord reasonably determines that the value of said property is so low that the cost of moving, storing and conducting a public sale would exceed the amount that would be realized from the sale. Tenant holds landlord harmless for loss of property and/or value of said property disposed of under these circumstances.

These are not "magic words." Any similar clause that clearly conveys this message will suffice under the statute. Feel free to use mine or compose your own, but be sure you put some type of provision addressing abandoned personal property into your rental agreement. When actually faced with the prospect of disposing of a tenant's abandoned property, I strongly recommend taking pictures of the property (before you "dispose" of it). A witness is also well advised.

(d) The rental agreement should provide for payment of expenses incurred to bring legal action.

The Act provides that after a Special Detainer action has been filed, the tenant may reinstate the rental agreement only by paying past due rent, late fees, attorneys' fees and court costs.[65] Your rental agreement should also include this language.

Similarly, your rental agreement should include language that entitles you to attorneys' fees and litigation expenses whether or not the action is contested. The reason for this is simple -- the statute does not adequately protect the landlord's interests. First, the statute provides that attorneys' fees *may* be awarded to the prevailing party in a lawsuit that arises from a contract (i.e., a rental agreement).[66] This statutory language means that an award of attorneys' fees is discretionary. Second, the statute only provides for an award of attorneys' fees in a "contested

65   A.R.S. § 33-1368(B) (West Supp. 1998).
66   A.R.S. § 12-341.01(A) (West 1992).

action."[67] Which means that if you get a judgment against a tenant by default, a very common occurrence, you are not entitled to your attorneys' fees. I find both of these situations completely unacceptable and so should you. Language as simple as this in your rental agreement should cure both problems:

> Landlord and Tenant agree that the prevailing party in any litigation, action or controversy arising from this Rental Agreement shall be entitled to an award of reasonable attorneys' fees, litigation expenses and court costs, without regard to whether or not the matter is contested.

This language, however, is not an iron-clad guarantee. I have seen some judges (normally in justice court) refuse to award attorneys' fees regardless of the language in the rental agreement. This practice is not fair and is certainly contrary to the express language of the contract (i.e., the rental agreement), but, unfortunately, the only way to correct this "bad decision" is to appeal the decision of the judge. The appeal process is normally not cost effective, in terms of time, effort and cost. Because of the myriad of variables involved, if your rental agreement provides for payment of attorneys' fees and you are denied an award of attorneys' fees, you should consult your attorney to discuss your (cost effective) options.

(e)   The rental agreement should provide for payment of "other expenses" incurred by the landlord.

It costs money to prepare and deliver notices (i.e., Five-Day Notice to Pay or Quit, etc.), but there is nothing in the Act that allows you to collect a fee for this effort. On the other hand, there is nothing in the Act that prohibits including a provision in the rental agreement that obligates the tenant to pay notice fees.[68] Furthermore, Arizona law permits parties to contract as they wish (except for contracts for illegal purposes or which are against public policy).[69] Consequently, you should consider including language in your rental agreement that allows you to collect a fee (i.e., $25.00, or some other "reasonable" amount) for preparation and service of notices. The key, however, is to enforce your rights; if the tenant decides to reinstate the rental agreement after a monetary default, then insist upon collecting *all* charges – the past due rent, the late charges, notice fees, etc. – make no exceptions.

You may also wish to assess and collect an "Application Fee." Keep in mind that because it is a fee, it is nonrefundable and, therefore, it must be designated as

---

[67]   A.R.S. § 12-341.01(A) (West 1992).

[68]   *See* A.R.S. § 33-1308 (West 1990).

[69]   A.R.S. § 33-1313(A) (West 1990).

a nonrefundable fee and the purpose of the fee must be stated in writing (i.e., on the Application Form).[70] (*See* Chapter 2(D)(1)(d), "Nonrefundable fee/charges must be stated in writing").

I have also heard of a landlord (i.e., a landlord for a single-family home, located some distance from his own home) who included a "drive-by fee" in his rental agreement, which he assessed when he was "forced" to travel to the rental unit to personally collect overdue rent, hand-deliver notices, or any time he had to physically visit the rental unit. Again, this type of provision is not expressly prohibited by the Act. Nevertheless, there is no guarantee that a court of law will enforce this provision or similar provisions merely because they are included in the rental agreement. You have a greater chance of succeeding in court if the fee charged is "reasonable" and assessment of the fee is tied to some type of default of the tenant.

(f)   The rental agreement should provide for the Tenant's maintenance obligations.

Unless specifically addressed in the rental agreement or stated in the Act,[71] your tenant will claim that you are responsible for certain items of maintenance, not s/he. Therefore, to avoid litigation, it behooves us to specifically address certain items.

Lawn care. Lawn care for a multi-unit complex is almost always the responsibility of the landlord. In the case of townhouses or condominiums, lawn care for common areas is usually the responsibility of the homeowners' association and lawn care for individually owned areas (i.e., fenced back yards, etc.) is usually the responsibility of the owner. In the case of a single-family house, the tenant is usually responsible for lawn care.

When you allocate responsibility for the lawn care (i.e., to the tenant or to the landlord), you should consider many factors, including your willingness to do or arrange for the lawn maintenance; the ease of access to the property for you or your lawn service; the complexity of the maintenance schedule (i.e., a small Bermuda grass lawn versus a tiff grass lawn, with one or more gardens of high maintenance flowers); the cost of providing lawn care for the tenant; and the potential cost to replace plants killed by the tenant if not properly maintained.

You may also wish to include language in your rental agreement that provides that the landlord may undertake responsibility for lawn care and bill the tenant for

---

70   A.R.S. § 33-1321(B) (West Supp. 1998).

71   A.R.S. § 33-1341 (West 1990).

the expense thereof, if the tenant fails to adequately maintain the yard after having been notified by the landlord on three prior occasions (i.e., three 10-Day Notices for Material Noncompliance).

Pool care/maintenance. Few tenants have the ability or inclination to properly perform pool maintenance. The financial risk of allowing the tenant to be responsible for pool care and maintenance is great. With very few exceptions, I recommend that the landlord retain responsibility for pool maintenance. This will ensure that the pool is properly maintained. The tenant may very well be willing to pay the added expense of having a pool service company perform regular care and maintenance. If not, your own peace of mind may be well worth absorbing the cost.

Pest control. Pest control is normally a landlord's responsibility when the rental unit is part of a multi-unit complex (i.e., an apartment complex) and the landlord has control over the adjoining units. On the other hand, when the rental unit is a single-family residence, pest control may be a tenant's responsibility. Make a decision regarding who will be responsible for pest control and include appropriate language in the rental agreement.

Light bulbs. You will be surprised how petty some tenants can be. It isn't so bad when a new tenant insists you replace a few light bulbs when s/he first moves in, but continued requests to replace bulbs can be annoying and tenants who take all the light bulbs with them when they vacate are absolutely exasperating. Conceivably, a tenant could reasonably argue that the landlord has the responsibility to "[m]aintain in good and safe working order ... all electrical ... facilities and appliances,"[72] including responsibility for replacing any inoperable light bulbs. To avoid this problem, allocate responsibility for light bulbs to the tenant and require that all bulbs be present and operable when the tenant vacates (this gives you express contractual authority to deduct the cost of light bulbs from the tenant's security deposit if the tenant fails to comply).

Air filters. Air filters are cheap. Nevertheless, tenants will not buy them and they will not replace them on a regular basis. Because the consequences of failing to regularly replace filters is so dire (i.e., the air conditioner or heat pump may become inoperable), the landlord should just accept this responsibility. This is not a burden; rather, it is a license to do a quick inspection of the premises every month. Put in the rental agreement that the landlord is responsible for replacing the air conditioning filter every month or as often as reasonably required. When you (or your maintenance man) go to the property to change the filter, you will have an opportunity to take a quick look at the condition of the premises and inquire about

---

72 A.R.S. §33-1324(A)(4) (West Supp. 1998).

anything you wish. Because your monthly visit will become "routine," you may catch the tenant off guard and discover unauthorized pets, unauthorized occupants, controlled substances in plain sight, and/or unauthorized use of the property (i.e., business operations, structural modifications, etc.). A word of caution, however, you must still give the tenant two days' advance notice of your intent to enter the rental unit.[73] In addition, you should state in your rental agreement that you inspect and/or replace air-conditioning filters monthly, so as to avoid any allegations by the tenant that you are harassing the tenant by conducting "too many" inspections.

Repairs and modifications. The landlord has the statutory duty to provide and maintain "fit premises."[74] Under certain circumstances, however, the landlord and tenant may agree to transfer "some" responsibilities:

A. The landlord shall:

1. Comply with the requirements of applicable building codes materially affecting health and safety.

2. Make all repairs and do whatever is necessary to put and keep the premises in a fit and habitable condition.

. . . .

5. Provide and maintain appropriate receptacles and conveniences for the removal of ashes, garbage, rubbish and other waste incidental to the occupancy of the dwelling unit and arrange for their removal.

6. Supply running water and reasonable amounts of hot water at all times, reasonable heat and reasonable air-conditioning or cooling where such units are installed and offered, when required by seasonal weather conditions, except where the building that includes the dwelling unit is not required by law to be equipped for that purpose or the dwelling unit is so constructed that heat, air-conditioning, cooling or hot water is generated by an installation within the exclusive control of the tenant and supplied by a direct public utility connection.

. . . .

C. The landlord and tenant of a single family residence may agree in writing, supported by adequate

---

73   A.R.S. § 33-1343(C) (West 1990).

74   A.R.S. § 33-1324 (West Supp. 1998).

consideration, that the tenant perform the landlord's duties specified in subsection A, paragraphs 5 and 6 of this section, and also specified repairs, maintenance tasks, alterations and remodeling, but only if the transaction is entered into in good faith, not for the purpose of evading the obligations of the landlord and the work is not necessary to cure noncompliances with subsection A, paragraphs 1 and 2 of this section.

D. The landlord and tenant of any dwelling unit other than a single family residence may agree that the tenant is to perform specified repairs, maintenance tasks, alterations or remodeling only if:

1. The agreement of the parties is entered into in good faith and not for the purpose of evading the obligations of the landlord and is set forth in a separate writing signed by the parties and supported by adequate consideration.

2.   The work is not necessary to cure noncompliance with subsection A, paragraphs 1 and 2 of this section.

3. The agreement does not diminish or affect the obligation of the landlord to other tenants in the premises.[75]

Only allow the tenant to perform repairs or modifications to the rental unit if you are confident that the tenant is qualified to perform the job and that s/he has the necessary tools available to do the job correctly. The statute requires that these types of agreements be written[76] and, in some cases, that it be a written agreement separate from the rental agreement.[77] I recommend that this type of written agreement be separate from the rental agreement *in all cases*. I also recommend that, in this separate written agreement, you address who assumes responsibility for injury to the tenant and/or others as a result of the tenant's construction efforts. Even if you allocate all risk and responsibility for liability to the tenant, make sure you are adequately insured. Then, re-think this decision one more time, to see if you *really* want to enter into this type of agreement with a tenant – I recommend against such agreements, except to transfer responsibility for minor maintenance (i.e., lawn maintenance, pool maintenance, pest control, etc.).

---

75   A.R.S. § 33-1324 (West Supp. 1998).

76   A.R.S. § 33-1324 (West Supp. 1998).

77   A.R.S. § 33-1324(D)(1) (West Supp. 1998).

(g)   The rental agreement should provide for regular inspections.

The Act allows the landlord access to the rental unit for inspections, repairs, alterations, improvements, etc.[78] The landlord, however, must provide the tenant with <u>at least</u> two days' advance notice of the landlord's intent to enter the premises and the landlord may enter the premises only at reasonable times.[79] It is possible that a monthly inspection could be interpreted by a judge as harassment and/or abuse of the landlord's right of access <u>unless</u> the rental agreement contains a specific provision regarding the frequency of inspections (i.e., monthly). It will be very difficult for a tenant to claim that monthly inspections are "too frequent," if the rental agreement, which the tenant read and signed *before* s/he moved in, specifically states that inspections will be conducted monthly. Consequently, if you plan to inspect your rental units frequently, then your rental agreement should disclose the frequency of your inspections (i.e., monthly, bi-monthly, quarterly, etc.).

(h)   The rental agreement should address "reasonable" modifications and alterations.

Generally, landlords do not allow any structural modifications and/or alterations to the rental unit. If, however, you do allow modifications and/or alterations, you should precisely define the limits of the tenant's right to modify and/or alter the property and, in any event, require written notice by the tenant to the landlord <u>before</u> any work is commenced. Naturally, all work should be performed by qualified and licensed workers.

The foregoing is the exception, not the rule. Most landlords do not permit modifications and/or alterations. What many landlords **do** encounter, however, are requests from tenants regarding: painting a wall, a room or the entire unit; putting hooks in the ceiling to hang plants; putting nails in the walls to hang pictures; installing closet organizers; etc. Obviously, the simple thing to do is to require landlord approval for **all** such modifications. The key, however, is getting the tenant to understand that putting a nail in the wall to hang a picture is a structural modification requiring landlord approval. This may be accomplished in the rental agreement or in separate rules and regulations, but is only effective if the tenant reads the form. Tenants will generally want to make these types of modifications immediately upon move-in. Consequently, you may wish to supplement your forms by posting a temporary notice inside the rental unit in a conspicuous spot (i.e., taped to the refrigerator, taped to the inside of the front door, etc.), that repeats these restrictions. In this way, the tenant will be reminded of these restrictions during move-in, which is when the tenant is most likely to violate (inadvertently or intentionally) these limitations.

---

[78]   A.R.S. § 33-1343(A) (West 1990).

[79]   A.R.S. § 33-1343(C) (West 1990).

(i)   The rental agreement should provide how <u>partial payments are applied to amounts due</u>.

Partial rent payments most frequently arise immediately after service of a Five-Day Notice to Pay or Quit. Many times, a tenant wants to stay, but, for whatever reason, s/he does not have the full amount due. If a tenant wants to reinstate the rental agreement after you have served a Five-Day Notice to Pay or Quit, but the tenant only has part of the amount due, <u>and you want to accept a partial payment</u> (you are not required to accept less than full payment), you are free to do so, but make sure you have the tenant sign some type of written agreement (i.e., "a contemporaneous writing").

For those instances where you wish to accept less than the full amount due (otherwise, how you apply payments is not an issue), your rental agreement should provide for *how* (i.e., to which of the amounts that are due) partial payments are to be applied. If it does not, but you wish to accept a partial payment, you should have your tenant sign a document that spells out how the partial payment is to be applied and that protects your rights (*see* Appendix B, Form 5). Partial payments should be applied as follows: first, to legal fees and court costs, then to accrued interest on any amounts owed to the landlord, then to late fees, then to amounts owed for damages to the property, then to any other amounts owed by the tenant to the landlord, then to unpaid past due rent, and finally to prepaid rent.

If your rental agreement provides for how partial payments are to be applied, it should also provide that you are *not obligated* to accept partial payments. This will prevent a "creative" tenants' lawyer from arguing that language in your rental agreement about how partial payments are applied, *implies* an **obligation** to accept partial payments.

So, what about partial payments? Can you accept a partial payment without waiving your rights? Yes, but be careful and "get it in writing." The Act was recently changed to allow landlords to accept partial payments without waiving the landlord's rights.

> A landlord is not required to accept a partial payment of rent or other charges. A landlord accepting a partial payment of rent or other charges retains the right to proceed against a tenant only if the tenant agrees in a **contemporaneous writing** to the terms and conditions of the partial payment with regard to the continuation of the tenancy. The written agreement shall contain a date on which the balance of the rent is due. The landlord may

proceed against a tenant in breach of this agreement or any other breach of the original rental agreement as provided in article 4 of this chapter and in title 12, chapter 8.[80]

If you accept a partial payment, the tenant must "agree in a contemporaneous writing"[81] that the landlord is reserving his/her right to collect the full amount due and to pursue all available legal action. The consequences of failing to do so are severe.

Acceptance of rent, or **any portion thereof**, with knowledge of a default by tenant or acceptance of performance by the tenant that varied from the terms of the rental agreement or rules or regulations subsequently adopted by the landlord **constitutes a waiver** of the right to terminate the rental agreement for that breach, except as specified in subsection A of this section.[82]

A simple form, such as a rent receipt book that shows the amount due, the amount paid, *and the amount remaining due*, will suffice. Merely have the tenant sign or initial the receipt, give the tenant a copy and retain the original for your records. This will satisfy the "contemporaneous writing" requirement of the statute. Alternatively, use Form 5, Appendix B.

If the tenant fails to pay the balance due on the due date specified in the "contemporaneous writing," and you have already served the Five-Day Notice to Pay or Quit, you need not serve another Five-Day Notice.

If the landlord has provided the tenant with a notice of failure to pay rent as specified in section 33-1368, subsection B [Five-Day Notice to Pay or Quit] prior to the completion of the agreement for partial payment, no additional notice under section 33-1368, subsection B is required in case of a breach of the partial payment agreement.[83]

---

80 A.R.S. § 33-1371 (West Supp. 1998) (emphasis added).

81 A.R.S. § 33-1371 (West Supp. 1998).

82 A.R.S. § 33-1371 (West Supp. 1998) (emphasis added).

83 A.R.S. § 33-1371 (West Supp. 1998).

(j) The rental agreement should provide for a reasonable late fee.

Late fees are only collectable if they are specified in a written rental agreement (another good reason to have a written rental agreement).[84] If you have an oral rental agreement or if your written rental agreement does not specifically state that the landlord may collect late fees and the amount thereof, the landlord **cannot** collect late fees. I frequently have landlords tell me that they have oral rental agreements and have collected late fees for many years. I have little doubt that this is true and, in fact, I believe this may be a common practice. If you ever go to court, however, the law does not permit the judge to award late fees to the landlord unless the late fee is stated in a written rental agreement.[85]

In addition to the foregoing, to be enforceable and collectable, late fees must be "reasonable."[86] What is "reasonable" will vary from unit to unit. I have seen a judge "strike" (i.e., deem unenforceable) a $5.00 per day late fee on a $500.00 per month rental and another judge find the same provision "reasonable." I have also seen a judge strike a $10.00 a day late fee on a commercial lease for $1,800.00 per month. Consequently, I cannot answer the question: "What is a reasonable late fee?" I can tell you, however, that judges tend to favor a late fee provision that is proportionate to the magnitude of the offense.

For example, assume you rent a property for $500.00 per month and that your late fee is expressed as a percentage (i.e., one percent) of the amount of rent outstanding, rather than as a flat rate (i.e., $5.00 per day). In this case, the amount of the late fee is proportionate to the offense – $5.00 a day late fee when the unpaid rent is $500.00. If the tenant had made a partial payment, $200.00 for instance, then the unpaid rent would be $300.00 and the late fee would only be $3.00 per day. In this way, the late fee is always proportionate to the size of the offense (i.e., the amount of due and unpaid rent). I cannot guarantee that a one, two or three percent late fee will always be enforceable. I cannot even guarantee that all judges will favor a percentage late fee over a flat rate late fee. I can tell you, however, that most judges that I have encountered have found a percentage late fee to be reasonable and that I have seen these same judges strike flat rate late fees. It is now up to you to decide whether you will use a flat rate, a percentage, or some other type of late fee. Whatever method you use, make sure you include *some type* of late fee. Otherwise, the tenant has no incentive to tender payment of rent on time.

---

84   A.R.S. § 33-1377(F) (West Supp. 1998).

85   A.R.S. § 33-1377(F) (West Supp. 1998).

86   A.R.S. § 33-1377(F) (West Supp. 1998).

In addition, the late fee should accrue on a daily basis. If your late fee provision states that a fee (i.e., flat rate or percentage) will be assessed if rent is not paid by the fifth day of the month, but does not provide for daily charges thereafter, there is no incentive for the tenant to pay the delinquent rent as soon as possible after the fifth day of the month.

(k) The rental agreement should provide for rental tax increases.

The Act provides that changes in the rental tax may be passed on to the tenant during the duration of an existing lease <u>provided</u> "the landlord's right to adjust rent pursuant to this subsection [is] disclosed in the rental agreement."[87] Therefore, it behooves you to include this type of provision in your rental agreement. The following will suffice:

> Pursuant to A.R.S. § 33-1314(E), Landlord may adjust rental tax with thirty days notice if changed by the municipality during the Term hereof.

(l) The rental agreement should include a liquidated damages provision.

Here is the scenario. The tenant has signed the rental agreement, paid you the first month's rent and the security deposit and then, for whatever reason, changes his mind or for some reason "cannot" move-in. What do you do? This tenant has broken the lease. There is no "three day cooling off period" or any other rule of law that allows the tenant to void the contract because of a job transfer, a death in the family or any other reason. Once the tenant signs the contract, the tenant is obligated to fulfill the terms thereof.

So what are your legal rights? The landlord may apply the security deposit to the payment of accrued rent and the amount of damages "actually" suffered as a result of the breach, subject to the landlord's obligation to mitigate (i.e., reduce) his/her damages.

What are your "actual" damages? The rent you will lose if the tenant does not move in, the advertising expenses you will incur to re-rent the property, any commissions that you paid to a real estate agent or broker that will not be refunded to you, and any other expense reasonably incurred to re-rent the property.

---

[87] A.R.S. § 33-1314(E) (West Supp. 1998).

If the tenant signs the rental agreement at 5:00 P.M. on Monday and then calls you at 8:00 A.M. on Tuesday and tells you that he will not or cannot move-in, what are your actual damages? Probably not very much. You will have to use your best judgment in assessing your actual damages.

As an alternative to actual damages, you may wish to consider a liquidated damages provision in the rental agreement. Because actual damages in these situations are oftentimes difficult to calculate, the law allows the parties to stipulate to an amount that will roughly approximate the damages the landlord will sustain in the event the tenant breaches the rental agreement by terminating the rental agreement before taking possession and/or before the end of the lease term. A liquidated damages provision will help in precisely this type of situation. An example follows:

> The parties hereby agree that in the event Tenant fails to take possession of the unit after signing the rental agreement or for any reason vacates the premises before the end of the rental term, then landlord may assess and collect a fee in the amount of $_____, which the parties hereby stipulate and agree is a reasonable approximation of landlord's damages. Tenant expressly authorizes landlord to deduct this fee from the security deposit.

So, how much should the fee be? A "reasonable amount," which may be an amount equal to one month's rent, one and one-half month's rent, two month's rent, or some other amount that you believe is a reasonable approximation of your damages. If it turns out that your actual damages are more or less than the amount stated in the rental agreement, the liquidated damages provision is still valid and binding.

Don't forget that you must nevertheless send the tenant an itemized statement of all deductions, including the liquidated damages amount, from his security deposit within fourteen business days.[88] (*See* Chapter 5, Section B(7)(b)).

(m)   The rental agreement should include waiver of jury trial.

Most landlords do not want a jury trial. Why? Because it delays trial of the action for possession until the Court can summon a jury, which will normally take several days and may take weeks. In addition, if the landlord is represented, a jury

---

[88]   A.R.S. § 33-1321(D) (West Supp. 1998).

will be an enormous expense. An ordinary forcible detainer action (if there is such a thing) will generally take less than one-half hour. A jury trial will take most of the day and can take much longer, depending on the number and complexity of issues involved.

Most tenants want a jury. Why? For the same reasons above. They want additional time and they want to put the landlord to as much expense as humanly possible.

How do we fix this problem? The right to a jury trial is found in the United States Constitution.[89] The Arizona State Legislature also granted tenants the right to a jury trial.[90] Parties to a contract, however, can agree to voluntarily waive the right to a jury trial. The question is will an Arizona judge will find that a tenant's agreement to waive a jury trial, in advance (i.e., at the time the rental agreement is signed, which will occur before any controversy arises), is enforceable?

This is "leading edge" stuff. The law is not clear on this issue.[91] The tenant may argue that a jury trial is a right given to him/her by the Act and, pursuant to A.R.S. § 33-1315(A)(1), the tenant cannot agree to "waive or forego rights or remedies under the [Act]."[92] The tenant's right to a jury trial, however, *is not* found in the Act; it is found in the forcible detainer statutes.[93] The Act does not state that the tenant cannot waive any of the rights given to him/her by the forcible detainer statutes and, therefore, the tenant's argument should fail. Moreover, case law and statutory law exists that says parties to a contract can agree, in advance, to waive their right to a jury trial.[94]

Several factors will be important in helping the judge reach the right decision: (1) the waiver provision must be written in clear and unambiguous language; (2) the waiver provision must be conspicuous; (3) the negotiability of all contract terms, including the waiver provision; (4) the disparity in the parties' bargaining power; (5) the knowledge and intelligence of the party opposing the waiver (i.e., whether the

---

89   U.S. Constitution, amendment VII.

90   A.R.S. § 12-1176(B) (West 1994).

91   *See* Broemmer v. Abortion Services of Phoenix, Ltd., 173 Ariz. 148, 840 P.2d 1013 (Ariz. 1992) (contract at abortion clinic waiving patient's right to jury trial and requiring arbitration was held unenforceable because the facts of the case revealed that the patient did not voluntarily waive a known right; the language of the decision, however, indicates that under appropriate facts, a party may contractually waive his/her right to a jury trial). *See also* Malan Realty Investors, Inc. v. Bea Harris, 1997 WL 10272 (Mo.App. WD, 1997) (provision waiving jury trial in commercial lease upheld by the court).

92   A.R.S. § 33-1315(A)(1) (West 1990).

93   A.R.S. §§ 12-1171 to 12-1183 (West 1994 & Supp. 1998).

94   A.R.S. § 12-1501 (West 1994).

tenant has an eighth grade education or whether s/he has a Ph.D.); (6) and the business experience of the party opposing the waiver. In short, the court will look for a voluntary waiver of a known right by a person who understood what s/he was waiving; waiver will never be implied.

So what provision will work? There are no guarantees. I have begun incorporating the following language in my rental agreements, but it has yet to be tested in court. Feel free to use the following provision, but recognize that some judges simply will not enforce such a provision.

> **To minimize delay and to reduce the cost of potential litigation, the parties hereby agree to waive their right to a trial by jury. The parties hereto understand that they are entitled to a jury trial for claims arising out of this rental agreement and/or the Arizona Residential Landlord and Tenant Act, but knowingly and voluntarily waive this right.**

I recommend that the foregoing provision be in bold type, in a type size as large or larger than the other portions of the rental agreement, and placed immediately above the signature line. You may even wish to have the tenants initial this provision separately.

3.   **Rental Agreement CANNOT's.**

(a)   **The landlord cannot require the tenant to waive the tenant's rights, agree to pay attorneys' fees, <u>or agree to limit the landlord's liability</u>.**

The Act specifically prohibits provisions within the rental agreement whereby the tenant: (1) waives the rights or remedies granted to the tenant under the Act, (2) agrees to pay the landlord's attorneys' fees (with two exceptions), and (3) agrees to limit the landlord's liability. Specifically, the Act provides:

Prohibited provisions in rental agreements

A. A rental agreement shall not provide that the tenant does any of the following:

1. Agrees to waive or to forego rights or remedies under this chapter [Chapter 10, which is the Arizona Residential Landlord and Tenant Act].

2. Agrees to pay the landlord's attorney's fees, except an agreement in writing may provide that attorney's fees may be awarded to the prevailing party in the event of court action and except that a prevailing party in a contested forcible detainer action is eligible to be awarded attorney fees pursuant to § 12-341.01 regardless of whether the rental agreement provides for such an award.

3. Agrees to the exculpation or limitation of any liability of the landlord arising under law or to indemnify the landlord for that liability or the costs connected therewith.

B. A provision prohibited by subsection A of this section included in a rental agreement is unenforceable. If a landlord deliberately uses a rental agreement containing provisions known by him to be prohibited, the tenant may recover actual damages sustained by him and not more than two months' periodic rent.[95]

These are the absolute taboos -- you <u>cannot</u> include these in your rental agreement. But otherwise, the sky is the limit (within reason). So draft your rental agreement to your benefit, but resist the temptation to go "too far."

(b)   The landlord cannot collect a security deposit equal to more than one and one-half month's rent.

"A landlord shall not demand or receive security, however denominated, including, but not limited to, prepaid rent in an amount or value in excess of one and one-half month's rent."[96] A "reasonable" nonrefundable cleaning or redecorating charge (not deposit) <u>is not</u> a security deposit.[97] Therefore, a landlord may require a security deposit less than or equal to, but not more than, one and one-half times the monthly rental amount, <u>plus</u> a "reasonable" nonrefundable cleaning, redecorating and/or other charge. For example, you rent a unit for $1,000 per month; you may collect a security deposit of $1,500 <u>plus</u> a "reasonable" nonrefundable cleaning or redecorating charge.

---

95   A.R.S. § 33-1315 (West 1990). *But see* A.R.S. § 33-1314(A) (West Supp. 1998) ("The landlord and tenant may include in a rental agreement terms and conditions not prohibited by this chapter [the Act] or other rule of law including rent, term of the agreement and other provisions governing the rights and obligations of the parties.").

96   A.R.S. § 33-1321 (West Supp. 1998).

97   A.R.S. § 33-1310(14) (West Supp. 1998) ("`Security' does not include a reasonable charge for redecorating or cleaning.").

"Reasonable" is a somewhat subjective term, but be sure the amount you charge passes the "straight face" test. The "straight face" test is the maximum amount that you can charge and still look the judge in the eye and announce, with a straight face, in a room full of people (including other landlords), that the amount is reasonable. Naturally, in addition to the straight face test, the judge will also require you to explain and/or demonstrate how you arrived at that figure (i.e., he may insist on seeing some empirical data). As a general "rule of thumb," you may be pushing the limits of what is "reasonable" if your cleaning or redecorating charge is more than one-half of the monthly rental amount.

Don't forget that if a cleaning, redecorating or other charge/fee is nonrefundable, it must be so stated in writing.[98] Also, you must state in writing (i.e., in the rental agreement or elsewhere) the purpose of your nonrefundable fees and charges. *See* Chapter 2, Section E(6) (Disposition of Deposit Form); Chapter 5, Section B(7)(b) (Security deposit).

(c)   The landlord cannot include provisions contrary to the Act.

The Act provides that the "lease agreement shall not contain any terms contrary to this section [wrongful failure to supply heat, air conditioning, cooling, water, hot water or essential services]."[99] This new language means that the landlord cannot take away any of the rights granted by this section of the Act. The full text of this section appears below.

> **A.** If contrary to the rental agreement or section 33-1324 the landlord deliberately or negligently fails to supply running water, gas or electrical service, or both if applicable, and reasonable amounts of hot water or heat, air-conditioning or cooling, where such units are installed and offered, or essential services, the tenant may give reasonable notice to the landlord specifying the breach and may do one of the following:
>
> 1.   Procure reasonable amounts of hot water, running water, heat and essential services during the period of the landlord's noncompliance and deduct their actual reasonable cost from the rent. If the landlord has failed to provide any of the utility services specified in this section due to nonpayment of the landlord's utility

---

98   A.R.S. § 33-1321(B) (West Supp. 1998).

99   A.R.S. § 33-1364(E) (West Supp. 1998).

bill for the premises, and if there is no separate utility meter for each tenant in the premises such that the tenant could avoid a utility shut-off by arranging to have services transferred to the tenant's name, the tenant may either individually or collectively with other tenants arrange with the utility company to pay the utility bill after written notice to the landlord of the tenant's intent to do so. With the utility company's approval the tenant or tenants may pay the landlord's delinquent utility bill and deduct from any rent owed to the landlord the actual cost of the payment the tenant made to restore utility services. The tenant or tenants may continue to make such payments to the utility company until the landlord has provided adequate assurances to the tenant that the above utility services will be maintained.

2. Recover damages based upon the diminution in the fair rental value of the dwelling unit.

3. Procure reasonable substitute housing during the period of the landlord's noncompliance, in which case the tenant is excused from paying rent for the period of the landlord's noncompliance. In the event the periodic cost of such substitute housing exceeds the amount of the periodic rent, upon delivery by tenant of proof of payment for such substitute housing, tenant may recover from landlord such excess costs up to an amount not to exceed twenty-five per cent of the periodic rent which has been excused pursuant to this paragraph.

B. A landlord shall provide all utilities and services specified in the lease agreement.

C. A landlord shall not terminate utility services as specified in subsection A of this section which are provided to the tenant as part of the rental agreement, except as necessary to make needed repairs or as provided in section 33-1368. Subsequent to the execution of the rental agreement, a landlord may not transfer the responsibility for payment of such utility services to the tenant without the tenant's written consent.

D. If a landlord is in violation of subsection C of this section, the tenant may recover damages, costs and reasonable attorneys fees and obtain injunctive relief. Nothing in this section shall preclude a tenant's right to recover damages as specified in section 33-1367.

E. A lease agreement shall not contain any terms contrary to this section.

F. In addition to the remedy provided in paragraph 3 of subsection A of this section, in the event the landlord's noncompliance is deliberate, the tenant may recover the actual and reasonable cost or fair and reasonable value of the substitute housing not in excess of an amount equal to the periodic rent.

G. If the tenant proceeds under this section, he may not proceed under section 33-1361 or section 33-1363 as to that breach, except as to damages which occur prior to the tenant proceeding under subsection A or B of this section.

H. The rights under this section do not arise until the tenant has given notice to the landlord and such rights do not include the right to repair. Such rights do not arise if the condition was caused by the deliberate or negligent act or omission of the tenant, a member of the tenant's family or other person on the premises with the tenant's consent.[100]

4. <u>Deposits.</u>

All that you need to know about **deposits** (security deposits, cleaning deposits and redecorating deposits) and **nonrefundable fees/charges** may be summarized as follows:

- You cannot collect deposits (*not* including nonrefundable fees or charges) equal to more than one and one-half month's rent.[101] Example: if rent is $500 per month, you cannot collect deposits (i.e., security deposit, cleaning deposit, redecorating deposit, pet deposit, key deposit, etc.) that total more than $750.

---

100   A.R.S. § 33-1364 (West Supp. 1998).

101   A.R.S. § 33-1321(A) (West Supp. 1998).

- Nonrefundable fees, charges and/or deposits must be clearly stated in writing, a copy of which must be given to the tenant.[102] In addition, the purpose of all nonrefundable fees, charges and/or deposits must be stated in writing.[103] Normally, this is addressed in the rental agreement, but if you do not have a written rental agreement (shame on you), you must nevertheless have some written document that clearly states which fees, charges and/or deposits are nonrefundable. If the landlord has not disclosed in writing that a fee, charge or deposit is nonrefundable and then fails to return the fee, charge or deposit to the tenant, the tenant may recover the deposit together with damages in an amount equal to **twice** the amount wrongfully withheld.[104] Also, the "label" the landlord chooses to use (i.e., fee, charge or deposit) is not as important as his/her intent. If money is collected from a tenant at the beginning of the rental period, with the understanding that it will be returned at the end of the rental period, provided certain things are done (i.e., property clean, keys returned, no pet damage, etc.), then it is a "security deposit."[105] If money is collected from a tenant at the beginning of the rental period, with the understanding that it **will not** be returned at the end of the rental period, regardless of any actions taken by the tenant, then it is a nonrefundable fee or charge.[106]

- Within fourteen business days, you must either: (1) refund 100% of the tenant's deposits that you are holding or (2) refund the amount due the tenant, if any, and provide a written notice that itemizes deductions from the tenant's deposits. The Act requires that you do either 1 or 2, above, within fourteen business days after: (1) termination of tenancy, (2) delivery of possession of the rental unit back to you, and (3) demand by the tenant. "Delivery of possession," means that the tenant has vacated the rental property and returned the keys to the landlord.[107] If the landlord does not comply by either failing to return the security deposit or to deliver a written itemization, the tenant may recover the property and money due him/her together with damages in an amount equal to **twice** the amount wrongfully withheld.[108] Consequently, you should be in the habit of refunding deposits and/or providing the required notice and/or refund within fourteen business days of termination of tenancy and delivery of possession of the unit, without regard

---

102 A.R.S. § 33-1321(B) (West Supp. 1998).

103 A.R.S. § 33-1321(B) (West Supp. 1998).

104 A.R.S. § 33-1321(D) (West Supp. 1998).

105 A.R.S. §§ 33-1310(14), -1321(A) (West Supp. 1998).

106 A.R.S. § 33-1321(B) (West Supp. 1998).

107 A.R.S. § 33-1310(3) (West Supp. 1998).

108 A.R.S. § 33-1321(D) (West Supp. 1998).

to whether or not the tenant makes a "demand." While demand by the tenant is technically a requirement, the courts are likely to impute demand from seemingly innocuous conduct (i.e., providing a forwarding address, etc).

- The law does not require the landlord to pay tenants interest on deposits.

The foregoing summarizes virtually all you need to know about security deposits. Nevertheless, you should read the portion of the Act that specifically addresses deposits (reprinted below).

A. A landlord shall not demand or receive security, however denominated, including, but not limited to, prepaid rent in an amount or value in excess of one and one-half month's rent. This subsection does not prohibit a tenant from voluntarily paying more than one and one-half month's rent in advance.

B. The purpose of all nonrefundable fees or deposits shall be stated in writing by the landlord. Any fee or deposit not designated as nonrefundable shall be refundable.

C. With respect to tenants who first occupy the premises or enter into a new written rental agreement after January 1, 1996, upon move-in a landlord shall furnish the tenant with a signed copy of the lease, a move-in form for specifying any existing damages to the dwelling unit and written notification to the tenant that the tenant may be present at the move-out inspection. Upon request by the tenant, the landlord shall notify the tenant when the landlord's move-out inspection will occur. If the tenant is being evicted for a material and irreparable breach and the landlord has reasonable cause to fear violence or intimidation on the part of the tenant, the landlord has no obligation to conduct a joint move-out inspection with the tenant.

D. Upon termination of the tenancy, property or money held by the landlord as prepaid rent and security may be applied to the payment of all rent, and subject to a landlord's duty to mitigate, all charges as specified in the signed lease agreement, or as provided in this chapter, including the amount of damages which the landlord has suffered by reason of the tenant's noncompliance with section 33-1341. Within fourteen days, excluding Saturdays, Sundays or other legal holidays, after termination of the tenancy and delivery of possession and demand by the tenant the landlord shall provide the tenant an itemized list of all deductions together with the amount due and payable to the tenant, if any. Unless other arrangements are made in writing by the tenant, the landlord shall mail, by regular mail, to the tenant's last known place of residence.

E. If the landlord fails to comply with subsection D of this section the tenant may recover the property and money due the tenant together with damages in an amount equal to twice the amount wrongfully withheld.

F. This section does not preclude the landlord or tenant from recovering other damages to which the landlord or tenant may be entitled under this chapter.

G. The holder of the landlord's interest in the premises at the time of the termination of the tenancy is bound by this section.[109]

---

[109] A.R.S. § 33-1321(A)-(D) (West Supp. 1998).

<u>Summary of last Section</u>

1. MUST's.
   Your rental agreement **must**:
   - Disclose the name of the manager and owner or owner's agent.
   - Be complete (i.e., all blank spaces filled in).
   - Be written, if longer than one-year.

   You **must**:
   - Deliver a signed copy of the written rental agreement to the tenant.
   - Give notice that Act is available free from the Arizona Secretary of State's Office.
   - Give tenant a move-in inspection form.
   - Give tenant notice that s/he may be present during move-out inspection.
   - Give notice of purpose of all nonrefundable fees, charges and/or deposits.
   - Give tenant a pool safety notice (if rental property includes a pool)
   - Give tenant a notice about lead-based paint and lead-based paint hazards

2. SHOULD's. Your rental agreement **should**:
   - Be written (regardless of length of tenancy).
   - Be comprehensive.
   - Provide for abandonment.
   - Provide for payment of expenses incurred to bring a legal action.
   - Provide for payment of "other expenses" incurred by the landlord.
   - Provide for tenant's maintenance obligations.
   - Provide for inspection of the rental unit.
   - Address "reasonable" modifications/alterations.
   - The rental agreement should provide how partial payments are applied to amounts due.
   - Provide for a reasonable late fee.
   - Provide for rental tax increases.
   - The rental agreement should include a liquidated damages provision.
   - The rental agreement should include waiver of jury trial.

3. CANNOT's. You or the rental agreement **cannot**:
   - Require the tenant to:
       - waive the tenant's rights;
       - agree to pay attorneys' fees; or
       - agree to limit the landlord's liability.
   - Collect a security deposit equal to more than one and one-half month's rent.
   - Include provisions contrary to the Act.

4. Deposits.
   - Not more than one and one-half times the monthly rent.
   - Nonrefundable fees, charges and/or deposits must be in writing.
   - Purpose of all nonrefundable fees, charges and/or deposits must be stated in writing.
   - Must refund deposit or provide written notice within fourteen business days.
   - No requirement to pay interest on deposits.

E.   PREPARE YOUR OTHER FORMS.

Okay, you have created or revised your written rental agreement. But, you are not finished yet. Next, you must prepare your "other" forms. While not exhaustive, the following is a list of necessary and commonly used forms.

- Tenant Application (*see* Chapter 3, Section D(1) and (2))
- Tenant Information Sheet (*see* Chapter 3, Section D(3))
- Property Inspection Checklist
- Personal Property Inspection Checklist
- Notice to Terminate Tenancy
- Disposition of Deposits
- Five-Day Notice to Pay or Quit
- Complaint Form
- Parking Violation
- Miscellaneous Notices
- Federal Debt Collection Practices Act Notices

There are four forms that are filled out every single time that you rent a unit: the Application, the Tenant Information Sheet, the Rental Agreement and the Property Inspection Checklist (which may include a personal property checklist). As previously discussed, the rental agreement is *the most important form* because it is the source of all your rights and your tenants' obligations. The other three forms are nevertheless very important because of the information they capture and the frequency that they are used.

Each form is discussed on the following pages. A sample form accompanies each discussion. Blank forms (except for the Personal Property Inspection Checklist), which you may reproduce and use, are included in Appendix B.

1.   Tenant Applications.

Tenant Applications are discussed at length in Chapter 3, Section D.

2.   Tenant Information Sheet.

Tenant Information Sheets are discussed at length in Chapter 3, Section D, in conjunction with Tenant Applications.

3.   Property Inspection Checklist.

Next to the rental agreement, the Property Inspection Checklist is probably the most important form. Apparently, the Arizona legislature felt the same way and, in July 1995, amended the Act to require that landlords provide tenants with a Property Inspection Checklist.[110] The precise structure and/or content of the form is not prescribed by the statute and, therefore, you may construct your own form. The design of the form is not as critical as the information that it is intended to capture. The purpose for the Property Inspection Checklist is to record the condition of the rental unit <u>before</u> the tenant moves in. The information recorded on this form is critical, even if you have only one rental unit.

Why all the fuss? First, this type of form is now required by law.[111] Second, as a practical matter, this form will help you if/when you end up in court. Here is the typical scenario: tenant moves out, the rental unit has sustained some type of damage (not normal wear and tear -- damage), the landlord alleges that the tenant has caused the damage and is responsible for repairs, the tenant asserts that the rental unit was damaged (i.e., in that condition) when he moved in. The typical courtroom colloquy goes something like this:

Judge:	"Mr. Tenant, did you cause this damage to the unit?"
Tenant:	"No Judge, it was that way when I moved in."
Judge:	"Mr. Landlord, do you have any evidence that demonstrates that the unit was not damaged when this tenant moved in?"
Landlord:	"I saw the unit before he moved in and it wasn't damaged."
Judge:	"Anything else, besides your word?"

Yes, I know, this dialogue is insulting because it questions the integrity of the landlord. But there are unscrupulous landlords as well as deadbeat tenants and the judge doesn't know either one of you. Enter the Property Inspection Checklist. Now, let us revisit the same scenario.

Judge:	"Mr. Tenant, did you cause this damage to the unit?"
Tenant:	"No Judge, it was that way when I moved in."

---

110 A.R.S. § 33-1321(C) (West Supp. 1998).

111 A.R.S. § 33-1321(C) (West Supp. 1998).

Judge:	"Mr. Landlord, do you have any evidence that demonstrates that the unit was not damaged when this tenant moved in?"
Landlord:	"Yes, your honor. Before Mr. Tenant moved in, I filled out this Property Inspection Checklist, noting all the property defects. Nowhere on this form does it report a `man-hole cover' size hole in the living room wall. Such a property defect certainly would have been recorded had it been there. Moreover, Mr. Tenant signed this form, acknowledging that it reflected the true condition of the rental unit on the date he moved in."
Judge:	"What about that, Mr. Tenant?"
Tenant:	"The hole was there, Judge, I must have neglected to write it on the inspection sheet."
Judge:	"Uh huh, right. I find for Mr. Landlord and enter judgment against Mr. Tenant."

The key points to remember about a Property Inspection Checklist are:

- Upon move-in (or before), the landlord must provide the tenant with a move-in inspection form.[112]

- It must be filled out before or shortly after the tenant moves in;

- It must be signed and dated by the tenant and you must provide the tenant with a signed copy of the form; and

- The form must be comprehensive.

On the next page is a completed Property Inspection Checklist. This form illustrates how detailed your notes should be. A blank copy of the Property Inspection Checklist, which you may copy and use, is included in Appendix B.

---

112   A.R.S. § 33-1321(C) (West Supp. 1998).

PROPERTY INSPECTION CHECKLIST

The premises located at: 111 North Maple Street, #2, Phoenix, Arizona, are clean, safe, in good repair and without defects, with only the following exceptions noted:

Exterior: ***Bedroom window cracked, south side of building needs paint (existing paint is peeling).***
(i.e., condition of the exterior structure, etc.)

Living room* : ***Hole in carpet (burn mark); stain on carpet, near door.***

Family room* : ***Hole in south hall; outlet cover missing.***

Kitchen: ***Cabinet above stove scratched; oven dented at bottom; faucet drips; 1 floor tile broken.***
(i.e., appliances, cabinets, walls, floor, ceiling, etc.)

Laundry room** : ***None.***

Hall: ***None.***

Hall bathroom** : ***Towel rack bent; light cover missing; bathtub porcelain chipped.***

Bedroom 1* : ***Door marred; hole in carpet, near window; drapes torn.***

Bedroom 2* : ***Light fixture doesn't work.***

Master Bedroom** : ***Carpet stain near closet; hole in wall behind door.***

When completed and signed, this form will be attached to your Rental Agreement. Costs to repair defects not noted on this checklist are the tenant(s)'s responsibility and will be deducted from the security deposit if not repaired prior to vacating the premises. MAKE A THOROUGH INSPECTION OF THE PREMISES & NOTE ALL DEFECTS!

Terry Tenant   (date)   *Larry Landlord*   (date)
(Tenants)   (Landlord/Owner)
* i.e., floor, carpet, walls, ceilings, doors, hardware, windows. ** i.e., fixtures, walls, ceilings, floor, outlets, door, windows.

4.   Personal Property Inspection Checklist.

A Personal Property Inspection Checklist is essentially the same as the property inspection form, except that it is typically used to record the condition of personal property that the tenant may rent, in addition to the rental unit itself, as in the case of a furnished apartment. Many times, where rental of real and personal property is the norm, the two forms are combined into one form.

5.   Notice to Terminate Tenancy.

Some landlords do not like to furnish tenants with a termination form, presumably because they don't want the tenants to terminate tenancy – ever. I, on the other hand, operate under the more reasonable assumption that all tenants will eventually terminate their tenancy – it is merely a question of when. That being the case, I want to supply them with a form for two very important reasons.

NOTICE TO TERMINATE TENANCY
(Voluntary termination by tenant)

In accordance with the Rental Agreement, I hereby submit my written notice to terminate tenancy for: _____ .

(rental property address)

TENANCY CANNOT BE TERMINATED IN THE MIDDLE OF THE RENTAL PERIOD. Example: Today is April 15 and you wish to terminate tenancy. Notice must be given on or before the last day of the present rental period; the present rental period is 1-30 April; therefore, notice must be given on or before April 30, and tenancy will terminate as of May 31.

I understand that I must give at least thirty (30) days' notice and that the thirtieth day of the notice must fall on or before the last day of the present rental period. I understand that return of any refundable deposits is conditional upon giving adequate notice to terminate and compliance with the other provisions of the Rental Agreement. I understand that any refundable deposits will be mailed within fourteen (14) days hereof or the date I/we vacate the unit, whichever occurs last. The check for the deposit(s) will be mailed to the address listed below, or, if none provided, to my last known address, less any amounts outstanding for past due rent, charges for cleaning in excess of my cleaning deposit, repairs, and any amounts owed by tenant(s) to the landlord. As previously agreed in the Rental Agreement, I will allow landlord access to the unit to show prospective tenants.

Date _____

_____   _____
(print names)   (Tenant's signature)

FORWARDING ADDRESS:

_____

_____

First, by giving them this form, I am telling them that I insist upon written notice of termination. In fact, in my rental agreement, the tenant expressly agrees that written notice to terminate will be given to the landlord and the tenant even acknowledges receipt of a form specifically for that purpose. Under these facts, a tenant has absolutely no excuse for not providing written notice of his/her intent to terminate tenancy.

Second, my Notice to Terminate Tenancy Form clearly explains how much notice is required and even provides an example. This is precisely the same language used in my rental agreement. By putting the same language from the rental agreement onto the Termination Form, it forces the tenant, one way or the other, to become familiar with my notice requirements. It also has the added benefit of obtaining his/her forwarding address, explaining my procedure for returning deposits, and obtaining permission to show the unit.

If you choose to use a form that repeats the termination language in your rental agreement, be sure to repeat the exact same language. Different words may import different meanings, which may cause a tenant to become confused or may allow a tenant to *claim* that s/he was confused.

DISPOSITION OF DEPOSITS

In accordance with the Arizona Residential Landlord and Tenant Act, specifically, A.R.S. § 33-1321, the following discloses the disposition of your deposit(s):

DEPOSITS
Nonrefundable fees, charges and/or deposits:

Cleaning fee (Nonrefundable)	$*0.00*
Redecorating fee (Nonrefundable)	$*100.00*
Other	$*0.00*
Total:	$*100.00*
Amount refundable:	$*0.00*

Refundable deposits:

Cleaning deposit (Refundable)	$*75.00*
Redecorating deposit (Refundable)	$*0.00*
Security deposit (Refundable)	$*300.00*
Other	$*0.00*
Total:	$*375.00*

DEDUCTIONS

Unpaid rent	$	*0.00*
Late charges	$	*0.00*
Damages	$	*65.00*
Other *Replace missing bathroom fixture*	$	*40.00*
TOTAL DEDUCTIONS		$*105.00*
AMOUNT OF REFUNDABLE DEPOSITS:		$*270.00*

■ Refund Due to Tenant ☐ Balance Due to Landlord; Payment immediately due.

Larry Landlord

This notice delivered this date *June 5, 1998* via:

☐ Certified mail
■ Regular first class mail
☐ Hand delivered

Acknowledgment of hand delivery and receipt hereof:
___N/A_____
(signature of tenant)   (date)

Notes for landlord:
Refund check #*1001* issued on *June 5, 1998*, for $*270.00*
Check made payable to: *Terry and Tina Tenant*
(should be made payable to all tenants on rental agreement, unless otherwise authorized)
Date tenant vacated the unit <u>and</u> returned keys: *May 31, 1998*
Date tenant requested (orally or in writing) return of deposit: *June 2, 1998*
Date tenancy terminated: *May 31, 1998*
A.R.S. § 33-1321(D) provides that refund must be "delivered to tenant ... within fourteen days after termination of the tenancy and delivery of possession and demand by the tenant."

---

6.   Disposition of Deposits.

As previously stated (Chapter 2, Section D(4)), within fourteen business days, you must either: (1) refund 100% of the tenant's deposits that you are holding or (2) refund the amount due the tenant, if any, and provide a written notice that itemizes deductions from the tenant's deposits.[113] Your notice should also be specific enough to refresh your recollection of the damage(s) done when/if the matter goes to court, which may be months or even years later.

This form (prior page) has served me well. Pay particular attention to the shaded portion, at the bottom of the form. This area is to be used by the landlord to document significant dates and will serve as a reminder that the landlord must refund deposits within fourteen days. A blank Disposition of Deposits form is included in Appendix B. I recommend, however, that you reproduce the shaded area of the form on the back of your form or on a separate sheet, so that this information is not accidently copied and sent to the tenant -- **the shaded area is intended for the landlord's use, not the tenant's**. This is particularly important if you failed (inadvertently, of course) to send the tenant his/her deposit within the fourteen day period.

7.   Five-Day Notice to Pay or Quit.

Alas, you will inevitably be required to send a ***Five-Day Notice to Pay or Quit***, a.k.a. the ***Five-Day Notice*** (previously known as the Seven-Day Notice to Pay or Quit).[114] Strangely enough, the Act does not prescribe the content of the Five-Day Notice, but some insight may be garnered from the Act:

> If rent is unpaid when due and the tenant fails to pay rent within five days after written notice by the landlord of nonpayment and the landlord's intention to terminate the rental agreement if the rent is not paid within that period of time, the landlord may terminate the rental agreement and file a special detainer action pursuant to § 33-1377.[115]

Once again, there are no magic words, but you must convey the appropriate message: rent is overdue and if not paid within five days, you (the landlord) intend to terminate the rental agreement. I use the following form (blank copy of this form is included in Appendix B, Form 9).

---

113   A.R.S. § 33-1321(D) (West Supp. 1998).

114   A.R.S. § 33-1368(B) (West 1990) (before 1995 amendment).

115   A.R.S. § 33-1368(B) (West Supp. 1998).

FIVE-DAY NOTICE TO PAY OR QUIT

Terry Tenant *123 North Oak Street* *Phoenix*, Arizona *85999*	Date: *July 2, 1998*

Notice to Tenant,

      Pursuant to Arizona Revised Statutes, Title 33, Chapter 10, Section 33-1368(B), you are hereby tendered five-days written notice to remit all due, but as yet unpaid, rent and other amounts owing, in the amount of: $*545.00* (calculated through *July 2, 1998*). The stated amount is calculated as follows:

$*500.00*	Rent for *July 1998*
$ *20.00*	Late charges (*$20 on 2d, plus 1%/day thereafter*)
$ *25.00*	Fee for preparing and serving Five-Day Notice.
$ _____	Other _____
$*545.00*	Total

The stated "Total" is exclusive of future accruing costs. Additional charges accrue after the date specified above at the daily rate of $5.00.

      In the event full payment is not tendered within five days after receipt of this notice, your right to possess and occupy the rental unit will be terminated and an eviction action filed against you to recover possession of the premises, rent, late fees, and any other amounts due under the rental agreement or available by law, including attorney's fees and court costs; your financial responsibility under the rental agreement will continue. Full payment within the five-day period will reinstate the rental agreement.

      THE FIFTH DAY FALLS ON: *JULY 9, 1998*

      Alternatively, you may vacate the premises on or before the fifth day. Vacating the premises, however, will not relieve you from your financial liability under the rental agreement. In the event you have any questions, contact <u>Larry Landlord</u> at *555-4444*.

                               (name)   (phone number)

                           Larry Landlord

This notice delivered this date _July 2, 1998_ via:

☐ Certified mail
☐ Regular first class mail
■ Hand delivered   Acknowledgment of hand delivery and receipt hereof:

                             Terry Tenant   *July, 2, 1998*
                             (signature of tenant)   (date)

8.   Complaint Form.

     Having tenants means having complaints: complaints from neighbors, other tenants and maybe even a few complaints of your own. Ergo, your cache of forms is not complete without some type of general purpose complaint form. Interestingly enough, this form actually gets results. But even when it doesn't, it helps document your file so that if you must evict this tenant, you have written evidence to justify your actions in court, if necessary.

NOTICE OF ☒ COMPLAINT ☐ VIOLATION

Terry Tenant
101 North Rental Avenue   Date: _(today)_
Phoenix, Arizona 85666

Notice to Tenant,

☒ Complaints have been made against you for:
Excessive noise; specifically, loud music played after 10:00 p.m.

☐ You are violating the following term(s) in your Rental Agreement:

☒ Your repeated violations of the same or similar nature constitute a material noncompliance with your Rental Agreement.
You must take action to remedy this/these problems immediately !

Your Rental Agreement will be terminated and you will be evicted if you fail to comply.

Larry Landlord

This notice delivered this date _____ via:
☐ Certified mail
☐ Regular first class mail
☒ Hand delivered   Acknowledgment of hand delivery and receipt hereof:
Terry Tenant _____ _____/date/_____
(signature of tenant)   (date)

---

9.   Parking Violation.

Your repertoire (collection) of forms is not complete without a parking violation form. Yes, inevitably, someone will park in your space, your manager's space or one of your tenants' spaces. And possibly, if you are having a particularly bad day, all of the above, on the same day. Naturally, a parking violation form will not remedy the situation, but it will make you feel a whole lot better. And, depending on the law in your local area, if the violator continue to ignore your warnings, you can probably have him/her towed away.

What is the law on towing away a vehicle that is parked on your property? Typically, towing of vehicles that are unlawfully parked on private property is governed by local law (i.e., city or town). Sometimes you must give written notice. Sometimes signs must be posted. Given the number of cities and towns in Arizona, I have not attempted to chronicle the various laws on this utterly fascinating subject. To find out the law in your area, call your lawyer. Alternatively, call a local towing company. Towing is their business – they will probably know what the law is, what the notice requirements are, and may even have signs and/or stickers that you can purchase from them to comply with the law. For those living in Phoenix, Arizona, I have reprinted, below, the Phoenix City Code.

Parking in driveway or private property; tow truck operators

A. No person shall park a vehicle in any private driveway or on private property or private parking areas without the express or implied consent of the owner or person in lawful possession of such property.

B. The owner or person in lawful possession of any private parking area shall be deemed to have given consent to unrestricted parking by the general public in such parking area unless such parking area is posted with signs as prescribed by this section which are clearly visible and readable from any point within the parking area and at each entrance thereto. Such signs shall contain, as a minimum, the following information:

(1) Restrictions on parking.

(2) Disposition of vehicles found in violation of parking restrictions.

(3) Maximum cost to the violator, including daily storage fees and other charges, that could result from the disposition of his unlawfully parked vehicle.

(4) Telephone number or address where the violator can locate his vehicle.

(5) Each sign shall state `Phoenix City Code Sec. 36-144.'

C. No tow truck operator acting under the authority of this section shall tow a vehicle from a private parking area unless the signs are posted as required by paragraph B and contain all the information specified in paragraph B, nor shall he charge fees in excess of the amounts specified on the signs.

. . . .

H. Not withstanding any other provision of this section an abandoned vehicle may be towed from any private parking area, pursuant to a written order from the real property owner or his agent. A tow truck operator shall not act as the agent of the real property owner. The real property owner or his agent shall sign the towing order, which shall specify each vehicle to be towed and shall not authorize the towing of an unknown vehicle at a future date. A tow truck operator shall not tow or transport a vehicle unless the towing order is in his possession. For purposes of this section an "abandoned vehicle" is a vehicle left in a private parking area more than fifteen (15) days, when it has not been left under a written contract of storage and has not, during that period been removed by the person leaving it.

I. A violation of subsection A of this section shall constitute a civil traffic violation, and the violator shall be subject to a civil sanction of not less than $50 or more than $250, provided that effective October 1, 1992, the minimum civil sanction shall be $65. Any other violations of this section shall constitute a Class I misdemeanor.[116]

PARKING VIOLATION

YOUR VEHICLE IS PARKED ON PRIVATE PROPERTY WITHOUT EXPRESS AUTHORIZATION.

UNAUTHORIZED USE OF THIS PRIVATE PROPERTY SUBJECTS YOUR VEHICLE TO IMPOUNDMENT AT YOUR EXPENSE, INCLUDING TOWING AND STORAGE FEES. IN ADDITION, Phoenix City Code, Section 36-144(A), provides that no person shall park a vehicle on private property without the express consent of the owner of such property.

VIOLATION OF SECTION 36-144 IS PUNISHABLE BY A FINE OF UP TO $250.
See PHOENIX, ARIZ., CITY CODE ART. XI, § 36-144(I) (1992).

WARNING: VEHICLE MAY BE TOWED ON NEXT VIOLATION!!

DATE:_____ LICENSE #_____ VEHICLE_____

WARNING TO THE READER: This Notice is provided merely as a sample. This warning, as written above, complies with the law in Phoenix, Arizona, provided you have signs posted in your parking area that restrict parking.[117] If you live in Phoenix, Arizona, and you do not have signs, you cannot tow away the violator's vehicle on the "next violation." Therefore, you will either need to get some signs or change the language on the Notice. You can, however, tow away an "abandoned" vehicle, as that term is defined in paragraph H (above).[118] If you live anywhere other than Phoenix, you should consult your attorney for the appropriate language to put in your notice.

---

116   PHOENIX, ARIZ., CITY CODE, ART. XI, § 36-144 (1992 & Supp. 1998).

117   *See* PHOENIX, ARIZ., CITY CODE art. XI, § 36-144(B) (1992 & Supp. 1998) (printed above).

118   *See* PHOENIX, ARIZ., CITY CODE art. XI, § 36-144(H) (1992 & Supp. 1997) (printed above).

10. Miscellaneous notices.

For the most part, the forms previously discussed will take care of 99% of your needs. Nevertheless, from time to time, you may have need of a form that has not been discussed. On the rare occasion when you need such a form, you can draft your own form, consult a fellow landlord or call your attorney.

11. Federal Debt Collection Practices Act Notices.

A common tactic used by delinquent tenants when they receive a Five-Day Notice to Pay or Quit and/or discover that you have obtained a judgment against them for rent and/or other amounts, is to have an attorney send you a letter stating that you have violated the Federal Debt Collection Practices Act and that you are now liable to the tenant in an amount that exceeds the judgment you have against the tenant. Don't let this tactic scare you into abandoning your right to collect the full amount due from your tenant. If you receive such a letter, immediately consult your attorney. To avoid ever getting such a letter, read on.

The Federal Debt Collection Practices Act (FDCPA)[119] prohibits certain conduct and requires that certain notices be given to the debtor (i.e., the tenant). The FDCPA encompasses several federal statutes and a thorough explanation of the cases interpreting the statutes and the various nuances of this area of the law could easily file an entire book. Nevertheless, what *you* need to know, as a landlord, is summarized below.

If *you* are the owner of the subject property and *you* are sending notices to tenants for past due rent, you do not need to worry about the FDCPA and/or provide your tenants with any of the notices that are required by the FDCPA. Stop, you are done; you need not read the remainder of this section.

If you are not the owner of the subject property, the FDCPA may apply to you. The FDCPA applies when someone, who is not the owner of the property (i.e., a collection agent, a property manager, etc.), attempts to collect past due rent from a tenant. Specifically, the FDCPA applies to the collection of "consumer debts" (which includes rent for a residence) by a "debt collector" (which includes collection agents and may include property managers, real estate agents acting on the owner's behalf, and even an attorney). Consequently, if you are sending a notice to a tenant that seeks to collect past due rent and/or possession of the rental property and you are not the owner of the subject property, you should comply with the requirements of the FDCPA.

---

[119] 15 U.S.C. §§ 1692a to 1692o (West 1982 & Supp. 1998).

It is possible that the FDCPA does not apply to some people and/or businesses that send notices to tenants on the owner's behalf, but to "err conservatively" (*see* Chapter 2, Section A), you should comply with the FDCPA *unless* you have a written legal opinion from your attorney that states the FDCPA does not apply to you and that you need not comply therewith.

A violation of the FDCPA may result in civil liability to the tenant equal to any actual damages sustained by the tenant, plus statutory damages of up to $1,000.00, and attorney's fees and costs.[120] (Note: the attorney's fees will normally be much more than the actual or statutory damages). Consequently, it is worth you while to comply with the FDCPA, thereby avoiding liability and, more importantly, avoiding litigation.

How do I comply with the FDCPA? The answer can sometimes be complex, but I have tried to simplify the actions you must take to comply with the FDCPA.

First, you must include the following notices with all notices that you send to the tenant that seek to collect past due rent or possession of the premises.

> This is an attempt to collect a debt. Any information obtained will be used for that purpose. Unless you dispute the validity of the debt, or any portion thereof, within 30 days of receipt of this letter, it will be assumed to be valid. If the dispute is received in writing, debt verification or a copy of judgment will be obtained and mailed to you. If requested in writing within 30 days of receipt of this letter, the original creditor's name and address will be provided. Pursuant to 15 U.S.C. Section 1692e(11), please be advised that this communication is from a debt collector.

Second, if you speak to the tenant orally in connection with collection of past due rent or to recover possession of the premises, you must tell the tenant: "I am a debt collector, attempting to collect a debt, and any information obtained will be used for that purpose."

Third, if the tenant requests "debt verification" or the name/address of the original creditor, send the tenant a copy of the rental agreement, a statement of his/her account (i.e., accrual of charges, when payments were received, and the amount presently due), and the name and address of the original creditor (i.e., the

---

120   15 U.S.C. § 1692k (West 1982).

owner). This will satisfy the tenant's request for information. Alternatively, you may send this information when you send the Five-Day Notice to Pay or Quit or any other notice that demands possession of the property, rather than wait for the tenant to request this information. The latter procedure has the benefit of avoiding the failure to timely respond to the tenant's request for information or defending an allegation that the tenant made a request (which you never received) and you did not timely respond. In any event, whether you just provide this information or wait for the tenant to request this information before supplying it, you must include the foregoing notice in all notices you send to the tenant that seek past due rent or possession of the subject property.

In addition, to comply with the FDCPA, you *must not*:

• Contact the tenant at "inconvenient" times.

• Contact the tenant as his/her place of employment, if it is known that this will cause a problem.

• Make any false or misleading representations (i.e., threatening to seize the tenant's personal property to satisfy payment of past due rent; seizing a residential tenant's personal property to pay for rent is not permissible).[121]

• Engage in any "unfair" debt collection practices (i.e., accepting a post dated check of more than five days; filing a lawsuit to collect past due rent after the statute of limitations has expired; etc.).

• Continue to contact the tenant if the tenant sends you a written notice requesting that you discontinue communicating with him/her (if you receive this type of notice, this is the time to turn the matter over to an attorney).

That, in a "nut shell," are the requirements to comply with the FDCPA. If you routinely engage in collecting past due rent (or other debts) for others, you should consult an attorney and ensure that you have sufficient office policies and procedures in place to avoid liability under the FDCPA.

---

121   A.R.S. § 33-1372 (West 1990).

CHAPTER 3

GETTING TENANTS

Summary of Chapter

- Prepare unit for new tenants
- Attract applicants -- Advertising
- Show the prospective tenants the unit
- Have the tenants fill out the application
- Select the best tenant; reject all others
- Term of tenancy

There is a series of specific steps that will help you to get good tenants. Common sense will tell you that the order of these steps is important. Naturally, you will want the unit (or complex) ready for occupancy before spending time and money attracting tenants. More important, however, is that you show prospective tenants the unit <u>before</u> having them fill out the application (*see* Chapter 3, Section C). And, of course, you will want to review the application and ask a few questions of the applicants before they leave (more on reviewing the application in Chapter 3, Section D).

A.   PREPARE UNIT FOR NEW TENANTS.

1.   Curb appeal.

The best advertisement and the one that will do the most good (or harm), is a well kept rental unit. Conversely, if the exterior looks bad, prospective tenants will just drive by. Remember, they plan on living there. Their friends and relatives will come to see them. They do not want to live in a slum, nor do they want other people to think that they live in a slum.

Put a little effort into "sprucing up" the exterior of the unit or complex. A little paint and cleanup goes a long way toward improving the curb appeal of your unit or complex.

2.   Interior appearance.

Normally, a rental unit that is clean and freshly painted will be more appealing to an applicant than a rental unit that is not. Likewise, a landlord can normally demand more rent for a rental unit that is clean and freshly painted than a rental unit that is not. In both cases, however, there are exceptions. For example, assume that you have two identical units: one is clean, freshly painted and ready to rent ("rental-ready"); the other is not clean (but not filthy), needs painting and some other "tidying up" before it is ready to rent. Your choices are: (1) pay someone to get the unit in rental-ready condition or (2) let your new tenants do the work and reduce the amount of their move-in cost.

The first option has the advantage of assuring you that the work is done, and done properly. But, the second option has three distinct advantages. First, your tenant can move in immediately and do the work over the next few days. This allows you to charge and collect rent for days that the unit would otherwise be vacant, thus reducing the "real" amount you are paying the tenant to do the repairs. Second, most tenants usually clean the premises as soon as they move in anyway, whether the unit is clean or not. This is a duplication of effort. Moreover, the tenant who will be living there is more likely to do a more thorough cleaning job than your regular cleaning crew. Third, assuming this tenant's only negative characteristic is a lack of sufficient capital to cover the advance rent and deposits, this option enables you to rent to a tenant that otherwise would not have been able to rent your unit. Even if the tenant does have sufficient funds to cover the move-in expenses, few tenants will turn down an opportunity to reduce their move-in expenses -- money they save can be spent elsewhere.

Several points are worth noting, however. First, make sure the tenant understands that the repairs must be done, must be done correctly and must be done by a specific date. Second, you must inspect the work. Third, do not allow them to perform work for which s/he is not qualified. Most people, but not everybody, can paint. Most people, however, cannot repair holes in the wall or replace electrical fixtures. One last item, this practice works best when you have at least two units available: one that is rental-ready and one that is not. That way, you can show the tenant what the unit will look like when it is clean and freshly painted. Otherwise, the only thing s/he will see is an unclean, dirty rental unit. Moreover, s/he will assume that the rest of your units look that way inside.

3.   Compliance with the law.

(a)   Safety.

Naturally, we want the property to look good, both inside and out, but we must also take care that the property is safe. *Caveat Emptor* (buyer beware, or in this case, tenant beware) is virtually dead in Arizona.[122] Therefore, it is up to you to make sure the property is safe and meets city code requirements. Some specific areas of concern include:

● Whether you are required to install <u>and maintain</u> smoke alarms. If you use battery operated smoke alarms, you may even be responsible for periodic inspection of the batteries, *in spite of* any attempt to transfer that responsibility to the tenant in the rental agreement.

● Compliance with local building codes. For example, all electrical, plumbing, gas, heating and air conditioning systems, and ventilating systems function properly and meet local building and safety codes. This is, perhaps, most important in the case of electrical wiring and gas pipes, where the potential for injury to occupants of the subject property is very great.

● Compliance with pool barrier laws. Pool barrier laws exist at the state, county and local level (i.e., city or town). Generally, pool barrier laws require the owner of a property with children and a swimming pool (but may also include spas and hot tubs) to install some type of barrier between the pool and the dwelling.[123] The parameters of the law may vary from city to city (or town). The specific ordinance will identify options, but may include installing a fence, a pool cover, or additional locks on doors that access the pool. Naturally, this is important if you rent a property with a pool to tenants with children, but it is <u>just as important</u> when you rent to tenants <u>without</u> children. Remember, tenants have guests over, especially when they have a pool, and guests may have children. Therefore, whether or not your tenant has children, you *should* install a pool barrier. Some local ordinances require a temporary barrier when children are visiting the property. Furthermore, because we presently live in a "lawsuit happy" society, I recommend installation of a pool barrier, <u>whether or not</u> required by law, for two reasons. First, the pool barrier laws are intended to, and do, prevent the drowning of young children. On this basis alone, you should install pool barriers. Second, this is consistent with our philosophy of avoiding litigation.

● Disclosure of "material" property information and your screening criteria. *See* Chapter 3, Section E(2) (applicant screening criteria); Chapter 3, Section A(4) (disclosure).

---

122 *See* <u>Hill v. Jones</u>, 151 Ariz. 81, 725 P.2d 1115 (App. 1986).

123 *See, e.g.*, PHOENIX, ARIZ., CONSTRUCTION CODE § 610.01 (1990).

(b)   Taxes.

(1)   Federal and state income tax.

Naturally, rental income must be reported on both your state and federal tax income tax return. The tax laws related to rental real estate could fill a separate volume and, therefore, no attempt is made to address those issues here. Suffice to say that rental income is taxable and that you should refer tax questions to your accountant.

(2)   Rental tax.

You may also be required to have a transaction privilege license (i.e., a rental tax license). There is no state rental tax on residential rental units. The requirement, if any, for a rental tax license will come from your local government (i.e., city or town). For example, in the City of Phoenix, a transaction privilege license is required for persons who rent three or more rental units in Arizona.[124] The rental tax is presently equal to 1.3% of the rental income.[125] To determine if you must pay a rental tax, contact the tax division of your local government.

4.   Disclosure.

Cross Reference
● *See* Chapter 3, Section A(5), Landlord Representations

The law in Arizona with respect to the <u>sale</u> of real property has clearly shifted from "buyer beware" (caveat emptor) to "seller must adequately disclose."[126] What this means is that anyone who sells real property in Arizona is under a duty to disclose certain facts to prospective buyers <u>before</u> the buyer purchases the property. Otherwise, the sale may later be rescinded on the basis of intentional or negligent misrepresentation.

What does this have to do with rental property? Creation of any type of tenancy (i.e., month-to-month, etc.) creates a "leasehold estate." The renting of real property is a "transfer" of real property; specifically, the transfer of a leasehold estate. A leasehold estate entitles the holder (i.e., the tenant) to exclusive use and possession of the subject property. This sounds like a lot of legal double-talk, doesn't it? Well, it is. What is important to remember is that renting real property

---

124   *See, e.g.,* PHOENIX, ARIZ., CITY CODE, ART. II, §§ 14-300 (Supp. 1995), 14-310 (Supp. 1994).

125   *See* PHOENIX, ARIZ., CITY CODE, ART. II, § 14-445 (Supp. 1996).

126   *See* <u>Hill v. Jones</u>, 151 Ariz. 81, 725 P.2d 1115 (App. 1986).

in Arizona is a transfer of an interest in real property. As such, there is a duty to disclose certain facts to the transferee (i.e., the recipient of the transfer – the tenant).

What are these "certain facts" that must be disclosed when *renting* real property? Some items that must be disclosed are clear. For example, you must make certain disclosures if the property you rent has a pool or if it contains any lead-based paint or lead-based paint hazards. (*See* Chapter 3, Section D(1)(i) {pool disclosure} and Section D(1)(j) {lead-paint disclosure}). Other items that may or should be disclosed are not as clear. Worse yet, the law is not crystal clear on this issue. Nevertheless, it would not be unreasonable for you to presume that the law will require disclosure of the same facts that must be disclosed when you *sell* real property (if that explanation is of any help). Defining what these "certain facts" are under the law is difficult because the courts have been somewhat vague in their analysis of what must be disclosed. In practice, however, the analysis is easy: **Disclose any fact about the property that *you* would want to know before you bought the property. Err on the side of disclosure -- if you have any doubt about a specific fact, disclose it.** It is that simple.

For example, assume the property is near an airport and planes occasionally (or frequently) fly overhead. This may constitute a significant noise problem, as in the case of a property near Sky Harbor International Airport, or may be a minor nuisance, as in the case of a property near Bullhead City airport. In either case, this fact concerns noise pollution affecting the subject property. The only distinction is the "degree" of pollution (i.e., frequency of, proximity to, and decibel level of the noise). Whether it "must" be disclosed or not will be determined by a court of law *if it is not disclosed* and the tenant complains. If disclosed, however, then there is no basis for a complaint or a lawsuit. Remember, your mission is to *avoid* litigation. By disclosing this fact, we avoid an intentional misrepresentation lawsuit (i.e., you knew about this fact and intentionally concealed it). In addition, by disclosing all facts that impact upon the subject property, you avoid a negligent misrepresentation lawsuit (i.e., you forgot to disclose something or you did not disclose a fact that was later determined to be material). The Arizona Association of Realtors (AAR) has promulgated a form called the "Seller's Property Disclosure Statement," which is intended to capture all the information that should be disclosed by property sellers.[127] This form would be an excellent guide for landlords to use and follow. The AAR form, however, is protected by copyright laws and, therefore, you may not reproduce and use the AAR form without express permission from AAR.

So, what *must* be disclosed and what *should* be disclosed? Some guidelines may be helpful. Keep in mind, however, inaccurate and/or misleading information

---

127 Arizona Association of Realtors, Form 1417-303, SPDS, March 1993.

is just as bad, and possibly worse, than failing to disclose. *See* Chapter 3, Section A(5), Landlord Representations (below).

 • Disclose "obvious" things (i.e., the property fronts a busy street, is right next to the airport, backs-up to a shopping center, is adjacent to a drainage ditch, is near a railroad track, etc.). You may say to yourself, "everyone knows that" or "everyone can plainly see that." First, if "everyone knows," then disclosing it shouldn't cause a problem. Second, "everyone" *may not* know or appreciate the potential hazards of a seemingly "obvious" condition. Remember, some applicants will be coming from out-of-town or out-of-state. Depending on an applicant's experience in life, it may or may not occur to him/her that: (1) noise from a busy street may continue day <u>and night</u> and/or close proximity to a busy street may pose a greater potential for harm to person and property as a result of a traffic accident on or near the subject property, (2) an airport means noise <u>and</u> a potential for harm to person and property as a result of a plane crash, (3) a property that backs-up to a shopping center means there may be frequent truck deliveries, at all hours of the day and night, very close to the rental property and/or that people (i.e., teenagers) may loiter on and around the shopping center and/or the rental property, and (4) close proximity to a drainage ditch means potential water damage if it overflows and poses a danger to children (even if dry).

 • Superfund sites <u>must</u> be disclosed (a superfund site is an area that has been identified by the federal government as having some type of environmental problem, such as a hazardous waste spill and/or groundwater contamination). The Arizona Department of Real Estate Commissioner, Jerry Holt, has taken the position that the fact that a piece of real property is located in a superfund site constitutes a "material fact" that must be disclosed to a prospective buyer/renter.[128] Consequently, licensed real estate agents are required to disclose this information to prospective buyers/renters. If the Arizona Department of Real Estate requires disclosure of this information, then a court of law will likely determine that disclosure of this information is required by all persons, whether or not they are licensed real estate agents.

 • High voltage power-lines in the area must be disclosed.

 • Poor water quality should be disclosed and, under certain facts, must be disclosed. If the water supply to the subject property, whether tap-water or well-water, is poor or contains high amounts of certain metals or minerals, you should disclose this information. If the water supply poses any type of potential hazard to

---

128 Arizona Administrative Code, Real Estate Department Commissioner's Rules, Rule R4-28-1101(B) (amended March 31, 1995). *See also* Arizona Department of Real Estate, Arizona Real Estate Bulletin, Volume XIX, No. 1, page 4 (March 1994).

those who use or consume the water and you know of the hazard, you must disclose this information.

- Potential water damage (i.e., frequent/occasional flooding because of rain and/or overflow of nearby drainage ditch, stream, river, lake, etc.; potential hazard because of upstream dam or dike; in/near flash flood area; etc.). Any potential harm from water should be disclosed. It rains almost everywhere, so a disclosure that it rains in your area is probably not necessary. But it may be necessary to disclose that rainwater pools excessively on the subject property, or that the property is in the middle of a natural run-off area, or is subject to frequent flooding, etc.

- Radon gas test results should be disclosed and, under certain facts, must be disclosed. If you have had a radon gas test performed on your property and the results are good (i.e., no or low levels of radon gas), you probably want to disclose this information, especially if radon gas is a concern in your area. Be sure to note in your disclosure that your representation is based on the test performed by XYZ Company, and that you believe it to be true and correct, but that tenants who deem this information material should run their own test. If you have done a radon gas test and the results are bad (i.e., high levels of radon gas), you *must* disclose this information and, depending on the specific facts, you may even be required to take remedial action (i.e., take steps to reduce the radon gas level). <u>Do not</u> simply order another test (of, perhaps, "dubious" reliability) and disclose only the most favorable test results.

- Problems with "pests" should be disclosed. "Pests" include insects and animals that are indigenous to that area and that either may or do present some level of nuisance. The nuisance may be indoors, outdoors, or both. For example, some areas are more prone to infestation by roaches, ants and/or crickets. Some areas are particularly prone to infestation by reptiles, rodents, and stinging or biting creatures (i.e., scorpions, bees, snakes, spiders, etc.). "Infestation" does not necessarily mean that the subject property is "overrun" with the little beasties (although it may), merely that certain pests may, from time-to-time, be encountered. In certain neighborhoods in the Phoenix metropolitan area, for example, as well as other Arizona locations, scorpions manage to penetrate the living quarters of many property owners. Some people consider them merely a nuisance; others, either because of allergic reactions or an irrational fear of them, consider them to be absolutely intolerable. Renting a property to a tenant that finds a particular pest intolerable, after the tenant moves in, without disclosing the problem in advance, may subject the landlord to damages for all expenses incurred by the tenant to relocate.

● Noise (i.e., nearby airports, busy streets, farming operations, industrial operations, railroad tracks and/or stations; barking neighborhood dogs; disruptive neighbors; etc.). List anything that may pose a potential problem – *especially* anything that has already been the subject of a complaint by a prior tenant.

● Noxious fumes (i.e., from nearby ranching, farming or industrial operations; nearby waste water treatment facility; chemical production plants; etc.). Failure to disclose real or potential problems, especially when the fumes pose a health risk, will almost certainly form the basis of a viable lawsuit against the landlord for misrepresentation and subject him/her to damages therefor.

● Proximity to nearby "attractive nuisances." An "attractive nuisance" is any condition upon property that may reasonably be considered to be a source of danger to children (i.e., drainage ditch, excavations site, condemned building, etc.).[129] You should also disclose the subject property's proximity to potentially dangerous conditions (i.e., railroad tracks, bodies of water, freeways, military installations, chemical and/or explosive manufacturing plants, etc.). Forgetting the legal liability for a moment, imagine how your life would change if a new tenant's child died as a result of your failure to disclose a nearby pond, which you knew to be secluded, not generally known, and a common swimming area for local children. Do yourself a favor, disclose more than you think is necessary and let the tenant make the decision as to whether or not they wish to rent the subject property.

● Known criminal activity. This has become a bigger problem in recent times. A tenant moves into a property and then finds out that the area has a very high incident of serious crime (i.e., rape, murder, drive-by shootings, etc.). Under appropriate facts, failure to disclose this information may subject the landlord to damages for all expenses incurred by the tenant to relocate – an extremely bad result for the landlord. The result could also be much worse; the landlord may be found legally and financially responsible for any injury suffered by the tenant. (*See* Chapter 4, Section (B)(6), for a discussion of state court cases concerning criminal activity). The solution – obtain a copy of the police report of criminal activity for the area. Such a report is available for a small fee in most cities in the Phoenix metropolitan area, at the appropriate police station. Many other towns/cities in Arizona also make such reports available. If such a report is not available, you should create your own report by keeping a running list of known criminal activity in the area.

---

129 Black's Law Dictionary 130 (6th Ed. 1990). *See, also,* MacNeil v. Perkins, 84 Ariz. 74, 324 P.2d 211 (1958) (specifically adopting the Restatement of Torts § 339 definition of attractive nuisance).

● Stigmatized properties. A stigmatized property is one that suffers from some stigma (i.e., a "haunted" house, owned/occupied by a notorious person, etc.). You may find a haunted house or a house once owned by Jesse James to be "quaint." Your tenant, however, may have very strong, and contrary, feelings about this fact. The best course of action is to simply make the disclosure and let the applicant make his/her own decision. What about crime scenes? The law was recently changed regarding this very issue.

> A. No criminal, civil or administrative action may be brought against a transferor of real property or a licensee acting on behalf of a transferor for failing to disclose that the property being transferred is or has been:

> i. The site of a natural death, suicide or homicide or any other crime classified as a felony.

> ii. Owned or occupied by a person exposed to the human immunodeficiency virus or diagnosed as having the acquired immune deficiency syndrome or any other disease that is not known to be transmitted through common occupancy of real estate.

> B. Failing to disclose any fact or suspicion as set forth in section A shall not be grounds for termination or recission of any transaction in which real property has been or will be transferred.[130]

The foregoing obviously resolves the issue with regard to felonies and certain types of deaths. But what about lesser crimes, for example, the theft of bicycle from the front yard of one or your rental units? What level of crimes must be disclosed? This is a very difficult question to answer. The theft of a bicycle does not cause a property to become stigmatized. Nevertheless, an argument can be made that even the theft of the bicycle from the front yard needs to be disclosed, not because this is a stigmatized property, but to make an adequate disclosure about the amount of crime in this area.

Two general rules should help you when deciding what to disclose. First, if you find yourself saying, "should I disclose this fact?" -- disclose it! Second, there is no penalty for disclosing "too much" information, but there may be dire consequences for disclosing "too little."

---

130   A.R.S. §32-2156 (West Supp. 1998).

Of course, to every rule there is an exception. The exception in this case is a prior or current tenant with the HIV or AIDS virus. You cannot discriminate against a person because they have a disability. AIDS is considered a disability under the Americans with Disabilities Act and, as a result, it is unlawful to discriminate against persons with the HIV or AIDS virus. And, the analysis goes, because it is unlawful to discriminate based on this disability, and disclosure of this information may cause others to unlawfully discriminate, there is no legal justification for disclosing that a prior tenant had or current tenants have the HIV or AIDS virus. In addition, the above cited statute expressly provides that this information need not be disclosed and because such information may reasonably be considered "confidential," as is a tenant's credit report, disclosure of this information without the tenant's express (i.e., written) consent may be unlawful and expose the landlord to civil liability. Bottom line - do not disclose that a prior tenant had, or current tenants have, the HIV or AIDS virus.

You are no doubt saying, "by the time I get done with all these disclosures, no one will rent the property." First, if that is the case, you may wish to re-evaluate whether you wish to continue owning that property. Second, your fears are probably unfounded. Have you ever read a prospectus for an offering of newly issued stock, by a newly formed corporation? Or, have you recently purchased a new home and received a copy of the public report? A prospectus discloses all sorts of seemingly irrelevant information and speaks in somewhat pessimistic and gloomy terms (i.e., "there may be no market for the corporation's new product and no profits whatsoever ..." ; "the investor may lose his entire investment ... ", etc.). Similarly, a public report contains all sorts of disclosures, disclaimers and warnings. After reading a typical prospectus or public report, you might reasonably conclude that no one in their right mind would purchase the subject investment -- but they do. Why? Either because they did not read the material or the material disclosed was not important to their decision to invest. In either event, there will be no legal basis for rescinding the investment based on information that appeared in the prospectus or report (unless inaccurate or misleading), only information that *did not* appear that *should have* appeared. Similarly, your tenants will not be able to claim intentional or negligent misrepresentation if you have made adequate disclosure.

You may be thinking, "so what if they have a problem with something I have disclosed?" Good! Before they sign the rental agreement is the time to address the problem, not after they move-in. Disclosure *will not* cost you any tenants. If it is important enough to cause them to not rent your property, it will be important enough for them to sue you after moving-in for failing to disclose a material fact. In either case, the tenant will eventually be gone, but in the latter case, you will also have a lawsuit on your hands.

You now have all the facts. You decide whether or not full disclosure is in your best interest.

5. Landlord Representations.

The law was recently changed. The Act now permits tenants to terminate a rental agreement and sue for damages that result from "material falsification of written information."[131]

> **A.** Except as provided in this chapter, if there is a material noncompliance by the landlord with the rental agreement, including a material falsification of the written information provided to the tenant, the tenant may deliver a written notice to the landlord specifying the acts and omissions constituting the breach and that the rental agreement will terminate upon a date not less than ten days after receipt of the notice if the breach is not remedied in ten days. If there is a noncompliance by the landlord with section 33-1324 materially affecting health and safety, the tenant may deliver a written notice to the landlord specifying the acts and omissions constituting the breach and that the rental agreement will terminate upon a date not less than five days after receipt of the notice if the breach is not remedied in five days. For the purposes of this section, material falsification shall include availability of the unit, except when a holdover tenant is in illegal possession or in violation of the rental agreement, the condition of the premises and any current services as represented by the landlord in writing as well as any written representation, as well as any representation regarding future services and any future changes regarding the condition of the premises, the provision of utility services and the designation of the party responsible for the payment of utility services. The rental agreement shall terminate and the dwelling unit shall be vacated as provided in the notice subject to the following:

> 1. If the breach is remediable by repairs or the payment of damages or otherwise and the landlord adequately remedies the breach prior to the date specified in the notice, the rental agreement will not terminate.

---

131 A.R.S. § 33-1361(A) (West Supp. 1998).

2. The tenant may not terminate for a condition caused by the deliberate or negligent act or omission of the tenant, a member of the tenant's family or other person on the premises with the tenant's consent.

B. Except as provided in this chapter, the tenant may recover damages and obtain injunctive relief for any noncompliance by the landlord with the rental agreement or section 33-1324.

C. The remedy provided in subsection B of this section is in addition to any right of the tenant arising under subsection A of this section.

D. If the rental agreement is terminated, the landlord shall return all security recoverable by the tenant under section 33-1321.[132]

This means that if you advertise (i.e., newspaper advertisements, fliers, brochures, etc.) that you have a pool, sauna, weight room, etc., that you must have these amenities and they must be available to the tenants. Similarly, if you represent that you will soon have these amenities (i.e., construction under way or will be started soon), these amenities must be constructed within the time frame represented. As another example, I heard about an apartment complex that distributed a brochure with a picture on the front of a guard house and a security guard. The complex had long since done away with the security guard, but the guard house remained. A tenant successfully terminated the rental agreement on the basis that the brochure represented that the complex employed a security guard, when, in fact, no security of any type was offered. The moral — periodically review your advertising material to ensure that it accurately represents the services and amenities that you offer.

B.   ATTRACT APPLICANTS – ADVERTISING.

● **Cross Reference,** Chapter 3, Section A(5), Landlord Representations

"What" you say about your rental unit is important; it may even be more important than how you say it or to whom you say it. Prospective tenants want to know location, price (exact monthly rental, not a "range"), square footage, and features. Floor plans are useful to show square footage and layout. Photographs may reveal the unit's "ambiance" (if it has any). The name of the complex (if any), the address and phone number should be easy to find in any type of advertisement. If helpful, a map or directions should be included. Proximity to shopping, schools,

---

132   A.R.S. § 33-1361 (West Supp. 1998).

transportation and other public services should be noted. Move-in specials, discounts, etc., should be highlighted and specific. Special features, such as pool, Jacuzzi, sauna, tennis court, etc., should be stressed. So should amenities like covered parking, laundry facilities, planned activities and the latest "high-demand" features (i.e., exercise rooms, security patrols, etc.).

"Where" you advertise, is equally important. The number of ways to advertise your unit or complex are limited only by your imagination and your advertising budget. Here are some of the more common methods.

Ways to advertise.

Free Advertising (or nearly free)
- Sign
- Appearance of property
- Present tenants
- Word of mouth

Paid Advertising
- Newspaper
- Billboards
- Specialized rental magazines
- Real estate brokers/agents

A few comments on each are in order.

1. Free advertising.

Some landlords do not spend much on advertising, yet they have a waiting list of applicants for units when/if they become available. What do these landlords do? These landlords have mastered the art of free advertising. The "art" of free advertising merely takes advantage of existing circumstances, employs resources that are already on hand and exploits efficiency. Some examples:

(a) A landlord with a rental unit that is on a well-traveled road can easily take advantage of that circumstance by using one or more well designed signs;

(b) A landlord may easily employ resources already on hand by using his personal computer to tie into an electronic bulletin board or the Internet to advertise;

(c) A landlord, because s/he normally has advance notice of when a unit is becoming available, may afford present tenants (in the case of an apartment complex) or neighbors (in the case of a single family home) an opportunity to influence who their new neighbors will be by notifying them when the unit will become available and asking them to refer applicants to you; and

(d) A landlord may develop a good reputation in the community by treating tenants fairly, charging a fair rate of rent, and keeping the grounds groomed -- traits that induce applicants to seek you out.

Important note -- free advertising is not limited to the four methods listed; your imagination is the only limitation on the number of methods to advertise your rental units free of charge (or nearly free).

One other point. Free advertising is usually more subtle than paid advertising (i.e., a sign versus a newspaper ad). Consequently, when an applicant sees your sign and stops, s/he feels that it was his/her idea, whereas a tenant that reads your newspaper ad feels more solicited and becomes unhappy when your unit does not live up to the accolades in your ad. Bottom line -- make maximum use of free advertising.

(a)   Sign.

Take advantage of free advertising -- use a sign!! Except for the (relatively) small initial cash outlay for a sign, advertising with an exterior sign is free. It is also one of the best methods. Many people select a part of town they wish to live in and then drive the area looking for a suitable place to live. If you don't display a sign, they won't know your unit is available. Moreover, many people answer newspaper and magazine advertisements, but are often disappointed with the advertised unit. Nevertheless, they may like the general area and drive around a bit. Your sign may snare an applicant that was drawn to your area by a competitor's advertisement.

Two last points. First, don't buy a cheap-looking sign. Spend a few dollars and get a professional-looking sign. The exterior of your unit or complex and your sign are the first things your prospective tenants see -- make a good impression or else they will just drive by. Second, before paying for a "huge" sign, check your local sign ordinances for size and placement limitations. For example, in Phoenix, unless the nature of your business and the zoning of your area allows a larger sign, a "For Sale" or "For Lease" sign cannot exceed six square feet (i.e., 2' x 3') and no higher than eight feet from the ground.[133] Violators may be subject to a $2,500 fine for each day of the violation.

---

133   PHOENIX, ARIZ., ZONING ORDINANCE § 705(B)(2)(o) (3/31/97).

(b) <u>Appearance of property</u>.

This was already covered in Chapter 3, Section A, but cannot be overstated.

(c) <u>Present tenants</u>.

Inform your present tenants of any vacancies and ask them to send you applicants. This is probably one of the best methods. First, it costs nothing. Second, you can let the word out before the unit actually becomes vacant, thereby not losing any other opportunities to advertise. Additionally, if a present tenant refers to you an acceptable tenant, you have saved some advertising expense and effort. Third, it gives your tenants an opportunity to influence who their new neighbor(s) will be and they will appreciate that. Fourth, assuming they refer a friend (as opposed to merely an acquaintance), both your present tenant and the new tenant will be more reluctant to move out because they will be leaving a friend behind. Avoid the temptation, however, to pay your tenants for referring applicants to you (or for referring applicants who actually become tenants); paying compensation to any person that is not a licensed real estate salesman or broker for real estate services is illegal.[134] Do not panic after having read the last sentence, if you are paying an on-site manager for leasing out your apartments and s/he happens to be unlicenced – there is an exception to this law for on-site managers.[135]

(d) <u>Word of mouth</u>.

Needless to say, free or inexpensive advertising is always desirable. Telling people you know and work with about your vacancies is absolutely free. While you may not wish to rent to a friend or co-worker (for whatever reason), these people may know someone else who is looking for a rental unit. Spread the word.

2. <u>Paid advertising</u>.

Paid advertising has some definite advantages over free advertising, but it should -- you paid for it. For example, you can reach a larger market (i.e., a newspaper ad versus a sign on the property) and you can target a specific sector of the market (i.e., young, old, families, professionals, etc.). Ineffective paid advertising, however, is a veritable "black hole" that sucks up all your money and returns nothing. Ineffective paid advertising includes employing the wrong medium to appeal to your target market (i.e., handbills distributed in an exclusive part of town for an inexpensive rental unit or vice versa), and employing the right medium,

---

134 A.R.S. §§ 32-2122, -2155(B) (West Supp. 1998).

135 A.R.S. § 32-2121(A)(6), -2121(A)(8) (West Supp. 1998).

but in an ineffective manner (i.e., poorly worded ad, poorly designed handbills or billboards, use of a realtor who is not skilled in leasing residential property, etc.). Bottom line – use paid advertising as necessary, when necessary, but use it effectively or don't use it at all.

(a) **Newspaper.**

There are two theories of newspaper advertising: a generalized ad that generates enormous response, or a specific ad that appeals only to the exact type of applicant that you will accept. The type you use will depend on the property (or properties) that you own. If you have 50 vacancies, you probably want as many responses as you can get. If, on the other hand, you have only one vacancy, and you don't allow pets, smokers, etc., you should run a very specific ad or else you will be deluged with applicants and will spend your valuable time taking applications from people who don't qualify to rent your unit in the first place.

The first thing I do when I run a newspaper advertisement is to look at, and improve upon, the competition. Buy a recent edition of the newspaper, rental magazine, etc., and look at advertisements for units similar to yours that are in your part of town. Find one or two ads that catch your attention and/or seem appealing. Copy one of the ads exactly (advertisements typically are not copyrighted), change it slightly and improve it, or combine portions of several ads. The key is to make your ad stand out more than the best ad in your section of the newspaper. Toward that end, try having the ad printed in **bold type**, or in ALL CAPITAL LETTERS. Also, you may consider putting your ad in more than one section of the newspaper (i.e., if your unit is in the Northwest part of town, advertise in the Northwest, North, and West sections of the newspaper). You may also wish to consider a "display ad" rather than a simple classified advertisement. Compare the difference.

```
2 bedroom, 1 bath, 900 sq.ft.,
Move-in Special.
Call 555-1212.
```

Classified Advertisement

MOVE IN SPECIAL

2 Bedroom, 1 bath

900 sq.ft.

CALL: 555-1212

Display Advertisement

In the case of a "display ad," the newspaper, magazine, etc., will generally make available the services of their design departments. These people will help you properly word the ad, design an eye-catching layout and make various other recommendations. Naturally, this costs more than a classified ad, but it may very well be worth it. Of course, only *you* can make that decision.

(b)   Billboards and specialized magazines.

These methods of advertising are obviously for landlords with large advertising budgets and many rental units. These methods are very effective if correctly employed.

Billboards should be located somewhat near the complex; most people are unlikely to travel many miles to find your property. Billboards, by definition, are typically located in high traffic areas, but some billboards are more visible than others. Make sure you are getting what you pay for.

Specialized magazines have the advantage of appealing to a specific segment of the population (i.e., prospective tenants). Members of this target market seek out these publications. The disadvantage is that your advertisement may be lost in a "flood" of advertisements. The challenge, then, is to design your advertisement to stick out from the rest. These publications typically have advertising design departments that will help you, but keep in mind that everyone is striving to attain the same goal – make their ad stick out.

Particularly when using billboard and specialized magazine advertising, keeping track of advertising results is crucial. Consequently, you must have some way of measuring the success of the various advertising methods you employ. After careful analysis, you can then focus your advertising funds on successful methods and discontinue the unsuccessful methods. Typically, advertising success is measured by surveying every applicant (not just every tenant) that comes through your door. *See* Appendix B, Form 1 (Tenant Application).

(c)   Real estate brokers/agents.

Real estate brokers and agents are indeed useful in marketing your rental properties. Nevertheless, they are not inexpensive.

There are two methods of employing a real estate broker: (1) hiring a broker as a property manager, who takes care of everything -- showing the property, screening tenants, preparing leases, collecting rent, and maintaining the property, and (2) hiring a broker for one rental unit and/or to perform only particular functions -- finding the applicants, but not screening the applicants, collecting rents or maintaining the property.

Typically, at least for smaller operations, a broker will list an individual rental unit and when (if) they lease it, they collect a real estate commission, which is usually calculated as a percentage of the lease term. This fee is charged merely for the service of finding an acceptable tenant. An additional real estate commission is normally charged for managing the property, including collecting the rent, maintaining the property, and various other routine functions. This fee is normally calculated on the amount of monthly rent collected.

Real estate commissions for leasing property and/or managing property are not set and are, in fact, negotiable, but both normally range between six and ten percent. When the broker finds a tenant and has the tenant sign a lease, the lease term can be any period, from month-to-month to several years. Because the broker knows that his commission is calculated on the total rent charged for the entire lease term, the broker will attempt to obtain the longest possible lease term. While this is good for the landlord, it is obviously also good for the broker.

For example, if a broker leases a rental unit to a tenant for a lease term of one year with monthly rent of $500, the total rent "charged" is $6,000. If the broker's real estate commission is ten percent (10%), then the commission equals $600.00. One other important point, the broker is paid up front (i.e., at the time the unit is first rented). Therefore, the broker's commission is calculated on the total rent charged, but not necessarily collected. If the tenant subsequently stops paying rent, including after the very first month, the broker is not legally obligated to refund any of the real estate commission, *unless* your agreement with him/her states otherwise. Therefore, in our example, if the tenant pays the broker the first month's rent, $600, the last month's rent, $600, and a $300 security deposit, for a total of $1,500, the broker will keep $600 and give the landlord $900.

NOTE: your listing agreement with the broker is the source of your legal obligation to pay the broker for his services. Many listing agreements for rental property provide that the broker is also due a commission for any renewals made by that tenant. Therefore, you may end up paying several commissions to the same broker without the broker performing any additional services. Perhaps you feel the broker is entitled to the additional commissions, perhaps not -- that is your decision. My point is make sure you know what you are signing.

In addition (or instead of) hiring a real estate agent/broker to help you market the property, you may wish to consider hiring someone to manage the property on a daily basis. Hiring an agent or property manager to manage your rental units has advantages (i.e., you don't have to be bothered with collecting rent or tenant problems), but it also has its disadvantages (i.e., it costs money and you "lose touch" with your tenants). This is a decision that only you can make. There is no requirement that an owner hire a local property manager, even if s/he lives out-of-state or out of the country. The only requirement is that the owner/landlord provide the tenant with a the name and address of someone who will receive notices and service of legal process.[136] If an out-of-state landlord fails to give the tenant an address where notices can be sent, then the Act allows the tenant to simply mail a copy of the notice and/or legal process to the Arizona Secretary of State, with a copy sent via certified mail to the owner's last known address. If this address is not correct, then the owner will not receive the notice and a judgment may be entered against him/her without him/her ever knowing there was a problem.

As a practical matter, it may make sense to have a local agent because a local manager can be more responsive to complaints, etc. Also, if there is an eviction, the local manager can provide testimony about the relevant facts. Otherwise, the out-of-state owner will need to personally appear in court to give testimony, which may be inconvenient and/or expensive (i.e., plane tickets, hotel room, meals, etc.). I have yet to see a judge award a landlord his/her travel expenses to appear in court.

C.   SHOW THE PROSPECTIVE TENANTS THE UNIT.

Show the apartment before having the applicants fill out an application. If they do not like it, you do not have to bother with an application. If they do like it, they are more motivated to accurately complete the application. The reverse is also true. If your practice is to have them fill out the application before showing them the unit, they are reluctant to take the time to fill out the entire application when they don't even know if they like your units. Moreover, if they do fill it out, they will do it in a hurried manner and not give you complete information. Work smarter, not harder -- show the unit first.

---

136   A.R.S. § 33-1309(B) (West 1990).

The down side of this practice, however, is that your advertising questionnaire, which is on the application, is not completed for every applicant. As previously discussed in Chapter 3, Section B(2)(b), when evaluating your advertising methods, you want to poll all applicants, not just a few. The simple solution is to ask each applicant what drew them to your unit and either put it on a separate form or on the application, which may or may not be filled out later. If you are in the position of having to evaluate the effectiveness of your advertising, my guess is that you will have no trouble resolving this small problem.

One other note, when showing an applicant a vacant rental unit, to protect yourself, both from personal harm and allegations about something you said or did to this applicant, you may wish to bring someone else with you (i.e., a co-worker, etc.) when you show the unit. It is also a good idea to make a copy of the applicant's driver's license, or other form of identification, and leave the copy in the office while you are showing the unit.

D.   HAVE THE TENANTS FILL OUT THE APPLICATION.

A word about gathering tenant information: The applicant is more likely to disclose all the things you want to know when filling out the tenant application than at any other time. This is especially true if you have already shown them the unit (which you should have done), they like it and want it. As soon as they are in, however, they no longer feel obligated to tell you all their personal business. And certainly, when they are behind in their rent, they won't tell you anything, including their name, because they know you want this information to chase them down later (I hate when they know what I'm up to). Moral – get all the information you can at the very beginning.

1.   The First Application - Step 1 (The Form).

You must look at the application process as an applicant eliminator. You will never approve an applicant just by looking at their application, but you will reject many without the need of further information or inquiry (*see* Chapter 3, Section E(2), regarding how and when to tell the applicant you have rejected his/her application). The information you ask for in the application is important; make sure you ask for the *right* information. I designed my own application to get the information applicants expect to divulge, the answers to some "deal breaker" questions, and several questions that I have learned, through experience, tell a lot about a person's character.

Examine the form on page 92. This is an application I designed and use. A cursory examination will reveal that it extracts very general information: no bank account numbers, no list of employers for the last five years, etc. Make no mistake, I want that information from my <u>tenants</u>, but not from every single <u>applicant</u> (*see* Chapter 3, Section D(3), immediately following, for the Tenant Information Sheet that I have acceptable applicants complete prior to accepting them as tenants). For now, though, I only need superficial personal data. The answers to my questions, the name and phone number of the last landlord, and the references are the most important information. This information alone will screen out <u>most</u> of the deadbeats.

Let's examine each of the areas I consider important (denoted by the double asterisk **) and why I think these areas are so critical (naturally, the asterisks do not appear on the actual application). This does not mean, however, that areas without the double asterisk are unimportant. For example, the "NAME" block does not have a double asterisk; nevertheless, if an applicant puts down John Doe, Billy the Kid, or anything else out of the ordinary, I give that matter my immediate attention. *Normally*, however, the areas without the double asterisk will not be cause for concern (but keep in mind that they could be).

Before we begin, let me answer a commonly asked question. What if, after the tenant moves in, you find out that s/he answered one or more questions on the application untruthfully? You may evict this tenant for making a material falsification to the landlord.[137] *See* Chapter 5, Section B(3)(a)(1).

<u>Home Phone number</u>. Are you a responsible person? Do you have a telephone at your home? My guess is that you answered yes to both questions. I would like to think of myself as a responsible person and yes, I too, have a telephone at home. Doesn't everybody? The real world answer is, "No, not everyone has a telephone at home." Who doesn't have a telephone at home and how do they live without one? Answer: deadbeats don't have a telephone at home. I don't know the answer to the second part of this question. Is it possible that someone could be responsible and make a very good tenant but not presently have a telephone at home? I suppose it is possible, but I will tell you that I have rejected applications without further investigation simply because the applicant did not have a telephone at home. Is it worth asking the applicant for an explanation as to why s/he doesn't have a telephone at home? Sure, but I have yet to receive an acceptable explanation. If you ever get what you consider to be an acceptable explanation, please write me and tell me what it was.

---

137 A.R.S. § 33-1368(A) (West Supp. 1998).

TENANT APPLICATION

HOW DID YOU YEAR ABOUT THIS RENTAL UNIT / COMPLEX?		
☐ Sign ■ Other Tenant ☐ Billboard	☐ Newspaper	☐ Friend
☐ Magazine ☐ Other:		

Do you wish to have a pet (of any type) on/in the rental property? ☐ Yes (type:) ■ No	Have you ever been evicted (as either a commercial or residential tenant)? ☐ Yes ■ No
Have you ever filed Bankruptcy? ☐ Yes ■ No If yes, when? What Chapter?	Have you ever been convicted of a crime (other than minor traffic)? ** ☐ Yes ■ No
How many vehicles do you wish to park on the Rental Property? *2*	Do you have a telephone at home? ■ Yes ☐ No Phone Number: *555-3333* **
Taking into account all your other expenses, can you afford the rent on this unit? ** ■ Yes ☐ No	When do you plan on moving in? ** *In 30 days.*
How long do you anticipate staying? *12 months* **	How is your credit? ** ■ Good ☐ Fair ☐ Ooops

Name: *Terry Tenant*	Name: *Tina Tenant*
Address: *(If less than 5 years, continue on back of form)* *222 North Oak Street, Anytown, AZ*	
Current Landlord's Name: *Bob Jones*	
Address: *(If less than 5 years, continue on back of form)* *112 North Oak Street, Anytown, AZ*	
Phone No.: *555-3333*	Present Rent: *$450.00* **
How Long There: *2 years* **	May I Call for Reference? ** ■ Yes ☐ No
Why are you Moving? *Job Transfer* **	
Current Employer: ** *OMNI Products, Inc.*	Work Phone Number: *555-4444*
Address: *505 West Ash Street, Anytown, AZ*	
Supervisor's Name: *Sarah Supervisor*	
Phone No.: *555-4444*	Gross Monthly Income: ** *$2,000.00*
How Long There: *5 years* **	May I Call for Reference? ** ■ Yes ☐ No

REFERENCES: (minimum two)		
Name: ** *Fran Friend*	How Known: (friend, boss, etc.) *Friend*	Phone No.: *555-5555*
Name: *Barry Boss*	How Known: (friend, boss, etc.) *Boss*	Phone No.: *555-6666*
Name: *Tom Tenant*	How Known: (friend, boss, etc.) *Your tenant/a friend*	Phone No.: *555-7777*

Applicants authorize Landlord to obtain information regarding credit history, confidential information and criminal record from any source and/or anyone listed on this form. Landlord charges a nonrefundable application fee; this fee is used to defray the administrative expense of processing and screening applications.

Signature: *Terry Tenant*	Signature: *Tina Tenant*

NOTE: Publish landlord's occupancy standard (i.e., 2 persons per bedroom) and landlord's minium acceptable applicant criteria on the back of this form or on a separate form.

You may wonder why I take such a hard line on this issue. The answer is simple. Analyzing a multitude of undesirable tenants (i.e., unreliable, late paying rent, not paying rent, moving out during the night, damaging the rental property, etc.), one of the common denominators was not having a telephone at home. No doubt someone out there (i.e., a statistics analyst) will be quick to point out that this may merely be a "correlation" and not necessarily a "direct relationship." Who really cares? Remember I told you to err conservatively (*see* Chapter 2, Section A); this is one of those times. If you still aren't convinced, forage through your own records and take another look at the applications of some of your own deadbeat tenants from days gone by. Trust me on this one, if they don't have a telephone at home, you need to look at the rest of their application very, very closely.

Present rent. This question yields useful information. For example:

- Is this applicant accustomed to making this amount of rental payment?

- Is my rent a substantial increase in his/her rent? If so, what makes him/her think s/he can now afford more (i.e., pay increase at work)?

These are the questions that should come to your mind when you see a great disparity in what this applicant was paying for rent and what his/her new rent will be. Ask your applicant to explain.

- Is this a substantial decrease?

People rarely move down. If they do, I verbally ask them why, and their answer better make sense. "I just want to save some money," won't do.

How long there? If less than one year, I verbally ask them how many times they have moved in the last three years. Stability is important. You do not want to prepare an apartment for this applicant to rent and then do it all over again in three months. Look for long-term tenants. And, I am not talking about people who will "sign" a long-term lease. Whether or not an applicant will sign a long-term lease is normally no indication of how long they will stay or how good/bad a tenant they will be (*see* Chapter 3, Section F, regarding month-to-month rental agreements versus long-term leases). Many people have irrational aversions to long-term leases, but end up staying many years. On the other hand, deadbeats have no problems signing long-term leases because they know they can skip out any time they want. Sure, you may get a judgment, but, as they say, you can't get blood out of a turnip (corollary: you can't collect a judgment from a deadbeat).

In addition to stability, you are looking for the number of prior addresses within the last five years and whether the prior properties were of comparable rent. You are also looking to see if there are any "mysterious gaps" in the applicant's prior addresses (i.e., incarceration).

<u>May I call for a reference?</u> This is a tricky area. If the tenant is leaving because the landlord is a jerk and the landlord truly is a jerk, he probably will not have anything good to say about anybody, much less a vacating tenant. In addition, the tenant may not have told the landlord he is leaving yet and may not want you to contact him. But remember, we are not looking to approve the applicant based on what the landlord says – we are trying to eliminate him/her. If we cannot contact the landlord, so be it. Move to the next question. On the other hand, if you do contact the landlord and he tells you that your applicant (his tenant) was always late paying his rent, caused severe damage to the rental unit, etc., STOP HERE. In any event, the next question is always very important.

<u>Why are you moving?</u> Verify their reason if you can. "No fault" reasons are good (i.e., job transfer, change of schools, move closer to work, etc.). Fault-based reasons are suspect. Some typical examples are given below with their respective translations immediately following.

Tenant:	"My landlord is/was a jerk."
Translation:	I was a jerk and my landlord evicted me.
Tenant:	"The unit was always breaking down."
Translation:	I broke everything in the unit and the landlord would not fix it.
Tenant:	"The neighbors were jerks."
Translation:	I was a jerk, the neighbors reported me and I was evicted.

And, finally,

Tenant:	"My roommate left without paying his share of the rent so I had to find a cheaper place."
Translation: or	I was the guy who left without paying rent.
	My roommate did leave without paying rent; therefore, I had to leave without paying rent -- my past landlord is looking for me.

<u>Current Employer</u>. This is good information for all the usual reasons. It also lets you screen applicants according to occupations. Some people do not like to rent to lawyers because they think they are likely to cause trouble (hard to imagine). Others like lawyers because they think they are responsible people. Who knows for sure. Recently, the construction market was slow. Maybe you want to pass on applicants that work for small or fledgling construction companies.

Yes, I hear you, "Can I discriminate based on occupation?" Yes. You cannot discriminate based on race, religion, national origin, sex, handicap or because the applicant has children, but discrimination based upon their occupation is not against the law. *See* Chapter 3, Section E(1), which addresses discrimination.

Gross monthly income. Naturally, you want to make sure s/he makes enough so that s/he can afford your rent. But, also look to see if s/he makes too much. Stop shaking your head and wondering if that is possible. If s/he makes $3,000 per month and your rent is $300 per month, there is something wrong with this picture (i.e., s/he is overstating her/his income or s/he is up to her/his earlobes in debt). At a minimum, too much income warrants a verbal question, followed by a plausible answer.

How long there (length of employment). Length of employment is just as important as length of his last tenancy – perhaps more. "Job hoppers" are typically poor risks. That is not to say that lengthy employment means an acceptable tenant. Remember, think elimination. Also, a "mysterious gap" in employment during the last five years may indicate schooling, a long vacation or incarceration – inquire further.

May I call for a reference? This is the same question you asked the applicant with respect to his landlord, but the answer is treated differently. A landlord can really only give you limited information because s/he typically sees the tenant once a month (to pay rent), if at all. A supervisor, on the other hand, sees the applicant all day long, five days a week (or more). This person knows a great deal about this applicant. I really want to talk to the applicant's supervisor; so should you. While declining to allow me to contact his/her current landlord may be acceptable under the circumstances, I can think of no acceptable reason for an applicant declining to allow me to talk to his/her supervisor. The truth is that bosses typically don't care if their employees move. If the applicant declines to give permission to contact his/her supervisor without an exceptionally well-reasoned explanation – ELIMINATE!

Taking into account all your other expenses, can you afford the rent on this unit? Sounds like a foolish question, right? You will be surprised at the answers you will get. Anything other than "yes" is unacceptable. Naturally, I inquire further to be sure s/he understood the question. On the other hand, if s/he *did* misunderstand this simple question, you may have another problem on your hands. While you do not need a building full of rocket scientists, insisting on at least average intelligence is a good idea. Anyone who does not know if they can afford their rent may easily be talked into buying a $2,000 vacuum cleaner at $500 per month and may no longer be able to pay your rent because they did not know whether or not they could afford the vacuum cleaner payments (Note: the vacuum cleaner salesman is unlikely to tell them). In addition, someone with less than average intelligence may be more likely to injure himself or others while on your premises (i.e., sticking his/her finger into a light socket).

When do you plan to move in? This will tell you if s/he is leaving his/her prior landlord "in a lurch." You may be next. If s/he indicates "right away," inquire whether s/he gave adequate notice.

How long do you anticipate staying? Any applicant with a modicum of intelligence will put at least six months, one year, or more. If, however, your applicant estimates his/her stay in terms of days or weeks, you may wish to pass. Anything less than six months deserves a hard look (*see* Chapter 3, Section F, regarding month-to-month rental agreements versus long-term leases).

How is your credit? Most people will tell you the truth on this question because they expect that you will check. And, they are more likely to divulge this information if the application prompts them. Prompt them, however, with choices that are not demeaning. For example:

How is your credit? (good, fair, "Oops" -- circle one).

Conversely, these choices will probably not yield good results:

How is your credit? (good, fair, slime-ball, dirtbag).

It goes without saying (although I feel compelled to say it) that people with a poor or unfavorable credit history typically do not make good tenants. On the other hand, if they had great credit, and any sense, they would be buying, not renting. Therefore, demanding "sterling" credit may be asking a bit too much. The point I wish to make, however, and one which may not be as obvious to the neophyte landlord, is that the more elaborate an applicant's explanation of why their credit history is not good, the more likely that s/he will be a troublesome tenant. Why? Hard to say for sure, but the fact is that applicants that give you long, convoluted, bizarre stories are the ones that you should stay away from. Chances are they are either making it up or their lives are truly this complicated. In either case, instead of giving you the rent each month they will give a new and incredible explanation of why they do not have the rent. What constitutes a "convoluted" or "bizarre" story? Use your best judgment, but err conservatively (*see* Chapter 2(A)).

I cannot leave this area without addressing the propriety of running credit checks on your applicants. The easy answer is always run a credit check. The harder question to answer is: Who pays for the credit check? The answer to this question is tied directly to the type of property you are renting and current market conditions. For example, if you rent luxury condominiums in an exclusive part of town, no doubt your applicants will be happy to pay for this expense. If, on the other hand, you rent run-of-the-mill apartments, surrounded by hundreds of other similar apartments, and those landlords <u>do not</u> require applicants to pay for this expense, you will undoubtedly have a difficult time collecting this fee from your applicants.

So, should you pay for the expense yourself? Yes. But what if you are a small landlord (very few units) and your profit margin, if you have a profit margin, is not very big; should you still pay to have a credit check on every applicant that traipses through the door? No, and actually, this applies equally to every landlord. You <u>do not</u> run a credit check on <u>every</u> applicant; only the ones that have already made it through your initial screening process and whom you are now considering as accepting as a tenant. And, of those, only the ones you have doubts about.

Approaching the credit check dilemma in this manner (i.e., following these steps) will save you some money.

Isn't it risky to accept a tenant without running a credit check? That depends on how you define risk. When it comes to being a landlord and accepting tenants, I am risk adverse (i.e., I do not like to take risks). Nevertheless, I have oftentimes rented units to applicants without running a credit check. You may ask, "Isn't that contradictory?" Not at all. The information I get from the application and the follow-up questions (assuming I don't eliminate them based on their answers) is normally more than enough to satisfy me that they are credit worthy. For example, if I receive an application from a professional person (i.e., doctor, lawyer, architect, engineer, etc.) who works for a company that I know employs responsible people and this applicant also successfully makes it through the application process (i.e., application and follow-up questions), I don't feel that I need to run a credit check. Keep in mind that although credit reporting agencies try to maintain accurate information, they are not infallible, and the information they render is not "gospel." I have rejected applicants with "good" credit reports based on other information in their application and/or the answers they provided to my questions. I have also accepted applicants with poor credit reports based on information and answers which I felt compensated for this shortcoming.

Do you disagree? Fine. You are the landlord. Your decision is final. The purpose of this book is merely to open your eyes to other methods of doing business; methods that perhaps may save you time and/or money. But, the decision is yours – as it should be.

Do you have a criminal record? The Fair Housing Act states that a landlord may refuse to rent to an applicant who would pose a health or safety risk to other tenants or whose tenancy would result in substantial physical damage to the property owners.[138] Further, case law expressly allows landlords to consider an applicant's past criminal actions that involved assaultive crimes (i.e., assault, rape, murder, etc.) or damage to property.[139] How you actually obtain this information, however, is another matter.

An amendment to the Violent Crime Control and Enforcement Act of 1994, commonly referred to as "Megan's Law," requires state and local law enforcement agencies to advise the public of sexually violent offenders in the community. But this applies only to "sex offenders." What about all the other criminals? Due to legal limitations requiring positive identification on criminal records, the three national consumer reporting agencies – Trans Union, TRW, and Equifax – do not collect and report information about criminal records. In addition, you cannot obtain a police clearance letter or report on a prospective tenant *directly* from a police department, county sheriff's office or the Arizona Department of Public

---

138 A.R.S. §§ 41-1442, -1491.19(C) (West 1992 & Supp. 1998).

139 *See* Talley v. Lane, 13 F.3d 1031 (7th Cir. 1994).

Safety. You may, however, lawfully require an applicant to obtain a copy of their own report and to provide or show you a copy thereof. But, let's face it, requiring every applicant to obtain and produce a copy of their criminal report will not be "well received" and will likely reduce the number of applications you get.

So, how do you get this information? Unfortunately, the only practical answer is to ask the applicant. Of course, an applicant may lie, but that is the case with every question on the form. The applicant, however, may not realize that you have no way of checking his/her answer and, therefore, may answer truthfully. This is especially true if the application indicates that this information will be verified. Is that it? Is that all I can do -- ask the applicant? No. You can also review the application for "clues" that indicate a criminal record. For example, a listed reference who is a prison warden or parol officer might be a clue. An inability to provide you with addresses or employers for the past five years (i.e., the applicant was incarcerated) is also a clue. A credit report that reflects a "gap" in credit or a string of missed payments on *all* accounts for the same length of time also suggests the applicant was "unable" to make payments (i.e., incarcerated). There are many things in an application that may "tip you off." If you have any doubt, verify the answer by asking the applicant again, directly and look them straight in the eye when they give you an answer. If you are still unsure or you get a "yes" answer, then you may wish to ask that applicant to provide you with a copy of his criminal file. An individual may obtain a report of his/her own criminal history (or lack thereof) by making a request to the Arizona Department of Public Safety, (602) 223-2222, and/or from the Federal Bureau of Investigation, (602) 279-5511.

Why go to all this trouble? In Chapter 4, Section B(6), I discuss several actual cases. The lesson of these cases is that the landlord has a duty to take "reasonable" steps to make the leased premises safe and secure. If you do absolutely nothing (i.e., not even asking a prospective tenant about his/her criminal record) and another party is harmed by one of your tenants, who has a criminal history of similar incidents, you may be held financially responsible. For example, in a California case regarding a commercial rental property,[140] the California Supreme Court found that a landlord owed a duty of care to its commercial tenants to take reasonable steps to secure the common areas under the landlord's control. Under the facts of this case, the landlord was found *not liable* for the rape of a tenant's employee. The Court stated that, absent some prior similar incident of violence on the property, the landlord had no duty to hire security guards. The message sent, however, is that if *there is* a history of violence, the landlord *may* be obligated to hire security guards.

In another California case,[141] a landlord was found responsible for drug activity *by third parties* on and *around* the subject property. A group of tenants in an apartment complex sued the owner because drug activity on and around the property made the property a public and private nuisance. The court concluded that

---

140 *See e.g.*, <u>Ann M. v. Pacific Plaza Shopping Center</u>, 863 P.2d 207 (Cal. 1993).

141 <u>Lew v. Superior Court of Alameda County</u>, 20 Cal.App.4th 866, 25 Cal.Rptr.2d 42 (1993).

drug activity could constitute a nuisance and did interfere with the plaintiffs' enjoyment of their property. The court stated, however, that the landlord would be liable only if he did not take reasonable steps to stop the problem. The landlord had posted "no trespassing" signs and installed new locks on some of the apartments. The court found these efforts inadequate and cited several more aggressive measures that could have been taken, such as employment of an on-site manager, secure fencing, and key-card gates. The court found the landlord responsible and awarded the plaintiffs monetary damages.

The landlord's liability may include criminal liability. In a Washington case,[142] a landlord was convicted of violating a state statute that prohibited knowingly renting space to tenants for manufacturing, delivering, selling, storing, or giving away any controlled substance. The landlord had visited his residential tenant's property a number of times, discovered that the tenant was growing marijuana in his basement, and did nothing about it. The tenant was arrested two months later. Had the landlord at least notified a law enforcement agency, he may have had a defense. In this case, however, the landlord "passively acquiesced" to the illegal activity and, therefore, the court found him criminally liable for his tenant's drug crime.

In Arizona, a law was passed in 1996 that makes it a crime, punishable by fine and imprisonment, if a landlord knows of criminal activity going on in his/her rental unit and does nothing to stop it.[143] If you *know* of criminal activity in your rental unit(s), it behooves you to take appropriate action.

References. Everyone has two references. Even people in the Federal Witness Protection Program will be able to give you two references. Anyone who cannot is either hiding something, or simply hiding.

Application Fee. If you charge a nonrefundable application fee, you must disclose – in writing – the purpose of the nonrefundable fee.[144] Language similar to that below will suffice. I recommend including this language on the Application Form.

The nonrefundable application fee is used to defray the administrative expense of processing and screening prospective applications.

Room for improvement? Can you improve on this simple application? Possibly. You will not bruise my ego by doing a complete make-over of my application or by scrapping it altogether. My simple, one-page application is the product of years of trial and error (mine and many others). I obtain favorable results by using this form, but you may not. Feel free to add to or modify the application

---

142   State v. Sigman, 826 P.2d 144 (Wash. 1992).

143   A.R.S. §§ 12-991.01, 12-994 (West Supp. 1998).

144   A.R.S. § 33-1321(B) (West Supp. 1998).

form given in this book or to construct your own application from scratch. <u>Bottom line</u> – the best application form is the one that you feel comfortable with and which yields <u>you</u> the best results.

2.   **The First Application - Step 2 (Ask Questions).**

This seemingly completes the application process -- not so. Here is the scenario: you have shown an applicant the unit. She likes it and wants it. She diligently fills out the application. You quickly scan the application to see if you can eliminate her without asking for any more information. Her application looks pretty good (assuming the information is true and correct – a huge assumption), so you do not immediately eliminate her. You ask, "What is the next step?" Answer: ask follow-up questions. Follow-up questions fall into two categories:

- Follow-up questions prompted by responses provided on the application. (previously discussed, *see* Chapter 3, Section D(1).

- Follow-up questions that you have prepared in advance (discussed below).

You may ask, "Why not merely include these questions on the application form?" Any bank loan officer will tell you that the written loan application is only part of the loan application. The loan officer's oral interview with the loan applicant, more times than not, is the deciding factor in whether or not the applicant receives a loan. This is no less true in the residential landlord setting. Applicants regard the written application as the "formal application." The truth is, everything they say and do is part of the application. Furthermore, because applicants typically do not regard oral questions as part of the formal application, they will generally be more truthful and give greater details when asked.

Answers to the following questions (and others of your own choosing, that you prepare in advance or that you think of during the interview) may reveal much about the character of your applicants.

- Why do they wish to live in this area/neighborhood?

- What attracted them to this unit? (Marketing information)

- If their application is approved, do they intend to install a telephone? (*See* Chapter 3, Section D(1))

- Do they have a checking account or other bank account? (*See* Chapter 3, Section D(3))

- Do they have a car?
  - What kind?
  - How many?
  - How much do they owe on it (them)?
  - What are their payments?

- What type of work do they do? (you know their employer, but not necessarily what they do – find out)
  - How long have they been performing that job? (to be distin-guished from "How long have they worked for that employer?")
  - How many jobs have they had in the last two years?

Listen to the answers. Don't merely go through the motions. Always listen very carefully to the answer when you ask an applicant a question. The answer must be reasonable and make sense to you. For example, you may ask an applicant why s/he wants to rent this particular unit and/or why s/he wants to be in that particular part of town. The average person will give you the usual answer (i.e., close to their children's school, close to their job, and/or close to friends or relatives). As previously stated (see Chapter 3, Section D(1), "How is your Credit?"), applicants that give you long, convoluted, bizarre stories are the ones that you should stay away from.

Unlike the questions on the Tenant Application form (just discussed in Chapter 3, Section D(1)), I have not provided you with "model answers" or "model wrong answers" for these questions. That is because *what* they say may not be as important as *how* they say it. You will be there; you must decide for yourself whether the applicant's answers are satisfactory.

3. The Second Application.

Examine the form on the following page. This is the second application form that I use, except that I call it a "Tenant Information Sheet." Have each occupant and each person who will sign the rental agreement (as in the case of a parent, who will sign the rental agreement but will not occupy the unit) complete this form. Again, the applicant's perception is important. If s/he believes the application process is over and that this form is merely "paperwork," s/he is more inclined to give complete and truthful answers. The reality is, however, the information s/he puts on this form will make or break his/her application.

No doubt, you are asking yourself, "How do I present them with this 'second' application?" Simple. After you have reviewed the first application and checked with his/her landlord, employer, references, etc., and have concluded that you cannot eliminate this applicant, you call him/her up and say that his/her application "looks pretty good," but that you need some additional information. Then either have him/her come by and complete the form or mail (or fax) it to him/her.

TENANT INFORMATION SHEET

Property Address: *123 N. Oak Street, Anytown, Arizona*	Home Phone No.: *555-2222* Work Phone No.: *555-1111*

TENANT INFORMATION	
(To be completed by each Adult Occupant)	

Name: *Terry Tenant*	
Place of Birth: *Tucson, Arizona*	Date of Birth: ** *June 1, 1950*
Social Security No.: ** *555-11-2222*	Driver's License No.: *555-22-9999*
Parents' Names: ** *Dick & Jane Tenant*	
Address: *111 North Elm Street, Anytown, AZ*	
Person to Notify in Case of Emergency: *Fran Friend*	
Address: *222 North 1st Avenue, Phoenix*	Phone No.: *555-5555*
Children: *Tanya Tenant* **	Age: *2*
Tony Tenant	Age: *7*
Have you ever filed Bankruptcy? ** ■ No □ Yes	When: Under what Chapters?
Have you ever been evicted? ** ■ No □ Yes	When:
Do you wish to have a pet? ** □ No ■ Yes	Type and Weight: *fish (1 ounce)*
Have you ever been convicted of a crime (other than minor traffic)? ■ No □ Yes	How many vehicles do you wish to park on the Rental Property? *2*
Will you park any commercial vehicles on the property? ■ No □ Yes	Do you presently have a telephone at home? *No* Number:
Taking into account all your other expenses, can you afford the rent on this unit? □ No ■ Yes	When do you plan to move in? *ASAP*
How long do you anticipate staying? *2 years*	How is your credit? ■ Good □ Fair □ Ooops

BANK INFORMATION	
Where do you bank? *First Interstate Bank*	Branch: *Main*
Checking Account No.: ** *01-2222*	Savings Account No.: *02-1111*
Other Account No.: *IRA - 03-4444*	Other Account No.:

VEHICLE INFORMATION			
(list information on each vehicle)			

Make: ** *Nissan*	Model: *Sentra*	Year: *1990*	License No.: *XYZ-111*
Lienholder: *Valley National Bank*	Balance Owed: *$6,000.00*		Monthly Payment: *$149.00*
Make: *Chevrolet*	Model: *Camaro*	Year: *1982*	License No.: *XYZ-222*
Lienholder: *None*	Balance Owed: *-0-*		Monthly Payment:

Once the Tenant Information Sheet is completed, review it carefully. As with the first application, this "second" application elicits information which may eliminate an applicant without further inquiry. The areas of concern are denoted by the double asterisk (**).

Parent's name. This information may or may not be available (i.e., parents deceased). The purpose for obtaining this information is merely to notify the tenant's parents in case of emergency (in addition to the person listed) and especially to assist you in locating the tenant if s/he leaves without giving you a forwarding address. In the case of a very young tenant (i.e., a college student), you may wish to have the parents sign the rental agreement with the student or have them sign a separate guarantee agreement (i.e., guarantying payment of the rent). You may not be able to collect a judgment from a college student, but you can probably collect a judgment from parents that can afford to send their kids to college. See Guarantee Form, Appendix B, Form 19.

Checking account, social security number and date of birth. I view a checking account much the same way as a telephone -- I want my tenants to have a telephone and, similarly, I want my tenants to have a checking account. Most responsible people have checking accounts. Granted, there are responsible people on the planet that don't have checking accounts (although I don't personally know any). Don't get the idea that I immediately turn people away if they don't have a checking account. It is merely one factor I consider important. If they are responsible people, but do not have a checking account, there will be other aspects of their application that will tell me they are okay.

Beyond being an indicator of responsibility, why do you need to know if they have a checking account? Your mission, as a landlord, is to get all the information you possibly can about your tenants at the very beginning. For example, make sure you make a copy of the first check they give you. Why? Because it tells you where they bank, which branch and even their account number. This will make garnishing their bank account much easier, should the need arise. I am not a pessimist, merely a realist. Similarly, their social security number and date of birth are key pieces of information that a "skip-tracer" will need. A skip-tracer is someone who is in the business of tracking down and finding people who have left you "high and dry" without paying their rent and/or leaving you a forwarding address or phone number.

Yes, I hear you, "What if they want to give you cash?" I typically don't take cash for two reasons. First, it makes me wonder if they have a checking account and, as discussed, I want my tenants to have a checking account. Second, I know that I don't keep a lot of cash around and I don't want anyone to think that I keep a lot of cash around. In addition, if the tenant doesn't have a checking account, that means at some point during every month, s/he is walking around with lots of cash in his/her possession. I don't want to be robbed and I don't want to hear that my tenant has been robbed of his/her "rent money." (I've always wondered why stolen currency is always "rent money" and not a tenant's "spending money" or car payment, etc.).

Type of car, etc. The type of car, the balance owed, the monthly payment and even the name of the lienholder yield very useful information. The old adage that the type of car you drive tells a lot about your personality is true. It also gives people an idea of how much you spend on transportation. I do not look favorably upon an applicant for a unit that rents for $300 per month who drives a Ferrari. Something tells me that this applicant may have some "unreported" income from an unsavory business. It may also suggest that this tenant will not be able to pay the rent by the time he gets done paying the car payment, the gasoline bill and that month's accumulation of speeding tickets. On the other hand, an applicant for an exclusive, single family home who drives a Ferrari may be acceptable. Bottom line -- the type of car the applicant drives should be consistent with the price range of property s/he wishes to lease.

The name of the lienholder may also be informative. A well-known financial institution is good. "Lurch's Pawn & Loan" may suggest that no one else on the planet would loan this applicant any money on a secured loan (meaning that the loan is secured by the car; if the car buyer doesn't make payments, the lender can repossess the car). As a landlord, you are an *unsecured* creditor. If this applicant becomes your tenant and he does not pay his rent on time, you have no collateral to secure the debt (i.e., to seize and sell, thus enabling you to apply the proceeds to the amount the tenant owes you). If no one else is willing to make this applicant a secured loan, you certainly don't need to be his unsecured creditor, and you don't need this applicant as a tenant. But don't jump to conclusions -- ask for an explanation (i.e., why didn't he get the loan from somewhere else). This applicant's name may be "Lurch," and he may own an entire chain of "Lurch's Pawn & Loan" establishments.

If the applicant has more than one car, have him/her continue on the back of the form. Be leery of people who "collect" and/or repair cars on your property.

Have you ever filed bankruptcy? Whether or not you automatically eliminate an applicant because s/he has filed bankruptcy is entirely up to you. Bankruptcy is obviously not a good sign, but it is certainly not as bad as some other problems (i.e., previous eviction). Keep in mind that although a bankruptcy destroys a person's credit, not all persons who file bankruptcy are intentionally evading their creditors (although, let's face it, most are). Actually, you may be interested to know that individuals who file bankruptcy and are discharged under Chapter 7, Chapter 11, Chapter 12 and Chapter 13 (under certain circumstances), cannot file another bankruptcy and receive a discharge under Chapter 7 for six (6) years[145] (although they could file under Chapter 13).[146] Moreover, after bankruptcy, they have no bills and are anxious to re-establish a good credit rating. Something to consider.

---

[145] Bankruptcy Reform Act of 1978, Pub.L. No 95-598, 11 U.S.C. §§ 727(a)(8) - (9) (1994).

[146] *See, generally*, 11 U.S.C. §§ 1301, *et seq.* (1994).

If, however, you absolutely know that you will never rent to an applicant that has filed bankruptcy, you may want to put this question on the first application or ask this question during the first interview, so that you find this out before you go to the trouble of calling the prior landlord, employer, references, etc.

Have you ever been evicted? You may be asking, "Why isn't this question on the initial application?" Actually, it is on the initial application. But this question (along with a few others) is repeated on the second form. Most applicants, if they have ever been evicted, will not answer this question truthfully on the initial application, but will *normally* answer truthfully when filling out the second application. Why? Who knows for sure. Perhaps they forgot how they answered on the first form. Or, perhaps, they feel that you have pretty much accepted them as tenants by allowing them to fill out the second application, which, of course, is absolutely not true, but we needn't tell them that. Whatever the reason, this question is more effective on the second application.

What about the answer? Is a "yes" an automatic elimination? Not necessarily. On more than one occasion, I have had reasonable and plausible explanations given for an eviction. For example, a young mother recently divorced, unemployed and unable to make the rent payments, but now has made the adjustment and is gainfully employed. A reasonable explanation will suffice, if I am confident that the circumstances will not recur (i.e., in the example just given, if the young woman had just remarried, had quit her job and told me that she and her new husband have been discussing divorce, I might pass on this applicant).

Children and pets. Historically, the predominating view was to avoid renting to people with children and pets. Today, however, there are good reasons for abandoning these past prejudices. First and foremost, discriminating against applicants because they have children violates the law,[147] except where the property is subject to a valid deed restriction or where the property lies within a subdivision designed, advertised and used as an adult community (i.e., Sun City, Arizona).[148] However, don't confuse rejecting an applicant because s/he has children with rejecting an applicant because s/he has *too many* children. You are certainly within your rights to turn down an application from a couple with three children who wish to rent your two-bedroom unit. This rejection is based upon the number of occupants, not the age of the occupants.[149] In fact, recent legislation has established a presumptively reasonable standard of two occupants per bedroom (*see* Chapter 3, Section E(1) (Discrimination)).[150]

Second, at least for those landlords who are looking to lease out a single family residence, tenants with children are typically married (although not always)

---

147   A.R.S. § 33-1317(A) (West Supp. 1998).

148   A.R.S. § 33-1317(B) (West Supp. 1998).

149   A.R.S. § 33-1317(D) (West Supp. 1998).

150   A.R.S. § 33-1317(F) (West Supp. 1998).

and generally more stable and responsible than single people. Conversely, as a general rule, single people are neither stable nor long-term tenants. Of course, there are exceptions to every rule, but unlike a married couple with children, single people are more susceptible to moves brought on by job opportunities, romance or whatever. Furthermore, single people typically are not good housekeepers because they are not home-oriented and, therefore, have no reason to be good housekeepers. For them, life is outside the home, where they can meet other singles. In addition, when they do stay home, they are more likely to party. And partying means wear and tear on your property. Single people also tend to have more temporary guests (i.e., roommates, boyfriends, girlfriends, etc.), none of whom feel any responsibility whatsoever for your property and greatly increase the wear and tear on your unit.[151]

Families, on the other hand, have an entirely different orientation. When they move in, they are more likely to put down roots and stay a while. They put their children in school, give their friends their new address and phone number, and are more likely to make friends with the neighbors. For them, home is the focal point of their lives. This is also a very good reason for making sure the property "shows well" before you advertise its availability. (*See* Chapter 3, Section A).

These notions of stability also apply to landlords who are attempting to lease out an apartment. However, because of the loss of privacy and noise associated with apartment living, families are less likely to apply.

As far as pets go, there is no "right" answer other than what you think is best. Not allowing pets reduces the number of people that are eligible to rent from you. On the other hand, allowing pets may increase the wear and tear on your property and, depending on the size and design of the complex, may result in numerous complaints and conflicts between tenants because of noise. You may also choose a middle ground and accept only certain types of pets and/or under a certain size. In any event, for many applicants, whether or not pets are allowed is a "deal breaker." Consequently, if you don't allow pets, you may wish to point this out on the first application form.

Keep in mind that an "assistance animal" (i.e., a seeing-eye dog, etc.) is not a "pet" and, therefore, even if you do not allow *any* pets, you cannot reject an applicant because s/he has an assistance animal. According to the Arizona Attorney General's Office, you cannot even require that a tenant with an assistance animal pay a pet deposit or fee. Rejecting an applicant because s/he has an assistance animal and/or requiring a pet deposit or fee is discriminatory.

So what is an "assistance animal"? This sounds like a simple question, but the answer is not always clear. No one would question the legitimacy of a blind person

---

151 The foregoing are reasons for not discriminating against families with children and are not intended to encourage landlords to discriminate against applicants who are single. Discrimination based on "familial status" (i.e., because an applicant is single, divorced or married) is unlawful. *See* Chapter 3, Section E(1) (Discrimination).

having a seeing-eye dog. This animal is not considered to be a pet. But what about a person who claims his/her doctor prescribed a pet for the purpose of calming the patient's nerves? How far can this go? What is to prevent a tenant from claiming s/he has a seeing-eye iguana?

There is no formal licensing or certification for "assistance animals." Yes, some animals undergo rigorous training and even come with papers that authenticate the nature of the animal's training. But there is no legal requirement that every assistance animal be trained and/or have certain papers. Consequently, there is no "bright line" standard for what is, and what is not, permissible. The best recommendation that I can give you is that a tenant or applicant with a legitimate need for an assistance animal should have no difficulty getting you a letter from his/her treating physician (i.e., a medical doctor, not a chiropractor) explaining why this person needs an assistance animal and the specific type of animal that the doctor prescribes. Requiring this information from tenants or applicants is not discriminatory and, in fact, is a good business practice. Applicants that cannot produce this information may legitimately be rejected.

E.   SELECT THE BEST TENANT; REJECT ALL OTHERS.

You now have all the information that you need. The application is complete, you have asked your follow-up questions, you have ordered and received your credit report, and you have verified the information in his/her application. You are now in an excellent position to make an informed decision as to whether or not this applicant is acceptable. If you have done all these things, your decision will rarely be that difficult. But, let's face it, in the real world, you can't always verify everything and/or some information is just not available. In short, sometimes you are forced to make a decision when you <u>do not</u> have all the information you need. In those cases, trust your own judgment and make a decision. Try to err conservatively (*see* Chapter 2, Section A). Fortunately, selecting good tenants is something you get better at.

1.   Discrimination.

Part of selecting a tenant is just math – can they afford the unit? Part is common sense – do they have a steady job, etc.? Most, however, is purely subjective. You may be surprised to learn just how much discretion you have when deciding the criteria for measuring the acceptability of applicants. There are, however, limits. Under the law you <u>cannot</u> use these factors in deciding whether to accept a tenant: race, color, religion, national origin, sex, handicap or familial status (i.e., because the applicant has children under the age of eighteen).[152]

---

152 Civil Rights Act of 1866, 42 U.S.C. § 1982 (1994) (prohibits racial discrimination in sale or rental of all property); 42 U.S.C. §§ 3601-3619 (1994) (unlawful to refuse to sell or rent a dwelling to any person because of race, color, religion, sex, familial status, or national origin); A.R.S. §§ 33-1317, 41-1491, 41-1491.01 to .36 (West 1992 & Supp. 1998).

<u>Anything else is okay</u>. Let me say that again. Anything else is okay. For example, you may decide that an applicant, who is an attorney, is undesirable and wish to refuse to rent to him/her because you believe (correctly or not) that s/he knows more about the law than you do and, therefore, may be likely to cause trouble. You <u>can</u> do it. You do not like the fact that an applicant's car is noisy because you live on the premises and it will disturb you every time they leave or arrive -- fine. You would rather not rent to a tenant who rides a noisy motorcycle because it will disturb other tenants or because you do not like "Bikers" -- no problem. Except for the factors just listed, you can refuse to rent to anyone for any reason.

Perhaps an actual court case can best demonstrate what I am saying. An unmarried black woman applied as a tenant to rent an apartment in New York and was turned down. She sued the landlord, charging the landlord with discrimination on the basis of race, sex and/or her marital status. The landlord's defense was that he did not discriminate because she was black, female or unmarried (in point of fact, he already had several tenants who were unmarried, black and/or women); he turned her down because she was a lawyer. The landlord stated outright that he openly discriminated against lawyers because he felt they were likely to cause trouble. The judge ruled in the landlord's favor stating that as long as the landlord was not discriminating on the basis of race, creed, color, national origin, sex, disability, or marital status, he was entitled to protect his own interests. Specifically, the Court said:

> Thus, this court concludes that there is nothing illegal in a landlord discriminating against lawyers as a group, or trying to keep out of his building intelligent persons, aware of their rights, who may give him trouble in the future.[153]

Okay, so perhaps you just learned that you have more discretion than you thought. Nevertheless, you must be very careful not to "unlawfully" discriminate. The rule is seemingly clear. And the goal of prohibiting discriminatory practices is certainly worthwhile. Compliance, however, is sometimes difficult. Not because landlords don't want to comply with the law, but because the laws are so complex and so numerous that a landlord may inadvertently run afoul of some obscure provision. Anti-discrimination laws may be found at the federal, state, county and local level. Most of these laws are complicated and use unfamiliar terms (i.e., familial status). In addition, newly identified "protected classes" and ever expanding definitions of previously identified "protected classes" make it very difficult to not inadvertently (i.e., without intending to) discriminate. Because the penalties can be so severe, however, comply with these laws you must. Here are some examples of conduct that may constitute "unlawful" discrimination.

---

153 <u>Kramarsky v. Stahl Management</u>, 92 Misc. 2d 1030, 401 N.Y.S.2d 943, 945 (1977).

- Refusing to show or rent a unit.
- Refusing to negotiate (if negotiation is normally afforded to others).
- Charging more rent or asking for a larger security deposit.
- Telling the applicant that the unit is no longer available, when it is.
- Denying services, amenities or use/access to facilities that are normally available.
- "Steering" applicants (i.e., directing applicants toward or away from specific areas) with children to "family areas."
- Refusing to allow handicap accommodations, assistive aides, assistive animal, parking, or reasonable physical modification to the property.

As with many areas of the law, whether or not particular conduct is discriminatory depends on the facts. Most people will tell you to call your attorney whenever you have a question about whether or not something you are doing, or want to do, is discriminatory. I am **not** going to do that. The Arizona Attorney General is the Governmental agency that receives and, if appropriate, files charges against landlords for discrimination under the state anti-discrimination statutes.[154] Therefore, my recommendation is that you call the Attorney General directly with your question. Certainly, you can call and ask your attorney, but if the Attorney General disagrees, it will be *you*, not your attorney, that is subject to sanctions. More important, a call to the Attorney General is free. Ideally, if you believe that a particular practice is going to ultimately result in a formal complaint, you should ask if you can get a written opinion from the Attorney General's Office. At a minimum, make note of the date, time and the name of the person with whom you spoke. You should also make note of the precise facts that you gave over the phone.

(a)   More about familial status.

The Federal Fair Housing Amendments Act of 1988 added two new protected classes to Title VIII of the Civil Rights Act of 1968, which prohibited housing discrimination based on race, color, religion, national origin or sex. The two new classes are "familial status" (i.e., people with children under eighteen years of age) and handicap.[155] The starting point for understanding "familial status" is knowing the federal and state law definition of "familial status."

Federal Law

"Familial status" means one or more individuals (who have not attained the age of 18 years) being domiciled with –

(1) a parent or another person having legal custody of such individuals or individuals; or

---

154 A.R.S. §§ 41-1491 to -1491.36 (West 1992 & Supp. 1998).

155 Fair Housing Amendments Act of 1988 § 804, 24 C.F.R. § 100.50 (1997).

(2) the designee of such parent or other person having such custody, with the written permission of such parent or other person.

The protections afforded against discrimination on the basis of familial status shall apply to any person who is pregnant or is in the process of securing legal custody of any individual who has not attained the age of 18 years.[156]

State Law

In this article, a discriminatory act is committed because of familial status if the act is committed because the person who is the subject of discrimination is:

1. Pregnant.

2. Domiciled with an individual younger than eighteen years of age in regard to whom the person either:

> (a) Is the parent or legal custodian.

> (b) Has the written permission of the parent or legal custodian for domicile with that person.

3. In the process of obtaining legal custody of an individual younger than eighteen years of age.[157]

The prohibition of discrimination based on "familial status" appears in federal and state law; state law is reprinted below.

> A. A person may not refuse to sell or rent after a bona fide offer has been made or refuse to negotiate for the sale or rental of or otherwise make unavailable or deny a dwelling to any person because of race, color, religion, sex, familial status or national origin.

> B. A person may not discriminate against any person in the terms, conditions or privileges of sale or rental of a dwelling, or in providing services or facilities in connection with the sale or rental, because of race, color, religion, sex, familial status or national origin.

---

156   42 U.S.C.A. § 3602 (West. 1995).

157   A.R.S. § 41-1491.01 (West 1992).

C. This section does not prohibit discrimination against a person because the person has been convicted under federal law or the law of any state of the illegal manufacture or distribution of a controlled substance.[158]

The Act, which is also state law, further provides:

A person who knowingly refuses to rent to any other person a place to be used for a dwelling for the reason that the other person has a child or children, or who advertises in connection with the rental a restriction against children, either by the display of a sign, placard or written or printed notice, or by publication thereof in a newspaper of general circulation, is guilty of a petty offense.[159]

To illustrate, by way of example, discrimination by "familial status," suppose a landlord takes an application from a married couple and then from a single woman (i.e., divorced or never married) with a small child. Assuming all other things are equal (i.e., credit, income, references, etc.), it is discriminatory for the landlord to prefer the married couple over the single woman because she has children or, said another way, because the married couple do not have children. In other words, the decision cannot turn on whether or not the applicant has children. If, however, the decision to accept the married couple's application is based on superior credit, income or other permissible criteria, *then there is no discrimination*.

Now, as a second example, assume the same facts, but that the single woman has two children, both over the age of two, and that both applicants are applying for a small, one bedroom apartment. Under these facts, the landlord may reject the single woman's application because acceptance of her as a tenant would exceed reasonable occupancy standards for that unit. The state law provides:

Nothing in this section [Section 33-1317] shall prohibit a person from refusing to rent a dwelling by reason of reasonable occupancy standards established by the owner or the owner's agent which apply to persons of all ages, and which have been adopted and published before the event in issue. An occupancy limitation of two persons per bedroom residing in a dwelling unit shall be presumed reasonable for this state and all political subdivisions of this state.[160]

---

158 A.R.S. § 41-1491.14 (West 1992).

159 A.R.S. § 33-1317(A) (West Supp. 1998). *See also* A.R.S. § 41-1491.01 (West 1992) (discrimination based on familial status prohibited).

160 A.R.S. § 33-1317(F) (West Supp. 1998).

The second sentence of the foregoing statute became effective July 17, 1994. The effect is to create a presumptively reasonable occupancy standard of two persons per bedroom. The language of the statute also indicates a legislative intent to preempt subordinate governmental units (i.e., counties, cities and towns) from adopting a different "reasonable standard." Notwithstanding the presumption, a landlord may establish a <u>higher</u> limitation: "[a] landlord may establish an occupancy limitation which exceeds two persons per bedroom residing in a dwelling unit."[161] Prior to July 1, 1995, infants under the age of twenty-four months could not be counted in determining an occupancy limitation.[162] When the Act was amended in July 1995, this language was omitted and, therefore, infants under twenty-four months old may (but do not have to be) counted in determining your occupancy limitation.

For the landlord to avail himself/herself of an occupancy standard limitation, the standard must be "adopted and published before the event in issue." In other words, the landlord must establish and adopt an occupancy standard and publish the standard before the applicant shows up at the door. I recommend publishing your occupancy standard with the landlord's minimum acceptable applicant criteria. And I recommend publishing this information on the back of the Application Form (or attached thereto). (*See* Chapter 3, Section E(2) (Saying No)).

(b) <u>More about handicap.</u>

Discrimination because the applicant has a handicap is also not permitted.[163] This includes discriminating because the handicapped applicant requires assistive aids and/or assistive animals. For example, you cannot discriminate because the applicant uses a wheelchair and/or crutches and you believe these assistive aids will increase the wear and tear on your property. Similarly, you cannot discriminate because the applicant wants or needs an assistive animal. Although it is true that certain assistive aids and/or assistive animals increase the wear and tear on the rental unit, nevertheless, discrimination on this basis is expressly prohibited at both the federal and state level.

The legislative intent of these laws is admirable and no one will argue that handicapped people are not entitled to housing, but these laws put the landlord at a severe disadvantage when confronted by someone who is not *really* handicapped and is merely trying to manipulate the system. For example, I know of one landlord who had a tenant who insisted that he must be allowed to have and park a modified school bus, purportedly an assistive aide, on the subject property. The Attorney General sided with the tenant, notwithstanding the fact that parking such a vehicle in this residential area violated a local ordinance (i.e., vehicles in excess of prescribed weight cannot be parked in residential area) and over the legitimate

---

161 A.R.S. § 33-1317(F) (West Supp. 1998).

162 1994 Ariz. Sess. Laws, Ch 355, § 3.

163 A.R.S. § 41-1491.19 (West 1992).

111

concerns of the landlord that the bus posed a safety hazard to children and other tenants because its placement when parked caused a dangerous "blind spot." As another example, a tenant claimed to have a mental disability and asserted that petting her pet ferret had a tranquilizing and calming effect on her. The tenant's doctor agreed and, therefore, so did the Attorney General. The potential for abuse is made clear by these examples.

No conscientious landlord would begrudge a blind person a seeing-eye dog. But when is a person blind and what makes a dog a "seeing-eye dog"? There is no law that prescribes a level of blindness entitling a person to a seeing-eye dog. Furthermore, you may be surprised to discover that in Arizona there is no certification or licensing of any type for seeing-eye dogs, or, for that matter, any other type of assistance animal. How, then, are landlords to defend themselves against tenants with 20/40 vision who claim they need the assistance of a "seeing-eye iguana" or self proclaimed mentally handicapped tenants who claim they are calmed only by petting their pet lemur. Absurd examples? Perhaps. But the startling absence of criteria for when a person is entitled to an assistive animal, the types of "acceptable" assistive animals, and certification or training for assistive animals, makes this area ripe for abuse.

As with any newly enacted law, subsequent amendments and case law will eventually give us guidance. In the meantime, a few tips may be helpful. Everyone with a heart problem would like their health spa dues and the cost of their swimming pool to be deductible from their taxes. The Internal Revenue Service takes a somewhat narrower view. Before such deductions are allowed, at a very minimum, the IRS will require that a medical doctor prescribe exercise and some explanation as to why swimming and a personally owned pool are necessary. Similarly, even the Arizona Attorney General will require some type of proof that the tenant is "truly" disabled. This type of proof normally comes from a medical doctor (i.e., a multiple-personality disorder, diagnosed by a chiropractor, probably won't suffice). So, the first step is for the landlord to ask for documentation that the applicant is disabled. The landlord is also entitled to proof that a medical doctor recommends specific assistive aids and/or assistive animals and, therefore, the second step is to ask for documentation that the specific aide is needed. Beyond these two items, however, there are no established and published criteria for documenting a handicap and/or the need for assistive aids and/or assistive animals.

(c) More about the Americans with Disabilities Act.

The Americans with Disabilities Act (ADA) requires landlords to make rental units accessible to disabled persons. The ADA provides:

> A disabled individual is one who has a physical or mental impairment that substantially limits one or more of his/her major life activities, has a record of such an impairment, or is regarded as having such an impairment even if in fact he/she does not have such an impairment.

"Major life activities" include "such things as caring for oneself, performing manual tasks, walking, seeing, hearing, speaking, breathing, learning and working."[164] "Substantially limited" means that the individual is unable to perform a major life activity that the average person in the general population can perform; or significantly restricted as to the condition, manner or duration under which an individual can perform a particular major life activity as compared to the condition, manner, or duration under which the average person in the general population can perform that same major life activity.[165]

As usual, the statutes are not a model of clarity. Perhaps specific examples will be more informative. People with physical and mental disabilities are disabled. Alcoholics and rehabilitated drug users/abusers are disabled. Persons with heart disease, cancer, epilepsy, cerebral-palsy, muscular dystrophy, multiple sclerosis, mental retardation, emotional illness, diabetes, and persons with the HIV or AIDS virus are disabled. On the other hand, current users of illegal drugs, homosexuals, bisexuals, transvestites, compulsive gamblers, and kleptomaniacs are not considered disabled.

The requirement to make rental units accessible is different for new and existing buildings. The ADA applies to "public accommodations," which means "a private entity that owns, leases or leases to, or operates a place of public accommodation."[166] Places of public accommodation designed and constructed for first occupancy after January 26, 1993, must be readily accessible to and usable by individuals with disabilities. For existing buildings, the ADA requires removal of architectural and communication barriers in existing buildings where such removal is "readily achievable." "Readily achievable" means easily accomplishable and able to be carried out without much difficulty or expense. A number of factors must be considered when determining whether or not a modification is readily achievable.[167] These factors concern the need, nature and cost of the modification, in comparison to the financial resources of the owner and the benefit that will be derived from the modification.

In short, if you are building a new rental property, your architect and builder should be well versed on the ADA requirements for new construction. To be sure, ask your architect and builder, preferably before s/he "breaks ground," what measures s/he has taken to comply with ADA. If s/he looks at you with a "blank" expression, you have a problem. If you own or are buying an existing building, contact the following agencies for additional information:

Americans with Disabilities Act Information Line   (202) 514-0301

Architectural and Transportation Barriers Compliance Board   (202) 272-5434
                     (accessibility guidelines)

---

164   29 C.F.R. § 1630.2(i) (1993).

165   29 C.F.R. § 1630.2(j) (1993).

166   42 U.S.C.S. § 12182(a) (1994).

167   42 U.S.C.S. § 12181(9) (1994).

(d)   Cohabitation.

So, what if you are faced with two applicants, of the opposite sex, who are not married? Can you say no to applicants who want to "live together"? The answer is *probably* yes.

In California, a landlord was fined by the California Fair Employment and Housing Commission for refusing to rent to an unmarried heterosexual couple because of his religious beliefs.[168] The California Supreme Court held that California law prohibited discrimination because of marital status and that it did not impinge upon the landlord's religious rights and, therefore, the landlord could not refuse to rent to the unmarried couple. The fine against the landlord was affirmed. The Court did not address sexual orientation (e.g., heterosexual, homosexual, bisexual), but it stands to reason that the result would have been the same if the landlord had refused to rent to a homosexual couple because of his religious beliefs. California, however, does not have a law that prohibits cohabitation, whereas Arizona *does* have a statute that prohibits cohabitation.[169]

In Washington, the Court of Appeals found that Washington state law, which made discrimination on the basis of marital status unlawful, did not preclude discrimination against a cohabitating heterosexual couple.[170]

So what is the answer in Arizona? The answer is not crystal clear in Arizona. Amazingly enough, today it is still unlawful to cohabitate with someone of the opposite sex.[171] Arizona does not recognize same sex marriages.[172] And there is no statute or case law in Arizona that prohibits discrimination against tenants who wish to cohabitate. Consequently, it is *my* legal opinion that, based on the current state of Arizona law, you may lawfully discriminate against a cohabitating heterosexual couple.

(e)   Liability for the discrimination of others.

If the foregoing hasn't scared you enough, this will. Not only are you responsible (and liable) for your own actions, you are responsible for your agent's actions. What this means is that you may win the State Fair Housing Award (if there is such a thing), but be fined by the Arizona Attorney General for the discriminatory

---

168   Smith v. Comm. of Fair Employment & Housing, 51 Cal.Rptr.2d 700, 913 P.2d 909 (1996). *See, also,* Foreman v. Anchorage Equal Rights Commission, 779 P.2d 1199 (Alaska 1989).

169   A.R.S. § 13-1409 (1989).

170   McFadden v. Elma Country Club, 26 Wash.App. 195, 613 P.2d 146 (1980). *See, also,* McReady v. Hoffius, 222 Mich.App. 210, 564 N.W.2d 493 (1997); Mister v. A.R.K. Partnership, 197 Ill.App.3d 105, 553 N.E.2d 1152, 143 Ill.Dec. 166 (1990); State by Cooper v. French, 460 N.W.2d 2 (Minn. 1990).

171   A.R.S. § 13-1409 (West 1989).

172   *See* A.R.S. § 25-101 (West 1991 & Supp. 1998).

practices of your property manager.[173] Consequently, you must not discriminate and you must ensure that no one acting on your behalf discriminates.

2. Saying No.

I never tell anyone "no" to his/her face, even if I know immediately that I consider his/her application unacceptable. Some people handle rejection well; some do not. I have not yet mastered the art of discerning, just by looking at them, which people take rejection well and which do not. Therefore, I only give people bad news (i.e., rejected application) over the phone. And it is a simple thing to do. Just say that you need to check the references before you make a decision, then call them later and diplomatically tell them "no." Make a note on the application why you rejected them and hold on to it for at least three (3) years.[174] Note: do this for all applications, not just applications from applicants in a protected class (i.e., minorities, etc.). Why? First, by keeping only rejected applications from protected class applicants, you are, in fact, treating them differently. Second, if those are the only applications you keep, all the rejected applications you have will be from protected class applicants – none from "ordinary" applicants. That will look very bad indeed.

One of the hardest lessons for the small landlord (someone who owns few units) to learn is to err conservatively (*see* Chapter 2, Section A). What do I mean by this? I will answer by way of an illustration. In the real world, there is a spectrum of tenant applicants. All tenant applicants will fall somewhere on that spectrum. At one end of the spectrum are the clear deadbeats – no job, no money, no car, no past address, no references, no anything. At the other end of the spectrum are the clearly good applicants -- people with good jobs, six figure bank accounts, new (and paid for) cars, one prior address since birth, and ten pages of kings and presidents as references. You will not have any trouble making a decision when an applicant comes to you that falls at, or even near, either end of the spectrum. The problem will only arise when they fall in that grey area right in the middle.

The large landlord (someone who owns many units) will merely establish certain criteria (*see* below) in advance and stick to it. All applicants are then measured against this criteria. They either pass or fail. If a few units, or even several units, go unrented because the landlord's criteria is exacting, it's no big deal. But for

---

173 *See e.g.,* <u>Cabrera v. Jakabovitz</u>, 24 F.3d 372 (2d. Cir. 1994) (jury found apartment owners liable for discriminatory practices of the real estate agency managing the property for the owners).

174 The statute of limitations for bringing a claim under the Civil Rights Act of 1866, 42 U.S.C. § 1982, is prescribed by the state law statute of limitations for personal injury, which in Arizona is two (2) years. A.R.S. § 12-542 (West 1992). The statute of limitations for bringing a claim under the Civil Rights Act of 1968, 42 U.S.C. §§ 3601-3619, is two years. The statute of limitations for a private citizen to bring a claim under A.R.S. § 41-1491.31 is two years. A.R.S. § 41-1491.31(A) (West 1992). Consequently, because an action may be filed within two years (the longest applicable statute of limitations) but not actually served until some time later (plaintiff has up to 120 days to serve the ***complaint***, pursuant to 16 A.R.S. Rules of Civ. Proc., Rule 4(i)), you should hold onto all applications for at least three (3) years.

the small landlord, this is a real problem. For example, you own three rental units. You have one unit vacant. If one goes unrented, that is one-third of your monthly rental income; a pretty hefty chunk. Joe Borderline shows up and fills out an application. You can't make up your mind about this guy; he seems to fall right in the middle. You have had only a few applicants this month and your ad has just run out. Here, then, is the dilemma. Do you say no, run another ad and wait it out, or do you take him? The answer: err conservatively -- reject Joe Borderline. The cheapest eviction you will ever do is to reject a borderline applicant. <u>Bottom line</u> -- establish your criteria for an acceptable tenant <u>in advance</u>, publish it (i.e., have it on a printed form), make it available to any applicant that asks for it, and, most important, stick to it. I recommend printing this information on the back of your Application Form (or attached thereto). Your criteria may look like this:

MINIMUM ACCEPTABLE CRITERIA

Monthly Income :	Four (4) times monthly rental amount
Employment :	One year or more with same employer
Credit :	Good
Pets :	Yes (but under 10 pounds)
Smokers permitted :	Yes
Assets/Savings :	Over $5,000.00
Attitude during application :	Good/pleasant/friendly
Occupancy Standard :	Two persons per bedroom

(Other Factors: phone, car, bankruptcy, vehicles, etc.)

<u>Develop good judgment</u>. The cornerstone of being a landlord is your own personal judgment. Face it, properly screening tenants is not a science -- it is an art. Many of your decisions will be based upon purely subjective evaluations. Learn to trust your own judgment. If you make a mistake, acknowledge that you "screwed up," learn from your mistake, take immediate corrective action and don't make the same mistake twice. You must have reasonably good judgment to have made it this far in life. Besides, you purchased this book -- you must have good judgment. In any event, even if your judgment could use some improvement, take comfort in knowing that properly screening tenants is something you get better at.

3.   <u>Saying Yes</u>.

How hard can this part be? One more thing you can (and should) do that will <u>prevent</u> many problems -- read the rental agreement to the tenant. Yes, read it to him/her. You do not want him/her to be surprised by any term or condition contained in the rental agreement <u>after</u> s/he has already moved in. You may think that reading the rental agreement to the tenant takes too much time. I assure you that you will be able to read <u>any</u> rental agreement to him/her in a shorter period of time than it will take to evict him/her or to defend the terms of your rental agreement in court. I have <u>never</u> had a tenant tell me that s/he did not have time for me to go over the entire rental agreement with him/her.

4. <u>Material Falsification of Information by the Tenant.</u>

One day it will happen. An applicant will give you information on the application which you later discover to be inaccurate or false. What do you do? For an applicant, the answer is simple — reject his/her application. If, however, the applicant has moved in and is now your tenant, the answer is different. Fortunately, the law was recently changed.

> **A.** Except as provided in this chapter [the Act], if there is a material noncompliance by the tenant with the rental agreement, including ***material falsification of the information provided on the rental application***, the landlord may deliver a written notice to the tenant specifying the acts and omissions constituting the breach and that the rental agreement will terminate upon a date not less than ten days after receipt of the notice if the breach is not remedied in ten days. For the purposes of this section, material falsification shall include the following untrue or misleading information about the:
>
> 1. Number of occupants in the dwelling unit, pets, income of prospective tenant, social security number and current employment listed on the application or lease agreement.
>
> 2. Criminal records, prior eviction record, current criminal activity. Material falsification of information in paragraph 2 of this subsection is not curable under this section.[175]

The answer, then, is to give your tenant a notice and evict the tenant if the s/he fails to cure the problem.

If you discover a falsification of information that falls within paragraph 2, above, then the tenant has no opportunity to cure the material falsification and must vacate within ten days. Notice, under these circumstances, is equivalent to a ten day notice to vacate.[176]

---

175 A.R.S. § 33-1368 (West Supp. 1998) (emphasis added).

176 A.R.S. § 33-1368 (West Supp. 1998).

117

If, however, you discover a falsification of information that falls within paragraph 1, above, then the tenant may cure the material noncompliance within ten days of your written notice.[177] Unfortunately, the statute does not specify how the tenant must correct the information. For example, if the tenant misrepresents his/her income (i.e., the tenant represented income of $2,000.00 per month, but had actual income of $1,000.00 per month), to cure the problem, must the tenant merely correct the application to reflect the tenant's true monthly income of $1,000.00? Or must the tenant obtain different or additional employment so that his/her income equals at least $2,000.00 per month. Although the latter may sound silly, what if your minimum acceptable criteria for applicants was income of $2,000.00? What good does it do you if the tenant is permitted to cure this material falsification of information, after the tenant has already moved in, merely by changing the information on the application? There is no guidance given in the statute and, as of yet, there are no cases that have interpreted this new language. Nevertheless, I offer the following as guidance.

- If the tenant misrepresented the number of occupants in the dwelling unit, the tenant must eliminate all occupants that are not specifically named in the rental agreement.

- If the tenant misrepresented that s/he had a pet, the type or number of pets, the tenant must eliminate all pets not disclosed on the application.

- If the tenant misrepresented his/her income, the tenant must disclose his/her present income. If the present income is below your minimum acceptable criteria, and has already demonstrated an inability to pay rent (i.e., recurring late payments), the tenant must secure different or additional employment, so that his/her income meets or exceeds your minimum income requirements. Alternatively, the tenant must provide additional assurances that the rent will be timely paid (i.e., another party to guarantee payment of all rent under the rental agreement).

- If the tenant misrepresented his/her social security number, the tenant must disclose the correct social security number.

- If the tenant misrepresented his/her current employment, the tenant must disclose the correct current employment. This may also impact upon the income represented by the tenant.

The foregoing are to be considered in light of all the facts and circumstances applicable to your situation. If you are in doubt as to how you should proceed, contact your attorney.

---

[177] A.R.S. § 33-1368 (West Supp. 1998).

F. **TERM OF TENANCY.**

Okay, you have decided to accept an applicant as a tenant. How long should you sign this tenant up for? You face the classic dilemma: long-term lease versus a month-to-month tenancy. The answer to this question is controlled by several practical considerations that vary depending on the types of rental units you own/manage.

1. **Exclusive, high dollar rental units.**

Practical considerations: You, as the landlord, have a much higher investment in these types of properties and, therefore, want low wear and tear and low tenant turnover. Similarly, the types of tenants interested in these types of properties are typically more affluent and they also want stability (i.e., they don't want to move again anytime soon).

Answer: The answer in this category is simple – yes, insist on a long-term lease. The fact is, tenants in this category may also insist on a long-term lease. It is not uncommon for leases in this category to be longer than one year (i.e., two to five years).

2. **Low priced rental units.**

Practical considerations: You, as the landlord, while having a significantly smaller per-unit investment, nevertheless want low wear and tear and low tenant turnover. Unfortunately, this is at odds with the expectations of the typical tenant for this category. The tenants in this category are typically younger, highly mobile and not financially stable (or worse). They are more mobile because they are not established in their careers (if they have one) and/or their relationships; therefore, they will move "at the drop of a hat" to change jobs or to cement or dissolve a relationship. On top of all that, these tenants typically abhor long-term commitments, especially long-term leases.

Now for a dose of reality. What is the point of a long-term lease? In theory, it assures that the tenant will remain in the unit for a long period of time. The consequence of breaking the long-term lease is financial liability for rent until the end of the lease or until the unit is re-rented. Are you beginning to see the light? Tenants in this category, because they typically have very little to begin with, are not concerned by the financial consequences of breaking a lease (i.e., you can't get blood out of a turnip). If they want to move out, they will merely move out -- it is that simple. Consequently, a long-term lease in this category really only binds the landlord – the landlord can't refuse to renew the rental agreement until it comes up for renewal (which, by definition, is a long time away), and the landlord can't terminate the rental agreement except when the tenant commits a material breach of the rental agreement. Correct me if I am wrong, but that does not sound like a good deal to me. Therefore, you may wish to consider a simple month-to-month tenancy. This allows you maximum flexibility (i.e., to not renew tenants who are or

119

become obnoxious). Also, because this is attractive to tenants in this category of rental units, you increase the number of applicants that apply, thereby increasing your chances of getting a good tenant. Remember, there are many good tenants out there that simply don't like long-term leases. These tenants oftentimes end up spending many years in the same place. The end result is what is important -- tenants that stay for a long time. What difference does it make how you achieve this result? The pragmatic landlord will recognize this approach as a "strategy" to get what s/he wanted in the first place -- tenant longevity.

Answer: Seriously consider offering month-to-month tenancies, thereby increasing the number of applicants who will apply and, thereby, increasing your odds of finding the type of tenant you wanted all along -- a tenant who will stay a long time. It just may be that a tenant who is interested in a month-to-month lease will stay a very long time, but merely have some irrational aversion to a long-term lease.

3.   Mid-range units.

I have addressed the mid-range level last because it is the most difficult to analyze.

Practical considerations: Naturally, you, as the landlord, want low wear and tear and low tenant turnover. Unfortunately, while tenants in this category are a little more stable than tenants in the lower level category, they generally are not any more anxious to commit to long-term leases. Perhaps they have just enough financial resources that the financial consequences of breaking a lease actually means something to them. Perhaps not too long ago they were in the lower level category and have not yet made the mental transition to wanting/accepting a long-term lease. Who knows for sure?

Answer: The answer depends on your area; not your city or town, but your area within that city or town. Sometimes you will be able to get away with insisting upon long-term leases. Sometimes you will only be able to sign up tenants if you offer month-to-month tenancies. In the latter case, the solution is to offer both long-term leases and month-to-month tenancies, with some type of financial incentive to tenants who opt for the lease (i.e., a monthly rental amount that is less than the amount charged to tenants who opt for the month-to-month tenancy).

NOTE: You may have noticed that I did not define "exclusive," "mid-range" and "lower level" rental units. I did not forget. Quantifying these terms in precise dollar amounts is futile because "exclusive" in Phoenix varies significantly from "exclusive" in Bisbee. You are familiar with your area. You know, much better than I do, what is "exclusive," "mid-range" and "lower level" in your area. Nevertheless, while the dollar amounts that define these categories may vary from area to area, the practical considerations for each of these three categories will not change, regardless of your location.

CHAPTER 4

MANAGING TENANTS EFFECTIVELY

Summary of Chapter

- The Art of Effectively Handling Tenant Problems
- Commonly Recurring Tenant Problems
- Problem Tenants

Depending on the number of rental units you have, attracting and screening applicants to obtain suitable tenants may occur very infrequently, as in the case of a landlord leasing out one single family residence, or may be an ongoing process, as in the case of a landlord for a large apartment complex. Nevertheless, in either case, at some point in time you will be faced with managing the property and managing your tenants.

The real estate industry has coined the phrase "property management." Property management, however, actually encompasses management of property problems (i.e., maintenance) and management of tenant problems (i.e., late rent payments, neighbor conflicts, etc.).

Effectively handling property problems (i.e., maintenance) does not take a rocket scientist. If something breaks and you have the "know-how" and tools to fix it yourself, then you fix it; otherwise, you call someone and pay them to fix it -- pretty straightforward. I am convinced, however, that effectively managing tenant problems is an art. Therefore, this section is devoted to a discussion of effective tenant management, which includes how to handle some of the most frequently occurring tenant problems (i.e., continual late payment of rent, noisy tenants, neighbor conflicts and parking problems).

Before proceeding further, I offer an observation: some of a landlord's time is spent handling <u>property</u> problems, but the bulk of a landlord's time is consumed handling <u>tenant</u> problems. I can tell you are not impressed by this revelation. Let me expound. I have discovered that there is a direct relationship between the number of tenant problems and the number of property problems; the higher the number of tenant problems, the higher the number of property problems. Why? The answer is really quite simple and logical -- property problems are normally the result of tenant problems. The fact is that rental units do not break their own windows, punch holes in their own doors, draw on the walls, or ruin their own carpet and flooring -- tenants do these things. Why? There are really only two reasons a tenant will indulge in such behavior: (1) this is the way s/he has always lived and you have done something to suggest that s/he can get away with it now, or (2) s/he has some reason to act vindictively toward you and/or your property. In either case, the fault lies with you. The point being, time and effort spent handling tenant problems <u>correctly</u> (i.e., effectively) tends to reduce the amount of property problems, thereby reducing the amount of time you spend on "property management."

A.   THE ART OF EFFECTIVELY HANDLING TENANT PROBLEMS.

Effectively handling tenant problems means, first, learning to <u>prevent</u> tenant problems and, second, learning how to control and resolve tenant problems once they develop.

1.   Prevent tenant problems.

In the event I have not heretofore clearly stated my position on this subject, I shall do so now: I subscribe to the notion that preventing a problem is infinitely more desirable than any conceivable solution to a problem. And the corollary, as previously stated (*see* Chapter 2, Section B), is that preventing or avoiding litigation is always better than winning litigation. Consequently, preventing tenant problems should be a top priority.

False expectations and a misunderstanding of important terms and conditions are the primary cause of tenant problems. Give your tenants a clear set of guidelines and expectations. Lay out your terms and conditions in your rental agreement in clear language and <u>read it to them before allowing them to sign it</u> (*see* Chapter 3, Section E(3)). If you have separate rules and regulations,[178] read those to them as well. Be straight with your tenants. Send a clear message -- you have specific rules, you follow those rules to the letter, and those who break the rules are penalized. In short, let them know that if they do not like the rules, they should not rent from you in the first place. Good tenants are not scared off by tough penalties. They do not plan on breaking the rules; therefore, they do not consider the penalties to be important. In short, let them know in advance what you will do and will not do for them as a landlord and, more importantly, what you expect them to do for you. This will avoid false expectations and misunderstandings in the future, thereby <u>preventing</u> an enormous amount of tenant problems.

The next critical step in preventing tenant problems is to implement a system for enforcing the terms of your rental agreement and your rules and regulations (if

---

178   *See* A.R.S. § 33-1342 (West Supp. 1998).

any). This means that you must first establish a method for discovering infractions quickly. For example, it does you no good to discover two weeks later that the tenant in unit six played loud music all night long -- disturbing all the surrounding tenants. You must establish a system whereby tenants may immediately report violations. Such a system must also allow anonymous reports, for those who desire to not identify themselves. In the case of an apartment complex, you might consider giving all your tenants a phone number to call to report disturbances. The key is to ensure that all tenants have the number and that all tenants know they are likely to be reported if they violate the rules. In the case of a single family residence, give both next-door neighbors and the three neighbors across the street a telephone number to contact (you or your property manager) in case of an emergency or some disturbance. Make sure you let your tenant know that all of his neighbors have this phone number -- this will help to keep the tenant "in line."

Similar to the first step in preventing tenant problems (which is to ensure that you inform the tenant of his/her obligations as a tenant), the final step in preventing tenant problems is ensuring that **you** know and understand the landlord's obligations. Article 2 of the Act spells out, in detail, the landlord's obligations with regard to security deposits, disclosures that must be made to the tenant, maintenance of the leased premises and more.[179] You must be intimately familiar with these sections of the statutes (see Appendix C). Failure to know and understand your obligations as a landlord will result in tenant problems and may result in civil liability. For example, if you fail to maintain the leased premises, the tenant may sue for damages or s/he may elect to repair the condition and deduct the cost of the repairs from the rent.[180]

2. Quickly and fairly resolve tenant problems.

Okay, in spite of all your efforts to prevent tenant problems, one has surfaced. Never make the mistake of assuming any tenant problem concerns only one tenant (unless you only own one rental unit). How you handle this tenant will eventually become known to the other tenants. Bend a rule one time and other tenants will ask you to do the same (i.e., waiving the late fee "just this one time"). Furthermore, if your inconsistent enforcement (i.e., okay for the tenant in unit one, but not okay for the tenant in unit two) of rental agreement terms, policy or rules and regulations is revealed in court, said term, policy, rule or regulation is likely to be declared unenforceable because you have established a habit of "selective enforcement."[181] Depending on the circumstances, selective enforcement may even be discriminatory.

The key to resolving tenant problems quickly and fairly is to follow the General Guidelines for Doing Business (see Chapter 2, Section A). Be honest, be

---

179   *See* A.R.S. §§ 33-1321 to -1329 (West 1990 & Supp. 1998).

180   *See* A.R.S. §§ 33-1324, -1361, -1363(A) (West Supp. 1998).

181   *See, e.g.,* Unif. Residential Landlord And Tenant Act, § 3.102; 7B U.L.A. 475 (1985).

straightforward, keep your forms and procedures simple, be businesslike, be authoritative, stay up-to-date and always err conservatively. Most of all, although you should strive to be fair, sometimes you must be unyielding. For example, if a tenant knew that you did not allow pets when she moved in, but now wants a "kitten," unless you are prepared to let all your tenants have pets, your answer must be NO.

Make your decision as soon as you have all the information you need upon which to base a valid judgment. In the case of the "kitten" (above), you have all the information you need right now, so make a decision right now – no or yes, as the case may be. Unnecessary delay may itself be an answer. If you tell your tenant you will let her know in a week, she may have the kitten in her house/apartment for that week. The primary reason for prohibiting pets in the first place is that they cause odors, which may linger indefinitely (i.e., cat boxes, kittens that are not yet house trained, etc.) and may cause damage to the rental unit (i.e., stains on carpet, snags in the drapes, etc.). Consequently, after one week, some damage may have already been done. Moreover, it will be much harder for this tenant to get rid of her kitten after having it around for a week than it would have been had you said no in the first place.

Conversely, if you need time to make a decision, take time and do not make a snap judgment. If a tenant wants to make some small structural modification (i.e., adding an inexpensive patio cover in the back yard), after you decide whether or not such an addition is desirable, you will need to determine whether the structure violates any zoning ordinances, deed restrictions and/or whether it requires a building permit. You should consider what you will do if all your tenants want to erect a patio cover (i.e., if you say yes, you may wish to allow only one type of design; otherwise, you will have as many different patio covers as you have tenants, which may or may not be desirable). You will also need to give some thought to who will pay for the materials, permits, etc., and what will become of the structure when that tenant leaves. All the details must be ironed out before you give approval. Furthermore, the agreement should be reduced to writing so that there is no controversy in the future.

One final point. Once you have made a decision, stick with it and do not change your mind (unless, of course, a significant fact changes). Tenants, like children, will challenge every decision you make that they do not like if they discover that continual pestering will cause you to change your mind. Similarly, if they know that once you have made up your mind, that is the end of it, they will not bring it up again.

3. Tenant survey.

A tenant survey is a management tool that helps to prevent future problems and to discover and cure existing problems. Like any tool, however, it is only effective if properly used. A Tenant Survey can help you: (1) measure current tenants' satisfaction with the leased premises, (2) discover the reason why vacating tenants are vacating, and (3) check the effectiveness of your management company.

TENANT SURVEY

The owners of the property are glad to have you as a tenant. This survey will help the owners evaluate the effectiveness of the property manager and measure your satisfaction with the leased premises, services and amenities. You may sign your survey or submit it anonymously. In either case, the property manager will not see your survey form and all data collected will be forwarded to the property owner. Please respond candidly.

What factor or factors were most important in your decision to rent at this property?

_____

If you are vacating, what factor or factors were most important in your decision to vacate this property?

_____

During your move (either in or out), did we make your move easier? ☐ Yes ☐ No
      What could we have done to make the move easier?

_____

Was your unit in satisfactory condition when you moved in?

_____

Did you provide the property manager with a list of items that needed to be remedied shortly after you moved in?
☐ Yes ☐ No
      Were all the items on the list remedied promptly? ☐ Yes ☐ No
      Which items were not remedied promptly?

_____

      Do you know why any items were not promptly remedied (or not remedied at all)?

_____

Other than as stated above, have your *subsequent* requests for service and repair been taken care of satisfactorily?
☐ Yes ☐ No. If no, please explain: _____

Are you presently pleased with the rental unit? ☐ Yes ☐ No. If no, please explain: _____

_____

Are you satisfied with the appearance of the exterior of the unit and/or the complex? ☐ Yes ☐ No

_____

Are you satisfied with the services and amenities provided? ☐ Yes ☐ No. If no, explain:

_____

Would you recommend this unit/complex to a friend? ☐ Yes ☐ No. If no, explain:

_____

Has any member of the property management company:
      • Been exceptionally helpful? ☐ Yes ☐ No. (Please provide name and details)

_____

      • Been rude or discourteous? ☐ Yes ☐ No. (Please provide name and details)

_____

What changes, if any, would you like to see made to your unit and/or the complex?

_____

Any other comments you wish to make: _____

_____

_____

Naturally, if one of the purposes is to check the effectiveness of your management company, you should not have the management company send out and receive the completed surveys. Otherwise, only "favorable" surveys may be forwarded to you. Instead, provide a self addressed stamped envelope, with the address on the return envelope being an address *other* than your property manager.

Shortly after move-in (i.e., within thirty days) and after the tenant has vacated, are very good times to send surveys. Most problems will normally surface immediately after move-in or during the move-out process. In the latter case, you may also discover the reason why the tenant is vacating. If, "I'm moving out because the property manager is a jerk," is a common theme, it may be time to reevaluate your property manager -- s/he is obviously driving away tenants and reducing your net profit by increasing turnover. Sometimes a "re-renting" fee gives the property manager an incentive to encourage high turnover, which is contrary to the owner's interests. Obviously, high turnover requires additional expense for advertising, preparing the unit for a new tenant, etc., and results in lost revenues while the unit remains unrented. Your survey form may look like the one on the prior page.

You may also wish to send a survey to all tenants at regular intervals (i.e., once a year, etc.). This will collect data from your most valuable tenants – the ones who have stayed a long time. One caveat – do not use a survey if you will not read and use the data. It is a waste of time and money and may even expose you to some type of liability. For example, if a tenant survey puts you on notice about another tenant improperly storing flammable material (i.e., paint, thinner, etc., on a back patio), and you take no action, you may be liable for any resulting damages.[182]

B. **COMMONLY RECURRING TENANT PROBLEMS.**

Summary of this Section

- Continually late rent payments
- "One time" or occasional past due rent
- Noisy tenants
- Neighbor conflicts
- Parking problems
- Security
- Accidents and incidents

"Okay, enough of this philosophical mumbo-jumbo," you say. "What are the most commonly occurring tenant problems and how do I deal with them effectively?" I am so glad you asked. The following pages discuss many of the most commonly occurring tenant problems and some suggested methods of effectively handling each of them.

---

182 *See, e.g.,* Klimkowski v. De La Torre, 175 Ariz. 340, 857 P.2d 392 (App. 1993).

1. Continually late rent payments.

Cross Reference:
- "One time" or occasional late payments, Chapter 4, Section B(2)
- How to evict a tenant for nonpayment of rent, Chapter 5, Section B

This section addresses how to handle the tenant who repeatedly pays his rent late, but not late enough for you to evict him. You know this guy; he is the one that you are forced to serve with a Five-Day Notice every single month, but he always pays the amount past due before a judgment is entered against him (a tenant may "pay and stay" anytime prior to entry of judgment; after entry of judgment, however, the landlord is not required to accept payment and/or permit the tenant to stay).[183]

First, do not try to understand this tenant – it cannot be done. By continually paying his rent late, he subjects himself to late fees and whatever charges you assess him for issuing the Five-Day Notice, filing the Special Detainer action, etc. (the source of your right to assess the tenant for these charges <u>after</u> you file the Special Detainer action is statutory,[184] <u>but</u> the source of your right to assess the tenant for these charges <u>before</u> you file the Special Detainer action is your rental agreement -- does your rental agreement address these charges?). I always find myself wondering why this tenant doesn't just pay the rent on time and save himself the hassle, not to mention the additional expense. It is almost like this guy has decided he wants to pay a higher rental amount than everyone else.

Rather than attempt to understand this tenant, you should simply make a policy decision, <u>in advance</u>, as to what you will do when this situation comes up. Your options are limited and simple: either you will live with it and enjoy the additional revenue each month (normally my choice) or you will not live with it. If you decide not to live with it, you will nevertheless be forced to endure it for some period of time.

(a) Month-to-month tenant.

If your tenant is on a month-to-month tenancy, your answer is simply to not renew his tenancy. Provide the tenant with the appropriate notice (which should be stated in your rental agreement) and tell him: (1) you have elected to not renew his tenancy, (2) his tenancy terminates on (give date tenancy ends), and (3) that he must be out no later than (same date). (*See* Appendix B, Form 12). If he fails to move out, he is a "holdover tenant" and you can evict him.[185] (*See* Chapter 5, Section B).

---

183 A.R.S. § 33-1368(B) (West Supp. 1998).

184 *See* A.R.S. § 33-1368(B) (West Supp. 1998).

185 A.R.S. § 33-1375(C) (West Supp. 1998).

(b) Long-term lease.

If your tenant is on a long-term lease and the term is not due to expire anytime soon (otherwise you would simply not renew his tenancy -- discussed immediately above), then it will take longer to get this guy out. You see, if the tenant always manages to pay before a court enters a judgment against him, then you cannot terminate his lease based on nonpayment of rent. Your rental agreement, however, may allow you to terminate his lease for a "material noncompliance" if he is continually late (what does your rental agreement say?). (*See* Chapter 5, Section B(3) for more about "material noncompliance"). "Continually" should be defined in the rental agreement (i.e., more than three consecutive months), but your definition must be "reasonable." Defining "continually" as being late one time will probably not hold up in court.[186]

If your rental agreement does not address this issue (a common occurrence), the "legal" answer is that you will be at the mercy of the judge that hears Special Detainer actions in your area. The key is to document your file with copies of notices that you have sent the tenant notifying him that his rent is late. Toward that end, always serve the Five-Day Notice when it should be served. After three consecutive months of late rental payments, send the tenant a notice stating that you consider his repeated late rental payments to be a material breach of the rental agreement and that any future occurrences will result in: (1) termination of his rental agreement and (2) a forcible detainer action[187] against him, if he fails to move out voluntarily, wherein you will ask the court to declare the tenant's right to possession of the rental unit forfeited (*see* Appendix B, Form 12). The <u>next time</u> he is late, terminate his rental agreement, send him notice of the termination, advise him of the day he must vacate the premises and <u>file the Special Detainer action</u> if he does not move out. Do not delay or give him another month -- if you have decided not to tolerate this behavior, <u>then follow through</u>. Now follow the steps for evicting a tenant for a material noncompliance with the rental agreement (*see* Chapter 5, Section B).

If you do delay and/or give him another month and then suddenly file a Special Detainer action, in all likelihood, the court will find that your delay effected a waiver of your right to declare late payment of rent a material breach. The judge will probably tell you that you must send the tenant another notice and will usually tell the tenant that he had better pay the rent on time because next time he will take the landlord's side. But you have still lost. You have lost time, money and, let's face it, whenever you lose a court case against a tenant (who, by virtue of winning, will remain a tenant and be around a while to tell all the other tenants of his spectacular victory) you lose face with your other tenants.

---

186 *See, e.g.,* A.R.S. §§ 33-1311, -1312, -1314 (West 1990 & Supp. 1998).

187 Although the proper term is "Special Detainer," I normally use the term "forcible detainer" in the notice because tenants are familiar with the term "forcible detainer."

2.   **"One time" or occasional past due rent.**

Cross Reference:
- How to handle continually late rent payments, Chapter 4, Section B(1)
- How to evict for material noncompliance with the rental agreement, noncompliance materially affecting health and safety, and material and irreparable breach, Chapter 5, Section B
- How to evict for nonpayment of rent, Chapter 5, Section B

This Section addresses how to handle a tenant who is not continually late paying his/her rent, but who, for some reason, is "behind" on paying the rent for this particular month and who, for whatever reason, you do not wish to evict (at least not yet). Perhaps this tenant, who has otherwise always been an exemplary tenant, has suffered some temporary financial calamity and you would prefer to help him/her through it, rather than evicting him/her and find a new tenant. This tenant owes you for past due rent and you want payment. What do you do? You already know the answer to this question. Turn to Chapter 5, Section B and begin the process for evicting the tenant for nonpayment of rent. Granted, you may not actually wish to evict this tenant, but you must start the process for two reasons. First, the process takes a while and you may work with this tenant for a couple weeks before concluding that a solution is not possible. If you wait to serve the Five-Day Notice to Pay or Quit and/or to file the Special Detainer action until after settlement negotiations have proven fruitless, you will have lost valuable time. Whereas, if you proceed immediately, once you have received a judgment against the tenant you can "drag your feet" a bit before asking the court to issue the Writ of Restitution and/or having the Sheriff physically evict the tenant. Second, as a landlord, you must strive to conduct yourself consistently, professionally and *predictably* (*see* Chapter 2, Section A). Failure to start the eviction process when a tenant fails to pay rent sends the wrong message to this tenant and *especially* to your other tenants.

After you serve the Five-Day Notice, try to negotiate partial payment of the amount due (*see* Appendix B, Form 5). In the partial payment agreement, you may give the tenant additional time to pay the remaining balance. Your imagination is the only limit on your ability to work out a solution. For example, if funds simply are not available, you may be able to have the tenant perform some type of maintenance or service in exchange for some or all of the money s/he owes you; or you may simply have the tenant execute a promissory note, to be paid at some predetermined future date. Naturally, effecting a workout of this type assumes that this tenant's financial crisis *truly is temporary*, that s/he will be able to make regular rent payments *soon* and soon thereafter make up any back payments.

You must be very careful, however, that you do not do this *too* often or else this tenant (and perhaps others) may expect you to "come to the rescue" every time s/he has a problem. This is where it pays to have a reputation as a landlord who is honest, straightforward and businesslike with his tenants (*see* Chapter 2, Section A). If your tenants know that you expect prompt payment of rent when it is due and that arrangements of this type are the exception, not the rule, then they will pay their rent on time.

If all else fails and you cannot work out some type of arrangement that is mutually acceptable, you have no choice but to complete the eviction process (although, I suppose, letting the tenant remain rent free is a theoretical option).

3.   Noisy tenants.

Practically all pre-printed rental agreement forms have some provision for the consequences of being a noisy tenant. In addition (or alternatively), you may have written rules and regulations that address noise and other disturbances.[188] Simply follow the procedures in your rental agreement and/or rules and regulations.

If you don't have rules and regulations and/or your rental agreement doesn't address noise or disturbances, your options are simple and straightforward. If the tenant is on a month-to-month tenancy or near the end of his long-term lease, simply do not renew his/her tenancy (*see* Appendix B, Form 12).

If your tenant is on a long-term lease (and not near the expiration date), follow these steps. First, pay the tenant a visit <u>while the disturbance is occurring</u> and tell him/her to stop. If you would rather not do this personally or if your personal visit was unsuccessful in quelling the disturbance, call the police and let them deal with the tenant. Incidently, a police report may be helpful later in court, when you are trying to justify to the judge why you are evicting this tenant. Second, whether or not your visit was successful, document your file by serving the tenant with a Ten-Day Notice of Material Noncompliance (i.e., disturbing his neighbor's peaceful enjoyment of the premises).[189] (*See* Appendix B, Form 11). If the disturbance is serious, you may be able to <u>immediately</u> terminate his lease (*see* Chapter 5, Section B(3)(c); Appendix B, Form 8). Naturally, the tenant will cure the noise problem well within the ten-day period. The Act provides, however, that upon a second occurrence of the "same or similar nature" anytime during "the term of the lease" the landlord may terminate the rental agreement with a ten-day notice.

> If there is an additional act of these types of noncompliance of the same or a similar nature during the term of the lease after the previous remedy of noncompliance, the landlord may institute a special detainer action pursuant to § 33-1377 ten days after delivery of a written notice advising the tenant that a second noncompliance of the same or a similar nature has occurred.[190]

---

188   *See* A.R.S. § 33-1342 (West Supp. 1998).

189   A.R.S. § 33-1341(7) (West 1990).

190   A.R.S. § 33-1368(A) (West Supp. 1998).

The <u>next time</u> he creates a disturbance, gather a list of people that witnessed the first disturbance and a list of people who witnessed the second disturbance, terminate his rental agreement, send him ten-day notice of termination and advise him of the day he must vacate the premises. (*See* Appendix B, Form 12). <u>File the Special Detainer action if he does not move out</u>. Do not delay or give him another month. If you have decided not to tolerate this behavior, then follow through (*see* Chapter 4, Section B(1), which discussed the consequences of not following through as your Notice to the tenant stated). Now follow the steps for evicting a tenant for a material noncompliance with the rental agreement (*see* Chapter 5, Section B(3)(a)).

4.   <u>Neighbor conflicts.</u>

This is probably one of the most common problems and one of the most difficult problems to solve. The difficulty arises from the fact that you rarely see this conflict from start to finish; therefore, you will never truly know who said and/or did what, who instigated the conflict, etc.

Sometimes (but rarely) the solution is simple. For example, a conflict over one tenant playing loud music late at night is easily resolved against the offending tenant because causing a disturbance normally violates the rental agreement and/or rules and regulations and, in any event, may be a violation of the law (i.e., disturbing the peace).[191]

The harder question is when the offending tenant (above) retaliates against the tenant that reported him by filing a complaint against her the next day for playing music during the day which is not particularly loud, but which can be heard outside her rental unit.

Your duty as a landlord in this situation and other similar situations is to resolve this matter as fairly as possible. Your best approach is to act as a mediator, not a judge. A judge decides who is right and who is wrong -- someone wins, someone loses. This only generates more animosity between tenants who obviously already have a conflict. A mediator's goal, on the other hand, is to achieve a result that is somewhere in between the positions taken by the opposing parties. In this case, the answer may be to ask the tenant to turn her music down "a little bit" and to remind the other tenant that during daylight hours a certain amount of noise is permissible under the terms of the rental agreement and/or rules and regulations. Then, remind <u>both</u> tenants that, as tenants, they have an obligation under the law to "conduct themselves in a manner that will not disturb [their] neighbors' peaceful enjoyment of the premises."[192] Both tenants may still dislike each other, but they are both aware that neither party "won." More important, chances are that neither tenant enjoyed being reminded by the landlord to conduct themselves as adults and, therefore, in the future, both may attempt to be more tolerant of the other.

---

191   A.R.S. § 13-2904(A) (West Supp. 1998) (unreasonable noise constitutes disorderly conduct).

192   The Act provides, "The tenant shall: . . . (7) Conduct himself and require other persons on the premises with his consent to conduct themselves in a manner that will not disturb his neighbors' peaceful enjoyment of the premises." A.R.S. § 33-1341(7) (West 1990).

131

Occasionally, you will run into the tenant I call "the antagonist." This tenant seems to get along with you, but can't (or doesn't want to) get along with other tenants. This guy has seemingly valid complaints, but he complains more than any other tenant and he complains about everyone and everything. There are only two solutions for dealing with this guy: (1) get rid of him or (2) retrain him. When I say "retrain," I mean that each time he brings a complaint, you must take the time to explain the parameters of acceptable and unacceptable behavior in that particular area and then explain whether or not you believe a violation has occurred. For example, in the prior scenario (i.e., marginally loud music played during the day), you may believe the tenant is clearly within her rights to play music during the day at that particular volume and, therefore, you would take a firm position with the complaining tenant and explain that her conduct is acceptable. You would also take this opportunity to point out that his conduct the previous night (loud music at night) was not acceptable. He may be unhappy, but he will have learned two things: (1) what you consider acceptable and unacceptable (at least with regard to volume of music) and (2) he cannot use you as a weapon to retaliate against other tenants. If he is truly unhappy, he will eventually move out, but my experience has been that "the antagonist" is happiest when he is unhappy.

5.   Parking problems.

Parking is such a significant source of problems that you should make a point of discussing it during the application process. Naturally, some types of parking problems are indigenous only to apartment complexes, some only to single family residential rentals and some parking problems are common to both.

The first dilemma you must face is whether you will have "assigned parking" (i.e., each parking stall is numbered and reserved for exclusive use by a particular tenant), or whether you will have "unassigned parking" (i.e., parking stalls are not numbered and any tenant may park wherever there is an empty stall). You may even have a combination of both (i.e., one numbered assigned parking stall for each tenant and many parking stalls that are not assigned, for use by tenants with more than one vehicle and guests).

You might think that parking problems would only occur if you have assigned parking stalls and someone parks in somebody else's assigned stall – false. The truth is that disputes over parking occur whether or not you have assigned parking stalls. This is the classic "no win" scenario – if you have assigned parking stalls, someone will want unassigned parking stalls and vice versa. The key to winning this argument with your tenants is to put it in your rental agreement (i.e., "tenant shall have two assigned {or unassigned} parking stalls"). If/when they complain, you simply point out that they knew they would be getting assigned (or unassigned) parking stalls when they signed the rental agreement. Moreover, you are absolutely certain you covered this point with them because you read the entire rental agreement to them before they signed it (see Chapter 2, Section A (Be Straightforward) and Chapter 3, Section E(3), regarding reading the rental agreement to the tenants before allowing them to sign it).

Besides wanting a parking system other than what you already have in place, some of the typical parking problems experienced by tenants and landlords include:

- A tenant is using too many spaces because: (1) a tenant owns more vehicles than his allotment of parking spaces, (2) a tenant or a tenant's guest is improperly parked, (3) a tenant or a tenant's guest is parked in another tenant's assigned parking stall, (3) a tenant frequently (or infrequently) has guests over to visit him/her and the guests take several or many of the unassigned parking stalls.

- Tenants or guests parking in areas not designated for parking.

- A tenant parking a commercial vehicle in one (or more) parking stall(s).

- A tenant leaving a disabled and/or unregistered vehicle in one space for a long period of time.

- A tenant frequently performing vehicle maintenance on his/her vehicle(s) while parked in parking stall(s).

Each will be discussed, with some suggestions on how to effectively resolve the problem.

(a) Tenants/guests improperly parked or taking too many spaces.

Whether parking is assigned or unassigned you will receive complaints that someone is taking too many parking spaces (i.e., the vehicle is improperly parked in two spaces or s/he has more vehicles parked on the property than their allotment of parking spaces). Whatever the reason precipitating this problem, the solution is simple. If someone is improperly parked, tell him/her to move. If the reason s/he has more vehicles on the property than his/her allotment of parking stalls is because of visiting guests, simply inform the tenant that: (1) neither tenants nor guests may park in parking stalls that are assigned to other tenants and (2) other tenants have priority over guests for unassigned parking stalls (if that is your policy).

You have a more serious problem if the reason s/he is taking too many parking stalls is because s/he owns more vehicles than his/her allotment of parking stalls. This should have been addressed at the time s/he signed the rental agreement; if not, this problem will arise shortly after the new tenant moves in and discovers that s/he has a problem. This problem also may arise when an existing tenant acquires an additional vehicle. Your options to solve this problem are few: (1) s/he must park on the street (assuming such parking is available and lawful), (2) s/he must find a tenant who is willing to give (or rent) him/her an unused parking stalls (or you may have to make this arrangement for him/her), or (3) s/he must either dispose of one vehicle or park it somewhere else.

If you have assigned parking, inevitably someone will park in your space, your manager's space or one of your tenants' spaces. And, if you are having a particularly bad day, all of the above on the same day. The answer is seemingly simple – ask him/her to move the vehicle – but this presumes you know who owns the vehicle that is improperly parked. If you do know, no problem – tell that tenant or guest to move his/her vehicle <u>and</u> send the tenant a written notice that s/he or one of his/her guests was improperly parked and not to do it again. (*See* Appendix B, Form 6). If you do not know who owns the vehicle (a common occurrence in large apartment complexes), you may not be able to achieve immediate results. Naturally, you can always put a "Parking Violation" notice on the vehicle. (*See* Appendix B, Form 7). But, let's face it, a parking violation form will not remedy the situation; it is merely a scare tactic to induce <u>future</u> voluntary compliance. It may, however, make you feel a whole lot better. On the other hand, you may be able to achieve immediate results if you are able to have the vehicle towed away, <u>if</u> the law so provides and <u>if</u> you have met the legal notice requirements (i.e., signs posted).

What is the law on towing away a vehicle that is parked on your property? Typically, towing of vehicles that are unlawfully parked on private property is governed by local law (i.e., city or town). Sometimes you must give written notice; sometimes signs must be posted. Given the number of cities and towns in Arizona, I have not attempted to reprint the various local laws. Nevertheless, for those with property in Phoenix, Arizona, I have reprinted the section of the Phoenix City Code that addresses unlawful parking on private property in Chapter 2, Section E(9). For those with property elsewhere, to find out the law in your area, call your lawyer. Alternatively, call a local towing company. Towing is their business -- they will probably know what the law is, what the notice requirements are and may even have signs and/or stickers that you can purchase from them to comply with the law.

(b)   Parking in areas not designated for parking.

Tenants parking in areas not designated for parking is a problem common to both apartment complexes (i.e., no parking zones, loading zones, driveways, etc.) and single family residences (i.e., on the lawn, in the back yard, etc.). As just discussed in the last Section (Chapter 4, Section B(5)(a)), your options are to: (1) ask the owner of the vehicle to move the vehicle (*if* you know who owns the vehicle), (2) place a "Parking Violation" notice on the vehicle, or (3) if the vehicle presents an immediate problem (i.e., parked in fire lane, etc.), have the vehicle towed away, pursuant to local law.

(c)   Parking of commercial vehicles.

Your rental agreement should address the propriety of parking commercial vehicles in assigned or unassigned parking stalls. You should be aware, however, that in some cases the parking of a commercial vehicle in a residential neighborhood is unlawful.[193] A commercial vehicle includes buses, tractors, semi-trailers, and vehicles with a rated capacity of over 1.5 tons. You will need to check local law (i.e., city or town) regarding parking commercial vehicles in your area.

(d)   Disabled and/or unregistered vehicles.

Local law may impose a fine for having an "abandoned vehicle" in a residential neighborhood. The definition of "abandoned vehicle" may be broader than you think. As such, a violation may be occurring without you realizing it. For example, under a Phoenix ordinance, a disabled and/or unregistered vehicle may be deemed an "abandoned" vehicle.[194] Generally, the owner of real property upon which the vehicle is located and the owner of the vehicle are both responsible for curing the problem and may both be subject to civil penalties. Obviously, you should avoid having abandoned vehicles on your property because of potential civil liability, but also because abandoned vehicles detract from the appearance of your property, thereby diminishing the aesthetic appeal and decreasing property/rental value.

(e)   Vehicle maintenance.

Your rental agreement should also address whether or not tenants may perform vehicle maintenance on the premises. In the case of an apartment complex (regardless of size), maintenance should not be allowed. In the case of a single family residence, you may feel the need to be a bit more lenient, but be very careful. While changing an air filter may be no big deal, changing the oil can leave a horrible mess if not properly performed. Environmentally speaking, engine oil, anti-freeze, brake fluid and automatic transmission fluid are hazardous materials and must be disposed of "properly," which does not mean down a storm drain, in the gutter, or poured over a dirt field. You can be assured that virtually no tenant will properly dispose of these substances. Consequently, you may end up with an environmental hazard on your property -- You Do Not Want an Environmental Hazard on Your Property!!!!!!!!!

An environmental hazard on your property brings federal and state environmental laws into play that will be your worst nightmare.[195] Environmental hazards may expose you to massive liability and are incredibly expensive to clean up. Bottom line -- prevent environmental hazards at all costs. Of secondary importance is the fact that all this oil and grease on your parking lot detracts from the appearance of the property and gets tracked into the rental units and onto carpets and floors by tenants and guests. In addition, allowing vehicle maintenance means

---

193 See, e.g., PHOENIX, ARIZ., CITY CODE, ART. XI, § 36-140 (1985); MESA, ARIZ., CITY CODE, TITLE 11 § 11-4-4(F) (1993).

194 PHOENIX, ARIZ., CITY CODE, ART. XI, Section 36-161 (1992 & Supp. 1997); Phoenix Development Guide, Section 500-C-8-e.

195 See, e.g., Comprehensive Environmental Response, Compensation, and Liability Act of 1980, 42 U.S.C. §§ 9601-9675 (1988); A.R.S. §§ 49-281 to -289 (West Supp. 1998).

that many vehicles will be left for long periods of time in various stages of disassembly with parts "temporarily" stored under, around and on top of vehicles; this, and a parking lot full of tenants working on their cars, negatively impacts on the image of your complex. Finally, in some instances, prolonged vehicle maintenance may even violate local law.[196]

6. Security.

A startling new trend is occurring in landlord/tenant law. More and more, landlords are becoming responsible for ensuring that the rented property, whether residential or commercial, is safe and secure. Essentially, this exposes the landlord to financial liability for any harm suffered by a tenant, guest, and/or neighboring property owner caused *by third parties* (i.e., criminals) and/or tenants, if the harm is the result of the landlord's failure to "act reasonably." Such harm may be the result of criminal activity by third parties, criminal activity by other tenants, or unsafe activity by other tenants or third parties.

For example, in a California case,[197] the California Supreme Court found that a landlord owed a duty of care to its commercial tenants to take reasonable steps to secure the common areas under the landlord's control. Under the facts of this case, the landlord was found not liable for the rape of a tenant's employee. The Court stated that, absent some prior similar incident of violence on the property, the landlord had no duty to hire security guards. The message sent, however, is that if *there is* a history of violence, the landlord *may* be obligated to hire security guards.

That was precisely the result in a Nevada case. In this case, a jury awarded $12.5 million to a woman for the murder of her son by another tenant. The jury found the owners liable for failing to provide adequate security for tenants and disregarding other safety procedures.

In another California case,[198] a landlord was found responsible for drug activity *by third parties* on and *around* the subject property. A group of tenants in an apartment complex sued the owner because drug activity on and around the property made the property a public and private nuisance. The court concluded that drug activity could constitute a nuisance and did interfere with the plaintiffs' enjoyment of their property. The court stated, however, that the landlord would be liable only if he did not take reasonable steps to stop the problem. The landlord had posted "no trespassing" signs and installed new locks on some of the apartments. The court found these efforts inadequate and cited several more aggressive measures that could have been taken, such as employment of an on-site manager, secure fencing, and key-card gates. The court found the landlord responsible and awarded monetary damages.

---

196 Phoenix, Ariz., City Code, Art. XI, Section 36-138 (1985).

197 *See e.g.*, Ann M. v. Pacific Plaza Shopping Center, 863 P.2d 207 (Cal. 1993).

198 Lew v. Superior Court of Alameda County, 20 Cal.App.4th, 25 Cal.Rptr.2d 42 (1993).

In an Arizona case,[199] a landlord was found responsible for damages resulting from a fire. The landlord and tenant had a verbal, month-to-month agreement. The neighboring property owner had warned the owner that the tenant's children were playing with cigarette lighters on the property, where gasoline, paints, thinners and other flammable materials were stored. Despite the warning, the landlord took no action and continued to rent to the tenant. Two months later, the neighboring property owner sustained damages as a result of a fire on the leased premises. The court observed that a landlord is generally not responsible for what a tenant does because the tenant's right of possession of the property is exclusive and, therefore, the landlord is powerless to enter the property and take corrective action. Because this was a month-to-month agreement, however, the landlord had the opportunity to require the tenant to remedy the problem as a condition of renewing the tenancy. The court concluded that the landlord's failure to take any action subjected him to liability for the harm resulting from his failure to act. The lesson to be learned is, if a landlord knows (or should know) about a nuisance on the leased premises and, thereafter, renews the tenancy without correcting the problem or requiring the tenant to correct the problem, he incurs liability for damages resulting from the nuisance. This is of particular importance to landlords with month-to-month tenants because such a tenancy renews every month.

The landlord's liability may include criminal liability. In a Washington case,[200] a landlord was convicted of violating a state statute that prohibited knowingly renting space to tenants for manufacturing, delivering, selling, storing, or giving away any controlled substance. The landlord had visited his residential tenant's property a number of times, discovered that the tenant was growing marijuana in his basement, and did nothing about it. The tenant was arrested two months later. Had the landlord at least notified a law enforcement agency, he may have had a defense. In this case, however, the landlord "passively acquiesced" in the illegal activity and, therefore, the court found him criminally liable for his tenant's drug crime.

Cases in other western states, especially California, are significant because Arizona courts often find them persuasive and reach similar conclusions. Consequently, you, as a landlord, should pay close attention to landlord/tenant cases in Arizona and other western states.

7.   Accidents and incidents.

Okay, you've done the best you can to make the property safe and secure (or not, as the case may be) and an accident or incident occurs anyway. What do you do next? The actions you take, or fail to take, immediately following an accident or incident may save you, or cost you, many thousands of dollars. Do the right things and you will save yourself time, money and a great deal of aggravation.

---

199   Klimkowski v. De La Torre, 175 Ariz. 340, 857 P.2d 392 (App. 1993).

200   State v. Sigman, 826 P.2d 144 (Wash. 1992).

An accident is simply that – an accident; arguably, nobody's fault. An incident normally involves intentional conduct (i.e., crimes against persons or property). In either event, the first priority, naturally, is to summon medical aid, if needed. Render medical aid yourself, while awaiting qualified medical aid, only if you are qualified to do so. The second priority is to immediately gather as much information as possible about what happened and the identity (i.e., name, address, phone number) of all persons involved in the accident/incident and the identity of all witnesses. Ideally, you should take photographs of any physical conditions that may be relevant.

For example, if the incident is the near-drowning of a child in an apartment complex pool, you would want to take photographs of the fence around the pool, any gates accessing the pool, close-up photographs of latches, locks, and posted signs, and photographs about anything else that would be *even remotely* relevant. With another witness present, you would want to immediately inspect all gates, latches and locks, to ensure they were operating properly. You would want to interview anyone who "saw" or "heard" actual events (i.e., saw the child wander into the pool area; heard the child call for help; heard the lifeguard say, "It's Miller time," and leave the area before his shift was through; etc.). Make a thorough inspection of the entire area and the surrounding area; take copious notes.

As a second example, if the incident was a burglary, you would want to take photographs of the "point of entry" (i.e., where the burglar gained entry into the rental unit) and close-ups of the lock or latch that secured the door or window, along with a statement from the tenant (or anyone with personal, first-hand knowledge) about whether the door/window was properly secured. An allegation that the locks/latches provided by the landlord were inadequate will not be successful if the lock/latch was not secured (i.e., locked). You will also want to get a comprehensive list of items taken and/or damaged, including photographs of the damaged items. This will keep the list of stolen/damaged property from "growing" after a few days, to include new stereos and "damage to all the carpet in the unit." If the burglary occurred at night, you will want to get photographs of exterior lighting and immediately note which lights were not operating, if any, and have this data verified independently by another witness. If there is an alarm system, test it immediately. If the alarm is monitored by an outside company, have them come out and test the system immediately.

You may be saying, "isn't this the police department's job?" Yes. But the police typically will not spend this much time and effort investigating these incidents. Besides, the police will approach the investigation from the "who done it" point of view. You, on the other hand, will be more concerned with "what others may allege *you* failed to do properly" (i.e., failed to properly secure pool, failed to provide adequate locks/latches, outdoor lighting or security). Face it, no one will have your best interests in mind – except you. Sure, your insurance company may do the same or similar investigation, but that may be days, weeks or months later. Many things may have changed by then and valuable witnesses may have moved or forgotten the facts.

After you have this information, contact your insurance agent and inform him/her that you have collected evidence in anticipation of litigation. Send copies (not originals) of your evidence to your insurance agent or the attorney assigned to defend the claim (original documents should be hand-delivered to the attorney). Most of your work is now over, but you must continue to follow-up and investigate any leads that arise later. In the case of serious or violent crimes, you should provide tenants in surrounding units (or neighbors, for a rental house) with the telephone number of the investigating officer and/or your own telephone number that they can call and leave an anonymous tip or message. Many people may be reluctant to openly give statements right after an incident, for fear of reprisal, but may freely give information at a later time, if they can do so in private or anonymously. Follow-up until a claim is made or the matter is forgotten. At a practical level, if some event occurs which reveals some type of problem, without regard to whether or not you incur liability as a result thereof, avail yourself of the opportunity to learn from the mistake and take immediate corrective action. Most of all, try to learn from other people's mistakes. If you hear about a lawsuit where the landlord was held liable because he failed to have adequate exterior lighting and your facts are similar to the facts in the lawsuit, then install some exterior lights -- don't wait to be sued.

C.   PROBLEM TENANTS.

Cross Reference:
- How to handle continually late rent payments, Chapter 4, Section B(1)
- How to evict for nonpayment of rent or some other type of noncompliance, Chapter 5, Section B

Sometimes, one tenant is a continuing source of grief. S/he does not get along with other tenants, does not get along with you or your other personnel and seems to be a continual source of both property problems and tenant problems. I refer to this condition between myself and this type of tenant as "irreconcilable differences." The cause of this dilemma is one or more of three possibilities:

1. You "Screwed up." Somehow, during the applicant screening process, you simply committed a colossal blunder and let an undesirable applicant become a tenant.

2. You Poisoned the Tenant. The second possibility is that this tenant was okay, but you did something to turn him/her against you after s/he moved into the property (i.e., failure to make promised repairs, etc.).

3. "The Bad Seed." The final and worst possibility is a tenant who has made a career out of being a bad tenant. Unless you lead an especially charmed life, you will eventually encounter "the tenant from Hell." "Not possible," you say, "because the screening process is designed to weed out these 'undesirables'." Yeah, right. I hate to break the news to you, but there exists in this world a breed of people whose purpose in life is to make other peoples' lives miserable. The worst part is

that the people who are *really* good at making life miserable are also the ones who are very good at getting through practically any screening process. For example, checking out an applicant's prior landlord is, of course, a good idea, provided the applicant actually wrote down his prior landlord and not his friend, who is waiting for your call. To fully appreciate how truly awful a "bad" tenant can be, go to your local video store and rent a movie video entitled <u>Pacific Heights</u>.[201] Michael Keaton epitomizes the quintessential "tenant from Hell."

The answer to all three types of tenants is simple. Do not dwell on "how you let this happen." If you made a mistake, make a mental note of it, do not do it again and move on. The priority, for now, is getting this problem solved. If it is within your power to make the tenant happy, then make the tenant happy, within reasonable economic limits, of course. But, when it becomes clear that no matter what you do, this tenant will not be happy, then get rid of him/her. Do whatever it takes, but get this problem out of your life. A phone call to your attorney at this moment should be all that is necessary to ascertain the options available to you, based on <u>your</u> facts. Some suggestions that come to mind: (1) if he is a month-to-month tenant, send him a notice that you are not renewing his/her tenancy and that s/he must be out at the end of the next full month (you must provide adequate advance notice; the notice should be in writing and either personally delivered or mailed by registered or certified mail)[202] and (2) if he is on a long-term lease, pay him to leave (*see* "Practical Approach to a `Real World' Dilemma," page 2; Chapter 5, Section B).

---

201 <u>Pacific Heights</u> (CBS/FOX Video 1990).

202 A.R.S. § 33-1313(B) (West 1990).

CHAPTER 5

TERMINATING TENANTS
AND
EVICTIONS

Summary of Chapter

- Normal terminations
  - Adequate notice
  - Damage to the unit
- Evictions
  - What CAN'T I do to evict a tenant?
  - What MAY I do to evict a tenant?
  - What notice must I prepare?
  - How do I serve the notice?
  - Where do I file the Special Detainer action?
  - How do I actually file the Special Detainer action?
  - Final steps
  - Appeals

A.   NORMAL TERMINATIONS.

Provided you have adequately screened your applicants, the bulk of your vacancies will be the result of "normal" terminations. A normal termination occurs when: (1) the tenant has provided you with adequate or inadequate notice that s/he intends to vacate on a specific date and does, in fact, voluntarily vacate on that date; (2) your rental agreement has provided for a specific termination date, that date has arrived and your tenant voluntarily vacates; or (3) the term of your rental agreement has expired, you have elected (for whatever reason) not to renew the rental agreement and the tenant voluntarily moves out. In all three cases, the key is that the tenant voluntarily vacates. Defined in this way, perhaps "uneventful" would be more appropriate than "normal." In any event, the only issues remaining in a normal termination are: (1) whether the tenant provided adequate notice and (2) whether the tenant damaged the unit.

1. Adequate notice.

If the end of the term of your rental agreement is approaching and you elect to not renew the rental agreement, it may be _you_ who must provide adequate notice; otherwise, you may be unable to forcibly remove a tenant who has not vacated. The answer will depend on the language in your rental agreement (where have you heard this before?). Typically, most rental agreements say that the party wishing to terminate, which in this case would be the landlord, must give notice. If, however, your rental agreement does not specifically address notice, but it does specify the lease start date _and_ the end date (i.e., January 1, 1998 - June 30, 1998), then you have created what is referred to as a "tenancy for years" (even though the actual term is less than one year). Unless otherwise stated elsewhere in the rental agreement, a tenancy for years _does not_ require the landlord _or_ the tenant to give notice of termination – the rental agreement has already done that. In the example, tenancy ends on June 30, 1998 and the tenant's obligation is merely to be out of the property by that date -- no prior notice by either party is necessary. Naturally, the rental agreement _may_ provide that notice _is_ required (what does your rental agreement say?). The message I am trying to convey to you is that, before you claim the tenant has failed to provide you with adequate notice, you should first make sure that the tenant, in fact, had an obligation to provide notice.

If the tenant has decided to terminate tenancy (i.e., to vacate), has provided you with notice thereof and the notice provided was adequate – no problem. If the tenant did not provide adequate notice, the first question is, "Why wasn't the notice adequate?" The answer is easily obtained by comparing the notice the tenant gave with the notice that is "required." If your rental agreement specifically addresses what notice must be given, is clear and understandable (understandable by "Joe Average," not you), then this is not an issue. Amazingly enough, however, many rental agreements either do not address what constitutes "adequate notice" or are confusing or ambiguous.[203]

So what happens if your rental agreement is confusing or ambiguous? (What, you have to ask?) Chances are the judge will conclude that any "reasonable" interpretation of the language in your rental agreement constitutes "adequate notice." The judge will probably ask the tenant how s/he interpreted the language of the rental agreement and then the judge will evaluate whether the tenant's interpretation was "reasonable." Alternatively, the judge may simply decide the language in your rental agreement is too confusing and conclude that "reasonable notice" is all that is necessary. The judge will then decide whether or not the notice actually given by the tenant was "reasonable notice." As you might have already guessed, unless the tenant takes an absolutely untenable position (i.e., one-hour advance notice probably won't fly), the judge will likely conclude that the tenant's interpretation was reasonable -- you lose. Once again, this goes back to the first thing I told you in this book – spend a little time and money to have your rental agreement properly prepared.

---

203 _See, e.g.,_ Falcon Research & Development v. Craddock, 679 P.2d 264 (N.Mex. 1984) (whether lease is ambiguous is question of law).

What happens if your rental agreement does not address notice at all? You probably will fare no better than those landlords who have confusing or ambiguous notice provisions. If the rental agreement is silent, the statute fills in the missing provisions, at least with regard to a month-to-month tenancy:

> The landlord or the tenant may terminate a month-to-month tenancy by a written notice given to the other at least thirty days prior to the periodic rental date specified in the notice.[204]

If tenancy is other than month-to-month, the Act provides no guidance. This is the notice provision that I use:

Termination. A "Notice to Terminate Tenancy" Form has been provided to the tenant; your signature below acknowledges receipt of this Form.

a. If the term of this agreement is for a specific term (i.e., six months or one year) and either party wishes <u>not</u> to renew the agreement for a period of time equal to the prior specified period, the party who wishes <u>not</u> to renew <u>shall</u> provide written notice thereof at least thirty (30) days <u>prior</u> to the termination date of the present term. In the absence of such a notice, tenancy shall automatically be renewed for a term of equal length (i.e., a six month term will renew for another six months; a one year term will renew for another year).

b. If the term of this agreement is month-to-month, either party may terminate hereunder upon thirty (30) days (or more) written notice. The thirty (30) day written notice shall be given on or before the last day of the present rental period and tenancy shall end on the last day of the <u>next</u> rental period. TENANCY CANNOT BE TERMINATED IN THE MIDDLE OF THE RENTAL PERIOD. Example: Today is April 15 and you wish to terminate tenancy. Notice must be given on the last day of the present rental period -- the present rental period is April 1 - April 30. Therefore, notice must be given on or before April 30. Tenancy will terminate on the last day of the next rental period -- the next rental period is May 1 - May 31. Therefore, tenancy will terminate on May 31.

---

[204] A.R.S. § 33-1375(B) (West Supp. 1998).

An example may transform language that is <u>not</u> clear or understandable into language that <u>is</u> clear and understandable. As shown above, my rental agreement always contains an example. In addition, on the day my tenants sign the rental agreement, I give them a "Notice to Terminate Tenancy" Form (*see* Appendix B, Form 13). <u>This form repeats the language of the rental agreement and contains the same example.</u> I have found that virtually no tenant consults the rental agreement before submitting his/her notice to terminate, but almost all of them remember that I gave them a form specifically for that purpose. And normally, upon reading the form, the tenants immediately know whether the notice they are giving is adequate. Interestingly enough, however, I have found that those who do not submit their notice to terminate on the form I provided for them usually submit inadequate notice. I suspect that these tenants read the form, realize they are providing inadequate notice, but figure that if they don't use the form, they can claim ignorance of the notice requirement -- they are wrong.

You also may wish to consider a provision in the rental agreement that, in the absence of a specific request by the tenant to renew for another period of equal or greater length, automatically converts the prior tenancy to a month-to-month tenancy. This eliminates the need for you to closely monitor rental agreement expiration dates, which could be disastrous. For example, suppose you have waited anxiously for Mr. Uncooperative's rental agreement to expire, but for whatever reason, you were "asleep at the switch" and failed to give him thirty days notice that you would not renew his rental agreement. Result: under the previously quoted provision, the term is automatically renewed for an equal period of time (i.e., one year). Not good. Therefore, you may prefer to change the last sentence in "Termination," subsection "a," from:

> In the absence of such a notice, tenancy shall automatically be renewed for a term of equal length (i.e., a six month term will renew for another six months; a one year term will renew for another year).

to:

> In the absence of such a notice, tenancy shall automatically convert to a month-to-month tenancy and, except for the rental term, all other provisions of this rental agreement shall continue in full force and effect.

Is either (or both) provision foolproof? I am convinced that <u>nothing</u> is foolproof. But I am reasonably confident that these provisions will suffice for most landlords. That is not to say that a judge in Pinetop may not find either or both provisions ambiguous, while, at the same time, a judge in Yuma finds both provisions to be models of clarity. In theory, the law is to be uniformly applied; in practice, the law is administered by judges, who are only human.

I have used these provisions without incident, but if you encounter a problem with either of these provisions, please write to me and let me know (I can be contacted at the address in the front of the book). For the most part, either of these should be okay. You may, however, wish to shorten or lengthen the notice time. Thirty (30) days is fine. Longer *may* be a problem, depending on *how much longer* -- six months is probably "too" long. One day is probably "too" short. If a judge finds your notice provision to be too long or too short, s/he may find the provision to be "unconscionable," which means that the judge will disregard your provision, no matter how clear, and substitute a "reasonable" time (isn't that a big surprise?).[205]

2. Damage to the unit.

If the tenant did not damage the unit – no problem. If the tenant did damage the unit, s/he is liable for the amount of those damages.[206] If you are holding a security deposit, you may deduct the amount of damages from the security deposit you hold, but you must provide the tenant with an itemized list of the damages within fourteen business days.[207] (*See* Chapter 2, Section D(4); Chapter 5, Section B(7)(b) ("Final Steps - Security Deposit"); Appendix B, Form 14). If the amount of damages exceeds the amount of the security deposit you are holding (you must still provide an itemized list), or if you are not holding a security deposit, you may file a lawsuit against the tenant to recover whatever amount remains due. Incidently, it is also a crime (class 2 misdemeanor) for a tenant to intentionally damage the rental unit or remove furnishings or fixtures.[208] In appropriate circumstances (use your discretion), you may wish to report the incident to the police. The police may be of immense assistance in locating the tenant (normally tenants who do damage do not leave a forwarding address). In addition, you may be able to convince the prosecutor to make restitution (i.e., payment of the damages by the tenant) a condition of any plea bargain the prosecutor may offer the tenant/defendant or a condition of the sentence imposed by the judge (if there is no plea bargain). This is a real benefit because you do not even have to file a lawsuit to recover your damages. The court, however, will not include past due rent in the amount of restitution the tenant/defendant must pay you. This is unfortunate because, normally, tenants that do damage to rental units are also behind in their rent. But now that you know where this guy is, you are free to file your own lawsuit to recover any other amounts due you, including past due rent.

NOTE: You cannot threaten criminal prosecution to coerce settlement of your civil lawsuit. For example, your tenant throws a chair through the living room window of his rental unit and you have several witnesses who saw the incident. You may report him to the police for criminal damage to your rental unit, but you are not required to report him. And, naturally, you can demand that the tenant pay for the damages, but if he does not wish to pay the damages, you cannot threaten

---

205 *See* A.R.S. § 33-1312(A) (West 1990).

206 A.R.S. §§ 33-1341(6), -1368(C), -1369 (West 1990 & Supp. 1998).

207 A.R.S. § 33-1321(C) (West Supp. 1998).

208 The statute provides, "Removal or intentional and material alteration or damage of any part of a building, the furnishings thereof, or any permanent fixture, by or at the instance of the tenant, without written permission of the landlord or his agent, is a class 2 misdemeanor." A.R.S. § 33-322 (West 1990).

criminal prosecution to force him to pay the damages. I can hear you: "My decision to prosecute or not will probably turn on whether he voluntarily pays the damages. Have I broken the law?" No, but this precise thought process cannot be communicated to the tenant because it sounds like a threat (i.e., pay the damages or I will prosecute). In truth, your thought process is really much closer to: "I want these damages paid for; either this tenant pays for the damages voluntarily, thereby bringing a quick and effortless resolution to this problem, or I will use the full weight of our judicial system, both criminal and civil, to compel this tenant to pay for the damages that s/he caused." In short, this is the exception to the rule that you should tell people what you are going to do and then do it. In this case, demand payment for the damages. If payment is not forthcoming and the circumstances merit criminal prosecution, then file criminal charges and ask the prosecutor to insist upon restitution as part of any plea bargain or sentence. And, if necessary (i.e., the tenant/defendant is not ordered to pay restitution or is found not guilty), file a civil lawsuit against him for the damages (the fact that s/he may have been found not guilty of criminal damages does not mean that you will not prevail in your civil lawsuit against him/her). The procedure for filing a civil lawsuit to recover for property damages (and any other amounts your wish to recover) is explained in Chapter 6, Section A. <u>Bottom line</u>: don't threaten criminal prosecution; if criminal charges are implicated and you are unsure how to proceed, get advice from your lawyer.

B. <u>EVICTIONS</u>.

What are the procedural steps for evicting a tenant? This is a short and seemingly simple question; the answer is very long and involves many steps. First, you must first know what you can and **cannot** do. Second, you must decide which notice is appropriate to your circumstances and serve it upon the tenant. Third, you must select the proper court. Finally, you must file and prosecute the Special Detainer action. If you have never been through the entire process of evicting a tenant, you should consult with your attorney. For those who have been through the process a few times <u>and</u> who feel confident they can proceed without an attorney, the following information should see you through each and every step.

1. <u>What CAN'T I do to evict a tenant?</u>

To keep you out of trouble, we begin with what you cannot do to evict a tenant. You cannot:

(1) Refuse to supply heat, air conditioning, cooling, water, hot water or essential services.[209]

(2) Lock the tenant out of the rental unit or otherwise exclude him/her from the property.[210]

---

[209] A.R.S. § 33-1364 (West Supp. 1998). *See, e.g.,* <u>State v. Main</u>, 159 Ariz. 96, 764 P.2d 1155 (App. 1988) (landlord cannot use self-help to evict tenant; only remedy is to bring an action for possession).

[210] A.R.S. § 33-1367 (West 1990).

(3) Turn off the power or disconnect other utility services until the day following execution of the Writ of Restitution. Nevertheless, disconnection of power and/or utility services may only be performed by a person authorized by the utility to perform that function.[211]

(4) Hold or seize the tenant's personal property to pay for rent or other amounts due.[212]

(5) Raise rent, decrease available services, evict a tenant or threaten to evict a tenant in retaliation for complaints made by the tenant to the landlord or to governmental agencies (i.e., reporting a housing code violation to the appropriate authority).[213]

2.   What MAY I do, under the Act, to evict a tenant?

Under the Act, once you reach the point where you are thinking about evicting a tenant, you have only two options: you may continue to work with the tenant to try to reach some mutually acceptable solution or you must file an action for possession of the leased premises. An action for possession under the Act is called a "Special Detainer" action (commonly referred to as a "forcible entry and detainer" action). A Special Detainer action is the legal process (the entire process is commonly referred to as an eviction) whereby the landlord obtains a Writ of Restitution, which grants the landlord the right to possession of the leased premises and also decrees that the tenant no longer has any possessory interest in the leased premises. Ultimately, the Writ is served and executed by the Sheriff or constable, forcibly removing the tenant from the leased premises.

3.   What notice must I prepare?

Okay, there has been some type of noncompliance with the rental agreement by the tenant. You have tried to work with the tenant, but to no avail. You resign yourself to the fact that you must evict this tenant via judicial process.

The first step is to serve the tenant with a written notice. The notice informs the tenant of the reason for the eviction and, if appropriate, gives the tenant an opportunity to cure the problem, thereby avoiding eviction.

"What type of notice must I provide?" The answer depends on the nature of the tenant's noncompliance (i.e., nonpayment of rent or some other type of noncompliance). Under the Act, a landlord may institute a Special Detainer action

---

211 A.R.S. § 33-1368(D) (West Supp. 1998).

212 A.R.S. § 33-1372 (West 1990).

213 A.R.S. § 33-1381 (West 1990).

against a tenant when there has been a **noncompliance** with the rental agreement by the tenant.[214] Noncompliance falls into three categories: (a) material noncompliance; (b) noncompliance materially affecting health and safety; and (c) material and irreparable breach. Nonpayment of rent is obviously a material noncompliance with the rental agreement, but the Act provides a special procedure for this type of noncompliance.[215]

Which category your situation falls into is very important because it determines whether or not you must give your tenant an opportunity to cure the noncompliance and, if so, how much time you must give your tenant to cure the noncompliance before you terminate the rental agreement. Your analysis should be as follows:

Is the noncompliance nonpayment of rent?

> Yes - *see* Chapter 5, Section B(3)(d).
> No - continue analysis.

Is this a material and irreparable breach (i.e., discharge of weapon on premises; infliction of serious bodily harm on landlord, his agent, or another tenant; imminent serious property damage, or some other type of criminal activity)?

> Yes - *see* Chapter 5, Section B(3)(c).
> No - continue analysis.

Is this a noncompliance that materially affects health and safety (i.e., premises not clean, dangerous/hazardous condition, etc.)?

> Yes - *see* Chapter 5, Section B(3)(b).
> No - continue analysis.

Is this: (1) a material falsification of information by the tenant on the tenant application, (2) a second noncompliance (either a material noncompliance or a noncompliance materially affecting health and safety) of the "same or similar nature" as a prior noncompliance, or (3) a "holdover" tenant?

> Yes - *see* Chapter 5, Section 3(a)(1) (material falsification of information by the tenant); Chapter 5, Section 3(e) (second noncompliance of the same or similar nature); Chapter 5, Section 3(f) (holdover tenants).
> No - handle as a material noncompliance; *see* Chapter 5, Section B(3)(a) (immediately below).

---

214 A.R.S. §§ 33-1368(A), (B), -1377 (West Supp. 1998).

215 A.R.S. § 33-1368(B) (West Supp. 1998).

(a)   Material noncompliance with rental agreement.

Cross Reference
- Flowchart for Nonpayment of Rent, Quick Reference Section, Procedures Section
- Sample and blank forms, Appendix B, Form 11

The notice requirements and steps for evicting a tenant for a material noncompliance (or breach) of the rental agreement are stated clearly (surprisingly enough) by the statute. A Ten-Day Notice must be given. The statute provides:

> Except as provided in this chapter [Chapter 10 is the Residential Landlord and Tenant Act; therefore, this sentence is properly read, `Except as provided elsewhere in the Act'], if there is a material noncompliance by the tenant with the rental agreement, including material falsification of the information provided on the rental application, the landlord may deliver a written notice to the tenant specifying the acts and omissions constituting the breach and that the rental agreement will terminate upon a date not less than ten [calendar] days after receipt of the notice if the breach is not remedied in ten [calendar] days. For the purposes of this section, material falsification shall include the following untrue or misleading information about the:
>
> 1. Number of occupants in the dwelling unit, pets, income of prospective tenant, social security number and current employment listed on the application or lease agreement.
>
> 2. Criminal records, prior eviction record, current criminal activity. Material falsification of information in paragraph 2 of this subsection is not curable under this section. ... However, if the breach is remediable by repair or the payment of damages or otherwise, and the tenant adequately remedies the breach prior to the date specified in the notice, the rental agreement will not terminate. If there is an additional act of these types of noncompliance of the same or similar nature during the term of the lease after the previous remedy of noncompliance, the landlord may institute a special detainer action pursuant to section 33-1377 [Special Detainer actions] ten [calendar] days after delivery of a written notice advising the tenant that a second noncompliance of the same or similar nature has occurred.[216]

---

[216] A.R.S. § 33-1368(A) (West Supp. 1998).

(1)   Material falsification of information.

A material noncompliance with the rental agreement will fall into one of two categories: (1) material falsification of information provided by the tenant on the rental application (discussed in this section)or (2) a general material noncompliance (discussed below). The statute (above) makes clear that false/inaccurate information provided by the tenant on the rental application is a material noncompliance.

False information relating to the tenant's criminal record, eviction record, and current criminal activity are "not curable."[217] The Ten-Day Notice of Material Noncompliance, in this case, effectively becomes a ten-day notice of termination because the tenant cannot cure the noncompliance and must move out within the ten day period. If the tenant does not move out, the tenant has become a holdover tenant. (*See* Chapter 5, Section 3(f) (holdover tenants).

False/inaccurate information relating to the number of occupants in the dwelling, pets, income, social security number, and employment are "curable."[218] Presumably, this means that the tenant may cure the material noncompliance within ten days of your written notice to the tenant of the noncompliance.[219] Unfortunately, the statute does not specify how the tenant must correct the information. For example, if the tenant misrepresents his/her income (i.e., the tenant represented income of $2,000.00 per month, but had actual income of $1,000.00 per month), to cure the problem, must the tenant merely correct the application to reflect the tenant's true monthly income of $1,000.00? Or must the tenant obtain different or additional employment so that his/her income equals at least $2,000.00 per month. Although the latter may sound silly, what if your minimum acceptable criteria for applicants was income of $2,000.00? What good does it do you if the tenant is permitted to cure this material falsification of information, after the tenant has already moved in, merely by changing the information on the application? There is no guidance given in the statute and, as of yet, there are no cases that have interpreted this new language. Nevertheless, I offer the following as guidance.

- If the tenant misrepresented the number of occupants in the dwelling unit, the tenant must eliminate all occupants that are not specifically named in the rental agreement.

- If the tenant misrepresented that s/he had a pet, the type or number of pets, the tenant must eliminate all pets not disclosed on the application.

- If the tenant misrepresented his/her income, the tenant must disclose his/her present income. If the present income is below your minimum

---

217 A.R.S. § 33-1368(A)(1) (West Supp. 1998).

218 A.R.S. § 33-1368(A)(1) (West Supp. 1998).

219 A.R.S. § 33-1368 (West Supp. 1998) (emphasis added).

acceptable criteria, and has already demonstrated an inability to pay rent (i.e., recurring late payments), the tenant must secure different or additional employment, so that his/her income meets or exceeds your minimum income requirements. Alternatively, the tenant must provide additional assurances that the rent will be timely paid (i.e., another party to guarantee payment of all rent under the rental agreement).

- If the tenant misrepresented his/her social security number, the tenant must disclose the correct social security number.

- If the tenant misrepresented his/her current employment, the tenant must disclose the correct current employment. This may also impact upon the income represented by the tenant.

The foregoing are to be considered in light of all the facts and circumstances applicable to your situation. If you are in doubt as to how you should proceed, contact your attorney.

(2)   General material noncompliance.

So what, precisely, is a "material noncompliance?" The "legal" answer is that a "material noncompliance" is a noncompliance that is not: (1) a material and irreparable breach or (2) a noncompliance materially affecting health and safety.[220] Therefore, if you encounter a noncompliance and it falls into one of the two aforementioned categories, then follow the procedure for that type of noncompliance, not the procedure for a material noncompliance. As usual, the "legal" answer is of marginal value. As a practical matter, you probably have a pretty good idea what constitutes a "material noncompliance." By definition, a "material noncompliance" is a noncompliance with a particular term in the rental agreement which is "material" (i.e., an important or key element of the agreement).

Keep in mind that not every noncompliance with the rental agreement is a "material noncompliance." Sometimes whether a noncompliance is material or not is really a "matter of degree." For example, when you leased your rental unit, you were adamant that pets were not allowed and clearly stated that you would immediately terminate the rental agreement of any tenant who violated this term. It is fairly clear that a tenant who gets a large dog has committed a "material noncompliance." On the other hand, although a tenant who gets one gold fish has not complied with the scriptures of your rental agreement, you may experience some difficulty convincing a judge (any judge) that this is a "material noncompliance" warranting termination of the tenant's rental agreement.

Some other examples of what *may* constitute a "material noncompliance" include: (1) occupants residing in the rental unit that are not listed on the rental agreement form, (2) "guests" that repeatedly stay for long periods of time, (3) parking

---

220   *See* A.R.S. § 33-1368(A) (West Supp. 1998).

more vehicles on the premises than the allotted spaces, (4) creating disturbances, constant noise and other conduct that disturbs the other tenants' quiet enjoyment of the premises, (5) failing to observe the landlord's rules and regulations (if you have rules and regulations), and (6) failing to pay any amount to the landlord, other than rent, which is due (i.e., deferred payment of all or part of the security deposit). This list is not exhaustive. Moreover, even infractions that are not a "material noncompliance" (i.e., playing loud music on one occasion) may become a "material noncompliance" if the tenant commits repeated violations after you notify him/her of the problem and instruct him/her to stop. *See* Appendix B, Form 6.

Keep in mind that this is not a "one-way street." If you commit a material noncompliance, the tenant may serve **you** with a notice and either terminate the rental agreement and move[221] or, if appropriate, have the problem corrected/repaired and deduct the cost thereof from the next month's rent.[222]

(b)   Noncompliance with the rental agreement materially affecting health and safety.

Cross Reference
- Flowchart for Nonpayment of Rent, Quick Reference Section, Procedures Section.
- Sample and blank forms, Appendix B, Form 10

Where the noncompliance "materially" affects "health and safety," the steps are the same, but the notice requirements (i.e., time limits) are shorter — a Five-Day Notice is required. The statute provides:

> If there is a noncompliance by the tenant with Section 33-1341 [tenant to maintain dwelling unit] materially affecting health and safety, the landlord may deliver a written notice to the tenant specifying the acts and omissions constituting the breach and that the rental agreement will terminate upon a date not less than five [calendar] days after receipt of the notice if the breach is not remedied in five [calendar] days. However, if the breach is remediable by repair or the payment of damages or otherwise, and the tenant adequately remedies the breach prior to the date specified in the notice, the rental agreement will not terminate. If there is an additional act of these types of noncompliance of the same or similar nature during the term of the lease after the previous remedy of noncompliance, the landlord may institute a special detainer action pursuant to

---

221   A.R.S. § 33-1361 (West Supp. 1998).

222   A.R.S. § 33-1363 (West Supp. 1998).

section 33-1377 [Special Detainer actions] ten [calendar] days after delivery of a written notice advising the tenant that a second noncompliance of the same or similar nature has occurred.[223]

A "noncompliance materially affecting health and safety" is somewhat easier to define than a "material noncompliance." To begin with, the statute (quoted directly above) specifically states that it must first be a noncompliance with Section 33-1341. Section 33-1341 is reprinted below:

Tenant to maintain dwelling unit

The tenant shall:

1. Comply with all obligations primarily imposed upon tenants by applicable provisions of building codes materially affecting health and safety.

2. Keep that part of the premises that he occupies and uses as clean and safe as the condition of the premises permit.

3. Dispose from his dwelling unit all ashes, rubbish, garbage and other waste in a clean and safe manner.

4. Keep all plumbing fixtures in the dwelling unit or used by the tenant as clean as their condition permits.

5. Use in a reasonable manner all electrical, plumbing, sanitary, heating, ventilating, air-conditioning and other facilities and appliances including elevators in the premises.

6. Not deliberately or negligently destroy, deface, damage, impair or remove any part of the premises or knowingly permit any person to do so.

7. Conduct himself and require other persons on the premises with his consent to conduct themselves in a manner that will not disturb his neighbors' peaceful enjoyment of the premises.[224]

---

223 A.R.S. § 33-1368(A) (West Supp. 1998).

224 A.R.S. § 33-1341 (West 1990).

The statute then states that only a violation of Section 33-1341 that *materially affects health and safety* constitutes a "noncompliance materially affecting health and safety."[225] In other words, it must meet both tests: (1) it must be a violation of Section 33-1341 *and* (2) it must materially affect health and safety. A noncompliance with Section 33-1341, paragraphs 1 - 6, probably constitutes a "noncompliance materially affecting health and safety." And, conceivably, a noncompliance with Section 33-1341, paragraph 7, could also constitute a "noncompliance materially affecting health and safety" (i.e., leaving a vehicle on "blocks" in the parking lot for several days may be a safety hazard; playing horseshoes or "yard darts" too close to buildings, property or people may be a safety hazard; etc.). The key, however, is that a noncompliance must *first* fall within Section 33-1341 and *then* must affect health and safety.

Again, this is not a "one-way street." If you commit a noncompliance with Section 33-1324 materially affecting health and safety, the tenant may serve **you** with a notice and either terminate the rental agreement and move[226] or, if appropriate, have the problem corrected/repaired and deduct the cost thereof from the next month's rent.[227]

(c)   **Material and irreparable breach.**

Cross Reference
* Flowchart for Nonpayment of Rent, Quick
  Reference Section, Procedures Section
* Sample and blank form, Appendix B, Form 8

Where the noncompliance is the result of egregious conduct or serious actual or potential harm, the Act provides for <u>immediate</u> termination of the rental agreement and an expedited issuance of the Writ of Restitution. In this case, the statute even provides several examples of what constitutes a "material and irreparable" noncompliance. This statute was amended in 1994 and 1995; these amendments significantly expanded applicability of this section. The statute provides:

> If there is a breach that is both material and irreparable and that occurs on the premises, including but not limited to an illegal discharge of a weapon, prostitution as defined in section 13-3211, criminal street gang activity as prescribed in section 13-105, activity as prohibited in section 13-2308, the unlawful manufacturing, selling, using, storing, keeping or giving of a controlled substance as defined in section 13-3451, infliction of bodily harm,

---

225 *See* A.R.S. § 33-1368(A) (West Supp. 1998).

226 A.R.S. § 33-1361 (West Supp. 1998).

227 A.R.S. § 33-1363 (West Supp. 1998).

threatening or intimidating as prohibited in section 13-1202, assault as prohibited in section 13-1203 or a breach of the lease agreement that otherwise jeopardizes the health, safety and welfare of the landlord, the landlord's agent or another tenant or involving imminent or actual serious property damage, the landlord may deliver a written notice for immediate termination of the rental agreement and shall proceed under section 33-1377 [Special Detainer actions].[228]

If you proceed under this Section of the Act, serve the tenant with the notice of immediate termination (*see* Appendix B, Form 8) and, simultaneously, file the Special Detainer action in court.

(d) Nonpayment of rent.

Cross Reference
- Flowchart for Nonpayment of Rent, Quick Reference Section, Procedures Section
- Sample and blank form, Appendix B, Form 9

The notice requirement for nonpayment of rent is five days. The statute provides:

> If rent is unpaid when due and the tenant fails to pay rent within **five days** after written notice by the landlord of nonpayment and his intention to terminate the rental agreement if the rent is not paid within that period of time, the landlord may terminate the rental agreement by filing a special detainer action pursuant to § 33-1377.[229]

(e) "Second occurrence" of the same or similar nature.

Cross Reference
- Flowchart for Nonpayment of Rent, Quick Reference Section, Procedures Section
- Appendix B, 12

Assume that there has been some type of noncompliance (i.e., a material noncompliance, or noncompliance materially affecting health and safety), if there is another occurrence of the noncompliance of the "same or similar nature" anytime during the "term of lease," which includes extensions and renewals of the original rental term,[230] then the landlord may terminate the tenancy and institute a Special

---

228   A.R.S. § 33-1368(A) (West Supp. 1998).

229   A.R.S. § 33-1368(B) (West Supp. 1998) (emphasis added).

230   A.R.S. § 33-1310(17) (West Supp. 1998).

Detainer action ten (10) days after delivery of a written notice advising the tenant that a second noncompliance has occurred.[231] (*See* Appendix B, Form 12). There is no "cure period" for the second noncompliance; if the landlord sends this notice, tenancy is terminated and the tenant must vacate.

(f)   "Holdover" tenant.

Cross Reference
- Flowchart for Nonpayment of Rent, Quick Reference Section, Procedures Section
- Appendix B, Form 12

A "holdover" tenant is a person who "remains in possession [of the rental unit] without the landlord's consent after expiration of the term of the rental agreement or its termination."[232] If a lease specifies that it ends on December 31, 1998 and the tenant does not vacate, the tenant is a "holdover" tenant. If the tenant commits some type of noncompliance, cures the noncompliance, and then commits a second noncompliance during the term of the rental agreement of the same or similar nature, then the landlord may terminate the tenant's tenancy by issuing a ten day notice of termination.[233] (*See* Chapter 5, Section 3(e), above). If the tenant fails to vacate after ten days, s/he is a "holdover tenant." This tenant may be evicted both as a "holdover tenant" and for a second noncompliance of the same or similar nature. Similarly, a tenant whose tenancy is terminated for a "material and irreparable breach" may also be considered a "holdover tenant" if s/he refused to vacate after receiving notice of the immediate termination.

If a tenant's holdover is willful and not in good faith, the landlord may, and should, seek to recover holdover damages equal to two months rent or twice the actual damages s/he sustains, whichever is greater.[234]

4.   How do I serve the notice?

You may serve the notice in person (i.e., hand-deliver) yourself or have someone serve it on your behalf (i.e., manager, friend, etc.). Ideally, you should have the tenant acknowledge receipt of the notice by having the tenant sign your file copy; give him/her the original. Alternatively, you may serve the notice by sending it certified mail, return receipt requested, but the time specified in the notice (i.e., 5-Day Notice, 10-Day Notice, etc.) does not start until the earlier of: (1) actual receipt of the letter or (2) five business days after it is mailed. You may also have a private process server or the Sheriff serve it. The latter method has the benefit of leaving a more lasting impression on your tenant to pay the rent when it is due, but is costly and may take several days before service is actually made.

---

231   A.R.S. § 33-1368(A) (West Supp. 1998).

232   A.R.S. § 33-1375(C) (West Supp. 1998).

233   A.R.S. § 33-1368(A) (West Supp. 1998).

234   A.R.S. § 33-1375(C) (West Supp. 1998).

5. Where do I file the Special Detainer action?

Cross Reference:
- How to handle continually late rent payments, Chapter 4, Section B(1)
- How to collect past due rent, Chapter 6, Section B

You have prepared and served the appropriate written notice. Your next questions are, "*Where* and *how* do I file the Special Detainer action and what happens next?" The simple and most recommended solution is to call your attorney and let him/her handle it. Nevertheless, let's face it, at some point in time you will merely make a business decision that it may be more cost effective to handle these matters without the assistance of an attorney (who, as we all know, is incredibly expensive) and lose a few cases, rather than always paying an attorney (who may also lose a few) to handle these matters. When you have reached the stage where you believe you can competently handle an eviction on your own, the following information will help you answer the foregoing questions; call your attorney if you have any doubts.

You first need to determine where you may/must file the Special Detainer action. Stated more precisely, "In which of three court systems shall I file my lawsuit: small claims court, justice court or superior court?" First, Special Detainer actions may only be brought in justice court or superior court and cannot be brought in small claims court.[235] The alternatives have thus been narrowed to two alternatives: justice court or superior court. Which of these two courts you select will turn on the amount of past due rent you are trying to recover and the monthly rental amount of your rental unit.

To file a Special Detainer action in justice court: (1) the damages sought (i.e., past due rent) must be $5,000.00 or less **and** (2) the monthly rental amount for your rental unit must not exceed $1000.00.[236] If you meet <u>both</u> criteria, you may file your Special Detainer action in justice court. Superior court has concurrent jurisdiction', which means that even though your lawsuit qualifies for filing in justice court, you may file your lawsuit in superior court, if you prefer.[237] Note: processing time is longer and court costs are higher in superior court than in justice court. As of January 1, 1998, the fee to file a Forcible Detainer action in superior court was $140.00, whereas the fee in justice court was $21.00.

If the amount sought in damages is more than $5,000 <u>or</u> your monthly rental amount for your rental is more than $1000.00, then you <u>must</u> file your lawsuit in superior court.[238]

---

235 A.R.S. § 22-503(B)(3) (West Supp. 1998).

236 A.R.S. § 22-201(C) (West Supp. 1998).

237 *See* A.R.S. §§ 12-123(A) (West 1992), 12-1175(A) (West 1994).

238 *See* A.R.S. § 22-201(C) (West Supp. 1998).

Okay, you have decided whether you will file in justice court or superior court. The next question is: which justice court or which superior court (i.e., which county)? This question raises the issue of **personal jurisdiction**. Personal jurisdiction can be a very complex matter. Nevertheless, in the "normal" landlord/tenant context, the following should resolve this issue. You cannot "go wrong" if you file in the court that has personal jurisdiction over the tenant/defendant. Where the tenant/defendant presently lives (i.e., at the time you file the lawsuit, not necessarily where s/he lived when s/he was your tenant) determines which court has personal jurisdiction over the tenant/defendant.

If you are filing a Special Detainer action, the rental unit and the place where the tenant/defendant resides should be the same. If you are bringing a civil action against a former tenant (or anyone else, for that matter), then the location of the rental unit and the defendant's present residence will be different and may even be in a different county or state.

If you are filing in superior court, you may file in the superior court for the county in which the rental property was located or the county in which the defendant now resides. If you are filing in justice court, you may file in the justice court that has jurisdiction over the rental property or the justice court that has jurisdiction over the property where the defendant now resides. (Note: the justice court clerks are pretty good about telling you whether or not a particular property address in located in their jurisdiction; *see* Appendix D for list of justice courts and phone numbers). If you have a question regarding jurisdiction, you should consult your attorney. If you file a lawsuit in the wrong court, the tenant/defendant may be able to have the case dismissed and you may end up paying the tenant/defendant's attorney's fees.

6.   How do I actually file the Special Detainer action?

"Enough of this 'nice guy' routine," you say, "let's get down to business. Tell me how to throw this deadbeat out on his ear." Spoken like a truly frustrated and frequently abused landlord. This is it – this is the section you have been waiting for. This is where you find out, "How do I get rid of that miserable *&%$#@ tenant?"

Most Arizona justice courts now have some type of instruction sheet, available from the clerk, which explains the precise procedure for filing and prosecuting a Special Detainer action in *that* court. "Wait a minute," you say. "If the Act is state law, shouldn't the procedure be the same in all courts?" In theory, that is true. But the truth is that judges perceive the law differently and from varying points of view (i.e., some judges are pro-tenant, some are pro-landlord). Moreover, each judge is given the discretion to dictate the "procedures" (not the substantive law) to be followed in his/her courtroom. Consequently, the procedure and forms made available by the court for Special Detainer actions may differ, in varying degrees, from one court to another. Telling the judge that things are done differently in another court will likely yield poor results. Therefore, you should read and follow the instructions provided by the court in which you filed your Special Detainer action.

JUSTICE COURT
[address / phone number]
REQUEST FOR REASONABLE ACCOMMODATIONS FOR PERSONS WITH DISABILITIES MUST BE MADE AT LEAST THREE WORKING DAYS BEFORE SCHEDULED COURT PROCEEDING.

_____ CASE NUMBER: _____

PLAINTIFF:	DEFENDANT:
Street:	Street:
City/State/Zip:	City/State/Zip:
Phone:	Phone:
ATTORNEY:	ATTORNEY:
Street:	Street:
City/State/Zip:	City/State/Zip:
Phone:	Phone:

SUMMONS AND COMPLAINT FORCIBLE / SPECIAL DETAINER
SUMMONS

STATE OF ARIZONA TO ABOVE NAMED DEFENDANTS:
You are summoned to appear and defend this action in the Court named above:
Trial date: _____ Time: _____
Courtroom number (if applies): _____

NOTICE TO DEFENDANT(S): You must appear at the date and time stated above and answer the allegations of the complaint. If you fail to appear, a judgment may be entered against you as requested in the complaint, including eviction from the premises.

DATE:_____   JUDGE: _____

COMPLAINT
Plaintiff(s) in this action alleges the following:
1. This court has jurisdiction over this action.
2. Plaintiff(s) is lawfully entitled to immediate possession which defendant(s) wrongfully withholds from Plaintiff: _____ (address).
3. On _____ (date), defendant(s) was served written notice to vacate the premises by ☐ Personal Service   ☐ Certified Mail.
4. Rent per _____ is $_____; and rent is due and unpaid since _____; for a total of $_____; plus late fees, per written rental agreement, court costs, attorney's fees, damages if proven at trial, and a Writ of Restitution to issue.
5. That defendant has failed to comply as follows: ☐ nonpayment of rent; ☐ material noncompliance (fill-in facts below); ☐ committed repeated violations during the term of the rental agreement; ☐ committed serious health or safety violations (fill-in facts below); ☐ threatened or committed serious harm to person or property as stated below, for which termination notice was give: _____
_____

WHEREFORE, Plaintiff(s) request(s) judgment against Defendant(s) for immediate possession of the premises, rent due, late fees, damages, court costs, attorney's fees, and that a Writ of Restitution be issued. I attest to the accuracy of the facts stated above based upon personal knowledge.
Plaintiff: _____   Notary/Clerk: _____
SUBSCRIBED AND SWORN before me this date: _____ Commission expires: _____

Sample Summons & Complaint Form

Notwithstanding the differences between courts, the general procedure is as follows. Ask the clerk for the forms for an eviction. The clerk will provide you with one or more multi-part forms. You will fill out some factual data on a form called a Complaint; it may also be called a Special Detainer Complaint or a Forcible Detainer Complaint. The factual data normally includes: the names of the parties, the amount of monthly rent, the reason for the eviction (i.e., nonpayment of rent or some type of noncompliance), the date written notices were delivered, and the relief you are seeking (i.e., possession of the rental property and, if applicable, due and unpaid rent). You must sign the Complaint. If not signed in the presence of the clerk, then your signature must be notarized. You must pay a fee to file the Complaint with the court. A sample complaint form is shown on the prior page; you will note that this form combines the summons and complaint on one form.

If anyone has guaranteed or co-signed the rental agreement for the tenants, you will need to decide at this stage whether to name the guarantors or co-signors as additional defendants (i.e., in addition to the tenants) or whether you would prefer to bring the action against the tenants first and, if they do not pay, to then bring a separate civil lawsuit against the guarantors or co-signors.[239] I recommend naming the guarantors or co-signors as additional defendants in the special detainer action. Why? Because it will cost more and take much longer if you file a second civil action later against only the guarantors or co-signors. A word of caution, however; a guaranty must be signed by both the husband and wife to be enforceable.[240] Naturally, if the guarantor is unmarried, this is not a problem. If you join the guarantors or co-signors as additional defendants, you must include additional language in your complaint, such as that which follows, and you must have a separate summons issued by the court and served upon each named defendant.

> Defendants John and Jane Parent signed the rental agreement as a guarantors (or co-signors). These Defendants are financially liable for all damages assessed against Defendants/Tenants John and Jane Tenant.

The clerk will then fill out the Summons, which may be a separate form or may be included on the bottom portion of the Complaint. The information the clerk will provide on the Summons is the date and time of the hearing, where the tenant will enter his/her plea (i.e., guilty or not guilty). The clerk then stamps the Summons with the official seal of the court and returns it to you.

You will deliver the Summons and Complaint to a process server. You may obtain the name of a process server from the Yellow Pages. Many courts have some type of bulletin board where local process servers advertise. Or you may seek a recommendation for a process server from your attorney or from another landlord.

---

239 Staffco, Inc. v. Maricopa Trading Co., 122 Ariz. 353, 357, 595 P.2d 31 (1979) (a guarantor of a lease may be joined as a defendant with the party in possession in a forcible detainer action).

240 A.R.S. § 25-214(C)(2) (West 1991).

The process server will hand-deliver (if possible) the Summons and Complaint to each tenant named in the Complaint. The Summons and Complaint must be served at least two days prior to the hearing date on the Summons.[241] Consequently, after filing the Complaint and having the Summons issued by the clerk, *waste no time getting these documents to the process server.* You must pay the process server directly for his/her services; the process server is not paid through the court.

That's it. The eviction process has begun. The next question is, "What are all the significant steps to prosecute a Special Detainer action?" The procedure you follow to evict a tenant will turn on whether you are evicting because of: (1) nonpayment of rent or (2) some other type of noncompliance with the rental agreement. The "Procedures" Section of the Quick Reference Section contains two flowcharts: one for nonpayment of rent and the second for noncompliance with the rental agreement (i.e., material noncompliance, noncompliance affecting health and safety, and material and irreparable breach). Each flowchart is followed by a thorough discussion of each step in the litigation process. Refer to the appropriate flowchart when you are ready to commence litigation. **Return to this section** when you have completed your lawsuit; the case may be over, but you are not done.

7.   FINIL STEPS -- What to do *AFTER* the eviction process.

Okay, you have evicted the tenant. You are done, right? Wrong. Whether you have evicted a tenant for nonpayment of rent or for any type of noncompliance, you need to observe the following procedures. These steps are critical. If not done or done improperly, you may lose the right to recover certain damages from the tenant. In some cases, **you** may even become liable *to the tenant* for failure to fulfill your obligations (i.e., failure to return all or part of the security deposit within fourteen days).

(a)   Inspection.

The Act was amended in 1995 and requires that you notify the tenant of the date/time of your move-out inspection *if* the tenant has requested this information.[242] Schedule your move-out inspection during your normal business hours or, if you desire, at a time that is convenient for the tenant. Conduct your post-eviction inspection of the rental unit. Take copious notes and photographs. If you observe damage to the premises, excessive wear and tear, etc., then photographs and/or video tape of the rental unit are highly recommended.

If utilities are in the tenant's name, check with the utility company to see if the utility (i.e., electric, gas, water, etc.) will allow a "temporary transfer" into your name, until the next tenant moves in, with either no transfer fee or a reduced fee.

---

241 A.R.S. §§ 33-1377(B) (West Supp. 1998); 12-1175(C) (West 1994),

242 A.R.S. § 33-1321(C) (West Supp. 1998).

(b)   Security deposit.

Within fourteen (14) days (business days), send the tenant a statement disclosing the disposition of his/her deposits (*see* Appendix B, Form 14 - Disposition of Deposit). Do not wait for the tenant to demand return of his/her deposit. If you are shaking your head in amazement that a tenant who has been evicted and put you through all this nonsense would have the audacity to request return of his deposit, you are not alone, but it happens frequently. If the tenant has left a forwarding address (an unlikely event), send the Disposition of Deposit statement to that address; otherwise, address it to the last known address (i.e., your rental unit). If/when the letter is returned, because no forwarding address was left (a common occurrence), place this letter in your file so that if it becomes necessary, at some future date, you can prove that you complied with the statutory requirements and that any failure of the tenant to receive the Disposition of Deposit statement is due to his/her own failure to leave a forwarding address with the landlord or to notify the post office.

(c)   Lawsuit for damages.

File a lawsuit against the tenant for:

(1) past due rent (if judgment for past due rent was not obtained in the Special Detainer action or if the judge only awarded a portion of the past due rent);

(2) for rent that accrued after entry of the Special Detainer judgment through the last date s/he occupied the rental unit (if not already included in the Special Detainer judgment);

(3) for damages to the rental unit (see below); and

(4) for any other amounts to which you are entitled under the law.

Be sure to check with the utility companies to see if the landlord is responsible for any unpaid balance on the account. For example, in Scottsdale and Glendale, the owner is responsible for a tenant's unpaid water bill and the water company will not turn-on the water for a new tenant until the full outstanding balance, including late penalties, is paid.

If the tenant has intentionally caused severe damage, you may wish to consider filing a criminal complaint with the police. Intentional property damage by a tenant may be prosecuted as a felony or a misdemeanor, depending on the severity of the damage.[243] If charges are filed against a tenant for criminal damage, you, as the victim, may request that restitution (i.e., reimbursement for the damage) be made a condition of the sentence or any plea agreement. In that way, you may be completely reimbursed without having to spend any money on a private attorney.

---

243 A.R.S. § 13-1602 (West 1989) (criminal damage).

If that does not work, you may wish to contact your property insurance company. Criminal damage may be covered as vandalism or under some other provision of your insurance policy.

If you don't recover from your insurance company and a complaint for criminal damage is not appropriate or the prosecutor either loses the case or refuses to file charges, you may still file a civil lawsuit to recover your damages. Depending on the amount in controversy, the lawsuit may be filed in small claims court (small claims court jurisdiction is limited to cases involving claims of not more than $2,500.00)[244] or in civil court (justice court jurisdiction is $5,000.00 or less;[245] for claims exceeding $5,000, the superior court has jurisdiction;[246] for amounts between $1,000.00 and $5,000.00, inclusive, the justice courts and the superior court have concurrent jurisdiction, which merely means that you may file in either court).[247] Depending upon the complexity of the issues involved, you may be able to do this yourself, without the assistance of a lawyer. If you have any questions, however, consult your lawyer. Normally, while it may not be economically feasible for your lawyer to try the case for you, s/he will help you with the steps you must take, the strategy you should pursue, etc.

(d) Obtain a Judgment.

Get a judgment against the tenant. While you may not be able to collect this judgment for some time, if ever, it will follow your tenant around for a very long time. Moreover, judgments show up on credit reports. Do yourself and your fellow landlords a favor: record the judgment with the county recorder's office and send a copy to local and/or national credit reporting agencies. Now, go to Chapter 6, Section B (Collecting Judgments).

8. APPEALS.

If you are a landlord long enough, you will eventually (or, perhaps, immediately) encounter a decision by a judge which you know to be incorrect. Either the judge made a mistake on the facts and evidence (i.e., wouldn't permit the presentation of certain evidence or witnesses at trial, misinterpreted certain evidence or documents, etc.) or s/he made a mistake on the law. In either event, you are convinced that not another soul on the planet would or could reach the same (erroneous) conclusion, and you want to appeal.

An appeal converts a fairly "user friendly" proceeding (i.e., the relatively informal procedures in a Special Detainer action) into a "formal" proceeding,

---

244 A.R.S. § 22-503(A) (West Supp. 1998).

245 A.R.S. § 22-201(B) (West Supp. 1998).

246 *See* Ariz. Const. article VI, § 14; A.R.S. §§ 12-123(A) (West 1992), 22-201(B) (West Supp. 1998).

247 *See* Ariz. Const. article VI, § 14; A.R.S. §§ 12-123(A) (West 1992), 22-201(B) (West Supp. 1998). *See also* Neely v. Brown, 177 Ariz. 6, 864 P.2d 1038 (1993).

governed by convoluted and cryptic rules of procedure. This is truly the time to seek the assistance of your attorney. Make sure your attorney is familiar with the appeal process for Special Detainer actions because it is different from criminal actions and other civil actions, and the deadlines are much shorter than in other appellate actions.

(a) Appeal by the landlord.

The first thing that must be done is to file the Notice of Appeal. In justice court, this must be done within five calendar days "after rendition of the judgment."[248] Which normally, but not always, is the date of the trial and the judge's oral announcement of his/her decision. If a written judgment is signed on another date, the time to appeal may be calculated differently, **but do not wait!** File your Notice of Appeal as soon as you receive the judge's decision. Failure to file the Notice of Appeal in a timely manner (i.e., within the five calendar days) is **absolutely, positively fatal** to your appeal.[249] The Notice of Appeal is filed in the court that rendered the judgment and you must send a copy of the Notice of Appeal to the other party (i.e., the tenant or his/her attorney).

You must also file a bond (i.e., either a cash bond or a surety bond) with the court, in an amount sufficient to cover the costs of the appeal.[250] In justice court, this amount is set by the court.[251] In superior court, the amount is $500.00, unless modified by the court.[252]

You may also need to file a supersedeas bond. A supersedeas bond stays (i.e., delays) execution of a judgment for possession or for money damages. Because you are the landlord, you will not need to post a bond to stay execution of the judgment for possession -- the tenant will retain possession of the rental unit until the appeal is complete. If, however, a judgment was entered against you for money damages (i.e., attorney's fees, failure to make repairs, diminished rental value, etc.), then you must post a supersedeas bond with the court in the full amount of the judgment.[253]

Next, you must order a copy of the trial transcript. The court should have made a "record" of the trial, either by tape recording the trial or by having a court reporter transcribe the trial testimony. In either case, you must order and pay for preparation of an official copy of the trial transcript. This is done by a court reporter. The court will give you instructions on how to order and pay for the trial transcript. Do this immediately (i.e., the same day you file the Notice of Appeal). You must have the transcript to prepare the Appellant's Memorandum, which *is* the appeal.

---

248 A.R.S. § 12-1179(A) (West Supp. 1998).

249 A.R.S. § 12-1179(A) (West Supp. 1998); 17B A.R.S. Civil Appellate Proc. Rules, Rules 5(b) and 9; 17B A.R.S. Super. Ct. Civil Appellate Proc. Rules, Rules 5(a) and 9.

250 A.R.S. § 12-1179(B) (West Supp. 1998).

251 17B A.R.S. Super. Ct. Civil Appellate Proc. Rules, Rule 10(a).

252 17B A.R.S. Civil Appellate Proc. Rules, Rule 10(a).

253 A.R.S. § 12-1179(C) (West Supp. 1998).

The only exception is when, for whatever reason, the "record" is defective (i.e., the tape failed to operate properly or the transcription is unintelligible). In that case, the appellate court may order a *trial de novo*, which means a new trial.

The Appellant's Memorandum must be filed within thirty (30) days of filing the notice of appeal and it will take the court reporter *some* amount of time to transcribe the trial testimony.[254] The point being, time is short, so order the transcript right away.

The next step is to prepare the Appellant's Memorandum. The person appealing the judgment (i.e., normally the person who lost the case) is the appellant. Preparation of the Appellant's Memorandum is critical; it will determine the success or failure of your appeal. It must also conform to a certain format (i.e., specific sections, in a certain order, not exceeding prescribed page limitations, etc.). Naturally, it must specify the particular findings or rulings that were in error and must refer to relevant pages of the trial transcript, but it must also cite (refer) to statutory and/or case law that supports your position and/or undermines the basis for the judge's ruling. Therefore, the Appellant's Memorandum *should* be done by an attorney familiar with the relevant issues and this area of the law.

The rules of procedure that you must follow depend on the court that will hear the appeal. The superior court hears appeals from justice courts and procedure is governed by the "Superior Court Rules of Appellate Procedure – Civil," found in volume 17B of Arizona Revised Statutes Annotated (these rules may be ordered from Consumer Law Books, *see* Order Form in the back of this book). The court of appeals hears appeals from the superior court and procedure is governed by the "Arizona Rules of Civil Appellate Procedure," also found in volume 17B of Arizona Revised Statutes Annotated.

After you file your Appellant's Memorandum, the tenant will have an opportunity to respond by filing his/her Appellee's Memorandum. In the Appellee's Memorandum, the tenant will explain to the appellate court why the trial court's decision was correct and why the arguments in your Appellant's Memorandum are without merit. Similarly, you may respond to the arguments in the Appellee's Memorandum by filing Appellant's Reply Memorandum.[255]

The appellate court (either the superior court or the court of appeals) may then order an "oral argument." This is not a new trial. Do not bring any witnesses with you or any new exhibits. The purpose of the oral argument is to highlight the strongest arguments in your brief (i.e., the Appellant's Memorandum and the Appellant's Reply Memorandum) and to answer any questions the judge(s) may have about the facts, evidence and/or proceedings that were not clear from the written

---

254   17B A.R.S. Civil Appellate Proc. Rules, Rule 15; 17B A.R.S. Super. Ct. Civil Appellate Proc. Rules, Rule 15.

255   17B A.R.S. Civil Appellate Proc. Rules, Rule 13; 17B A.R.S. Super. Ct. Civil Appellate Proc. Rules, Rule 13.

briefs. The appellate court will then normally render a written decision and the parties will receive notice thereof via regular mail. On rare occasion, a decision will be rendered orally, in open court, on the day of the oral argument, with the court's legal analysis appearing in a subsequent written decision.

If you are unhappy with the appellate court's decision, you may appeal the decision of the court of appeals to the Supreme Court of Arizona, but there is no further right of appeal from an appellate decision of the superior court.[256] Your only remedy, in the latter case, is to file a "Special Action." If you reach this stage, you most certainly will need an attorney to help you with the appeal to the Supreme Court or to file a Special Action.

(b)   Appeal by the tenant and how to oppose the appeal.

The first thing the tenant must do is file the Notice of Appeal. The Notice of Appeal is filed in the court that rendered the judgment and the tenant must send you (or your attorney) a copy of the notice. The Notice of Appeal must be filed within <u>five calendar</u> days "after rendition of the judgment."[257] Which is normally, but not always, the date of the trial and the judge's oral announcement of his/her decision. If a written judgment is signed on another date, the time to appeal may be calculated differently. Failure to file the Notice of Appeal in a timely manner (i.e., within the five days) is **absolutely, positively fatal** to the tenant's appeal.[258]

If your tenant has appealed and the Notice of Appeal was filed more than five calendar days "after rendition of judgment," you should file a "Motion to Dismiss Appeal." If you are representing yourself, you can probably get away with something as simple as the sample on page 169.

This simple one-page motion fulfills the substantive requirements of court procedure. This motion should be typed, double-spaced on plain 8.5" x 11" paper. If that is not possible, you can probably get away with legible handwriting. Keep in mind that people representing themselves in court are *supposed* to be held to the same standards as attorneys.[259] In truth, most judges give unrepresented parties a larger margin for error and, therefore, *minor* errors may be overlooked (i.e., handwritten instead of typed motions), but some errors (i.e., one day late filing a Notice of Appeal), which you may perceive as being minor, are fatal and judges will not and cannot make an exception because the party is unrepresented.

The tenant, when filing the Notice of Appeal, must file a bond (i.e., either a

---

256 17B A.R.S. Super. Ct. Civil Appellate Proc. Rules, Rule 20(b).

257 A.R.S. § 12-1179(A) (West Supp. 1998).

258 A.R.S. § 12-1179(A) (West Supp. 1998); 17B A.R.S. Civil Appellate Proc. Rules, Rules 5(b) and 9; 17B A.R.S. Super. Ct. Civil Appellate Proc. Rules, Rules 5(a) and 9.

259 <u>Smith v. Rabb</u>, 95 Ariz. 49, 386 P.2d 649 (1963) (appellants who conducted their entire case in propria persona were held to same familiarity with required procedures and same notice of statutes and local rules as would be attributed to qualified member of bar).

cash bond or a surety bond) for costs on appeal. In justice court, the amount of this bond is set by the judge and is generally equal to the opposing party's costs on appeal. In superior court, the amount of the bond is $500.00, unless modified by the court. Under appropriate circumstances, the tenant may file an affidavit requesting waiver of the cost bond and giving specific reasons therefor. If such a waiver is requested, the landlord may object to the affidavit within five business days. Thereafter, a hearing thereon shall be held within five business days. If the waiver is denied, the tenant must post the cost bond within five business days.[260]

The tenant must also file a supersedeas bond. A supersedeas bond stays (i.e., delays) execution of a judgment for possession (i.e., the Writ of Restitution). The amount of the bond must equal (or exceed) "the amount of rent accruing from the date of the judgment until the next periodic rental date, together with costs and attorney's fees, if any."[261]

For example, let us assume that monthly rent is $620.00 per month and you obtained a judgment against Terry Tenant on January 15, 1998. In addition to rent, the judgment included $60.00 late fees, $150.00 attorney's fees, and $50.00 court costs. The supersedeas bond to stay execution of the judgment for possession must be at least $520.00 (rent for January 16 - 31, 1998, which is 16 days @ $20/day, equals $320, plus $150.00 attorney's fees and $50.00 court costs).

The tenant may also need to post a supersedeas bond to stay execution of the money judgment entered against him/her. In the example above, you have a judgment against the tenant for $1,190.00 ($930 past due rent, $60.00 late fees, $150.00 attorney's fees, and $50.00 court costs). If the tenant wishes to stay execution of the money judgment (i.e., to prevent garnishment of wages, bank account, etc.), the tenant must post another supersedeas bond. The amount of this bond would normally be $1,190.00 ($930 rent, $60.00 late fees, $150.00 attorney's fees, and $50.00 court costs), but because the tenant has already posted a bond that included the $150.00 for attorney's fees and $50.00 for court costs, the maximum amount of this supersedeas bond is $990.00 ($930.00 rent and $60.00 late fees). The parties may stipulate to a lesser amount. If the parties cannot reach an agreement on the amount of this bond, the court will hold a hearing within five business days after one of the parties advises the court that a stipulation cannot be reached; the court will then determine the amount of this bond.[262]

If your tenant has appealed and has failed to file the cost bond or the supersedeas bond is inadequate, you should file a "Motion to Dismiss Appeal" (see example, next page).

---

260 A.R.S. § 12-1179(B) (West Supp. 1998); 17B A.R.S. Civil Appellate Proc. Rules, Rule 10; 17B A.R.S. Super. Ct. Civil Appellate Proc. Rules, Rule 10.

261 A.R.S. § 12-1179(D) (West Supp. 1998).

262 A.R.S. § 12-1179(D) (West Supp. 1998); 17B A.R.S. Civil Appellate Proc. Rules, Rule 7; 17B A.R.S. Super. Ct. Civil Appellate Proc. Rules, Rule 7.

Larry Landlord
123 N. Central Avenue
Anytown, Arizona 85000
(602) 555-0000
Plaintiff / *Pro per*

SUPERIOR COURT OF ARIZONA, MARICOPA COUNTY

LARRY LANDLORD,)	Superior Court Case No. CV98-00001
)	Justice Court Case No. CV98-00001 FD
Plaintiff,)	
vs.)	
)	
TERRY and TINA TENANT,)	**MOTION TO DISMISS APPEAL**
husband and wife, and DOES 1-10,)	and Request for Accelerated Hearing
)	
Defendants.)	
_____)	

Plaintiff/Appellee hereby moves this Court to dismiss the appeal filed by Defendants/Appellants. This Motion is supported by the attached Memorandum.

MEMORANDUM OF POINTS AND AUTHORITIES

Plaintiff moves this Court to dismiss Defendants' appeal on the grounds that Defendants' appeal is untimely.

1. <u>The notice of appeal is untimely</u>.

Judgment was entered on February 1, 1998 (copy attached). The Notice of Appeal was filed on February 15, 1998 -- more than five calendar days "after rendition of judgment." *See* A.R.S. § 12-1179(A). Therefore, this appeal must be immediately dismissed -- the Court does not have jurisdiction to hear an untimely appeal. A.R.S. § 12-1179(A).

2. <u>CONCLUSION</u>.

For the foregoing reasons, Plaintiff moves for dismissal of Defendants' appeal. Plaintiff requests and expedited hearing on this matter.

DATED this 16th day of February 1998.

_____
Larry Landlord

Original filed this date with the Clerk of the Court;
Copy mailed this date to:
Judge High N. Mighty (address)
Copy mailed this date to:
Terry and Tina Tenant (property address)

Next, the tenant must order a copy of the trial transcript. The court should have made a "record" of the trial, either by tape recording the trial or by having a court reporter transcribe the trial testimony. In either case, the tenant must order and pay for preparation of an official copy of the trial transcript. This is done by a court reporter. The tenant **must** have the transcript to prepare the Appellant's Memorandum, which *is* the appeal. The only exception is when, for whatever reason, the "record" is defective (i.e., the tape failed to operate properly or the transcription is unintelligible). In that case, the appellate court may order a *trial de novo*, which means a new trial.

The Appellant's Memorandum must be filed within thirty (30) days of filing the notice of appeal.[263] Because it will take the court reporter some time to transcribe the trial testimony, if the tenant has not ordered a copy of the transcript within two weeks of filing the notice of appeal, s/he may have lost interest in the appeal. This is known as "abandonment" of the appeal and is grounds for dismissal. Consequently, if the tenant has not filed the Appellant's memorandum by the thirtieth day after filing the Notice of Appeal, you should file a "Motion to Dismiss Appeal." Again, if you are representing yourself, something like this (shown on the next page) should suffice. This example combines several grounds for dismissal.

The next step for the tenant is to prepare the Appellant's Memorandum. The person appealing the judgment (i.e., normally the person who lost the case) is the appellant. Preparation of the Appellant's Memorandum is critical; it will determine the success or failure of the appeal. It must also conform to a certain format (i.e., specific sections, in a certain order, not exceeding prescribed page limitations, etc.). It must specify the particular findings or rulings that were in error and must refer to relevant pages of the trial transcript, but it must also cite (refer) to statutory and/or case law that supports the tenant's position and/or undermines the basis for the judge's ruling.

The rules of procedure that you and the tenant must follow depend on the court that will hear the appeal. The superior court hears appeals from justice courts and procedure is governed by the "Superior Court Rules of Appellate Procedure -- Civil," found in volume 17B of Arizona Revised Statutes Annotated. The court of appeals hears appeals from the superior court and procedure is governed by the "Arizona Rules of Civil Appellate Procedure," also found in volume 17B of Arizona Revised Statutes Annotated (these rules may be ordered from Consumer Law Books, *see* Order Form in the back of this book).

---

[263] 17B A.R.S. Civil Appellate Proc. Rules, Rule 15; 17B A.R.S. Super. Ct. Civil Appellate Proc. Rules, Rule 15.

Larry Landlord
123 N. Central Avenue
Anytown, Arizona 85000
(602) 555-0000
Plaintiff / *Pro per*

SUPERIOR COURT OF ARIZONA, MARICOPA COUNTY

LARRY LANDLORD,   )
)
                    Plaintiff,   )
vs.   )
)
TERRY and TINA TENANT,   )
husband and wife, and DOES 1-10,)
)
                    Defendants.   )
_____)
	Superior Court Case No. CV98-00001
	Justice Court Case No. CV98-00001 FD
	
	MOTION TO DISMISS APPEAL
	and Request for Accelerated Hearing

Plaintiff/Appellee hereby moves this Court to dismiss the appeal filed by Defendants/Appellants. This Motion is supported by the attached Memorandum.

<u>MEMORANDUM OF POINTS AND AUTHORITIES</u>

Plaintiff moves that Defendants' appeal be dismissed on the following grounds: (1) no cost bond has been posted, (2) the bond for possession is inadequate, (3) Defendants have failed to pay rent into the court during pendency of the appeal, and (4) Appellants have failed to provide a transcript of the trial court proceedings.

1. <u>No cost bond has been posted</u>.

The statute is very specific, "A party seeking to appeal a judgment **shall** file with the notice of appeal a bond for costs on appeal ... ." A.R.S. § 12-1179(B) (emphasis added). The form filed by Defendants, "Forcible/Special Detainer Appeal" (copy attached hereto), and the Court's records, clearly reveal that **no cost bond** has been posted. Consequently, Defendant's appeal must be dismissed.

The statute provides that the hearing for this matter *shall* be scheduled within five days. A.R.S. § 12-1179(B).

2. <u>The supersedeas bond for possession is inadequate</u>.

The statute provides, "The party seeking to stay the execution of the judgment for possession shall file a supersedeas bond in the amount of rent accruing from the date of the judgment until the next periodic rental date, together with costs and attorney's fees, if any." A.R.S. § 12-1179(C). Judgment was entered on January 15, 1998. The Judgment awarded Plaintiff $150.00 for attorney's fees and $50.00 for court costs. Rent is $620.00 per month. Therefore, the supersedeas bond for possession must be at least $520.00 (rent for January 16 - 31, 1998, which is 16 days @ $20/day, equals $320, plus $150.00 attorney's fees and $50.00 court costs).

Landlord v. Tenant, CV98-00001 (Continued)

3. <u>Defendants have failed to pay rent while the appeal is pending</u>.

"The tenant shall pay to the clerk of the superior court, on or before each periodic rental due date during the pendency of the appeal, the amount of rent due under the terms of the lease or rental agreement." A.R.S. § 12-1179(D). Tenants/Appellants have not paid into the Superior Court rent that became due on February 1, 1998 and/or provided Plaintiff with proof thereof. Consequently, Plaintiff hereby moves this Court to lift the stay of execution of the Judgment for possession and to dismiss the appeal.

4. <u>Defendants have failed to file Appellant's Memorandum within thirty days</u>.

Defendants must file the Appellant's Memorandum within thirty days of filing the Notice of Appeal. 17B A.R.S. Super. Ct. Civil Appellate Proc. Rules, Rule 15(a). The Notice of Appeal was filed January 15, 1998. Today is March 1, 1998 and, to date, no Appellant's Memorandum has been filed. Consequently, Defendants' appeal should be dismissed pursuant to 17B A.R.S. Super. Ct. Civil Appellate Proc. Rules, Rule 15(c).

<u>CONCLUSION</u>.

For the foregoing reasons, Plaintiff moves for dismissal of Defendants' appeal. Pursuant to A.R.S. § 12-1179(B), Plaintiff requests an accelerated hearing.

DATED this 16th day of February 1998.

_____
Larry Landlord

Original filed this date with the Clerk of the Court;
Copy mailed this date to:
Judge High N. Mighty (address)
Copy mailed this date to:
Terry and Tina Tenant (property address)

After the tenant files the Appellant's Memorandum, you will have the opportunity to respond by filing your Appellee's Memorandum. In the Appellee's Memorandum, you will explain to the appellate court why the trial court's decision was correct and why the arguments in the Appellant's Memorandum are without merit. Thereafter, the tenant may respond to the arguments in the Appellee's Memorandum by filing Appellant's Reply Memorandum.[264]

The success or failure of the appeal will turn on the content of the Appellant's Memorandum, your Appellee's Memorandum, and the Appellant's Reply Memorandum. Consequently, you must make sure that your Appellee's Memorandum (the one and only opportunity you have to explain to the court why

---

[264] 17B A.R.S. Civil Appellate Proc. Rules, Rule 13; 17B A.R.S. Super. Ct. Civil Appellate Proc. Rules, Rule 13.

the trial court judgment should be affirmed) adequately rebuts the arguments made by the tenant/appellant and that you cite relevant statutes and/or case law that supports your position. Toward that end, I strongly recommend that you hire an attorney for this task.

The appellate court (either the superior court or the court of appeals) may then order an "oral argument." This is not a new trial. Do not bring any witnesses with you or any new exhibits. The purpose of the oral argument is to highlight the strongest arguments in your brief (i.e., the Appellee's Memorandum) and to answer any questions the judge(s) may have about the facts, evidence and/or proceedings that were not clear from the written briefs. The appellate court will normally render a written decision and the parties will receive notice thereof via regular mail. On rare occasion, a decision will be rendered orally, in open court on the day of the oral argument, with the court's legal analysis appearing in a subsequent written decision.

If you are unhappy with the appellate court's decision, you may appeal the decision of the court of appeals to the Supreme Court of Arizona, but there is no further right of appeal from an appellate decision of the superior court.[265] Your only remedy, in the latter case, is to file a "Special Action." If you reach this stage, you most certainly will need an attorney to help you with the appeal to the Supreme Court or to file a Special Action.

---

[265] 17B A.R.S. Super. Ct. Civil Appellate Proc. Rules, Rule 20(b).

CHAPTER 6

COLLECTING

Summary of Chapter

- Lawsuit for damages
    - Which court?
    - File the lawsuit
    - Service of the Summons and Complaint
    - Answer or default
    - Counterclaim
    - Disclosure statement
    - Trial date
    - Judgment
- Collection of judgments
    - Writs of Garnishment
    - Writs of Execution
    - Other states -- "full faith & credit"

A.　LAWSUIT FOR DAMAGES.

Time to get down to business. You may have already been through the court system with a particular tenant (i.e., Special Detainer action), but the tenant still owes you for additional rent (i.e., rent accruing after entry of judgment in the Special Detainer action until the tenant actually vacated), damages to the rental unit and/or owes you money for some other reason. You must now file a separate lawsuit against the tenant to recoup these amounts.

> What happens first?
> What do you do then?
> Where do you go to get things started?

The answer to all these questions, and more, follow.

1.　Which court?

Typically, you first need to determine, "In which of three court systems shall I file my lawsuit: small claims court, justice court or superior court?" The answer will turn on the type of lawsuit and the amount you are seeking.

(a)   Special Detainer actions.

Special Detainer actions may be brought only in justice court or superior court and cannot be brought in small claims court.[266] To file a Special Detainer action in justice court: (1) the damages sought (i.e., past due rent) must be $5,000.00 or less **and** (2) the monthly rental amount for your rental unit must not exceed $1000.00.[267] If you meet both criteria, you may file your Special Detainer action in justice court. Superior court has concurrent jurisdiction, which means that even though your lawsuit qualifies for filing in justice court, you may file your lawsuit in superior court -- if you prefer.[268] If the amount sought in damages is more than $5,000 or your monthly rental amount for your rental is more than $1000.00, then you must file your lawsuit in superior court.[269]

If you are seeking to obtain a judgment against a tenant for rent and other amounts due to you *after* you have evicted the tenant or after the tenant has already voluntarily vacated the rental unit, you cannot file a Special Detainer action. The primary purpose of a Special Detainer action is to obtain possession of the rental unit. A money judgment for rent and/or other amounts due is secondary. Consequently, if you already have possession of the rental unit and all you are seeking is a money judgment against the former tenant, then you must file a civil lawsuit.

(b)   Civil lawsuits.

The court in which you will file all other civil lawsuits (that you will be concerned with) is determined by the amount you are trying to recover. If the amount sought in your complaint (i.e., the amount you are trying to recover) is:

(1) Not more than $2,500.00, you may file in small claims court (which is a special division of the justice court), or in justice court; if more than $2,500.00, you cannot file in small claims court.[270]

(2) More than $1,000.00 and less than $5,000.00, you may file in justice court or superior court, whichever you prefer.[271]

(3) More than $5,000.00, you must file in superior court.[272]

---

266 *See* A.R.S. § 22-503(B)(3) (West Supp. 1998).

267 A.R.S. § 22-201(C) (West Supp. 1998).

268 *See* Ariz. Const. article VI, § 14; A.R.S. §§ 12-123(A) (West 1992), -1175(A) (West 1994).

269 A.R.S. § 22-201(C) (West Supp. 1998).

270 A.R.S. § 22-503(A) (West Supp. 1998).

271 *See* Ariz. Const. article VI, § 14; A.R.S. §§ 12-123(A) (West 1992), 22-201(B) (West Supp. 1998). *See also* Neely v. Brown, 177 Ariz. 6, 864 P.2d 1038 (1993).

272 *See* Ariz. Const. article VI, § 14; A.R.S. §§ 12-123(A) (West 1992), 22-201(B) (West Supp. 1998).

(c)   Distinctions between the three courts.

What is the distinction between small claims court, justice court and superior court and why would you want one rather than the other? First, superior court judges and commissioners[273] are attorneys, whereas judges in justice court (who hear both the justice court cases and small claims cases) may or may not be attorneys. Is that important? It may be. On the other hand, under certain circumstances, it may be better to have a non-lawyer as a judge. Second, you may know the judge, commissioner or justice of the peace personally or, at least, know that person to be "fair." Third, the physical location of either the justice court or superior court may be more convenient. Finally, processing time is longer and court costs are higher in superior court than in justice court. There is no "right" answer that will apply to everyone. The answer for you is tied directly to the specific facts of your situation. If, after considering your own facts, you still do not know where you should file your lawsuit, call your attorney and ask his/her advice.

The distinction between small claims court and justice court is that attorneys are not permitted in small claims court (except where the attorney is one of the parties – the plaintiff or the defendant) and the decision is not appealable. My personal opinion is that you, as a landlord, *never* want to be in small claims court. Judges in small claims court are capable of being entirely wrong on the law and deciding against you (i.e., had your case been heard by anyone else on the planet, you would have won). Because the judgment cannot be appealed, you are stuck with a truly unjust decision. I hear you, "Doesn't the tenant face the same problem?" Technically, yes; effectively, no. Most tenants will not appeal a judgment. Consequently, by bringing the lawsuit in small claims court, you are the only one who is giving up the right to appeal. Moreover, for the tenant to appeal (which would mean that the judge ruled against him and judgment was entered against him/her), the tenant must post a bond in an amount to pay the full amount of the judgment entered against him. What are the odds that your tenant is going to fork over the money to post a bond -- even if s/he is convinced that s/he is right? You, the landlord, on the other hand, may not need to post a bond (or, perhaps, only a nominal cost bond) to appeal because no judgment was entered against you. This is a good deal for the landlord. Take advantage of it. Don't file in small claims court.

2.   File the lawsuit.

The lawsuit is commenced by filing a document called the ***complaint***. Go to the appropriate courthouse and ask the clerk for a summons and complaint. If you intend to file in small claims court, which is merely a special division in the justice court, be sure to tell the clerk you want to file in the Small Claims Division of the Justice Court (the forms are typically different for small claims court and justice court).

---

273 Commissioners, rather than judges, normally hear Special Detainer actions in superior court.

Fill out the forms completely and specify in the body of your complaint why you (the plaintiff) believe that the tenant (the defendant) owes you money. If you have never done this before, this would be a good time to call your attorney. If you screw up and put the incorrect or insufficient information in the complaint, you may lose the case just on that basis alone. As a practical matter, however, if you are only trying to recover $200.00, consulting with your attorney to ensure that you properly fill out the complaint may (and probably will) cost more than the $200.00 you hope to recover. At this point it becomes a business decision -- do you call the attorney or just give it your best shot? Only you can answer that question. If you feel comfortable without legal advice, "go for it"; if you don't feel comfortable, there are two reasons why you might wish to consider "going for it" anyway. First, judges in small claims court are sensitive to the fact that everyone in small claims court is a non-lawyer and, therefore, they (typically) do not require rigid adherence to court procedure and do not penalize you for technical imperfections in your complaint. Nevertheless, the judge will probably not allow your claim for damages to the rental unit if your complaint only states that you are seeking past due rent. Second, although attorneys' fees may be awarded in contract actions, such an award is completely discretionary -- the judge is not required to award attorneys' fees.[274] Moreover, attorneys' fees, even if awarded, may not be awarded "dollar-for-dollar" (i.e., your attorneys' bill may be more than the amount of attorneys' fees awarded by the judge). Consequently, although attorneys' fees are *theoretically* recoverable, you should not count on any such award -- especially where the amount in controversy is very small (judges are very reluctant to award $500 in attorneys' fees for a $200 claim).

3. Service of the Summons and Complaint.

The summons and complaint must be served upon the defendant(s) by the Sheriff or someone authorized by law to serve legal papers. This procedure is known as **service of process**. Typically, a private process server is used. You may also serve the defendant by mailing, via first-class mail (not certified, not registered and no return receipt is required), a copy of the summons and complaint, two copies of a "Notice and Acknowledgment of Receipt of Summons and Complaint," and a return envelope, postage prepaid and addressed to the sender.[275] If, however, the defendant refuses to accept service by this latter method, you must have him personally served.

4. Answer or default.

The defendant(s) is required to file a document with the court called an **answer**. The answer must be filed within twenty calendar days after the defendant is served with the summons and complaint.[276] If no answer is filed, ask the clerk of

---

274 A.R.S. § 12-341.01(A) (West 1992).

275 16 A.R.S. Rules of Civil Procedure, Rule 4.1(c)(1).

276 16 A.R.S. Rules of Civil Procedure, Rule 12(a).

the court for a "Notice of Default," fill it out and file it with the court. If no answer is received within ten business days after filing the Notice of Default, the court may enter judgment against the defendant for the amount claimed in the complaint.

5.   Counterclaim.

A *counterclaim*, if one is filed by the defendant, must be filed at the same time the defendant files the answer (assuming the counterclaim is somehow related to your complaint).[277] If a counterclaim is filed against you by the defendant, <u>you must file a reply to the counterclaim</u> within twenty (20) calendar days of service upon you of the answer and counterclaim. Otherwise, you, too, are subject to default.[278]

6.   Disclosure statement.

The Arizona Rules of Civil Procedure were amended in July 1992, and a new rule of procedure, specifically Rule 26.1, went into effect. Essentially, this rule requires both parties to disclose to the other party their legal theories, damage calculations, defenses, witnesses, and documents to be used at trial.[279] In justice court, the court will provide you with a disclosure statement form, which you merely need to fill out and mail to the other party. In superior court, you are expected to provide your own form and know how and when to prepare and serve the disclosure statement. Failure to make complete and/or timely disclosure (disclosure statements must be provided to the other party forty days after the answer is filed) may result in the court imposing sanctions (i.e., a penalty), including not allowing you to use at trial any of the witnesses and/or documents that you failed to disclose.

7.   Trial date.

Assuming an answer is filed, the court will assign a trial date. Do not miss your trial date. If there is a good reason why you cannot be in court on that date, give the court as much advance notice as possible and request a continuance. Failure to appear on your appointed trial date normally causes one of two results: (1) dismissal of the complaint, if the plaintiff fails to appear or (2) entry of judgment, if the defendant fails to appear. Note, however, that if the defendant fails to appear, the judge still will ask the plaintiff to present whatever evidence s/he has to prove his contention that the defendant owes him money because the plaintiff has the burden of proof. Consequently, <u>it is possible to lose your lawsuit even if the defendant fails to appear</u>. Make sure you bring all witnesses, exhibits and documents you need to prove your case. Whether the defendant is present or not, present your case to the judge in an organized, logical manner. Keep it simple.

---

[277] 16 A.R.S. Rules of Civil Procedure, Rule 13(a).

[278] 16 A.R.S. Rules of Civil Procedure, Rule 12(a).

[279] 16 A.R.S. Rules of Civil Procedure, Rule 26.1.

Normally, in small claims court and justice court, if you have been less than clear and the judge has some questions, s/he will simply ask you or the defendant (if present) whatever s/he wants to know -- the procedure is relatively informal. Nevertheless, never address the judge in small claims court, justice court or superior court in a casual manner. Always call the judge "Your Honor."

8. Judgment.

The judge may render his verdict immediately after presentation of evidence by both parties or may take the matter "under advisement," which merely means that s/he will make a decision soon and the court will notify both parties by mail.

A victorious plaintiff receives a document called a *judgment*. The judgment specifies the amount the defendant owes the plaintiff, including court costs and attorneys' fees (if awarded). The defendant may or may not tender immediate voluntary payment (normally not); if not, go to Chapter 6, Section B (collection of judgments through Writs of Garnishment and/or Writs of Execution).

A victorious defendant receives a judicial determination dismissing the plaintiff's complaint **with prejudice** (which means that the plaintiff cannot file another complaint against the same defendant, based on the exact same facts). The judge may or may not award the defendant his/her attorneys' fees. If so, the defendant will receive a judgment against the plaintiff. Similarly, if the defendant filed a counterclaim against the plaintiff and was victorious, the defendant may receive a judgment for the amount claimed in the counterclaim. Where there is both a complaint and a counterclaim and both parties are successful, the two amounts will be "netted" against each other and only one judgment rendered. For example, if the plaintiff's complaint seeks $1,000 for damages to the rental unit and the defendant's counterclaim seeks $500 for work he performed for the plaintiff but was never paid, and both the plaintiff and defendant win, one judgment is rendered to the plaintiff in the amount of $500.

Presuming that you now have a judgment, either from a Special Detainer action or from a separate civil lawsuit, your next step is to collect the judgment.

B.   COLLECTION OF JUDGMENTS.

Summary of this Section
- Writs of Garnishment - Writs of Execution - Other States -- Full Faith & Credit

Okay, you have a judgment against a tenant (or anyone, for that matter). What do you do? How do you collect?

The process to elicit payment of sums owed to you is simple and straightforward. Obtaining results, however, is dependent upon: (1) how you ask for payment, (2) your tenant's knowledge of the law, (3) your tenant's inclination to pay (i.e., is s/he a responsible person?), (4) your tenant's ability to pay (remember, you can't get blood out of a turnip), and (5) your tenacity.

Again, this is where it pays to have a reputation as a landlord who is honest, straightforward and businesslike with his tenants (*see* Chapter 2). If your (former) tenants know that you say what you mean, mean what you say and will follow through tenaciously with whatever actions you have promised to take, they are more likely to pay voluntarily. Under these circumstances, a simple letter to the judgment debtors (your former tenants), asking for voluntary payment and stating that if payment is not made voluntarily you will compel involuntary payment, may be sufficient to elicit voluntary payment. Therefore, the first step is to make a demand for voluntary payment.[280] (*See* Appendix B, Form 15). If, however, they simply do not have the money and cannot get the money, you must pursue *involuntary* payment.

The two most common methods for compelling involuntary payment are Writs of Garnishment and Writs of Execution. Most of the courts have packets of forms for obtaining a Writ of Garnishment or a Writ of Execution. Simply ask the court clerk for these forms. As you might have guessed, the clerk will normally refuse to assist you in completing the forms (s/he will tell you that assisting you in filling out forms is the practice of law and s/he is prohibited from offering legal advice; whether or not true, the clerk's statement normally gets him/her out of explaining the forms). The good news is that the forms are fairly self-explanatory.

Now all you need to do is decide whether you want a Writ of Garnishment or a Writ of Execution (if you have any doubts, a phone call to your attorney should answer any questions you may have).

1.   **Writs of Garnishment.**

A garnishment is an order from a court ordering a person who owes money to the judgment debtor (a person with a judgment against him/her is called the judgment debtor, i.e., your tenant), to pay that money directly to you, instead of paying that money to the judgment debtor.

The most common example is an employer who employs your tenant and owes him/her wages. The Writ of Garnishment commands the employer, known as the garnishee, to pay the money directly to you. In the case of garnishment of wages, the judgment creditor (the person in whose favor the judgment is rendered is called the judgment creditor, i.e., the landlord), is only entitled to a percentage of

---

280   In the case of garnishment of wages, a demand for voluntary payment is a prerequisite to issuance of a Writ of Garnishment. *See* A.R.S. § 12-1598.03(2) (West Supp. 1998).

the total wages due from the employer to the employee.[281] But something is better than nothing.

To obtain a Writ of Garnishment, you must first make a demand upon the judgment debtor for voluntary payment[282] (i.e., send the judgment debtor a letter asking for voluntary payment; the letter also should state that if voluntary payment is not received, you will compel involuntary payment). If you used the Post-Judgment Letter to Tenants (see Appendix B, Form 15), this demand is already included and you need not send another demand.

Garnishment of wages is normally governed by state law. In at least one instance, however, state law is preempted (i.e., displaced by other law). In the case of an Indian, who lives and works on an Indian reservation, state law is preempted by tribal law. Consequently, a state court cannot issue a Writ of Garnishment to a judgment creditor (i.e., a landlord), even though he holds a valid judgment against a judgment debtor, if the judgment debtor is an Indian who lives and works on an Indian reservation. Instead, the judgment creditor must look to tribal courts and tribal law. In the case of Navajo law (i.e., the Navajo Tribal Code), garnishment of wages is not permitted.[283]

Another common example is a bank that holds funds belonging to your tenant (i.e., a savings or checking account). For an account in one person's name, the first one hundred fifty dollars ($150) is exempt from garnishment; you are entitled to everything over $150, up to the amount of your judgment.[284] For a joint account, the first three hundred dollars ($300) is exempt from garnishment; you are entitled to everything over $300, up to the amount of your judgment.[285] If your judgment is against one person and he is married, but the judgment does not also name his spouse, community property laws will apply and you may not be able to collect the entire amount of your judgment from a joint account.

There are some other, more creative avenues to pursue with a Writ of Garnishment. An escrow/title company that holds a tenant's earnest money on a house s/he is buying is holding funds belonging to the judgment debtor. The escrow/title company may be served with a Writ of Garnishment and compelled to pay the money to you, the judgment creditor. Similarly, escrow agents and account servicing agents also are potential garnishees. Some tenants may have funds coming to them from the sale of property somewhere. If you are fortunate enough to know where and who the escrow agent is, you can garnish the amounts the escrow agent is holding. Likewise, if your tenant is receiving a monthly check from an account servicing agent (i.e., they sold property some time ago and are receiving monthly

---

281 See A.R.S. § 33-1131(B) (West 1990).

282 A.R.S. § 12-1598.03(2) (West Supp. 1998).

283 Begay v. Roberts, 167 Ariz. 375, 807 P.2d 1111 (App. 1990), review denied.

284 A.R.S. § 33-1126(A)(7) (West Supp. 1998).

285 See generally A.R.S. § 33-1126(A)(7) (West Supp. 1998).

payments via a second mortgage), you can garnish these amounts as well.

Be creative. Practically anyone who owes your judgment debtor money may be served with a Writ of Garnishment.

2. **Writs of Execution.**

A Writ of Execution is a court order directing the Sheriff to seize property belonging to the judgment debtor (i.e., the tenant), sell it at an auction and pay the proceeds to the judgment creditor (i.e., the landlord holding a judgment against the tenant). The types of property the Sheriff may seize and sell include cars, furniture, real estate, etc. Certain property is exempt from execution (i.e., tools of one's trade; wedding rings, up to a certain dollar amount; etc.).[286]

Normally, before proceeding with a Writ of Execution, you should order an **asset search** from a business that performs this service. An asset search may cost anywhere from $50 to $250 (more, if you want to search other counties). But the information obtained will enable you to direct the Sheriff to specific pieces of property. It will also tell you whether it is worth your time and trouble to pursue a Writ of Execution.

If the judgment debtor has few assets or only has property that is exempt from execution, there is no point in proceeding -- at least not now. In that case, record the judgment in the county where the judgment debtor lives, sit back and wait. Your judgment remains valid for five (5) years.[287] And you can renew the judgment. So, after the judgment is four years and nine months old, but before the end of the fifth year, merely renew the judgment.[288] Your judgment will hang around his/her neck like an anchor. I point this out so that, while you may never receive payment on your judgments, you may rejoice in the knowledge that your recorded judgment has quite possibly made this tenant's life a living hell.

Your judgment can only be wiped out by being paid off or by being discharged by a bankruptcy court. S/he may not have any property now, but s/he may someday and you will be there to execute on it when s/he does. In the meantime, your judgment is accruing interest at the legal rate (currently ten percent per annum) and recording the judgment will prevent him/her from selling or buying any real property until s/he pays you off. In addition, the judgment may show up on his/her credit report. To ensure that it does, send a copy of the judgment to credit reporting agencies (i.e., TRW, Equifax, Trans Union; addresses may be found in the yellow pages). Have no fear that you are committing libel or slander; court judgments are factual determinations by a court of law and are matters of public record. Consequently, threats made by judgment debtors (your former tenants) that

---

286 A.R.S. §§ 33-1121 to -1133 (West 1990 & Supp. 1998).

287 A.R.S. §§ 12-1611 to -1613 (West 1994).

288 A.R.S. § 12-1612(B) (West 1994).

they will sue you for damaging their credit are without merit.

Someday it will occur to your ex-tenant that life would be much more pleasant if s/he would just pay you off. Many times, being turned down for a loan or being denied credit for some other reason is enough to elicit spontaneous payment after several years of stonewalling. Some day you will record a judgment and forget it. Several years later a title insurance company may contact you asking for a payoff amount because the judgment debtor wants to buy or sell real property and s/he must pay you off before the transaction can close escrow. The title company then sends you a check, including interest accrued from the date of the judgment to the date of payoff -- sweet!

3. Other states -- "full faith and credit."

The typical scenario goes like this: you finally get a judgment against Joe Deadbeat and then he moves to another state. Now what?

Judgments rendered in any court in Arizona are entitled to the "full faith and credit" under the law of every other state in the country.[289] What this means to you is that you can still collect your judgment against this guy, even though he has moved to another state. As a practical matter, however, it may not be particularly convenient. Typically, you must go through a process called "domesticating" your judgment in the state where the judgment debtor has moved. Each state has different procedures on how to do this. Contact the clerk of the court in the county where your judgment debtor has moved; the clerk may or may not be helpful. If not, contact an attorney in that state.

---

[289] U.S. Const. art. IV, § 1; 28 U.S.C.A. § 1738 (West 1994).

CHAPTER 7

COMMERCIAL LEASES

Summary of Chapter

- Other relevant material
- Preparation
  - Review your business practices
  - Controlling law
  - Review/create your lease
  - Review/create your other forms
- Tenants and tenant problems
- Terminating tenants and evictions
  - Notices
  - Eviction procedure
- Commercial forms

This chapter appears for the first time in this edition. The difference between commercial and residential landlord/tenant law is not merely the difference between day and night, it is the difference between a breezy Summer afternoon on Maui and nuclear winter on the dark side of Jupiter. Consequently, it is somewhat unrealistic to expect that I will be able to include everything you need to know about commercial leases in one chapter. The topic of commercial leases could fill a separate volume (or several volumes). Nevertheless, I believe that I have included in this chapter the issues that will most commonly arise and the information that will be crucial to most commercial landlords.

A.   OTHER RELEVANT MATERIAL.

This chapter is "self-contained." By that, I mean that all the information in this book that relates to commercial leases will be found in this chapter, including sample forms, and blank forms, which normally would be found in the Procedures Section or in Appendix B (forms). This is to prevent residential landlords from accidentally following the wrong flowchart and/or using the wrong form. Nevertheless, there is information in the other chapters of this book that apply equally to residential and commercial landlords. Specifically, much of the general information in Chapter 1 (Preliminary Matters) and Chapter 2 (Preparation) applies to both residential and commercial landlords. Similarly, much of Chapter 3 (Getting Tenants) and Chapter 4 (Managing Tenants Effectively) apply to both. And certainly, the information in Chapter 6 (Collecting) applies to both residential and commercial landlords.

The simple truth is that a commercial landlord could ignore this chapter and follow the practices and procedures set forth in the other chapters of this book and would not violate the law. The contrary, however, is not true (i.e., a residential landlord cannot lawfully follow the practices and procedures in this chapter). That is because residential tenants are granted many rights by the Act,[290] whereas commercial tenants have virtually no rights granted by law.[291] A commercial landlord is free to treat a commercial tenant as a residential tenant and give that tenant additional rights (i.e., follow the residential procedures), but a residential landlord cannot treat a residential tenant as a commercial tenant and take away rights that are granted by the Act.

To ignore this chapter, however, would be unwise. The Arizona Legislature has decided that commercial and residential tenants should be treated differently and should be governed by two entirely separate bodies of law. It is in your own best interest to take advantage of the additional rights available to commercial landlords. These rights are discussed below.

B.   PREPARATION.

1.   Review Your Business Practices.

The sections "General Guidelines for Doing Business" (Chapter 2, Section A) and "Legal Advice to Landlords" (Chapter 2, Section B) are worth reviewing.

2.   Controlling Law.

The statutes that control commercial landlord/tenant law are found in Arizona Revised Statutes, Sections 33-301 through 33-381. (See Appendix C for complete text of these statutes). These are state statutes and apply equally in all parts of the state, except where preempted. (See Chapter 2, Section C). In addition, commercial landlord/tenant law is also controlled by case law (case law is a rule of law determined by a court of law in an actual court case; see "Conventions," Chapter 1, Section D).

3.   Review/Create Your Lease.

The common term for the document establishing tenancy in residential landlord/tenant law is "rental agreement," but the common term for the same

---

290   A.R.S. §§ 33-1301 to -1381 (West 1990 & Supp. 1998).

291   See A.R.S. § 33-301 to -381 (West 1990).

document in a commercial setting is "lease." In Chapter 2, Section D, I help residential landlords create a residential rental agreement. Most residential rental agreements are pretty straightforward and normally do not exceed two or three pages. Commercial leases are rarely "straightforward" and normally range in length from five to fifty pages. For the most part, the complexity of the lease turns on the nature of the property. For example, a small space in a strip-mall would have a substantially different lease than a lease for an anchor tenant at a large shopping mall. The information necessary to cover all the conceivable properties could easily fill two books. Consequently, the only feasible recommendation that I can give you about reviewing or creating a commercial lease is to refer you to your attorney, so that a commercial lease can be drafted to fit you and your specific property. I strongly recommend against attempting to purchase a standard commercial lease form from an office supply store; these forms generally do not address all the necessary issues and are not intended to favor the landlord.

4. **Review/Create Your Other Forms.**

(a) **Application, Tenant Information, Property Inspection Checklist.**

You will need a tenant application and a property inspection checklist, similar to those provided in Appendix B (Forms) for residential landlords. Naturally, you will need to tailor the property inspection checklist to suit your property and, at a minimum, your rental application should capture all the information found in both the residential Tenant Application (Form 1, Appendix B) and the Tenant Information Sheet (Form 2, Appendix B). As with the lease form, you will want to have these forms drafted to suit your specific needs.

(b) **Balance Sheet, Profit and Loss, Guaranty.**

Most commercial landlords insist that the tenant provide (and I recommend you obtain) a current balance sheet and a current and/or projected profit and loss analysis, submitted to you by a Certified Public Accountant. You should also insist upon personal guarantees from the principals of business entity tenants (i.e., corporations, partnerships, limited liability companies, etc.). The guaranty form in Appendix C should suffice. (*See* Appendix C, form 19).

(c) **Five Day Notice to Pay or Quit and similar forms.**

The Five Day Notice to Pay or Quit and similar forms are discussed in Section D(1), below; sample forms are provided in Section E, below.

C. **TENANTS AND TENANT PROBLEMS.**

Chapters 3 (Getting Tenants) and 4 (Managing Tenants Effectively) contain information about getting tenants and managing tenants that, for the most part, will apply to commercial landlords. Recognize, however, that commercial landlords generally receive fewer tenant complaints than residential landlords and do not receive the same types of tenant complaints (i.e., pest control, broken faucet, etc.) because most commercial leases transfer virtually all of the maintenance and upkeep of the leased premises to the tenant.

D. TERMINATING TENANTS AND EVICTIONS.

Terminating a commercial tenancy may be virtually identical to terminating a residential tenancy, as in the case when the landlord provides a notice of default and then files a lawsuit for possession, or may be completely different, as in the case when the landlord locks the tenant out of the leased premises (a remedy that is not available to residential landlords).

1. Notices.

(a) Service of the notice.

Service of notices may be controlled by your lease. You may be required to send it via regular or certified mail to a specific address. If your lease does not address how notices must be served, you may serve the notice in person (i.e., hand-deliver) yourself or have someone serve it on your behalf (i.e., manager, friend, etc.). Ideally, you should have the tenant acknowledge receipt of the notice by having the tenant sign your file copy; give him/her the original. You may also have a private process server or the Sheriff serve it.

Alternatively, you may serve the notice by sending it certified mail, return receipt requested. Generally, when serving a notice via certified mail, the time given to the tenant to cure the default (i.e., five days for nonpayment of rent) does not begin to run until the notice is actually received or five days after it was mailed, whichever occurs first.

> Example 1: you mail the tenant a five day notice for nonpayment of rent on the second day of the month and the tenant receives and signs for the notice on the third day of the month; the five days will begin to run on the fourth day of the month and the tenant has until the eighth day of the month to cure the default.

> Example 2: you mail the tenant a five day notice for nonpayment of rent on the second day of the month and the rent either fails or refuses to accept the notice; the five days will begin to run five days after you mailed the notice, which is the seventh day of the month, and the tenant has until the twelfth day of the month to cure the default.

Because mailing may add up to five days, your first choice should be hand-delivery of the notice.

FIVE-DAY NOTICE TO PAY OR QUIT

Terry Tenant
123 North Oak Street
Phoenix, Arizona 85999

Notice to Tenant,   Date: *July 2, 1998*

Pursuant to Arizona Revised Statutes, Title 33, Chapter 8, Section 33-361(A), you are hereby tendered five-days written notice to remit all due, but as yet unpaid, rent and other amounts owing, in the amount of: *$545.00* (calculated through *July 2, 1998*). The stated amount is calculated as follows:

$*1,500.00*	Rent for *July 1998*
$*50.00*	Late charges (*$50 on 2nd, plus 1% per day thereafter*)
$*25.00*	Fee for preparing and serving Five-Day Notice.
$*1,575.00*	Total

The stated "Total" is exclusive of future accruing costs. Additional charges accrue after the date specified above at the daily rate of *$5.00 (1%)*.

In the event full payment is not tendered within five days after receipt of this notice, your Rental Agreement will be terminated and an eviction action filed against you to recover possession of the premises, rent, late fees, and any other amounts due under the rental agreement or available by law, including attorney's fees and court costs. Full payment within the five-day period will reinstate the rental agreement. Assuming this notice is delivered on the date specified above, **THE FIFTH DAY FALLS ON: *July 7, 1998*.**

Alternatively, you may vacate the premises on or before the fifth day. Vacating the premises, however, will not relieve you from liability for the outstanding balance. In the event you have any questions, please contact me.

Larry Landlord
Larry Landlord (602) 555-1111
123 N. Main Street, Anytown, Arizona 85000

This notice delivered this date *July 2, 1998*   via:
☐ Certified mail
☐ Regular first class mail
■ Hand delivered

Acknowledgment of hand delivery and receipt hereof:

Terry Tenant _____   *July 2, 1998*
(signature of tenant)   (date)

(b)   **Five Day Notice to Pay or Quit.**

A commercial landlord is not required to give a commercial tenant a five-day notice to pay or quit, unless this requirement appears in the lease. If, however, the commercial landlord wishes to give the commercial tenant a five-day notice to pay or quit, s/he may do so without violating the law. The residential form (Form 9, Appendix B), minus the citations to the Arizona Residential Landlord and Tenant Act, will suffice.

Keep in mind, this is the "nice guy" approach. Under commercial landlord/tenant law, you may simply lock the tenant out of the property;[292] you are not required to give a written notice of default (i.e., nonpayment of rent), unless you have signed a lease that includes a provision requiring the landlord to give a written notice of default to the tenant (*but see* Section D(1)(e), below). Moreover, you are not required to give the tenant an opportunity to cure the default and reinstate the lease, unless your lease so provides.

(c)   **Lock-out.**

Rather than provide a five-day notice to pay or quit, the commercial landlord may simply lock a defaulting commercial tenant out of the rental property. The law provides:

> When a tenant neglects or refuses to pay rent when due and in arrears for five days, or when tenant violates any provision of the lease, the landlord or person to whom the rent is due, or his agent, may re-enter and take possession, or, without formal demand or re-entry, commence an action for recovery of possession of the premises.[293]

Caution: you must be absolutely sure that a default has occurred. If, for example, you lock a commercial tenant out because you believe that s/he has not paid rent and it turns out that rent had actually been paid (i.e., you forgot, rent was paid to your manager, etc.), you will be liable to the tenant for any damages sustained by the tenant, which may include damages to his/her business and/or reputation. Similarly, if rent is due, but the tenant is entitled to various offsets which exceed the amount of rent due, then locking the tenant out is not lawful and you will be liable to the tenant for damages.

If you resort to this remedy, you should change the locks, post the following notice (preferably on a window, so that it may be read from outside, but cannot be removed), and mail a copy of the notice via certified mail to the tenant's address (your lease should specify an address where all legal notices to the tenant may be sent). In appropriate circumstances, you should hire a security guard to ensure that the tenant does not attempt to re-enter the premises.

---

[292] A.R.S. § 33-361(A) (West 1990).

[293] A.R.S. § 33-361(A) (West 1990).

NOTICE OF TERMINATION

Terry Tenant
123 North Oak Street
Phoenix, Arizona 85999

Notice to Tenant,   Date: *July 2, 1998*

You have:

☐   Failed or refused to remit all due, but as yet unpaid, rent
      and other amounts owing under the lease;

☐   Violated a material provision of your lease, specifically:

_____

_____

You are hereby notified that your landlord has terminated your right to possess and occupy the premises and, pursuant to Arizona Revised Statutes, Title 33, Chapter 8, Section 33-361(A), has re-entered the premises and taken possession thereof. This action has been taken by the landlord to mitigate his/her damages. Reasonable efforts will be made to re-rent the premises on your behalf. The landlord has not and will not accept a surrender of the premises. Although your right to possess and occupy the premises has been terminated, your lease has not been terminated and your obligations (financial and otherwise) under the lease shall continue until the end of the lease term or until the premises are re-rented, whichever occurs first.

Pursuant to A.R.S. § 33-361(D), the landlord has a lien on all personal property located on/in the leased premises and may cause the same to be sold at public auction if all amounts due (if any) are not paid within sixty days hereof. To reclaim your personal property and/or arrange payment of any amounts which may remain due, contact **Larry Landlord, at 555-1111.**

The locks to the premises have been changed and your right to enter and/or occupy the premises terminated. If you enter (or attempt to enter) these premises, criminal charges may be brought against you for breaking and entering, criminal damage, burglary, trespass, and/or any other charges warranted by the facts.

Larry Landlord
Larry Landlord (602) 555-1111
123 N. Main Street, Anytown, Arizona 85000

This notice delivered this date *July 2, 1998*   via:
■ Certified mail
☐ Regular first class mail
☐ Hand delivered

Acknowledgment of hand delivery and receipt hereof:

_____
(signature of tenant)   (date)

NOTICE OF DEFAULT

Terry Tenant
123 North Oak Street
Phoenix, Arizona 85999

Notice to Tenant,   Date: *July 2, 1998*

You have:

☐   Failed or refused to remit all due, but as yet unpaid, rent and other amounts owing under the lease;

☐   Violated a material provision of your lease, specifically:

_____

_____

You must cure the foregoing default within _____ days after: ☐ receipt hereof ☐ the date of this letter (above). If the default is not cured within the time provided, your landlord may: (1) terminate your right to possess and occupy the premises (your obligations, financial and otherwise, under the lease shall continue until the end of the lease term or until the premises are re-rented, whichever occurs first) and, pursuant to Arizona Revised Statutes, Title 33, Chapter 8, Section 33-361(A), enter and take possession thereof, or (2) file a lawsuit to recover possession, rent and damages. If you have any question, you may contact **Larry Landlord, at 555-1111.**

                       Larry Landlord
                       Larry Landlord (602) 555-1111
                       123 N. Main Street, Anytown, Arizona 85000

This notice delivered this date *July 2, 1998*   via:
■ Certified mail
☐ Regular first class mail
☐ Hand delivered

Acknowledgment of hand delivery and receipt hereof:

_____
(signature of tenant)   (date)

(d)   **Notice of Default.**

Under many circumstances, you will want to provide a notice to the tenant and an opportunity to cure the default:

- If you have any doubts whatsoever about the tenant's default.

- If the tenant has a "reasonable" argument about not being in default.

- If your lease requires a notice of default.

- If you prefer to resolve the problem via the courts, rather than by locking the tenant out.

If in doubt, serve a notice of default and give the tenant an opportunity to cure the default. It is a better way to do business and, more importantly, if you lose (for whatever reason), your liability will be greatly reduced (i.e., no damages for damage to the tenant's business and/or reputation). Keep in mind, if you elect to lock the tenant out, you are now responsible for safeguarding all of the tenant's possessions. If there is a fire or theft while you control the tenant's possessions, you may be liable for all financial losses suffered by the tenant.

The Notice of Default (above) is different than the Termination of Tenancy form (above). The Notice of Default form may be used for either nonpayment of rent (thereby replacing the "Five Day Notice to Pay or Quit" form, above) or for a nonmonetary default (i.e., failure to provide proof of insurance, failure to provide tenant estoppel certificate, etc.).

(e) Lawsuit for Possession.

There are times when the plain language of the statute is contrary to the procedure you must follow. This is one of those times. Two different statutes seem to say that the landlord need not give notice to the tenant before commencing a lawsuit to recover possession:

> A lease from month to month may be terminated by the landlord giving at least ten days notice thereof. In case of nonpayment of rent <u>notice is not required</u>.[294]

> When a tenant neglects or refuses to pay rent when due and in arrears for five days, or when tenant violates any provision of the lease, the landlord or person to whom the rent is due, or his agent, may re-enter and take possession, or, <u>without formal demand</u> or re-entry, commence an action for recovery of possession of the premises.[295]

---

[294] A.R.S. § 33-341(B) (West 1990).

[295] A.R.S. § 33-361(A) (West 1990) (emphasis added).

Nevertheless, the Supreme Court of Arizona has declared that a demand for possession must be given before a lawsuit for possession can be filed to evict a tenant for nonpayment of rent.

> Although A.R.S. § 33-341(B) requires no notice in order to effectuate a termination of a month to month tenancy, once rent is due and unpaid, if the landlord intends to commence forcible entry and detainer proceedings to enforce his right to possession of the premises, he must make a written demand upon the tenant to surrender the property. The forcible entry and detainer proceedings cannot be commenced until five days after giving of this notice. See A.R.S. § 12-1173(A)(1).[296]

The statute cited by the Supreme Court, A.R.S. § 12-1173(A)(1), provides:

> There is a forcible detainer if:

> 1. A tenant at will or by sufferance or a tenant from month to month or a lesser period whose tenancy has been terminated retains possession after his tenancy has been terminated or after he receives written demand of possession by the landlord.[297]

Consequently, if you intend to file a lawsuit to recover possession of the leased premises because the tenant has failed to pay rent, without regard to whether your lease requires a written notice, you must provide the tenant with a demand after rent becomes due and remains unpaid. You may use the "Five Day Notice to Pay or Quit" form (above) or the "Notice of Default" form (above).

If you intend to file a lawsuit to recover possession of the leased premises because the lease has expired or because tenancy has been terminated, the language of the statute indicates that no written demand is required.[298] Nevertheless, the conservative approach requires that you provide a written demand for possession. Otherwise, you run the risk of a trial judge reading the Alton case[299] as holding that a demand for possession is a prerequisite for a lawsuit for possession for *any* reason (i.e., nonpayment of rent, nonmonetary default, holdover tenant, etc.). You may use the "Notice of Default" form (above). In short, if you are going to file an eviction action, serve a written notice.

---

296 Alton v. Tower Capital Co., Inc., 123 Ariz. 602, 604, 601 P.2d 602, 604 (1979).

297 A.R.S. § 12-1173(A)(1) (West 1994).

298 *See* A.R.S. § 12-1173(A)(1) (West 1994).

299 Alton v. Tower Capital Co., Inc., 123 Ariz. 602, 604, 601 P.2d 602, 604 (1979).

2. **Eviction Procedure.**

(a) **Where to file the Forcible Detainer action?**

You have prepared and served the appropriate written notice. Your next questions are, "*Where* and *how* do I file the Forcible Detainer action and what happens next?" The simple and most recommended solution is to call your attorney and let him/her handle it. Nevertheless, let's face it, at some point in time you will merely make a business decision that it may be more cost effective to handle these matters without the assistance of an attorney (who, as we all know, is incredibly expensive) and lose a few cases, rather than always paying an attorney (who may also lose a few) to handle these matters. When you have reached the stage where you believe you can competently handle an eviction on your own, the following information will help you answer the foregoing questions; call your attorney if you have any doubts.

You first need to determine where you may/must file the Forcible Detainer action. Stated more precisely, "In which of three court systems shall I file my lawsuit: small claims court, justice court or superior court?" First, Forcible Detainer actions may only be brought in justice court or superior court and cannot be brought in small claims court.[300] The alternatives have thus been narrowed to two alternatives: justice court or superior court. Which of these two courts you select will turn on the amount of past due rent you are trying to recover and the monthly rental amount of your rental unit.

To file a Forcible Detainer action in justice court: (1) the damages sought (i.e., past due rent) must be $5,000.00 or less **and** (2) the monthly rental amount for your rental unit must not exceed $1000.00.[301] If you meet <u>both</u> criteria, you may file your Forcible Detainer action in justice court. Superior court has concurrent jurisdiction', which means that even though your lawsuit qualifies for filing in justice court, you may file your lawsuit in superior court, if you prefer.[302] Note: processing time is longer and court costs are higher in superior court than in justice court. As of January 1, 1998, the fee to file a Forcible Detainer action in superior court was $140.00, whereas the fee in justice court was $21.00.

If the amount sought in damages is more than $5,000 <u>or</u> your monthly rental amount for your rental is more than $1000.00, then you <u>must</u> file your lawsuit in superior court.[303] As a general rule, most commercial evictions, because of the monthly rent and/or the total amount of damages sought, are filed in superior court.

Okay, you have decided whether you will file in justice court or superior

---

300 A.R.S. § 22-503(B)(3) (West Supp. 1998).

301 A.R.S. § 22-201(C) (West Supp. 1998).

302 *See* A.R.S. §§ 12-123(A) (West 1992), 12-1175(A) (West 1994).

303 *See* A.R.S. § 22-201(C) (West Supp. 1998).

court. The next question is: which justice court or which superior court (i.e., which county)? This question raises the issue of **personal jurisdiction**. Personal jurisdiction can be a very complex matter. Nevertheless, in the "normal" landlord/tenant context, the following should resolve this issue. You cannot "go wrong" if you file in the court that has personal jurisdiction over the tenant/defendant. Where the tenant/defendant presently lives (i.e., at the time you file the lawsuit, not necessarily where s/he lived when s/he was your tenant) determines which court has personal jurisdiction over the tenant/defendant. Under certain circumstances, you may be able to file in the court that has jurisdiction over the leased premises (if in doubt, consult your attorney).

If you are filing in superior court, you may file in the superior court for the county in which the rental property was located or the county in which the defendant now resides. If you are filing in justice court, you may file in the justice court that has jurisdiction over the rental property or the justice court that has jurisdiction over the property where the defendant now resides. (Note: the justice court clerks are pretty good about telling you whether or not a particular property address in located in their jurisdiction; *see* Appendix D for list of justice courts and phone numbers). If you have a question regarding jurisdiction, you should consult your attorney. If you file a lawsuit in the wrong court, the tenant/defendant may be able to have the case dismissed and you may end up paying the tenant/defendant's attorney's fees.

(b)   How to file and serve the Forcible Detainer action.

Generally, the superior court will not provide you with a Forcible Detainer Complaint and/or Summons form. You will need to obtain these forms from another source. Most Arizona justice courts, however, will provide you with the necessary forms and most justice courts now have some type of instruction sheet, available from the clerk, which explains the precise procedure for filing and prosecuting a Forcible Detainer action in *that* court. "Wait a minute," you say. "If the landlord and tenant statutes are state law, shouldn't the procedure be the same in all courts?" In theory, that is true. But the truth is that judges perceive the law differently and from varying points of view (i.e., some judges are pro-tenant, some are pro-landlord). Moreover, each judge is given the discretion to dictate the "procedures" (not the substantive law) to be followed in his/her courtroom. Consequently, the procedure and forms made available by the court for Forcible Detainer actions may differ, in varying degrees, from one court to another. Telling the judge that things are done differently in another court will likely yield poor results. Therefore, you should read and follow the instructions provided by the court in which you filed your Forcible Detainer action.

Notwithstanding the differences between courts, the general procedure is as follows. Ask the clerk for the forms for an eviction. The clerk will provide you with one or more multi-part forms. You will fill out some factual data on a form called a Complaint; it may also be called a "Special Detainer / Forcible Detainer Complaint." The factual data normally includes: the names of the parties, the amount of monthly rent, the reason for the eviction (i.e., nonpayment of rent or some type of noncompliance), the date written notices were delivered, and the relief you are seeking (i.e., possession of the rental property and, if applicable, due and unpaid rent). You must sign the Complaint. If not signed in the presence of the clerk, then your signature must be notarized. You must pay a fee to file the Complaint with the court. A copy of a sample complaint form is shown below; you will note that this form combines the summons and complaint on one form. You may also note that this form may be used for either a residential or commercial eviction.

If anyone has guaranteed or co-signed the rental agreement for the tenants, you will need to decide at this stage whether to name the guarantors or co-signors as additional defendants (i.e., in addition to the tenants) or whether you would prefer to bring the action against the tenants first and, if they do not pay, to then bring a separate civil lawsuit against the guarantors or co-signors.[304] I recommend naming the guarantors or co-signors as additional defendants in the Forcible Detainer action. Why? Because it will cost more and take much longer if you file a second civil action later against only the guarantors or co-signors. A word of caution, however; a guaranty must be signed by both the husband and wife to be enforceable.[305] Naturally, if the guarantor is unmarried, this is not a problem. If you join the guarantors or co-signors as additional defendants, you must include additional language in your complaint, such as that which follows, and you must have a separate summons issued by the court and served upon each named defendant.

Defendants John and Jane Parent, at all times material hereto were husband and wife and residents of this county. Mr. & Mrs. Parent signed the rental agreement as a guarantors (or co-signors). These Defendants are financially liable for all damages assessed against Defendants/Tenants John and Jane Tenant.

The clerk will then fill out the Summons, which may be a separate form or may be included on the bottom portion of the Complaint. The information the clerk will provide on the Summons is the date and time of the hearing, where the tenant will enter his/her plea (i.e., guilty or not guilty). The clerk then stamps the Summons with the official seal of the court and returns it to you.

You will deliver the Summons and Complaint to a process server. You may obtain the name of a process server from the Yellow Pages. Many courts have some type of bulletin board where local process servers advertise. Or you may seek a recommendation for a process server from your attorney or from another landlord.

---

304 Staffco, Inc. v. Maricopa Trading Co., 122 Ariz. 353, 357, 595 P.2d 31 (1979) (a guarantor of a lease may be joined as a defendant with the party in possession in a forcible detainer action).

305 A.R.S. § 25-214(C)(2) (West 1991).

[NAME OF COURT]

REQUEST FOR REASONABLE ACCOMMODATIONS FOR PERSONS WITH DISABILITIES MUST BE MADE AT LEAST THREE WORKING DAYS BEFORE SCHEDULED COURT PROCEEDING.

_____ CASE NUMBER: _____

PLAINTIFF:	DEFENDANT:
Street:	Street:
City/State/Zip:	City/State/Zip:
Phone:	Phone:

ATTORNEY:	ATTORNEY:
Street:	Street:
City/State/Zip:	City/State/Zip:
Phone:	Phone:

SUMMONS AND COMPLAINT FORCIBLE / SPECIAL DETAINER

SUMMONS

STATE OF ARIZONA TO ABOVE NAMED DEFENDANTS:

You are summoned to appear and defend this action in the Court named above:

Trial date: _____ Time: _____

Courtroom number (if applies): _____

NOTICE TO DEFENDANT(S): You must appear at the date and time stated above and answer the allegations of the complaint. If you fail to appear, a judgment may be entered against you as requested in the complaint, including eviction from the premises.

DATE: _____ JUDGE: _____

COMPLAINT

Plaintiff(s) in this action alleges the following:

1. This court has jurisdiction over this action.

2. Plaintiff(s) is lawfully entitled to immediate possession which defendant(s) wrongfully withholds from Plaintiff: _____ (address).

3. On _____ (date), defendant(s) was served written notice to vacate the premises by ☐ Personal Service   ☐ Certified Mail.

4. Rent per _____ is $_____; and rent is due and unpaid since _____; for a total of $_____; plus late fees, per written rental agreement, court costs, attorney's fees, damages if proven at trial, and a Writ of Restitution to issue.

5. That defendant has failed to comply as follows: ☐ nonpayment of rent; ☐ material noncompliance (facts filled-in below); ☐ committed repeated violations during the term of the rental agreement; ☐ committed serious health or safety violations (facts filled-in below); ☐ threatened or committed serious harm to person or property as stated below, for which termination notice was give: _____

_____

WHEREFORE, Plaintiff(s) request(s) judgment against Defendant(s) for immediate possession of the premises, rent due, late fees, damages, court costs, attorney's fees, and that a Writ of Restitution be issued. I attest to the accuracy of the facts stated above based upon personal knowledge.

Plaintiff: _____ Notary/Clerk: _____

SUBSCRIBED AND SWORN before me this date: _____ Commission expires: _____

Sample Summons & Complaint Form

The process server will hand-deliver (if possible) the Summons and Complaint to each tenant named in the Complaint and, if applicable, to each guarantor. The Summons and Complaint must be served at least two days prior to the hearing date on the Summons.[306] Consequently, after filing the Complaint and having the Summons issued by the clerk, *waste no time getting these documents to the process server.* You must pay the process server directly for his/her services; the process server is not paid through the court.

That's it. The eviction process has begun. The next question is, "What are all the significant steps to prosecute a Special Detainer action?" The procedure you follow to evict a tenant will turn on whether you are evicting because of: (1) nonpayment of rent or (2) some other type of noncompliance with the lease.

(c)   The eviction process -- Step-by-Step.

This is it -- this is the section you have been waiting for. This is where you find out, "How do I get rid of that miserable *&%$#@ tenant?"

What are the procedural steps for evicting a tenant? This is a short and seemingly simple question; the answer is very long and involves many steps. First, you must decide if you will merely lock the tenant out or file a lawsuit for possession. Second, if filing a lawsuit for possession, you must decide which notice is appropriate to your circumstances and serve it upon the tenant. Third, you must select the proper court. Finally, you must file and prosecute the Forcible Detainer action. If you have never been through the entire process of evicting a tenant, you should consult with your attorney. For those who have been through the process a few times <u>and</u> who feel confident they can proceed without an attorney, the following information should see you through each step.

(1)   Notice of Default.

TIME FRAME: Day 1

Step 1: Prepare a Five-Day Notice to Pay or Quit or a Notice of Default (both notices were discussed above). The notice must fairly apprise the tenant of the nature of the default (i.e., monetary or otherwise) and inform the tenant how to cure the default, if curable.

Step 2: Serve the notice on the first day of the default (i.e., if for nonpayment of rent that is due on the first of the month, then you may serve the notice on the second day of the month). Do not wait a few days. Be consistent. If your tenants know that they can be late a few days without consequence, they will be late. By being methodical and predictable, your tenants get in the habit of paying the rent before it is past due. NOTE: If your rental agreement provides for late fees and/or a "notice fee," you should assess and collect these charges as well. (For an example, *see* Chapter 2, Section D(2), which pertains to residential rental agreements).

---

306   A.R.S. §§ 33-1377(B) (West Supp. 1998); 12-1175(C) (West 1994),

Residential landlord/tenant law provides that after a Special Detainer action has been filed, the tenant may reinstate the rental agreement only by paying past due rent, late fees, attorneys' fees and court costs.[307] The commercial tenant does not have this right. You may accept rent after the Forcible Detainer action has been filed, if you wish, but you are not required to do so.

If the tenant only has part of the amount due and you want to accept a partial payment (you are not required to accept less than full payment), you are free to do so, but to protect your rights you must have the tenant execute a "Partial Payment Agreement." (*See* Appendix B, Form 5). Your rental agreement should provide for how partial payments are to be applied. If not, the Partial Payment Agreement should specify how the partial payment is to be applied, thereby protecting your rights. Partial payments should be applied as follows: first, to legal fees and court costs, then to accrued interest on any amounts owed to the landlord, then to late fees, then to amounts owed for damages to the property, then to any other amounts owed by the tenant to the landlord, then to unpaid past due rent, and finally to prepaid rent. If the tenant thereafter fails to pay the balance due on the date specified in the Partial Payment Agreement, you *do not* need to serve another Five-Day Notice to Pay or Quit, merely proceed with the eviction process.

(2)   Tenant Pays.

TIME FRAME: Specified in your notice of default.

The tenant can stop the eviction process by curing the default within the time specified in your notice of default. After the cure period expires and you have terminated the tenant's tenancy, the tenant is not entitled to reinstate the lease. Naturally, the landlord may elect to allow the tenant to reinstate the rental agreement if s/he wishes.

Do not accept any payments from the tenant after entry of judgment and before the tenant vacates without having the tenant execute a form that specifies the terms upon which payment is being accepted (i.e., payment being accepted with the understanding that the tenant may stay or with the understanding that the tenant must still vacate). *See* Appendix B, Form 5.

(3)   Tenant Moves.

TIME FRAME: Anytime prior to execution of Writ of Restitution.

Naturally, anytime from day one to the day the Writ of Restitution is executed, the tenant can voluntarily move out. This will not necessarily stop the eviction process and you may still have a separate legal cause of action against the tenant for past due rent, money damages for breach of the rental agreement, damages to the rental unit, etc. To proceed against the tenant for these claims, you must

---

307 A.R.S. § 33-1368(B) (West Supp. 1998).

initiate a separate lawsuit. The purpose of a Forcible Detainer action is to restore possession of the rental property to the landlord; if the tenant moves before you file the Forcible Detainer action and voluntarily transfers possession of the premises to you (i.e., gives you the keys), possession is restored and the court will dismiss a subsequently filed Forcible Detainer action. Go to Chapter 6, Section A, filing a lawsuit against the tenant for damages. Similarly, the court may dismiss the Forcible Detainer action if the tenant voluntarily transfers possession to you after you have file the Forcible Detainer action and before the hearing date.

IMPORTANT NOTE: You should also be cognizant of the distinction between: (1) a tenant voluntarily moving out, transferring possession to you, and you accepting possession on the tenant's behalf for the purpose of mitigating your damages and (2) the tenant offering to surrender possession and the landlord accepting surrender of possession of the premises. The tenant's conduct of voluntarily moving out does not automatically equate to an acceptance of surrender of possession of the premises by the landlord. Why is this important? A Forcible Detainer action is a lawsuit to recover possession of rental property. Consequently, if the tenant voluntarily surrenders possession of the rental unit and you accept the surrender of possession before the hearing date, the court will dismiss the Forcible Detainer action. Why is that important? Because you lose the opportunity to get a judgment against the tenant for past due rent. Moreover, acceptance of surrender by the landlord may be (and usually is) deemed a waiver of the landlord's right to pursue the tenant for all damages (i.e., past due rent, damages to the unit, etc.). This is why it is **very important** that you not accept surrender of the premises unless you are fully prepared to give up all rights to pursue this tenant. If you want the Forcible Detainer action to go forward (i.e., you want a money judgment against the tenant for past due rent), do not accept a surrender of possession under any circumstances and do not accept a voluntary transfer of possession of the rental unit until after the hearing. Naturally, the tenant may voluntarily move out anytime s/he wishes, but the landlord is not required to accept surrender of possession of the premises. As long as the landlord does not have possession, the Forcible Detainer action may go forward. "Acceptance" of surrender turns on the landlord's intent. For example, abandonment of the premises by the tenant and depositing the keys in the landlord's mail slot does not "force" the landlord to accept surrender of the premises.

(4)   **File the Forcible Detainer action.**

TIME FRAME: Upon expiration of the cure period in the notice of default.

If serving a Five-Day Notice to Pay or Quit, you may file the Forcible Detainer action on the sixth day. If you mailed the notice, you must wait additional time. *See* Section D(1)(a), above. The day that the notice is served or received in the mail is not counted.

Example 1: file the Forcible Detainer action on the eighth day of the month if the notice was hand-delivered on the second day of the month.

Example 2: file the Forcible Detainer action on the ninth day of the month if the notice was mailed via certified mail, return receipt requested, on the second day of the month and received by the tenant on the third day of the month.

(5)   Have tenant served.

TIME FRAME: Hearing date, minus two (2) business days.

The **summons** and **complaint** must be served on the tenant. The complaint is the legal document that you filed with the court to commence the Forcible Detainer action. The summons commands the tenant to appear in court on a particular date and time. Service of the summons and complaint is known as **service of process**. Service of process must be served by a person authorized by law to deliver legal papers. Typically, this is the Sheriff or a private **process server**. Service must be completed at least two business days (not calendar days) before the entry of the tenant's plea on the hearing date/trial date.[308] The hearing and/or trial date (also known as the "return date") is entered on the summons by the clerk of the court at the time the complaint is filed and the summons issued.

Procedural Note: Call your process server and give him/her the papers to serve on the same day you file the Forcible Detainer action. Some process servers will even pick up the summons and complaint (after you have filled out and signed the documents), file the Forcible Detainer action on your behalf with the court and then serve the summons and complaint on the tenant (this will save you a trip to the courthouse – you know, that incredibly efficient place where you never have to wait and are greeted by scores of friendly, courteous people). If you anticipate that the tenants will evade service (a common occurrence), instruct the process server to immediately make an attempt at service and, if unsuccessful, to "post and mail." "Post and mail," means to post a copy of the summons and complaint on the property and to mail a copy via certified mail, return receipt requested. The problem, however, is that although residential landlord/tenant law allows service via "post and mail," there is no parallel provision in commercial landlord/tenant law (unless this type of service is expressly permitted in your lease). Consequently, at best, "post and mail" will give the court jurisdiction over the leased premises (known as *in rem* jurisdiction) and allow the court to give you a judgment for possession, but will not give the court jurisdiction to enter a money judgment against the tenant. You will need to file a separate civil lawsuit to recover rent, damages, etc. (*see* Chapter 6, Section A), but at least you will recover possession.

---

[308]   A.R.S. § 12-1175(C) (West 1994).

(6) "Hearing Date" / "Return Date".

TIME FRAME: Five business days after filing of Forcible Detainer.

"Hearing date" or "return date" - this is the date entered on the summons by the clerk of the court at the time the complaint is filed and the summons issued. The Forcible Detainer statutes provide that the hearing date cannot be more than five business days after the Forcible Detainer complaint is filed.[309] The landlord and tenant statutes, however, provide that the trial shall be conducted not less than five business days after the Forcible Detainer complaint is filed, nor more than thirty calendar days after the Forcible Detainer complaint is filed.[310] In practice, it will probably be close to thirty days before your eviction action is scheduled for trial.

Go to court on the hearing date scheduled for your Forcible Detainer action. Do not miss this date. If you miss this date without a really good excuse and/or prior notice to the court to continue the hearing date, the case will be dismissed and you must file another Forcible Detainer complaint, pay another filing fee and incur several days of delay. You may also be liable for the tenant's defense costs (if any), if the tenant appears and you do not.

(7) Tenant enters plea.

TIME FRAME: "Hearing Date" / "Return Date".

Entry of the tenant's plea occurs on the "hearing date" (also known as the "return date"). The tenant will enter his plea -- guilty or not guilty. If guilty, judgment is immediately entered for the landlord; if not guilty, the matter is set for trial. Either party may request a jury trial. Requesting a jury trial will normally add at least four hours to the trial and will delay scheduling of the trial date.

(8) Tenant requests and court grants continuance/postponement.

Only upon "good cause" shown, supported by affidavit, may the tenant request a postponement of the trial. If the postponement is granted, the postponement may be no longer than three (3) calendar days in justice court or ten (10) calendar days in superior court.[311] In justice court, if a request for postponement is not made or not granted, trial may (and typically does) immediately follow entry of the tenant's plea, on the hearing date. In superior court, if a request for postponement is not made or granted, a trial date is normally scheduled for a few days later.

---

309 A.R.S. § 12-1176(A)(West 1994).

310 A.R.S. § 33-361(B) (West 1990).

311 A.R.S. § 12-1177(C) (West 1994).

(9)   **Trial.**

TIME FRAME: "Hearing date" / "return date" or subsequently scheduled "trial date."

In justice court, unless a postponement was granted (see above), trial immediately follows entry of the plea. In superior court, whether or not a postponement is granted, trial is normally scheduled for a few days later.

If you are evicting for nonpayment of rent (if you are evicting for a non-monetary default, see below), before you walk into the court room for trial, be sure that you know this information: (1) why you are evicting tenant (i.e., nonpayment of rent); (2) when rent was last paid; (3) whether the written rental agreement provides for late fees; (4) the precise amount of rent, late fees and any other amounts that you are seeking to recover (be prepared to explain your calculations); (5) the date you served your written notice (i.e., the 5-Day Notice) and have an extra copy with you; (6) how the notice was served (i.e., hand-delivered, certified mail, etc.); (7) when the tenant was served with the Forcible Detainer summons and complaint; (8) how service of the Forcible Detainer summons and complaint was accomplished (i.e., personal service); and (9) any other facts specific to your eviction action.

If you are evicting for a non-monetary default, before you walk into the court room for trial, be sure that you know this information: (1) why you are evicting tenant (i.e., the precise nature of the non-monetary default); (2) when rent was last paid; (3) any amounts that are presently due (i.e., rent, late fees, common area expenses, etc.), even though these amounts may not be in default and/or you are not evicting for nonpayment of rent; (4) the date you served your written notice (i.e., the Notice of Default) and have an extra copy with you; (5) how the notice was served (i.e., hand-delivered, certified mail, etc.); (6) when the tenant was served with the Forcible Detainer summons and complaint; (7) how service of the Forcible Detainer summons and complaint was accomplished (i.e., personal service, "post & mail"); and (8) any other facts specific to your eviction action.

The purpose of a Forcible Detainer action is to provide landlords with a speedy legal proceeding to recover possession of the rental property.[312] Counterclaims are not permitted and the only issue the court will examine in a Forcible Detainer action is which party is entitled to immediate possession of the premises.[313] The court will not consider issues regarding who has the right to title.[314] There is case law that allows counterclaims and inquiry into title in residential landlord/tenant cases, but this practice has not yet spread to commercial landlord/tenant law.[315] Nevertheless, a commercial tenant may assert any defense

---

[312]   *See* Andreola v. Arizona Bank, 26 Ariz.App. 556, 550 P.2d 110 (1976).

[313]   *See* Taylor v. Stanford, 100 Ariz. 346, 414 P.2d 727 (1966).

[314]   A.R.S. § 12-1177(A) (West 1994).

[315]   *See* Moreno v. Garcia, 169 Ariz. 586, 821 P.2d 247 (App. 1991) (issues of title may be raised in forcible detainer action following foreclosure of property and/or other events specified in A.R.S. § 12-1173.01).

which, if proven, preserves his/her right to possession and/or prevents the landlord from recovering possession.[316] Generally, there are few defenses available to the tenant. The more common defenses include:

- The notice was improperly served or the notice itself was defective (i.e., lacks required information).

- The Forcible Detainer complaint was filed before expiration of the cure period (i.e., five day, ten day, etc.) stated in the notice.

- The summons and complaint were improperly served.

- The tenant no longer lives in the rental unit and the landlord has accepted a surrender of possession.

- There was a justification for nonpayment of rent, based on some type of breach of the rental agreement by the landlord (i.e., failure to provide tenant improvements, etc.).

- The Forcible Detainer action was filed in the wrong court. *See* Chapter 5, Section B(5).

- The landlord inconsistently enforces the terms in the rental agreement (i.e., s/he allows some tenants to be late with rent, but not others). If the tenant can demonstrate to the court that s/he is the victim of "selective enforcement," the court may dismiss the action.

- The language of the rental agreement provides (or suggests) that the landlord **must** accept partial rent payments, but the landlord has refused to accept a partial payment.

Judgment is typically entered for the prevailing party at the conclusion of the trial. If the tenant wins, the court will enter judgment in the tenant's favor, the tenant will be entitled to retain possession of the unit and the tenant is entitled to judgment against the landlord for his/her attorneys' fees and court costs (pretty grim). On the other hand, if the landlord wins, the court will enter judgment in the land-lord's favor and the judgment will restore the landlord's legal right of possession to the rental unit. Unfortunately, while the court has now determined that you are entitled to possession of the rental unit, the **Writ of Restitution** – the legal paper that grants you the right to possession – will not be issued by the court until five calendar days after entry of judgment.[317]

---

316 Magna Inv. & Dev. Corp. v. Brooks Fashion Stores, Inc., 137 Ariz. 247, 669 P.2d 1024 (App. 1983).

317 A.R.S. § 12-1178(C) (West Supp. 1998).

If the landlord fails to appear at the trial, the judge will dismiss the Forcible Detainer action (that means you start over -- do not pass go, do not collect $200). If the tenant fails to appear at the trial, the landlord must still prove to the judge that s/he is entitled to judgment in his/her favor. Assuming the landlord presents sufficient evidence to prove his/her case, the judge will enter judgment in the landlord's favor. This process is known as obtaining a judgment by default (i.e., in the tenant's absence). If judgment is obtained by default and the tenant was personally served with the summons and complaint, the judgment for possession may, at the landlord's option, include a specific monetary amount representing past due rent.[318] Actual eviction (i.e., removal of the tenant from the rental unit) cannot be initiated until a **Writ of Restitution** is issued by the court; the earliest a that Writ of Restitution may issue is five calendar days after the date of judgment.[319]

If you get a judgment against the tenant, send copies to the credit reporting agencies and, if you believe it cost-effective, record the judgment in the county recorder's office. This will ensure the judgment shows up on the tenant's credit report and will deter him/her from buying or selling real property in the county in which the judgment is recorded until the judgment is paid.

(10)   Letter to tenant.

TIME FRAME: Date of Judgment

After judgment is rendered, but before the Writ of Restitution is issued (five calendar days after entry of judgment), send the tenant a copy of the judgment and a letter informing the tenant s/he must vacate within calendar five days or you will obtain the Writ of Restitution on the fifth day and direct the Sheriff (or constable) to forcibly remove him/her. See sample letter in Appendix B, Form 15. This letter normally works -- I have rarely had to pay the Sheriff to forcibly remove a tenant.

(11)   Writ of Restitution issued.

TIME FRAME: Judgment plus five calendar days

The Writ of Restitution will not issue until five calendar days (not business days) after entry of judgment.[320] Issuance of the Writ is not automatic; you must request (i.e., pay a fee and fill out a form) the court to issue the Writ of Restitution. Upon receiving the Writ, you must deliver the Writ to the Sheriff or constable.

(12)   Writ of Restitution: service and execution.

Service and execution of the Writ of Restitution may be a two-step process.

---

318 A.R.S. § 12-1178(A) (West Supp. 1998).

319 A.R.S. § 12-1178(C) (West Supp. 1998).

320 A.R.S. § 12-1178(C) (West Supp. 1998).

The precise time of service/execution of the Writ after you deliver the Writ to the Sheriff or constable will depend on the present backlog – it may be one day; it may be three weeks. Actual eviction, as conducted by the Sheriff or constable, and no one else (not you; not a process server), may not be initiated until a Writ of Restitution is issued by the court and delivered to the Sheriff or constable (the Sheriff serves and executes the Writ in superior court cases; the constable serves and executes the Writ in justice court cases) along with a payment of the fee (the Maricopa County Sheriff requires a $150 deposit to serve the Writ; for constables, the amount of deposit may vary; the final charge, which may be more or less than the deposit, will depend on the number of attempts the Sheriff/constable must make to serve the Writ, the mileage from the courthouse to the property, etc.). The Sheriff/constable has the legal authority to forcibly remove the tenant (a rare occurrence), but the task of removing the tenant's personal property falls on the landlord. If you are actually driven to this step, you should talk with the Sheriff or constable on the telephone before s/he shows up to forcibly remove the tenant. Typically, the Sheriff or constable goes to the tenant's door, tells the tenant to get out within twenty-four (24) hours or s/he will forcibly remove the tenant and his/her belongings. This normally produces the desired results (i.e., the tenant moves out). If it does not, the Sheriff or constable shows up the next day and forcibly removes the tenant.

Although you may want the tenant's property thrown into the street, this will not happen. The landlord is responsible for arranging for the moving and storage of the tenant's personal property. Numerous companies provide this service and are familiar with the process, but this is why you should speak with the Sheriff or constable beforehand, so that you may coordinate the arrangements in advance. You will be required to pay their fees up front. You may be tempted to simply store the tenant's personal property in the rental unit. This is usually a bad idea. Tenant's oftentimes break into "their" rental unit, recover some or all of their property, and then sue the landlord for the value of their property because the landlord was responsible for safeguarding their property. Moving the tenant's property to another location prevents this problem. In appropriate circumstances, hiring a security guard to watch the premises until the tenant calms down (i.e., two or three weeks) may be a viable alternative to moving and storing the tenant's property. In any event, you should have a locksmith present to immediately re-key the unit.

If the tenant subsequently returns and attempts to re-enter the premises, call the police: the tenant has committed criminal trespass upon your property. If the tenant actually re-enters the rental unit (i.e., breaks in), call the police: the tenant has committed criminal trespass, breaking and entering, criminal damage and burglary. Above all, do not get into any physical confrontation with the tenant.

To dispose of abandoned or seized property (i.e., seized by landlord by locking the tenant out of the unit), follow the procedure in the Quick Reference Section, Procedures (What are the procedural steps for conducting a public sale of abandoned personal property?). The distinction, however, is that a commercial landlord has a landlord's lien upon all nonexempt property on/in the leased premises.[321] This means that if you are forced to conduct an auction of all personal property found on/in the leased premises, you may apply it toward any amounts due to the landlord under the lease (i.e., rent, damages, late fees, etc.).

(13)   Additional Important Notes.

• The entire process, from the date the notice is served until the tenant is "forcibly evicted" by the Sheriff or constable, cannot take less than fifteen (15) days and could take as long as sixty (60) days. Naturally, there is nothing that prevents the tenant from voluntarily moving out sooner.

• I know you are anxious to get these impecunious or "noncomplying" tenants out of your rental unit and out of your life, but make sure you follow the proper procedure. The tenant has very few defenses available in a Forcible Detainer action. Most are procedural. Don't "jump the gun" or try to "short-cut" the process.

• Depending on your situation, you may wish to consider paying the tenant to leave. I can hear you shrieking, "Pay this deadbeat to leave? What, have you lost your mind?" Business is business; the goal is to get him/her out – grit your teeth and do whatever you must do to get him/her out, voluntarily or otherwise. Sit down and "pencil out" a few numbers: how much it will cost you to go through the whole process, including having the Sheriff or constable forcibly removing this tenant, versus how much it will "cost" to pay this tenant to leave. The truth is, it just may be cheaper to pay the deadbeat (*see* "Practical Approach To A `Real World' Dilemma," at the very beginning of this book). Even if the amount you must pay the tenant is almost as much, as much, or even a little more than what it would cost to go through the judicial system, paying the tenant has two major benefits: (1) the tenant is out right now and (2) you do not have to go through the hassle. Keep in mind, depending on the facts, there is a chance that you could go through the whole process and lose for some reason (i.e., you committed some procedural blunder, the judge believed the tenant's fabricated story, etc.). Paying the tenant to leave has the distinct advantage of providing certainty that the tenant will be out. This may be done at practically any stage of the process, prior to actual physical eviction of the tenant by the Sheriff or constable.

• You should consult with your attorney before filing or pursuing a Forcible Detainer action.

(d)   FINAL STEPS -- What to do *AFTER* the eviction process.

Okay, you have evicted the tenant. You are done, right? Wrong. Whether you have evicted a tenant for nonpayment of rent or for any type of noncompliance, you need to observe the following procedures. These steps are critical. If not done or done improperly, you may lose the right to recover certain damages from the tenant.

---

[321]   A.R.S. § 33-362 (West 1990).

(1) <u>Inspection.</u>

Conduct a post-eviction inspection of the rental unit. Take copious notes. If you observe damage to the premises, excessive wear and tear, etc., then photographs and/or video tape of the rental unit are highly recommended.

If utilities are in the tenant's name, check with the utility company to see if the utility (i.e., electric, gas, water, etc.) will allow a "temporary transfer" into your name, until the next tenant moves in, with either no transfer fee or a reduced fee.

(2) <u>Security deposit.</u>

Send the tenant a statement disclosing the disposition of his/her deposits (see Disposition of Deposit form, below).

DISPOSITION OF DEPOSITS

The following discloses the disposition of your deposit(s):

DEPOSITS
Nonrefundable deposits:

Cleaning deposit (Nonrefundable)	$	*100.00*
Other	$	*0.00*
Total:	$	*100.00*
Amount refundable:	$	*0.00*

Refundable deposits:

Cleaning deposit (Refundable)	$	*75.00*
Security deposit (Refundable)	$	*300.00*
Total:	$	*375.00*

DEDUCTIONS

Unpaid rent	$	*0.00*
Late charges	$	*0.00*
Damages	$	*65.00*
Other *Damage to entrance door*	$	*40.00*
TOTAL DEDUCTIONS	$	*105.00*
AMOUNT OF REFUNDABLE DEPOSITS:	$	*270.00*

■ Refund Due to Tenant   ☐ Balance Due to Landlord; Payment immediately due.

Larry Landlord

This notice delivered this date *June 5, 1998* via:

Larry Landlord (602) 555-1111
ABC Commercial Properties

☐ Certified mail
■ Regular first class mail
☐ Hand delivered

123 N. Main Street, Anytown, Arizona 85000

Acknowledgment of hand delivery and receipt hereof:
_____N/A_____
(signature of tenant)   (date)

If the tenant has left a forwarding address, send the Disposition of Deposit statement to that address; otherwise, address it to the last known address (i.e., your rental unit or the address specified for delivery of notices in the lease). If/when the letter is returned, because no forwarding address was left (a common occurrence), place this letter in your file so that if it becomes necessary, at some future date, you can prove that you attempted to return the tenant's deposits and that any failure of the tenant to receive the Disposition of Deposit statement is due to his/her own failure to leave a forwarding address with the landlord or to notify the post office.

(3) Abandoned/Seized personal property.

To dispose of abandoned or seized property (i.e., seized by landlord by locking the tenant out of the unit), follow the procedure in the Quick Reference Section, Procedures (What are the procedural steps for conducting a public sale of abandoned personal property?). The distinction, however, is that a commercial landlord has a landlord's lien upon all nonexempt property on/in the leased premises.[322] This means that if you are forced to conduct an auction of all personal property found on/in the leased premises, you may apply it toward any amounts due to the landlord under the lease (i.e., rent, damages, late fees, etc.).

(4) Lawsuit for damages.

File a lawsuit against the tenant for:

• Past due rent (if judgment for past due rent was not obtained in the Forcible Detainer action or if the judge only awarded a portion of the past due rent);

• Rent that accrued after entry of the Forcible Detainer judgment through the last date s/he occupied the rental unit (if not already included in the Forcible Detainer judgment);

• Damages to the rental unit (see below); and

• For any other amounts to which you are entitled under the law.

Be sure to check with the utility companies to see if the landlord is responsible for any unpaid balance on the account. For example, in Scottsdale and Glendale, the owner is responsible for a tenant's unpaid water bill and the water company will not turn-on the water for a new tenant until the full outstanding balance, including late penalties, is paid.

If the tenant has intentionally caused severe damage, you may wish to consider filing a criminal complaint with the police. Intentional property damage by a tenant may be prosecuted as a felony or a misdemeanor, depending on the severity of the damage.[323] If charges are filed against a tenant for criminal damage, you, as the victim, may request that restitution (i.e., reimbursement for the damage)

---

322 A.R.S. § 33-362 (West 1990).

323 A.R.S. § 13-1602 (West 1989) (criminal damage).

be made a condition of the sentence or any plea agreement. In that way, you may be completely reimbursed without having to spend any money on a private attorney. If that does not work, you may wish to contact your property insurance company. Criminal damage may be covered as vandalism or under some other provision of your insurance policy.

If you don't recover from your insurance company and a complaint for criminal damage is not appropriate or the prosecutor either loses the case or refuses to file charges, you may still file a civil lawsuit to recover your damages. Depending on the amount in controversy, the lawsuit may be filed in small claims court, justice court or superior court. Small claims court jurisdiction is limited to cases involving claims of not more than $2,500.00.[324] Justice court jurisdiction is $5,000.00 or less.[325] For claims exceeding $5,000, the superior court has jurisdiction.[326] For amounts between $1,000.00 and $5,000.00, inclusive, the justice courts and the superior court have concurrent jurisdiction (which merely means that you may file in either court).[327] Depending upon the complexity of the issues involved, you may be able to do this yourself, without the assistance of a lawyer. If you have any questions, however, consult your lawyer. Normally, if it is not economically feasible for your lawyer to try the case for you, s/he will help you with the steps you must take, the strategy you should pursue, etc.

(5)   Obtain a Judgment.

Get a judgment against the tenant. While you may not be able to collect this judgment for some time, if ever, it will follow your tenant around for a very long time. Moreover, judgments show up on credit reports. Do yourself and your fellow landlords a favor: record the judgment with the county recorder's office and send a copy to local and/or national credit reporting agencies. Now, go to Chapter 6, Section B (Collecting Judgments).

e.   Appeals.

If you are a landlord long enough, you will eventually (or, perhaps, immediately) encounter a decision by a judge which you know to be incorrect. Either the judge made a mistake on the facts and evidence (i.e., wouldn't permit the presentation of certain evidence or witnesses at trial, misinterpreted certain evidence or documents, etc.) or s/he made a mistake on the law. In either event, you are convinced that not another soul on the planet would or could reach the same (erroneous) conclusion, and you want to appeal.

An appeal converts a fairly "user friendly" proceeding (i.e., the relatively informal procedures in a Forcible Detainer action) into a "formal" proceeding,

---

324 A.R.S. § 22-503(A) (West Supp. 1998).

325 A.R.S. § 22-201(B) (West Supp. 1998).

326 *See* Ariz. Const. article VI, § 14; A.R.S. §§ 12-123(A) (West 1992), 22-201(B) (West Supp. 1998).

327 *See* Ariz. Const. article VI, § 14; A.R.S. §§ 12-123(A) (West 1992), 22-201(B) (West Supp. 1998). *See also* Neely v. Brown, 177 Ariz. 6, 864 P.2d 1038 (1993).

governed by convoluted and cryptic rules of procedure. This is truly the time to seek the assistance of your attorney. Make sure your attorney is familiar with the appeal process for Forcible Detainer actions because it is different from criminal actions and other civil actions, and the deadlines are much shorter than in other appellate actions.

If you are determined to conquer the appeal process without a lawyer, refer to Chapter 5, Section B(8).

E.   APPENDIX OF COMMERCIAL FORMS

So that commercial forms are not accidentally used by residential landlords, all commercial blank forms are included in this chapter.

```
FORM 1 - Notice of Default
FORM 2 - Notice of Termination
FORM 3 - Five Day Notice to Pay or Quit
FORM 4 - Disposition of Deposit(s)
```

NOTICE OF DEFAULT

_____

_____

_____

Notice to Tenant,   Date:_____

     You have:

☐   Failed or refused to remit all due, but as yet unpaid, rent and other amounts owing under the lease;

☐   Violated a material provision of your lease, specifically:

     _____

     _____

     You must cure the foregoing default within _____ days after: ☐ receipt hereof ☐ the date of this letter (above). If the default is not cured within the time provided, your landlord may: (1) terminate your right to possess and occupy the premises (your obligations, financial and otherwise, under the lease shall continue until the end of the lease term or until the premises are re-rented, whichever occurs first) and, pursuant to Arizona Revised Statutes, Title 33, Chapter 8, Section 33-361(A), enter and take possession thereof, or (2) file a lawsuit to recover possession, rent and damages. If you have any question, you may contact _____ at

_____ .

                                    _____

                                    _____

                                    _____

This notice delivered this date _____   via:
☐ Certified mail
☐ Regular first class mail
☐ Hand delivered

                       Acknowledgment of hand delivery and receipt hereof:

                _____

                    (signature of tenant)   (date)

NOTICE OF TERMINATION

_____

_____

_____

Notice to Tenant,   Date:_____

　　　You have:

　　　☐　　Failed or refused to remit all due, but as yet unpaid, rent
　　　　　and other amounts owing under the lease;

　　　☐　　Violated a material provision of your lease, specifically:

　　　　　_____

　　　　　_____

　　　You are hereby notified that your landlord has terminated your right to possess and occupy the premises and, pursuant to Arizona Revised Statutes, Title 33, Chapter 8, Section 33-361(A), has re-entered the premises and taken possession thereof. This action has been taken by the landlord to mitigate his/her damages. Reasonable efforts will be made to re-rent the premises on your behalf. The landlord has not and will not accept a surrender of the premises. Although your right to possess and occupy the premises has been terminated, your lease has not been terminated and your obligations (financial and otherwise) under the lease shall continue until the end of the lease term or until the premises are re-rented, whichever occurs first.

　　　Pursuant to A.R.S. § 33-361(D), the landlord has a lien on all personal property located on/in the leased premises and may cause the same to be sold at public auction if all amounts due (if any) are not paid within sixty days hereof. To reclaim your personal property and/or arrange payment of any amounts which may remain due, contact _____ at _____.

　　　The locks to the premises have been changed and your right to enter and/or occupy the premises terminated. If you enter (or attempt to enter) these premises, criminal charges may be brought against you for breaking and entering, criminal damage, burglary, trespass, and/or any other charges warranted by the facts.

　　　　　　　_____

　　　　　　　_____

　　　　　　　_____

This notice delivered this date _____ via:
☐ Certified mail
☐ Regular first class mail
☐ Hand delivered

　　　　　　　Acknowledgment of hand delivery and receipt hereof:

　　　　　　　_____
　　　　　　　(signature of tenant)　　　　　　　　　　(date)

FIVE-DAY NOTICE TO PAY OR QUIT

_____

_____

_____

Notice to Tenant,   Date:_____

    Pursuant to Arizona Revised Statutes, Title 33, Chapter 8, Section 33-361(A), you are hereby tendered five-days written notice to remit all due, but as yet unpaid, rent and other amounts owing, in the amount of: _$_____ (calculated through_____). The stated amount is calculated as follows:

    $_____   Rent for _____

    $_____   Late charges (_____)

    $_____   Fee for preparing and serving Five-Day Notice.

    $_____   Total

The stated "Total" is exclusive of future accruing costs. Additional charges accrue after the date specified above at the daily rate of _$_____ .

    In the event full payment is not tendered within five days after receipt of this notice, your Rental Agreement will be terminated and an eviction action filed against you to recover possession of the premises, rent, late fees, and any other amounts due under the rental agreement or available by law, including attorney's fees and court costs. Full payment within the five-day period will reinstate the rental agreement. Assuming this notice is delivered on the date specified above, **THE FIFTH DAY FALLS ON: _____ .**

    Alternatively, you may vacate the premises on or before the fifth day. Vacating the premises, however, will not relieve you from liability for the outstanding balance. In the event you have any questions, please contact me.

_____

_____

_____

This notice delivered this date _____ via:
☐ Certified mail
☐ Regular first class mail
☐ Hand delivered

Acknowledgment of hand delivery and receipt hereof:

_____
(signature of tenant)   (date)

DISPOSITION OF DEPOSITS

The following discloses the disposition of your deposit(s):

DEPOSITS

Nonrefundable deposits:

Cleaning deposit (Nonrefundable)	$	_____
Other	$	_____
Total:	$	_____
Amount refundable:	$	**_0.00_**

Refundable deposits:

Cleaning deposit (Refundable)	$	_____
Security deposit (Refundable)	$	_____
Total:	$	_____

DEDUCTIONS

Unpaid rent	$_____
Late charges	$_____
Damages	$_____
Other _____	$_____
Other _____	$_____
Other _____	$_____

TOTAL DEDUCTIONS	$ _____
AMOUNT OF REFUNDABLE DEPOSITS:	$ _____

☐ Refund Due to Tenant   ☐ Balance Due to Landlord; Payment immediately due.

This notice delivered this date _____ via: _____

_____

☐ Certified mail

☐ Regular first class mail   _____

☐ Hand delivered   Acknowledgment of hand delivery and receipt hereof:

_____

(signature of tenant)	(date)

QUICK
REFERENCE
SECTION

The Quick Reference Section is divided into two sections: Section I — Questions and Answers, and Section II — Procedures. The Question and Answer Section will give you quick, practical answers to each question and then refer you to the section of the book that discusses that particular issue or topic in depth. Frequently arising questions have been categorized into eight major areas. Listed on the next page are these eight major areas and the questions addressed within each area. The Procedures Section will give you step-by-step instructions for specific procedures.

I. QUESTIONS AND ANSWERS

A. THE ARIZONA RESIDENTIAL LANDLORD AND TENANT ACT.
- Does the Act apply to me?
- Where does the Act apply?
- Does the Act apply to my on-site manager?
- Can I call all my tenants "on-site managers" and have the Act not apply?
- Must an out-of-state owner/landlord have a local property manger?

B. THE APPLICATION.
- How do I get good tenants?
- May I discriminate against certain people when evaluating whether or not to accept an applicant as a tenant?

C. FORMS.
- What are the most important forms?
- Where do I get forms?

D. THE RENTAL AGREEMENT.
- Is an oral rental agreement binding?
- What "must," "should" and "cannot" be in a written rental agreement?
- Should I insist on a long-term lease or is month-to-month better?
- What if the tenant signs the rental agreement, but fails to move-in?

E. DEPOSITS.
- What is the maximum security deposit I can collect?
- Must I pay the tenant interest on his/her security deposit during the time that I hold it?

F. COMMON TENANT PROBLEMS.
- What legal advice can you offer landlords?
- What business advice can you offer landlords?
- How do I handle a noisy tenant?
- What are some other common problems and how do I handle them?

G. NONPAYMENT OF RENT.
- What do I do when rent is late?
- How do I handle a tenant that repeatedly pays rent late?
- May I shut off the tenant's utilities for non-payment of rent?
- May I lock a tenant out of his/her unit and/or seize his/her personal property for non-payment of rent?
- Can a tenant legally make repairs and deduct the cost of repairs from his/her rent?

H. EVICTION.
- How do I serve a notice to the tenant?
- When can I serve the Five-Day Notice to Pay or Quit?
- What must be contained in the Five-Day Notice to Pay or Quit for the notice to be legally sufficient?
- Other than nonpayment of rent, what other basis is there for evicting a tenant?
- How do I know whether a noncompliance is: a material noncompliance, a noncompliance that materially affects health and safety, or an immediate and irreparable breach?
- How do I evict a tenant?
- In which court do I file my Special Detainer action: small claims, justice or superior court?
- How do I know which court has **personal jurisdiction** over the tenants/-defendants?

II. PROCEDURES

- What are the procedural steps for evicting a tenant?
  1. Eviction Process for: Nonpayment of Rent.
  2. Eviction Process for:
      - (1) Material Noncompliance with the Rental Agreement;
      - (2) Noncompliance with the Rental Agreement that Materially Affects Health and Safety; and
      - (3) Material and Irreparable Breach of the Rental Agreement.
- What do I do *AFTER* the eviction process?
- What are the procedural steps for issuing 5-Day and 10-Day Notices to tenants?
- What are the procedural steps for reclaiming an abandoned rental unit?
- What are the procedural steps for conducting a public sale of abandoned personal property?
- What are the procedural steps for collecting money from tenants?
- What if the tenant files bankruptcy?

I. QUESTIONS AND ANSWERS

A.   **THE ARIZONA RESIDENTIAL LANDLORD AND TENANT ACT.**

● **Does the Act apply to me?**

The Act applies to the rental of dwelling units. Therefore, generally speaking, if you rent a residential dwelling, the Act applies to you, but there are some exclusions.

See Chapter 2, Section C.

● **Where does the Act apply?**

The Act is state law and is applicable statewide. The only exceptions are instances where state law is preempted by federal law (i.e., on Indian reservations, Section 8 housing, etc.).

See Chapter 2, Section C.

● **Does the Act apply to my on-site manager?**

Maybe. On-site managers are specifically excluded from the scope of the Act. Nevertheless, you may elect to have the Act apply if you so desire. Furthermore, most landlords have their on-site managers sign the same form of rental agreement as the regular tenants sign. Most rental agreements state that the Act applies. Consequently, by having your on-site manager sign your usual rental agreement form, you have elected to have the Act apply in a case where it need not apply.

See Chapter 2, Section C(1).

● **Can I call all my tenants "on-site managers" and have the Act not apply?**

No.

See Chapter 2, Section C(1).

● **Must an out-of-state owner/landlord have a local property manger?**

No, but if you do not have a local agent, the tenant may serve you with notices and court documents by sending them to you via certified mail and by delivering a copy to the Arizona Secretary of State. As a practical matter, it makes sense to have a local agent because s/he can be more responsive to complaints, etc. Also, if there is an eviction, the local manager can provide testimony about the relevant facts, otherwise the out-of-state owner will need to personally appear to give testimony.

See Chapter 3, Section B(2)(c).

B.   THE APPLICATION.

● **How do I get good tenants?**

To get good tenants, you must properly prepare your business, properly prepare the rental unit, properly prepare the surrounding area (i.e., the apartment complex), effectively attract large numbers of qualified applicants, gather and evaluate the applications submitted, and then select the best and most qualified applicant.

> *See* Chapters 2 and 3.

● **May I discriminate against certain people when evaluating whether or not to accept an applicant as a tenant?**

Yes, but you <u>cannot</u> discriminate against an applicant based on race, color, religion, national origin, sex, handicap or familial status (i.e., because the applicant has children). You may discriminate against an applicant on any other basis. For example, you may deny to accept an applicant because s/he has insufficient income, drives a motorcycle or because s/he is a lawyer.

> *See* Chapter 3, Section E(1).

C.   FORMS.

● **What are the most important forms?**

The rental agreement is the most important form. It is the source of all your legal rights and remedies, except the meager rights and remedies provided by the Act. The rental agreement forms available from the local stationery store do not favor the landlord, are too generic, contain too many blank spaces and, as a general rule, will not do an adequate job of protecting your rights and property. **Spend a few dollars; have a good rental agreement drafted *specifically for you* by an attorney**.

> *See* Chapter 2, Sections B and D.

The Tenant Application, Property Inspection Checklist and Tenant Information Sheet are also important because they are used every time you sign up a new tenant and because of the information they capture. In 1995, the Property Inspection Checklist became a required form. Because of the potential consequences to children, the pool safety notice and the lead-based paint disclosure form are also very important.

> *See* Chapter 2, Section E.

- **Where do I get forms?**

Your rental agreement should be drafted by your own attorney; s/he can also provide you with the other forms that you will need. Alternatively, you may obtain virtually all other forms (except for the rental agreement) from a local stationery store (these other forms are normally adequate). *See* Chapter 2, Sections B, D and E. You may also use the forms contained in the Arizona Landlord's Deskbook.

> *See* Appendix B.

D. THE RENTAL AGREEMENT.

- **Is an oral rental agreement binding?**

Yes, but I strongly recommend against oral rental agreements.

> *See* Chapter 2, Section D.

- **What must, should and cannot be in a written rental agreement?**

A written rental agreement ***must***: disclose the name of the manager and the owner or owner's agent; inform the tenant that a copy of the Act is available free of charge from the Arizona Secretary of State's Office; inform the tenant that s/he may be present during the move-out inspection; be completely filled out; state which deposits are nonrefundable and state the purpose for each nonrefundable deposit, charge or fee; be in writing, if longer than one year; and a signed copy must be delivered to the tenant. In addition, the landlord *must* provide the tenant with a move-in inspection form when tenancy begins.

The rental agreement ***should***: be written; be comprehensive; provide for abandonment; describe the tenant's maintenance obligations, limitations on alterations/modifications; provide for regular inspections; provide for payment of expenses incurred to bring legal action, late fees, notice fees and how partial payments are to be applied; include a liquidated damages provision, a jury waiver provision, a lead based paint disclosure, and a pool safety notice (if the property has a pool); and allow for rental tax increases.

The rental agreement ***cannot***: require the tenant to waive his/her rights, include any provision contrary to the Act, agree to pay attorney's fees (with an exception), agree to limit the landlord's liability, and/or require a security deposit greater than one and one-half month's rent.

> *See* Chapter 2, Section D. *See also* Appendix A, Checklist 2.

- **Should I insist on a long-term lease or is month-to-month better?**

  The answer to this question is controlled by the type of rental units you own/manage.

    See Chapter 3, Section F.

- **What if the tenant signs the rental agreement, but fails to move-in?**

  The tenant has broken the lease. The landlord may apply the security deposit to the payment of accrued rent and the amount of damages suffered as a result of the breach, subject to the landlord's obligation to mitigate (i.e., reduce) his/her damages. If the rental agreement includes a reasonable and enforceable liquidated damages provision, this amount may be deducted from the security deposit *instead* of the foregoing damages. In either case, the landlord must still send an itemized statement of deductions made from the tenant's security deposit within fourteen days.

    See Chapter 2, Section D(2)(l) (liquidated damages).

E.   DEPOSITS.

- **What is the maximum security deposit I can collect?**

  You cannot collect a security deposit equal to more than one and one-half month's rent. A security deposit *does not* include *non*refundable cleaning or redecorating fees, but *does* include refundable cleaning and redecorating deposits (or any other type of refundable deposit, i.e., refundable pet deposit). Therefore, in addition to the security deposit, you may also require the tenant to pay a "reasonable" charge or fee for cleaning and/or redecorating.

    See Chapter 2, Section D(4).

- **Must I pay the tenant interest on his/her security deposit during the time that I hold it?**

  There is no requirement in the Act for the landlord to pay interest on security deposits.

    See Chapter 2, Section D(4).

F. **COMMON TENANT PROBLEMS.**

● **What legal advice can you offer landlords?**

The best legal advice you will ever receive is advice that helps to prevent and/or avoid problems and litigation. Toward that end, I strongly recommend that you: (1) get a lawyer, (2) get the right lawyer, (3) have this lawyer prepare or review your rental agreement and other forms, (4) discuss asset protection with your attorney, and (5) review your insurance needs with your insurance agent.

See Chapter 2, Section B.

● **What business advice can you offer landlords?**

Be honest, straightforward, businesslike, and authoritative. Keep your business procedures and the language in your forms as "simple" as is reasonably possible. Stay up-to-date on the laws that affect you. Learn to err conservatively. These general guidelines will help you avoid problems and litigation and go a long way toward building and maintaining good rapport with your tenants.

See Chapter 2, Section A.

● **How do I handle a noisy tenant?**

If your rental agreement addresses noise, merely follow the remedies prescribed by your rental agreement. If not and the tenant is on a month-to-month tenancy, simply refuse to renew the tenancy. Otherwise, either seek the tenant's voluntary compliance or begin documenting your file with complaint forms, etc., to use as evidence in a subsequent eviction proceeding.

See Chapter 4, Section B(3).

● **What are some other common problems and how do I handle them?**

Common problems include: continually late rent payments, "one time" or occasional incidents of late rent, noisy tenants, tenant conflicts with other tenants and/or neighbors, parking problems, vehicle problems, security issues, and accidents/incidents.

See Chapter 4, Section B.

G.   NONPAYMENT OF RENT.

• **What do I do when rent is late?**

Serve the tenant with a Five-Day Notice to Pay or Quit.

> *See* Chapter 4, Section B(1) and B(2); Chapter 5, Section B.

• **How do I handle a tenant that repeatedly pays rent late?**

Either assess and collect late fees and tolerate the problem or decide that you will not tolerate the problem. If the latter, and the tenant is on a month-to-month tenancy, simply refuse to renew the tenancy. If the tenant is on a long-term lease and you have properly documented your file, you may be able to evict the tenant.

> *See* Chapter 4, Section B(1).

• **May I shut off the tenant's utilities for non-payment of rent?**

No, no, no (get the picture?).

> *See* Chapter 5, Section B(1).

• **May I lock a tenant out of his/her unit and/or seize his/her personal property for non-payment of rent?**

No. Distraint for rent is prohibited under the Act.

> *See* Chapter 5, Section B(1).

• **Can a tenant legally make repairs to the unit and deduct the cost of repairs from his/her rent?**

Yes, but the tenant must provide the landlord with a written notice of his/her intent to effect such repairs, the repairs must be done by a licensed contractor and the amount of the deduction may not exceed the greater of $300.00 or one-half month's rent.

> *See* Chapter 5, Section B(3)(a) and B(3)(b).

H.   EVICTION.

● **How do I serve a notice to the tenant?**

All notices to the tenant should, and in most cases must, be written. A written notice may be hand-delivered by you or someone on your behalf or may be sent via certified mail, return receipt requested.

> *See* Chapter 5, Section B(4).

● **When can I serve the Five-Day Notice to Pay or Quit?**

You may serve the Five-Day Notice on the first day after rent is due and remains unpaid. For example, if rent is due on the first day of the month, you may serve the Five-Day Notice on the second day of the month, even though your rental agreement provides that rent is not delinquent until the fifth day of the month.

> *See* Chapter 5, Section B(3)(d). *See also* Quick Reference Section, Procedures Section, Flowchart and discussion for Nonpayment of Rent.

● **What must be contained in the Five-Day Notice to Pay or Quit for the notice to be legally sufficient?**

The Five-Day Notice must inform the tenant that rent has not been paid and that the landlord intends to terminate the rental agreement if due and unpaid rent is not paid within five days of the notice.

> *See* Quick Reference Section, Procedures Section, Flowchart and discussion for Nonpayment of Rent. *See also* Appendix B, Form 9.

● **Other than nonpayment of rent, what other basis is there for eviction?**

You do not need any reason to not renew a tenancy. Therefore, if your tenant is on a month-to-month tenancy, you may choose to not renew for any reason whatsoever (any reason that is not discriminatory or retaliatory).

> *See* Chapter 5, Section A.

Eviction must be based on one of four categories of tenant conduct: (1) a material noncompliance with the rental agreement, which includes material falsification of information by the tenant on the rental application, (2) a noncompliance that materially affects health and safety, (3) a breach that is both material and irreparable and (4) nonpayment of rent.

> *See* Chapter 5, Section B.

- **How do I know whether a noncompliance is: a material noncompliance, a noncompliance that materially affects health and safety, or an immediate and irreparable breach?**

  The purpose for asking this question is to determine the amount of notice you must give (i.e., 5-Day Notice, 10-Day Notice, or a notice of immediate termination). There are many factors to consider and the consequences of issuing the wrong notice may mean being "thrown out of court." Consequently, it is important that you answer this question correctly. The proper approach is contained in Chapter 5.

  > *See* Chapter 5, Section B(3).

- **How do I evict a tenant?**

  In short, you must first know what you can and cannot do. Then you must serve the appropriate written notice. Then you must select the proper court. And, finally, you must file and prosecute the Special Detainer action. If you have never been through the entire process, you should consult with your attorney. For those who have been through the process a few times <u>and</u> who feel confident they can proceed without an attorney, Chapter 5, Section B and the Flowcharts in the Quick Reference Section, provide thorough discussions of the eviction process; the two <u>flowcharts</u> may be especially helpful.

  > *See* Chapter 5, Section B(1) and B(2) (what you can and cannot do).
  > *See* Chapter 5, Section B(3) (which notice to serve).
  > *See* Chapter 5, Section B(5) (selecting the proper court).
  > *See* Chapter 5, Section B(6) and B(7) (prosecuting the Special Detainer).

- **In which court do I file my Special Detainer action: small claims, justice or superior court?**

  You cannot file a Special Detainer action in small claims court.[328] Justice court and superior court have concurrent jurisdiction, which means you may file in either, **but** if the monthly rental amount is more than $1,000.00 per month **or** the amount you are trying to recover from the tenant is more than $5,000, then you **must** file in superior court.[329]

  > *See* Chapter 5, Section B(5).

- **How do I know which court has *personal jurisdiction* over the tenants?**

  If you are filing a Special Detainer action, the rental unit and the place where the tenant/defendant resides should be the same. If you are bringing a civil action against a former tenant (or anyone else, for that

---

[328] A.R.S. § 22-503(B)(3) (West. Supp. 1998).

[329] A.R.S. § 22-201(C) (West Supp. 1998).

matter), then the location of the rental unit and the defendant's present residence will be different and may even be in a different county or state. If you are filing in superior court, you may file in the superior court for the county in which the rental property was located or the county in which the defendant now resides. If you are filing in justice court, you may file in the justice court that has jurisdiction over the rental property or the justice court that has jurisdiction over the property where the defendant now resides. (Note: the justice court clerks are pretty good about telling you whether or not a particular property address in located in their jurisdiction; *see* Appendix D for a list of justice courts in Arizona, including phone numbers).

See Chapter 5, Section B(5).

II. PROCEDURES

- **What are the procedural steps for evicting a tenant?**

This is a short and seemingly simple question; the answer is long and involves many steps. First, you must first know what you can and **cannot** do. Second, you must decide which notice is appropriate to your circumstances and serve it upon the tenant. Third, you must select the proper court. Finally, you must file and prosecute the Special Detainer action. If you have never been through the entire process of evicting a tenant, you should consult with your attorney. For those who have been through the process a few times <u>and</u> who feel confident they can proceed without an attorney, the following information should see you through each step.

The procedure you follow to evict a tenant will turn on whether you are evicting because of: (1) nonpayment of rent or (2) some other type of noncompliance with the rental agreement. Following are two flowcharts. The first shows you the significant events of the eviction process for nonpayment of rent. I have included a few "tips" that apply to the nonpayment of rent situation that may not apply to other situations. The second flowchart discusses the significant events to evict a tenant for: (1) material noncompliance with the rental agreement, including material falsification of information on the rental application by the tenant, (2) noncompliance with the rental agreement that materially affects health and safety, and (3) material and irreparable breach of the rental agreement. Each flowchart is followed by a thorough discussion of each step in the eviction process.

1.   **Eviction Process for: <u>Nonpayment of Rent</u>.**

Cross Reference:
- Nonpayment of rent, Chapter 5, Section B(3)(d)
- What you can and cannot do to evict a tenant, Chapter 5, Sections B(1) and B(2)
- Which notice must be served on the tenant, Chapter 5, Sec. B(3)
- How the notice must be served, Chapter 5, Section B(4)
- In which court to file the Special Detainer action, Chapter 5, Section B(5)

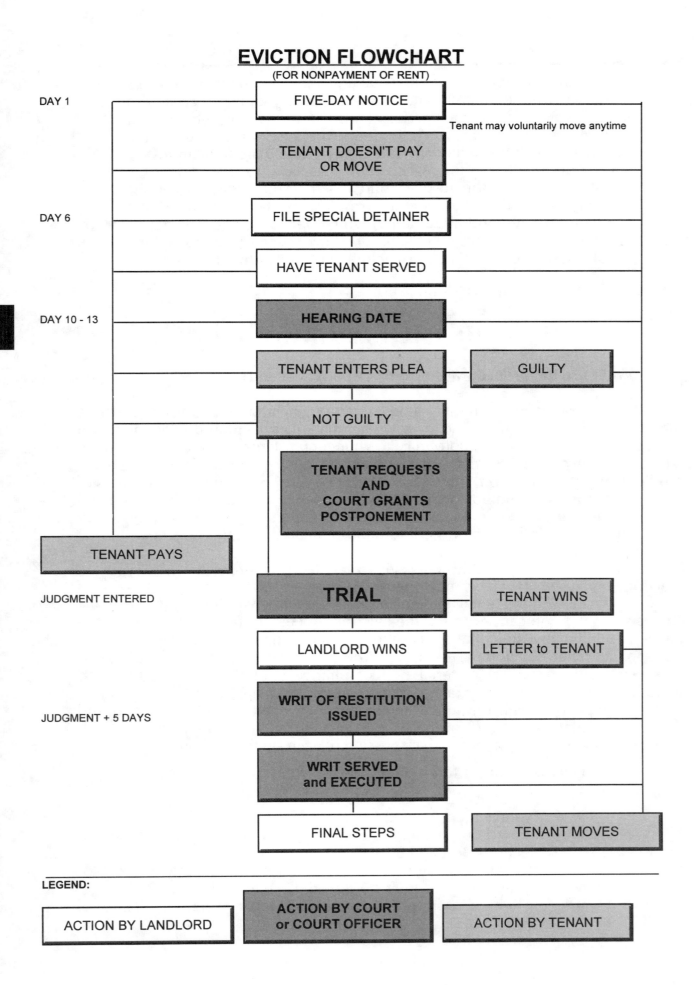

EVICTION FLOWCHART
(FOR NONPAYMENT OF RENT)

DAY 1 — FIVE-DAY NOTICE

Tenant may voluntarily move anytime

TENANT DOESN'T PAY OR MOVE

DAY 6 — FILE SPECIAL DETAINER

HAVE TENANT SERVED

DAY 10 - 13 — HEARING DATE

TENANT ENTERS PLEA → GUILTY

NOT GUILTY

TENANT REQUESTS AND COURT GRANTS POSTPONEMENT

TENANT PAYS

JUDGMENT ENTERED — TRIAL → TENANT WINS

LANDLORD WINS → LETTER to TENANT

JUDGMENT + 5 DAYS — WRIT OF RESTITUTION ISSUED

WRIT SERVED and EXECUTED

FINAL STEPS   TENANT MOVES

LEGEND:

ACTION BY LANDLORD | ACTION BY COURT or COURT OFFICER | ACTION BY TENANT

Before beginning, be sure that you understand: what you can and cannot do to evict a tenant, which notice must be served on the tenant, how the notice must be served, and in which court you should/must file the Special Detainer action. Then, and only then, should you proceed.

The first flowchart is to be used only when you are evicting a tenant for nonpayment of rent. The second flowchart is to be used when you are evicting a tenant for a material noncompliance with the rental agreement, a noncompliance that materially affects health and safety, and/or a material and irreparable breach of the rental agreement. The flowcharts and accompanying discussion are similar, but there are some important distinctions -- make sure you use the correct flowchart. Both flowcharts have been carefully engineered to help you achieve your goal -- evict the tenant.

Each box depicted on the flowchart is fully discussed on the following pages and linked to a precise or approximate time when the action must or should occur. Again, if you have any questions, you should call your attorney.

The first flowchart and the following steps have been carefully designed to elicit voluntary payment, if possible, or, alternatively, to either convince the tenant to vacate the premises voluntarily or to compel involuntary eviction of the tenant for nonpayment of rent and reacquire possession of your rental unit. Naturally, all steps comply with applicable Arizona law, but some steps serve strategic purposes rather than satisfy legal requirements.

FIVE-DAY NOTICE

TIME FRAME: Day 1

Step 1: Prepare a *Five-Day Notice to Pay or Quit* (a.k.a. *Five-Day Notice*). For a Five-Day Notice to be legally sufficient it must give notice of: (1) the nonpayment of rent and (2) the landlord's intention to terminate the rental agreement if rent is not paid

FIVE-DAY NOTICE

within the five-day period.[330] In addition, I recommend that the Five-Day Notice show: (1) the amount of past due rent, (2) the total amount of late charges accumulated to date __and__ (3) the amount of late charges that accrue each day. The purpose for showing the total accumulated late charges and the daily late charges is to bring to the tenant's attention the fact that s/he has the power to stop additional late charges from accruing simply by paying the amount due. The predominate reason tenants don't pay the rent is because they have some other debt that needs to be paid. What they fail to realize is that their debt to you is accumulating much larger late charges and at a faster rate than their other competing debt. By showing the daily late charge, you prompt the tenant to make the "right" decision (i.e., pay the

---

330 A.R.S. § 33-1368(B) (West Supp. 1998).

past due rent and let the other debt go unpaid). *See* Appendix B, Form 9, for a sample Five-Day Notice.

Step 2: Serve the Five-Day Notice on the first day that rent is past due. Do not wait a few days. Be consistent. If your tenants know that they can be late a few days without consequence, they will be late. By being methodical and predictable, your tenants get in the habit of paying the rent before it is past due. NOTE: If your rental agreement provides for late fees and/or a "notice fee," you should assess and collect these charges as well. (*See* Chapter 2, Section D(2)).

The Act provides that after a Special Detainer action has been filed, the tenant may reinstate the rental agreement only by paying past due rent, late fees, attorneys' fees and court costs.[331] Similarly, the tenant has an absolute right to reinstate the rental agreement before you file the Special Detainer action by paying all past due rent, late charges, and any other charges stated in the written rental agreement. Enforce your rights; if the tenant decides to reinstate, collect all charges. If the tenant only has part of the amount due and you want to accept a partial payment (you are not required to accept less than full payment), you are free to do so, but to protect your rights you must have the tenant execute a "Partial Payment Agreement." (*See* Appendix B, Form 5). Your rental agreement should provide for how partial payments are to be applied. If not, the Partial Payment Agreement should specify how the partial payment is to be applied, thereby protecting your rights. Partial payments should be applied as follows: first, to legal fees and court costs, then to accrued interest on any amounts owed to the landlord, then to late fees, then to amounts owed for damages to the property, then to any other amounts owed by the tenant to the landlord, then to unpaid past due rent, and finally to prepaid rent. If your rental agreement provides for how partial payments are to be applied, it should also provide that <u>you are not obligated to accept partial payments</u>. This will allow you to refuse to accept a "token payment." If the tenant thereafter fails to pay the balance due on the date specified in the Partial Payment Agreement, you *do not* need to serve another Five-Day Notice to Pay or Quit,[332] you may merely proceed with the eviction process.

TENANT PAYS

TIME FRAME: Anytime, up to entry of judgment on the trial date.

The tenant can stop the eviction process by paying all amounts due, including all past rent, late fees, attorneys' fees and court costs; the landlord <u>must</u> accept tender of said payment by tenant.[333] If this is a recurring problem

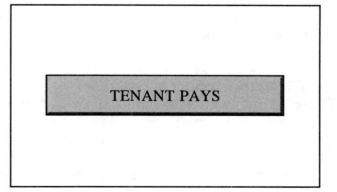

---

331   A.R.S. § 33-1368(B) (West Supp. 1998).

332   A.R.S. § 33-1371(A) (West Supp. 1998).

333   A.R.S. § 33-1368(B) (West Supp. 1998).

(i.e., repeated late payments) and your rental agreement defines repeated late payment of rent as a material noncompliance (i.e., three late payments within one year), you *may* be able to proceed with a Special Detainer action for a material noncompliance with the rental agreement if the tenant commits a subsequent similar noncompliance (i.e., late payment of rent) during the "term of the lease" (*see* Chapter 5, Section B(3)(a)).[334] You should consult your attorney before proceeding under this theory.

After entry of judgment in the landlord's favor, the tenant is not entitled to reinstate the rental agreement and the landlord is not obligated to let the tenant remain in the rental unit after tendering full payment of all amounts due. Naturally, the landlord may elect to allow the tenant to reinstate the rental agreement is s/he wishes. Do not, however, accept any payments from the tenant after entry of judgment and before the tenant vacates without having the tenant execute a form that specifies the terms upon which payment is being accepted (i.e., payment being accepted with the understanding that the tenant may stay or with the understanding that the tenant must still vacate). *See* Appendix B, Form 5.

TENANT MOVES

TIME FRAME: Anytime prior to execution of Writ of Restitution.

TENANT MOVES

Naturally, anytime from day one to the day the Writ of Restitution is executed, the tenant can voluntarily move out. This will not necessarily stop the eviction process <u>and</u> you may still have a <u>separate</u> legal cause of action against the tenant for past due rent, money damages for breach of the rental agreement, damages to the rental unit, etc. To proceed against the tenant for these claims, you must initiate a separate lawsuit. The purpose of a Special Detainer action is to restore <u>possession</u> of the rental property to the landlord; if the tenant moves, possession is restored and the court may dismiss the Special Detainer action. Go to Chapter 6, Section A, filing a lawsuit against the tenant for damages.

IMPORTANT NOTE: You should be aware of the distinction between: (1) a tenant voluntarily moving out and (2) the tenant offering to surrender possession <u>and</u> the landlord accepting surrender of possession of the premises. The tenant's conduct of voluntarily moving out <u>does not</u> automatically equate to an acceptance of surrender of possession of the premises by the landlord. Why is this important? A Special Detainer action is a lawsuit to recover possession of rental property. Consequently, if the tenant voluntarily surrenders possession of the rental unit <u>and you accept</u> the surrender of possession before the hearing date, the court will dismiss the Special Detainer action. Why is that important? Because you lose the opportunity to get a

---

judgment against the tenant for past due rent. Moreover, acceptance of surrender by the landlord may be (and usually is) deemed a waiver of the landlord's right to pursue the tenant for <u>all</u> damages (i.e., past due rent, damages to the unit, etc.). This is why it is **very important** that you not accept surrender of the premises unless you are fully prepared to give up all rights to pursue this tenant. If you want the Special Detainer action to go forward (i.e., you want a money judgment against the tenant for past due rent), do not accept surrender of possession of the rental unit. Naturally, the tenant may voluntarily move out anytime s/he wishes, but the landlord is not required to accept surrender of possession of the premises. As long as the landlord does not have possession, the Special Detainer action may go forward. "Acceptance" of surrender turns on the landlord's intent. For example, abandonment of the premises by the tenant and depositing the keys in the landlord's mail slot does not "force" the landlord to accept surrender of the premises.

FILE SPECIAL DETAINER

TIME FRAME: Day 6

You must wait five days (calendar days, not business days) <u>after</u> serving the Five-Day Notice before you may file the Special Detainer action; therefore, the sixth day after service of the Five-Day Notice is the earliest day that you may file the lawsuit. Do not count the day that the Five-Day Notice is served. Example: Five-Day Notice is served on the second day of the month; the earliest the Special Detainer action may be filed is the eighth day of the month.

FILE SPECIAL DETAINER

Have the Five-Day Notice personally served. If you cannot personally serve the Five-Day Notice, you may serve it via registered or certified mail, return receipt requested, but you must then add five days (for mailing) to the five days in the notice. If, however, the tenant signs for the notice in less than five days, you may begin counting the five days in the notice on the day after the tenant signed for delivery of the letter. Example 1: The Five-Day Notice is mailed via certified mail, return receipt requested, on the second day of the month; the tenant does not sign for the letter; the earliest the Special Detainer action may be filed is the thirteenth day of the month (five days for mailing and five days in the Five-Day Notice). Example 2: The Five-Day Notice is mailed via certified mail, return receipt requested, on the second day of the month; the tenant signs for the letter on the fourth day of the month; the earliest the Special Detainer action may be filed is the tenth day of the month (five days after delivery of the notice on the fourth day of the month).

File the Special Detainer action against the tenant on the sixth day after service of the Five-Day Notice. Again, be methodical and predictable. The Act provides that after a Special Detainer action has been filed, the tenant may reinstate the rental agree-

agreement only by paying past due rent, late fees, attorneys' fees and court costs.[335] Enforce your rights; if the tenant decides to reinstate, collect all charges – the past due rent, the late charges, etc. If s/he only has part of the amount due and you want to accept a partial payment (you are not required to accept less than full payment), you are free to do so, but to protect your rights you must have the tenant execute a "Partial Payment Agreement." (*See* Appendix B, Form 5). You are not obligated to accept a partial payment. If the tenant thereafter fails to pay the balance due on the date specified in the Partial Payment Agreement, you *do not* need to serve another Five-Day Notice to Pay or Quit.[336] Merely proceed with the eviction action.

HAVE TENANT SERVED

TIME FRAME: Hearing date, minus two (2) business days.

The **summons** and **complaint** must be served on the tenant. The complaint is the legal document that you filed with the court to institute the Special Detainer action. The summons commands the tenant to appear in court on a particular date and time.

```
HAVE TENANT SERVED
```

Service of the summons and complaint is known as **service of process**. Service of process must be served by a person authorized by law to deliver legal papers. Typically, this is the Sheriff or a private **process server**. Service must be completed at least two business days (not calendar days) before the entry of the tenant's plea on the hearing date/trial date. The hearing and/or trial date (also known as the "return date") is entered on the summons by the clerk of the court at the time the complaint is filed and the summons issued. Procedural Note: Call your process server and give him/her the papers to serve on the day you file the Special Detainer action. Some process servers will even pick up the summons and complaint (after you have filled out and signed the documents), file the Special Detainer action on your behalf with the court and then serve the summons and complaint on the tenant (this will save you a trip to the courthouse – you know, that incredibly efficient place where you never have to wait and are greeted by scores of friendly, courteous people). If you anticipate that the tenants will evade service (a common occurrence), instruct the process server to immediately make an attempt at service and, if unsuccessful, to "post and mail." "Post and mail," means to post a copy of the summons and complaint on the property and to mail a copy via certified mail, return receipt requested. The problem, however, is that for "post and mail" to be effective, the summons and complaint must be mailed within one day of issuance of the summons.[337] Therefore, you and the process server must act promptly.

---

[335] A.R.S. § 33-1368(B) (West Supp. 1998).

[336] A.R.S. § 33-1371(A) (West Supp. 1998).

[337] A.R.S. § 33-1377(B) (West Supp. 1998).

HEARING DATE

TIME FRAME: Day 10 - 13

"Hearing date," "trial date," or "return date" - this date is entered on the summons by the clerk of the court at the time the complaint is filed and the summons issued. This date cannot be less than three business days nor more than six business days from the date

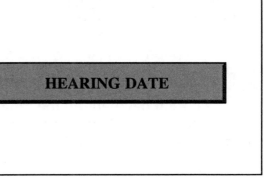

HEARING DATE

the summons was issued.[338] Go to court on the hearing date scheduled for your Special Detainer action. Do not miss this date. If you miss this date without a <u>really</u> good excuse and/or prior notice to the court to continue the hearing date, the case will be dismissed and you must file another Special Detainer complaint, pay another filing fee and incur several days of delay. You may also be liable for the tenant's defense costs (if any), if the tenant appears and you do not.

TENANT ENTERS PLEA

Entry of the tenant's plea occurs on the hearing date. The tenant will enter his plea – guilty or not guilty. If guilty, judgment is immediately entered for the landlord; if not guilty, the matter is set for trial.

TENANT ENTERS PLEA

TENANT REQUESTS AND COURT GRANTS POSTPONEMENT

TENANT REQUESTS AND COURT GRANTS POSTPONEMENT

Only upon "good cause" shown, may the tenant request a postponement of the trial. If the postponement is granted, the postponement may be no longer than three (3) business days in justice court or five (5) business days in superior court.[339] In justice court, if a request for postponement is not made or not granted, trial may (and typically does) immediately follow entry of the tenant's plea on the hearing date. In superior court, if a request for postponement is not made or granted, a trial date is scheduled for a few days later.

---

338 A.R.S. § 33-1377(B) (West Supp. 1998).

339 A.R.S. § 33-1377(C) (West Supp. 1998).

TRIAL

TIME FRAME: Day 10 - 13, or
if postponement granted, Day 14 - 19

In justice court, unless a postponement was granted, trial immediately follows entry of the plea. In superior court, whether or not a postponement is granted, trial is scheduled for a few days later.

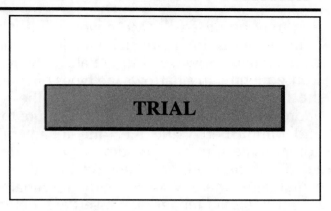

Before you walk into the court room for trial, be sure that you know this information: (1) why you are evicting tenant (i.e., nonpayment of rent); (2) when rent was last paid; (3) whether the written rental agreement provides for late fees; (4) the precise amount of late fees accrued through the "periodic rental period"[340] (which, generally, means through the end of the month {see example, below}; be prepared to explain your calculations); (5) the date you served your written notice (i.e., the 5-Day Notice) and have an extra copy with you; (6) how the notice was served (i.e., hand-delivered, certified mail, etc.); (7) when the tenant was served with the Special Detainer summons and complaint; (8) how service of the Special Detainer summons and complaint was accomplished (i.e., personal service, "nail & mail"); (9) any other facts specific to your eviction action; and (10) the precise amount of rent that is presently due and unpaid.

> Example: The tenant has a one year lease that terminates December 31. Rent is paid at the beginning of each month. Today (the day of trial) is September 10. Rent was last paid on July 1. Rent is $600.00. The precise amount of rent that is presently due and unpaid, through "periodic rental period" is $1,200.00 ($600 for August; $600 for the entire month of September).[341]

The purpose of a forcible detainer action is to provide landlords with a speedy legal proceeding to recover possession of the rental property.[342] Traditionally, counterclaims were not allowed and the only issue the court would examine in a Special Detainer action was which party was entitled to immediate possession of the premises.[343] The court did not consider issues regarding who had the right to title.[344] Recent case law, however, indicates that, under appropriate facts, issues relating to

---

340 A.R.S. § 33-1377(F) (West Supp. 1998).

341 A.R.S. § 33-1377(F) (West Supp. 1998).

342 See Andreola v. Arizona Bank, 26 Ariz.App. 556, 550 P.2d 110 (1976).

343 See Taylor v. Stanford, 100 Ariz. 346, 414 P.2d 727 (1966).

344 A.R.S. § 12-1177(A) (West 1994).

title may be raised.[345]   Moreover, the Act specifically allows the tenant to assert counterclaims in a Special Detainer action for nonpayment of rent.[346]   The counterclaim, however, must relate to the rental agreement or arise under the Act.[347] Consequently, this narrows the types of counterclaims that may be asserted against the landlord. As a practical matter, these types of counterclaims will normally address habitability (i.e., landlord's failure to make the rental unit fit and habitable) and diminished value (i.e., the tenant may claim rent should be reduced to compensate him/her for some property defect, which the landlord should have fixed). If there are no counterclaims, then it is merely a question of whether the rental agreement was properly terminated (i.e., was rent due and unpaid?). Nevertheless, a tenant may assert any defense which, if proven, preserves his/her right to possession and/or prevents the landlord from recovering possession.[348] Generally, there are few defenses available to the tenant; these constitute most of the defenses the tenant may raise:

- The Five-Day Notice was improperly served or the Notice itself was defective (i.e., lacks required information).

- The Special Detainer complaint was filed before the five day period (after service of the Five-Day Notice) had expired.

- The summons and complaint were improperly served.

- The tenant no longer lives in the rental unit and the landlord has accepted surrender of possession.

- The Special Detainer action is an unlawful retaliation against the tenant (i.e., retaliation for reporting building code violations, retaliation for the tenant making complaints about the property and/or requesting repairs, etc.).

- There was a justification for nonpayment of rent, based on some type of breach of the rental agreement by the landlord (i.e., failure to repair, failure to provide heat/cooling, etc.).

- The Special Detainer action was filed in the wrong court. *See* Chapter 5, Section B(5).

- The landlord inconsistently enforces the terms in the rental agreement (i.e., s/he allows some tenants to be late with rent, but not others). If the tenant can demonstrate to the court that s/he is the victim of "selective enforcement," the court may dismiss the action.

---

345 *See* <u>Moreno v. Garcia</u>, 169 Ariz. 586, 821 P.2d 247 (App. 1991) (issues of title may be raised in forcible detainer action following foreclosure of property and/or other events specified in A.R.S. § 12-1173.01).

346 A.R.S. § 33-1365(A) (West Supp. 1998).

347 A.R.S. § 33-1365(A) (West Supp. 1998).

348 <u>Magna Inv. & Dev. Corp. v. Brooks Fashion Stores, Inc.</u>, 137 Ariz. 247, 669 P.2d 1024 (App. 1983).

- The language of the rental agreement provides (or suggests) that the landlord **must** accept partial rent payments, but the landlord has refused to accept a partial payment.

Judgment is typically entered for the prevailing party at the conclusion of the trial. If the tenant wins (i.e., s/he shows just cause for nonpayment of rent), the court will enter judgment in the tenant's favor, the tenant will be entitled to retain possession of the unit and the tenant is entitled to judgment against the landlord for his/her attorneys' fees and costs (pretty grim). On the other hand, if the landlord wins, the court will enter judgment in the landlord's favor and the judgment will restore the landlord's legal right of possession to the rental unit. Unfortunately, while the court has now determined that you are entitled to possession of the rental unit, the **Writ of Restitution** – the legal paper that grants you the right to possession -- will not be issued by the court until five calendar days after entry of judgment.[349]

If the landlord fails to appear at the trial, the judge will dismiss the Special Detainer action (that means you start over -- do not pass go, do not collect $200). If the tenant fails to appear at the trial, the landlord must still prove to the judge that s/he is entitled to judgment in his/her favor. Assuming the landlord presents sufficient evidence to prove his/her case, the judge will enter judgment in the landlord's favor. This process is known as obtaining a judgment by default (i.e., in the tenant's absence). If judgment is obtained by default and the tenant was personally served with the summons and complaint or served via "post & mail," the judgment for possession may, at the landlord's option, include a specific monetary amount representing past due rent.[350] Actual eviction (i.e., removal of the tenant from the rental unit) cannot be initiated until a **Writ of Restitution** is issued by the court; the earliest a Writ of Restitution may issue is five calendar days after the date of judgment.

If you get a judgment against the tenant, send copies to the credit reporting agencies and, if you believe it cost-effective, record the judgment in the county recorder's office. This will ensure the judgment shows up on the tenant's credit report and will deter him/her from buying or selling real property in the county in which the judgment is recorded until the judgment is paid.

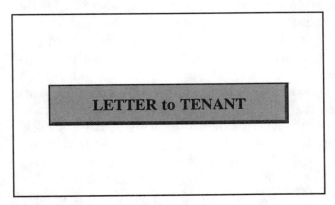

LETTER to TENANT

LETTER TO TENANT

TIME FRAME: Date of Judgment

After judgment is rendered, but before the Writ of Restitution is issued (five calendar days after entry of judgment), send the tenant a copy of the judgment and a letter informing the tenant s/he must vacate within calendar five days

---

349   A.R.S. § 12-1178(C) (West Supp. 1998).

350   A.R.S. § 33-1377(F) (West Supp. 1998).

or you will obtain the Writ of Restitution after the fifth day and direct the Sheriff to forcibly remove him/her. *See* sample letter in Appendix B, Form 15. This letter normally works – I have rarely had to pay the Sheriff to forcibly remove a tenant.

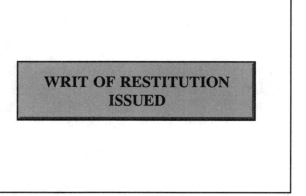

WRIT OF RESTITUTION ISSUED

TIME FRAME: Judgment + 5 days

The Writ of Restitution will not issue until five calendar days (not business days) after entry of judgment. Issuance of the Writ is not automatic; you must request (i.e., pay a fee and fill out a form) the court to issue the Writ of Restitution. Upon receiving the Writ, you must deliver the Writ to the Sheriff or constable.

WRIT SERVED and WRIT EXECUTED

Service and execution of the Writ may be a two-step process. The precise time of service/execution of the Writ of Restitution after you deliver it to the Sheriff or constable will depend on the present backlog – it may be one day; it may be three weeks. Actual eviction, as conducted by the Sheriff or constable, and no one else (not you; not a process server), may not be initiated until a Writ of Restitution is issued by the court and delivered to the Sheriff or constable (the Sheriff serves and executes the Writ in superior court cases; the constable serves and executes the Writ in justice court cases) along with a payment of the fee (the Maricopa County Sheriff requires a $150 deposit to serve the Writ; for constables, the amount of deposit may vary; the final charge, which may be more or less than the deposit, will depend on the number of attempts the Sheriff/constable must make to serve the Writ, the mileage from the courthouse to the property, etc.). The Sheriff/constable has the legal authority to forcibly remove the tenant (a rare occurrence), but the task of removing the tenant's personal property falls on the landlord. If you are actually driven to this step, you should talk with the Sheriff or constable on the telephone before s/he shows up to forcibly remove the tenant. Typically, the Sheriff or constable goes to the tenant's door, tells the tenant to get out within twenty-four (24) hours or s/he will forcibly re-move the tenant and his belongings. This normally produces the desired results (i.e., the tenant moves out). If it does not, the Sheriff or constable shows up the next day and forcibly removes the tenant. Although you may want the tenant's property thrown into the street, this will not happen. The landlord is responsible for arranging for the moving and storage of the tenant's personal property. Numerous companies arranging for the moving and storage of the tenant's personal property. Numerous companies provide this service and are familiar with the process, but this is why you should speak with the Sheriff or constable beforehand, so that you may coordinate the arrangements. You will, however, be required to pay their fees up front. You should also have a locksmith present to immediately re-key the unit. If the tenant subsequently returns and attempts to re-enter the premises, call the police: the tenant has committed criminal trespass upon your property. If the tenant, in fact, re-enters the rental unit, call the police: the tenant has committed criminal trespass, breaking and entering, criminal damage and burglary. Above all, do not get into a physical confrontation with the tenant.

Additional Important Notes.

• The entire process, from the date the Written Notice is served until the tenant is "forcibly evicted" by the Sheriff or constable, cannot take less than fifteen (15) days and could take as long as sixty (60) days. Naturally, there is nothing that prevents the tenant from voluntarily moving out sooner.

• I know you are anxious to get these impecunious or "noncomplying" tenants out of your rental unit and out of your life, but make sure you follow the proper procedure. The tenant has very few defenses available in a Special Detainer action. Most are procedural. Don't "jump the gun" or try to "short-cut" the process.

• Depending on your situation, you may wish to consider paying the tenant to leave. I can hear you shrieking, "Pay this deadbeat to leave? What, have you lost your mind?" Business is business; the goal is to get him/her out – grit your teeth and do whatever you must do to get him/her out, voluntarily or otherwise. Sit down and "pencil out" a few numbers: how much it will cost you to go through the whole process, including having the Sheriff or constable forcibly removing this tenant, versus how much it will "cost" to pay this tenant to leave. The truth is, it just may be cheaper to pay the deadbeat (*see* "Practical Approach To A `Real World' Dilemma," at the very beginning of this book). Even if the amount you must pay the tenant is almost as much, as much, or even a little more than what it would cost to go through the judicial system, paying the tenant has two major benefits: (1) the tenant is out right now and (2) you do not have to go through the hassle. Keep in mind, depending on the facts, there is a chance that you could go through the whole process and lose for some reason (i.e., you committed some procedural blunder, the judge believed the deadbeat's fabricated story, etc.). Paying the tenant to leave has the distinct advantage of providing certainty that the tenant will be out. This may be done at practically any stage of the process, prior to actual physical eviction of the tenant by the Sheriff or constable.

• The "Eviction Flowcharts" and the foregoing discussion are intended as a road map of the critical stages of a Special Detainer action by a landlord against a tenant, but they are not exhaustive. You should consult with your attorney before filing or pursuing a Special Detainer action.

You are now done with the eviction process, but you are not done; go to Chapter 5, Section B(7), you must still complete a few more steps, including sending the tenant an itemized statement of deductions that you made from his/her security deposit.

EVICTION FLOWCHART

(For material noncompliance, noncompliance affecting health & safety, and material and irreparable breach)

```
                        WRITTEN NOTICE

                   TENANT DOESN'T CURE
                        OR MOVE

                   FILE SPECIAL DETAINER

                   HAVE TENANT SERVED

                       HEARING DATE

                   TENANT ENTERS PLEA  ───────  GUILTY

                        NOT GUILTY

                   TENANT REQUESTS
                        AND
                   COURT GRANTS
                   POSTPONEMENT

  TENANT CURES**

                         TRIAL  ───────────  TENANT WINS

                   LANDLORD WINS  ──────────  LETTER to TENANT

                   WRIT OF RESTITUTION
                        ISSUED

                   WRIT SERVED
                   and EXECUTED

                       FINAL STEPS                TENANT MOVES
```

LEGEND: ** If another occurrence anytime thereafter, landlord may file Special Detainer action after 10-Day Notice.

| ACTION BY LANDLORD | ACTION BY COURT or COURT OFFICER | ACTION BY TENANT |

2. **Eviction Process for:**
   (1) **Material Noncompliance with the Rental Agreement;**
   (2) **Noncompliance with the Rental Agreement that Materially Affects Health and Safety; and**
   (3) **Material and Irreparable Breach of the Rental Agreement.**

   Cross Reference:
   - Eviction for some type of noncompliance, Chapter 5, Section B(3)
   - What you can and cannot do to evict a tenant, Chapter 5, Sections B(1) and B(2)
   - Which notice must be served on the tenant, Chapter 5, Sec. B(3)
   - How the notice must be served, Chapter 5, Section B(4)
   - In which court to file the Special Detainer action, Chapter 5, Section B(5)

Before beginning, be sure that you understand: what you can and cannot do to evict a tenant, which notice must be served on the tenant, how the notice must be served, and in which court you should/must file the Special Detainer action. Then, and only then, should you proceed.

This flowchart is to be used only when you are evicting a tenant for a material noncompliance with the rental agreement, including material falsification of information on the rental application by the tenant, a noncompliance that materially affects health and safety, and/or a material and irreparable breach of the rental agreement. If you are evicting a tenant for nonpayment of rent, refer to the prior flowchart. The two flowcharts and accompanying discussion are similar, but there are some important distinctions -- make sure you use the correct flowchart.

This flowchart has been carefully engineered to help you achieve your goal -- evict the tenant. Naturally, all steps comply with applicable Arizona law, but some steps serve strategic purposes rather than satisfy legal requirements.

Each box depicted on the flowchart is fully discussed on the following pages and linked to a precise or approximate time when the action must or should occur. Again, if you have any questions, you should call your attorney.

WRITTEN NOTICE

Serve the tenant with the proper written notice. For the written notice to be legally sufficient it must specify the acts or omissions constituting the breach.

In the case of a material noncompliance with the rental agreement, including material falsification of the

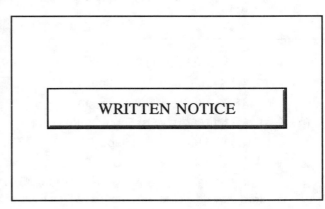

239

information in the rental application by the tenant, the written notice must state that the rental agreement will terminate if the breach is "curable" and is not remedied within ten (10) calendar days.[351] If the breach is "not curable," then the Ten-Day Notice of Material Noncompliance is actually a Ten-Day Notice of Termination.[352]

In the case of a noncompliance with the rental agreement that materially affects health and safety, the written notice must state that the rental agreement will terminate if the breach is not remedied within five (5) calendar days.[353]

In either case (i.e., material noncompliance or noncompliance materially affecting health and safety), the statute provides that if the noncompliance is cured before the date specified in the written notice (i.e., the tenth of fifth day, respectively), the rental agreement will not terminate.[354] Nevertheless, if there is another occurrence of the noncompliance of the "same or similar nature" anytime during the "term of lease," which includes extensions and renewals of the original rental term,[355] then the landlord may terminate the tenancy and institute a Special Detainer action ten (10) days after delivery of a written notice advising the tenant that a second noncompliance has occurred.[356] (*See* Appendix B, Form 12). There is no "cure period" for the second noncompliance; if the landlord sends this notice, tenancy is terminated and the tenant must vacate.

TENANT CURES

Except in the case of a second noncompliance of the "same or similar nature" (discussed immediately above), if the noncompliance is remediable by repair, payment of damages or otherwise, the tenant can stop the eviction process by taking said remedial action prior to the date specified in the written notice; but, the tenant <u>cannot</u> stop the eviction process for a material and irreparable breach.[357] Key Point: If the noncompliance is curable and the tenant cures the noncompliance, ensure that you adequately document the file. A similar noncompliance anytime thereafter during the "term of lease" is sufficient basis to evict this tenant and/or to refuse to renew this tenant's lease.[358]

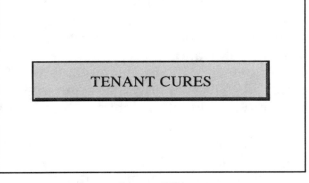

---

351 A.R.S. §§ 33-1368(A), (E) (West Supp. 1998).

352 A.R.S. § 33-1368(A)(2) (West Supp. 1998).

353 A.R.S. §§ 33-1368(A), (E) (West Supp. 1998).

354 A.R.S. § 33-1368(A) (West Supp. 1998).

355 A.R.S. § 33-1310(17) (West Supp. 1998).

356 A.R.S. § 33-1368(A) (West Supp. 1998).

357 *See* A.R.S. § 33-1368(A) (West Supp. 1998) (for a breach that is both material and irreparable, the landlord may deliver to the tenant a written notice for immediate termination of the rental agreement).

358 A.R.S. § 33-1368(A) (West Supp. 1998).

TENANT MOVES

Naturally, anytime prior to actual "forcible" eviction by the Sheriff, the tenant may elect to voluntarily move. When this happens, you may still have a legal cause of action against him/her for past due rent, money damages for breach of lease, damages to the rental unit, etc. To proceed against the tenant for these claims, you must

TENANT MOVES

initiate a separate lawsuit. Go to Chapter 6, Section A, for information relating to filing a lawsuit against the tenant for damages.

IMPORTANT NOTE: You should be aware of the distinction between: (1) a tenant voluntarily moving out and (2) the tenant offering to surrender possession and the landlord accepting surrender of possession of the premises. The tenant's conduct of voluntarily moving out does not automatically equate to an acceptance of surrender of possession of the premises by the landlord. Why is this important? A Special Detainer action is a lawsuit to recover possession of rental property.[359] Consequently, if the tenant vacates prior to the time you file the Special Detainer action, the court must dismiss the action.[360] Similarly, if the tenant voluntarily surrenders possession of the rental unit and you accept the surrender of possession after filing the Special Detainer action and before the hearing date, the court will dismiss the Special Detainer action. Why is that important? Because you lose the opportunity to get a judgment against the tenant for past due rent. Moreover, acceptance of surrender by the landlord may be (and usually is) deemed a waiver of the landlord's right to pursue the tenant for all damages (i.e., past due rent, damages to the unit, etc.). This is why it is **very important** that you not accept surrender of the premises unless you are fully prepared to give up all rights to pursue this tenant. If you want the Special Detainer action to go forward (i.e., you want a money judgment against the tenant for past due rent), do not accept surrender of possession of the rental unit. Naturally, the tenant may voluntarily move out anytime s/he wishes, but the landlord is not required to accept surrender of possession of the premises. As long as the landlord does not have possession, the Special Detainer action may go forward. "Acceptance" of surrender turns on the landlord's intent. For example, abandonment of the premises by the tenant and depositing the keys in the landlord's mail slot does not "force" the landlord to accept surrender of the premises.

---

359 Andreola v. Arizona Bank, 26 Ariz.App. 556, 550 P.2d 110 (1976).

360 See Moore v. Blackstone, 20 Ariz. 328, 329, 180 P. 526, 527 (1919); Byrd v. Peterson, 66 Ariz. 253, 257, 186 P.2d 955 (1948).

FILE SPECIAL DETAINER

The day after the date specified in your written notice, you may file the Special Detainer action. When calculating the ten or five days, do not count the day that the written notice was served. Example: on the first day of the month, you, as landlord, issue a written notice for a material noncompliance, specifying that the breach must be cured

```
┌─────────────────────────────┐
│   FILE SPECIAL DETAINER     │
└─────────────────────────────┘
```

within ten calendar days or the rental agreement will terminate on the tenth calendar day. The earliest the Special Detainer action may be filed is the eleventh day of the month.

HAVE TENANT SERVED

The **summons** and **complaint** must be served on the tenant. The complaint is the legal document that you filed with the Court to institute the Special Detainer action. The summons commands the tenant to appear in court on a particular date and time. Service of the summons and complaint is known as **service of process**. Ser-

```
┌─────────────────────────────┐
│     HAVE TENANT SERVED      │
└─────────────────────────────┘
```

vice of process must be served by a person authorized by law to deliver legal papers. Typically, this is the Sheriff or a private **process server**. Service must be completed at least two business days (not calendar days) before the entry of the tenant's plea on the hearing date/trial date.[361] The hearing and/or trial date (also known as the "return date") is entered on the summons by the clerk of the court at the time the complaint is filed and the summons issued.

Procedural note: Call your process server and give him/her the papers to serve on the day you file the Special Detainer action. Some process servers will even pick up the summons and complaint (after you have filled out and signed the documents), file the Special Detainer action with the court on your behalf and then serve the summons and complaint on the tenant (this will save you a trip to the courthouse -- you know, that incredibly efficient place where you never have to wait and are greeted by scores of friendly, courteous people). If you anticipate that the tenants will evade service (a common occurrence), instruct the process server to immediately make an attempt at service and, if unsuccessful, to "post and mail." "Post and mail," means to post a copy of the summons and complaint on the property and to mail a copy via certified mail, return receipt requested. The problem, however, is that for "post and mail" to be effective, the summons and complaint must be mailed within one day of

---

361 A.R.S. §§ 12-1175(C) (West 1994), 33-1377(B) (West Supp. 1998).

issuance of the summons.[362]   Therefore, you and the process server must act promptly.

HEARING DATE

"Hearing date," "trial date," or "return date" – this date is entered on the complaint by the clerk of the court at the time the complaint is filed and the summons issued. This date cannot be less than three (3) business days nor more than six (6) business days from the date the summons was issued (i.e., the date you filed the Special Detainer).[363] Go to court on the hearing date scheduled for your Special Detainer action. Do not miss this date. If you miss this date without a really good excuse and/or prior notice to the court to continue the hearing date, the case will be dismissed and you must file another Special Detainer complaint, pay another filing fee and incur several more days of delay. You may also be held liable for the tenant's defense costs (if any), if the tenant appears and you do not.

TENANT ENTERS PLEA

Entry of the tenant's plea occurs on the hearing date. The tenant will enter his/her plea -- guilty or not guilty. If guilty, judgment is immediately entered for the landlord; if not guilty, the matter is set for trial.

TENANT REQUESTS AND COURT GRANTS POSTPONEMENT

Only upon "good cause" shown, may the tenant request a postponement of the trial.   If the postponement is granted, the postponement may be no longer than three (3) business days in justice court or five (5) business days in superior court.[364] In justice court, if

---

362 A.R.S. § 33-1377(B) (West Supp. 1998).

363 A.R.S. § 33-1377(B) (West Supp. 1998).

364 A.R.S. § 33-1377(C) (West Supp. 1998).

a request for postponement is not made or not granted, trial may (and typically does) immediately follow entry of the tenant's plea on the hearing date. In superior court, if a request for postponement is not made or granted, a trial date is scheduled for a few days later.

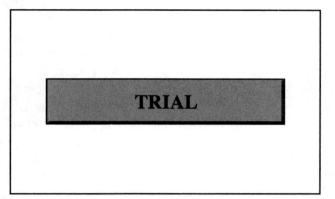

TRIAL

In justice court, unless a postponement was granted, trial immediately follows entry of the plea. In superior court, whether or not a postponement is granted, trial is scheduled for a few days later.

Before you walk into the courtroom for trial, be sure that you know this information: (1) why you are evicting tenant (i.e., material noncompliance, noncompliance materially affecting health and safety, immediate and irreparable breach); (2) if rent is also overdue, when rent was last paid, the amount due through the current "periodic rental period" (which, generally, means through the end of the current month),[365] and any applicable late and/or notice fees; (3) the precise nature of the noncompliance (i.e., noise, pets, unauthorized occupants, drug activity, etc.); (4) the date you served your written notice (i.e., the 10-Day or 5-Day Notice) and have an extra copy with you; (5) how the notice was served (i.e., hand-delivered, certified mail, etc.); (6) when the tenant was served with the Special Detainer summons and complaint; (7) how service of the Special Detainer summons and complaint was accomplished (i.e., personal service, "post & mail"); and (8) any other facts specific to your eviction action.

Traditionally, the only issue the court would examine in a forcible detainer action was which party was entitled to immediate possession of the premises.[366] Counterclaims were not allowed in Special Detainer actions. Today, however, the Act specifically allows the tenant to assert counterclaims in a Special Detainer action for *nonpayment of rent*.[367] Because we are evicting for reasons other than nonpayment of rent, the court should not allow any counterclaims. Essentially, this reduces the issues down to a question of whether the rental agreement was properly terminated (i.e., was there a material noncompliance, a noncompliance that materially affects health and safety, or a material and irreparable breach?). Nevertheless, a tenant may assert any defense which, if proven, preserves his/her right to possession and/or prevents the landlord from recovering possession.[368] There are very few defenses available to the tenant; these constitute most of the defenses the tenant may raise:

---

365 A.R.S. § 33-1377(F) (West Supp. 1998).

366 *See* Taylor v. Stanford, 100 Ariz. 346, 414 P.2d 727 (1966).

367 A.R.S. § 33-1365(A) (West Supp. 1998).

368 Magna Inv. & Dev. Corp. v. Brooks Fashion Stores, Inc., 137 Ariz. 247, 669 P.2d 1024 (App. 1983).

- The noncompliance did not occur or was not material and, therefore, not grounds for terminating the rental agreement.

- The Notice was improperly served or the Notice itself was defective (i.e., lacks required information).

- The Special Detainer complaint was filed before the applicable period had expired (i.e., ten or five days).

- The summons and complaint were improperly served.

- The tenant no longer lives in the rental unit and the landlord has accepted surrender of possession.

- The Special Detainer action is an unlawful retaliation against the tenant (i.e., retaliation for reporting building code violations, requests for repairs, etc.).

- Rent was paid and accepted after service of the Notice, thereby waiving the breach.

- There was a justification for the tenant's conduct (i.e., the landlord or his/her agent authorized the conduct; the conduct was necessary for the tenant to protect himself/herself and/or the rental property; etc.).

- The Special Detainer action was filed in the wrong court. *See* Chapter 5, Section B(5).

- The landlord inconsistently enforces the terms in the rental agreement (i.e., s/he allows some tenants to have pets, unauthorized occupants, etc., but not others). If the tenant can demonstrate to the court that s/he is the victim of "selective enforcement," the court may dismiss the action.

- The noncompliance has been cured.

Judgment is typically entered for the prevailing party at the conclusion of the trial. If the tenant wins (i.e., s/he shows just cause for the noncompliance, that the breach was curable and s/he cured the breach, etc.), the court will enter judgment in the tenant's favor, the tenant will be entitled to retain possession of the unit and the tenant is entitled to judgment against the landlord for his/her attorneys' fees and costs (pretty grim). On the other hand, if the landlord wins, the court will enter judgment in the landlord's favor and the judgment will restore the landlord's legal right of possession to the rental unit. Unfortunately, while the court has now determined that you are entitled to possession of the rental unit, the **Writ of Restitution** -- the legal paper that grants you the right to possession -- will not be issued by the court until five calendar days after entry of judgment.[369]

---

[369] A.R.S. § 12-1178(C) (West Supp. 1998).

If the landlord fails to appear at the trial, the judge will dismiss the Special Detainer action (that means you start over -- do not pass go, do not collect $200). If the tenant fails to appear at the trial, the landlord must still prove to the judge that s/he is entitled to judgment in his/her favor. Assuming the landlord presents sufficient evidence to prove his/her case, the judge will enter judgment in the landlord's favor. This process is known as obtaining a judgment by default (i.e., in the tenant's absence). If judgment is obtained by default and the tenant was personally served with the summons and complaint or served via "post and mail," then the judgment for possession may, at the landlord's option, include a specific monetary amount, representing past due rent.[370] Actual eviction (i.e., removal of the tenant from the rental unit), however, cannot be initiated until a **Writ of Restitution** is issued by the court; the earliest a Writ of Restitution may issue is five calendar days after entry of judgment.

If you get a judgment against the tenant, send copies to the credit reporting agencies and, if you believe it cost-effective, record the judgment in the county recorder's office. This will ensure that the judgment shows up on the tenant's credit report and will deter him/her from buying or selling real property in the county in which the judgment is recorded until the judgment is paid.

LETTER TO TENANT

LETTER to TENANT

After judgment is rendered, but before the Writ of Restitution is issued (five calendar days after entry of judgment), send the tenant a copy of the judgment and a letter informing the tenant that s/he must vacate within five calendar days or you will obtain the Writ of Restitution after the fifth day and direct the Sheriff to forcibly remove him/her. *See* Appendix B, Form 15 (sample letter). This letter normally works -- I have rarely had to pay the Sheriff to forcibly remove a tenant.

WRIT OF RESTITUTION ISSUED

WRIT OF RESTITUTION ISSUED

The Writ of Restitution will not issue until five calendar days (not business days) after entry of judgment. Issuance of the Writ is not automatic; you must request (i.e., pay a fee and fill out a form) the court to issue the Writ of Restitution. Upon receiving the Writ, you take the Writ to the Sheriff or con- stable to be served on the tenant.

---

370 A.R.S. § 33-1377(F) (West Supp. 1998).

WRIT SERVED and WRIT EXECUTED

Service and execution of the Writ may be a two-step process. The precise time of service/execution of the Writ of Restitution after you deliver it to the Sheriff or constable will depend on the present backlog – it may be one day; it may be three weeks. Actual eviction, as conducted by the Sheriff or constable, and no one else (not you; not a process server), may not be initiated until a Writ of Restitution is issued by the court and delivered to the Sheriff or constable (the Sheriff serves and executes the Writ in superior court cases; the constable serves and executes the Writ in justice court cases) along with a payment of the fee (the Maricopa County Sheriff requires a $150 deposit to serve the Writ; for constables, the amount of deposit may vary; the final charge, which may be more or less than the deposit, will depend on the number of attempts the Sheriff/constable must make to serve the Writ, the mileage from the courthouse to property, etc.). The Sheriff/constable has the legal authority to forcibly remove the tenant (a rare occurrence), but the task of removing the tenant's personal property falls on the landlord. If you are actually driven to this step, you should talk with the Sheriff or constable on the telephone before s/he shows up to forcibly remove the tenant. Typically, the Sheriff or constable goes to the tenant's door, tells the tenant to get out within twenty-four (24) hours or s/he will forcibly remove the tenant and his/her belongings. This normally produces the desired results (i.e., the tenants move out). If it does not, the Sheriff or constable shows up the next day and forcibly removes the tenant. Although you may want the tenant's property thrown into the street, this will not happen. The landlord is responsible for arranging for the moving and storage of the tenant's personal property. Numerous companies provide this service and are familiar with the process, but this is why you should speak with the Sheriff or constable beforehand, so that you may coordinate the arrangements. You will, however, be required to pay their fees up front. You should also have a locksmith present to immediately re-key the unit. If the tenant subsequently returns and attempts to re-enter the premises, call the police: the tenant has committed criminal trespass upon your property. If the tenant, in fact, re-enters the rental unit, call the police: the tenant has committed criminal trespass, breaking and entering, criminal damage and burglary. Above all, do not get into a physical confrontation with the tenant.

Additional Important Notes.

• The entire process, from the date the Written Notice is served until the tenant is "forcibly evicted" by the Sheriff or constable, cannot take less than fifteen (15) days and could take as long as sixty (60) days. Naturally, there is nothing that prevents the tenant from voluntarily moving out sooner.

• I know you are anxious to get these impecunious or "noncomplying" tenants out of your rental unit and out of your life, but make sure you follow the proper procedure. The tenant has very few defenses available in a Special Detainer action. Most are procedural. <u>Don't "jump the gun"</u> or try to "short-cut" the process.

• Depending on your situation, you may wish to consider paying the tenant to leave. I can hear you shrieking, "Pay this deadbeat to leave? What, have you lost your mind?" Business is business; the goal is to get him/her out – grit your teeth and do whatever you must do to get him/her out, voluntarily or otherwise. Sit down and "pencil out" a few numbers: how much it will cost you to go through the whole process, including having the Sheriff or constable forcibly removing this tenant, versus how much it will "cost" to pay this tenant to leave. The truth is, it just may be cheaper to pay the deadbeat (*see* "Practical Approach To A `Real World' Dilemma," at the very beginning of this book). Even if the amount you must pay the tenant is almost as much, as much, or even a little more than what it would cost to go through the judicial system, paying the tenant has two major benefits: (1) the tenant is out <u>right now</u> and (2) you do not have to go through the hassle. Keep in mind, depending on the facts, there is a chance that you could go through the whole process <u>and lose</u> for some reason (i.e., you committed some procedural blunder, the judge believed the deadbeat's fabricated story, etc.). Paying the tenant to leave has the distinct advantage of providing certainty that the tenant will be out. This may be done at practically any stage of the process, prior to actual physical eviction of the tenant by the Sheriff or constable.

• The "Eviction Flowcharts" and the foregoing discussion are intended as a road map of the critical stages of a Special Detainer action by a landlord against a tenant, <u>but they are not exhaustive</u>. You should consult with your attorney before filing or pursuing a Special Detainer action.

You are now done with the eviction process, but you are not done -- go to Chapter 5, Section B(7), you must still complete a few more steps, including sending the tenant an itemized statement of deductions that you made from his/her security deposit.

● **What do I do *AFTER* the eviction process?**

Whether you have evicted a tenant for nonpayment of rent or for any type of noncompliance, you need to take certain steps *after* the case is over. Go to "Final Steps," Chapter 5, Section B(7).

● **What are the procedural steps for issuing 5 and 10-Day Notices to tenants?**

See Quick Reference Section, Procedures Section (5-Day Notice discussed in eviction process for Nonpayment of Rent) (continued on next page)

See Quick Reference Section, Procedures Section (5-Day and 10-Day Notices discussed with eviction process for: Material Noncompliance with the Rental Agreement; Noncompliance with the Rental Agreement that Materially Affects Health and Safety; and Material and Irreparable Breach of the Rental Agreement).

- **What are the procedural steps for reclaiming an abandoned rental unit?**

First, decide whether the rental unit has been "abandoned," as that term is used in the Act. The Act provides:

> In this section "abandonment" means either the absence of the tenant from the dwelling unit, without notice to the landlord for at least seven days, if rent for the dwelling unit is outstanding and unpaid for ten days and there is no reasonable evidence other than the presence of the tenant's personal property that the tenant is occupying the residence *or* the absence of the tenant for at least five days, if the rent for the dwelling unit is outstanding and unpaid for five days and none of the tenant's personal property is in the dwelling unit.[371]

If the tenant has "abandoned" the unit, then you must deliver a notice to the tenant.

> **A.** If a dwelling unit is abandoned ..., the landlord shall send the tenant a notice of abandonment by certified mail, return receipt requested, addressed to the tenant's last known address and to any of the tenant's alternate addresses known to the landlord. The landlord shall also post a notice of abandonment on the door to the dwelling unit or any other conspicuous place on the property for five days.[372]

The notice must be posted and mailed via certified mail, return receipt requested. (*See* Appendix B, Form 16 -- Notice of Abandonment). After five business days have passed, the landlord may re-enter the property and retake possession.

> **B.** Five days after notice of abandonment has been both posted and mailed, the landlord may retake the dwelling unit and rerent the dwelling unit at a fair rental value if no personal property remains in the dwelling unit. After the

---

371   A.R.S. § 33-1370(H) (West Supp. 1998) (emphasis added).

372   A.R.S. § 33-1370(A) (West Supp. 1998).

> landlord retakes the dwelling unit, money held by the landlord as a security deposit is forfeited and shall be applied to the payment of any accrued rent and other reasonable costs incurred by the landlord by reason of the tenant's abandonment.[373]

As a practical matter, the first thing you should do when you retake possession is to change the locks or rekey the existing locks. This will deter, but not necessarily prevent, the tenant from returning and recovering possession. Second, document the condition of any personal property remaining on the premises <u>no matter how worthless it may appear</u>. This is best done via video tape, but may also be documented with photographs. You may <u>also</u> (not instead) wish to have a witness with you during this process. Third, inventory all personal property left on the premises. Finally, move all the personal property to another location (i.e., a storage room, another vacant rental unit, etc.). If you leave the personal property in the unit, the prior tenant is much more likely to break in and recover it. This is probably because the tenant still regards the rental unit as "his place" and breaking into "his place" may not seem quite as bad as breaking into a storage room or another rental unit. Whatever the reason, you will be much better off if you move the personal property to another location.

The next question is, "What do I do with all this junk?" Rarely, if ever, will a tenant leave anything of "real value" behind. If your rental agreement contains an important provision (*see* Chapter 2, Section D(2)(c)) and the value of the personal property is less than what it will cost to move, store and sell the property, then you may dispose of the personal property any way you wish.[374]

> If provided by a written rental agreement, the landlord may destroy or otherwise dispose of some or all of the property if the landlord reasonably determines that the value of the property is so low that the cost of moving, storage and conducting a public sale exceeds the amount that would be realized from the sale.[375]

If your rental agreement does not contain this provision, you must store it for ten days and then sell it at public auction.[376] *See* "Procedural Steps for Conducting a Public Sale," below.

---

373   A.R.S. § 33-1370(B) (West Supp. 1998).

374   A.R.S. § 33-1370(E) (West Supp. 1998).

375   A.R.S. § 33-1370(E) (West Supp. 1998).

376   A.R.S. § 33-1370(E) (West Supp. 1998).

- **What are the procedural steps for conducting a public sale of abandoned personal property?**

You may need to do a public sale of abandoned property after an eviction or after you have declared the premises to be abandoned.

The first step is to determine whether you **must** do a public sale or whether you may simply dispose of the personal property. If your rental agreement contains an important provision (*see* Chapter 2, Section D(2)(c)) and the value of the personal property is less than what it will cost to move, store and sell the property, then you may dispose of the personal property any way you wish.[377]

If your rental agreement **does not** contain this provision, then you must hold the personal property for a prescribed period of time and then conduct a public auction. The holding periods are as follows: (a) after an abandonment, you must store it for ten (10) days and then sell it at public auction[378]; (b) after an eviction, you must store it for twenty-one (21) days and then sell it at public auction.[379]

> The landlord shall hold the tenant's personal property for a period of ten [business] days after the landlord's declaration of abandonment. The landlord shall use reasonable care in holding the tenant's personal property. If the landlord holds the property for this period and the tenant makes no reasonable effort to recover it, the landlord may sell the property, retain the proceeds and apply them toward the tenant's outstanding rent or other costs which are covered in the lease agreement or otherwise provided for in title 33, chapter 10 [the Act] or title 12, chapter 8 and have been incurred by the landlord due to the tenant's abandonment. Any excess proceeds shall be mailed to the tenant at the tenant's last known address. A tenant does not have any right of access to that property until the actual removal and storage costs have been paid in full, except that the tenant may obtain clothing and the tools, apparatus and books of a trade or profession and any identification or financial documents, including all those related to the tenant's immigration status, employment status, public assistance or medical care.[380]

> Example 1 (Abandonment): declaration of abandonment occurs on May 15; the ten business days begin to run on May 16; ten business days later, you may conduct your sale, but you must also fulfill additional notice requirements (see below).

---

377 A.R.S. § 33-1370(E) (West Supp. 1998).

378 A.R.S. § 33-1370(E) (West Supp. 1998).

379 A.R.S. § 33-1368(E) (West Supp. 1998).

380 A.R.S. § 33-1370(E) (West Supp. 1998).

After an eviction, you must store the tenant's property for twenty-one (21) days and then sell it at public auction.

E. The landlord shall hold the tenant's personal property for a period of twenty-one days beginning on the first day after a writ of restitution or writ of execution is executed as prescribed in section 12-1181. The landlord shall use reasonable care in moving and holding the tenant's property and may store the tenant's property in an unoccupied dwelling unit owned by the landlord, the unoccupied dwelling unit formerly occupied by the tenant or off the premises if an unoccupied dwelling unit is not available. If the tenant's former dwelling unit is used to store the property, the landlord may change the locks on that unit at the landlord's discretion. The landlord shall prepare an inventory and promptly notify the tenant of the location and cost of storage of the personal property by sending a notice by certified mail, return receipt requested, addressed to the tenant's last known address and to any of the tenant's alternative addresses known to the landlord. To reclaim the personal property, the tenant shall pay the landlord only for the cost of removal and storage for the time the property is held by the landlord. Within five days after a written offer by the tenant to pay these charges the landlord must surrender possession of the personal property in the landlord's possession to the tenant upon the tenant's tender of payment. If the landlord fails to surrender possession of the personal property to the tenant, the tenant may recover the possessions or an amount equal to the damages determined by the court if the landlord has destroyed or disposed of the possessions before the twenty-one days specified in this section or after the tenant's offer to pay. The tenant shall pay all removal and storage costs accrued through the fifth day after the tenant's offer to pay is received by the landlord or the date of delivery or surrender of the property, whichever is sooner. Payment by the tenant relieves the landlord of any further responsibility for the tenant's possessions.

F. A tenant does not have any right of access to that property until all payments specified in subsection E of this section have been made in full, except that the tenant may obtain clothing and the tools, apparatus and books of a trade or profession and identification or financial documents including all those related to the tenant's immigration status, employment status, public assistance or medical care. If the landlord holds the property for the twenty-one day period and the tenant does not make a reasonable effort to recover it, the landlord, upon the expiration of twenty-one days as provided in this subsection, may administer the personal property as provided in section 33-1370, subsection E. The landlord shall hold personal property after a writ of restitution or writ of execution is executed for not more than twenty-one days after such an execution. Nothing in this subsection shall preclude the landlord and tenant from making an agreement providing that the landlord will hold the personal property for a period longer than twenty-one days.[381]

Example 2 (Eviction): eviction occurs on May 15; the twenty-one days begin to run on the day after the Writ of Restitution is executed by the Sheriff or constable, which, in this example, is May 16; twenty-one calendar days later, you may conduct your sale, but you must also fulfill additional notice requirements (see below).

There are other notice requirements that you must fulfill before you conduct the public auction.

A. ... [W]hen possession of any property described in this article or any other personal property held under lien without provision at law for foreclosure of the lien has continued for twenty days after the charges accrue and remain unpaid, the person holding the property may notify the owner, if in the county where the property is located, to pay the charges. Upon failure of the owner within ten days thereafter to pay the charges, the holder of the property may sell it at public auction and apply the proceeds to payment of the charges. The balance of the proceeds shall be paid to the person entitled thereto. If the owner's residence is not in the county where the property is located, the holder is not required to give the ten days' notice before proceeding to sell.

B. Five days' notice of sale shall be given to the owner if he can be found, and if not, then by two publications in a newspaper published in the county.[382]

As seen above, you must give a ten-day notice and then a five-day notice. For the ten-day notice, simply state the amount of the moving and storage charges the tenant must pay to reclaim his/her property, inform him/her that if not paid within

---

381 A.R.S. § 33-1368(E) and (F) (West Supp. 1998).

382 A.R.S. § 33-1023 (West Supp. 1998).

ten business days you will sell the property at public auction, and provide the tenant with the means to contact you (i.e., phone number, address, etc.). For the five-day notice, simply state the date, time and location of the public sale and provide the tenant with at least five business days' advance notice. (*See* Appendix B, Forms 17 and 18).

As a final note, I strongly recommend <u>against</u> conducting your own auction. First, if the tenant shows up, things may get "ugly" in a hurry. Second, there may be subsequent allegations by the tenant that you failed to conduct the sale in a "commercially reasonable manner," which, unless you are an auctioneer or regularly conduct public auctions, may have some merit. I find that the best way to avoid problems is to call a local auction company and let them handle the entire matter. This will reduce the chance of any problems arising if the tenant shows up, will help preclude allegations that the sale was not conducted in a commercially reasonable manner, will probably yield more money from the sale (which is good for you), and significantly reduces the burden on you. All you have to do is notify the tenant of the date/time of the sale.

- ### What are the procedural steps for collecting money from tenants?

  The various methods for collecting past due rent is discussed in Chapter 4, Section B. The procedural steps for collecting on a judgment are discussed in Chapter 6, Section B.

- ### What if the tenant files bankruptcy?

  Bankruptcy is a landlord's nightmare. The safest and best, but not the cheapest, course of action if a tenant files bankruptcy is to call your attorney at let him/her deal with the problem. Nevertheless, I shall endeavor to give you a brief overview of your options.

A tenant may file under various different chapters of the Bankruptcy Code. Typically, you will encounter: (1) Chapter 7, liquidation (tenant/debtor sells all non-exempt assets and uses proceeds and cash on-hand to pay creditors), (2) Chapter 13, wage earner reorganization (tenant/debtor files a plan that provides for adjustment and payoff of debts), and (3) Chapter 11, reorganization (typically for businesses; tenant/debtor files a plan that provides for adjustment and payoff of debts). In all instances, once the petition (referred to as the Order for Relief) is filed with the Bankruptcy Court, the "automatic stay" immediately goes into effect.[383] The "automatic stay" prohibits all creditors, including landlords, from taking *any* action to collect pre-petition debt (i.e., due and unpaid rent accruing prior to the filing of the petition). This means that you cannot even send notices to the tenant while the stay is in effect. Moreover, the landlord can take no action to evict the tenant

---

[383] 11 U.S.C. § 362 (1989).

without obtaining "permission" from the Bankruptcy Court.[384] "Permission" is known as "relief from the automatic stay." To obtain relief from the automatic stay, the creditor (i.e., the landlord) must file a Motion to Lift Stay with the Bankruptcy Court. Thereafter, the tenant/debtor will have an opportunity to object to the Motion. If there is no objection, the court will grant the motion. If there is an objection, and you just know that there *will be*, then the matter is set for a hearing. The court will receive evidence on the relevant issues and render a decision. Once the Bankruptcy Court grants the landlord relief from the automatic stay, the landlord must then proceed under state law. Which means the landlord must then file the forcible detainer action in the appropriate state court (i.e., justice court or superior court) and obtain a judgment for possession from the state court. There is no "short-cut." Knowingly violating the automatic stay may subject the violator (i.e., the landlord) to substantial sanctions.[385]

If the foregoing sounds relatively simple, it is only because I have omitted *many* steps and many alternative results. For example, in the case of a lease, which, under the Bankruptcy Code, falls under the category of "executory contracts" (i.e., contracts that have not been fully performed), the tenant/debtor may chose to "assume" the lease (i.e., reaffirm the lease and continue to rent the leased premises), "assign" the lease (i.e., sell the lease to another party, which the debtor may do whether or not your lease prohibits assignments), or "reject" the lease (i.e., break the lease and move out).[386] The debtor's ability and/or desire to pursue each option will turn on the specific facts. But this much is certain, it is going to take a couple of months just to get the relief from the automatic stay, *assuming* all goes well. If there are problems, it may take *many* months to obtain stay relief. Because of the myriad of issues and the cryptic and convoluted rules of procedure in Bankruptcy Court, if you have a tenant that files bankruptcy, I strongly encourage you to seek out and retain an attorney familiar with both bankruptcy law and landlord/tenant law.

---

[384] 11 U.S.C. § 362 (1989).

[385] 11 U.S.C. § 362 (1989).

[386] 11 U.S.C. § 365 (1989).

APPENDIX A

CHECKLISTS

Okay, you have read this entire book, or at least the parts you feel apply to you. No doubt, your head is now spinning with all the things I told you to do. You liked many of the ideas, but you are not sure you remember them all. Fear not -- much of what you need to know has been condensed for you into four handy checklists. These checklists should serve you well.

CHECKLIST 1 - What to do when you have finished reading this book and are ready to rent your units.

CHECKLIST 2 - Review your rental agreement.

CHECKLIST 3 - "Quick Start" for new landlords and "Checklist" for existing landlords.

CHECKLIST 4 - Getting Tenants.

CHECKLIST NUMBER 1

<u>What to do when you have finished reading this book and are ready to rent your units</u>

    a. Follow the Legal Advice to Landlords (*See* Chapter 2).

        - Get a lawyer.
        - Get the right lawyer.
        - Have your lawyer prepare (or revise) your rental agreement and other forms. This is the source of your legal rights; does it say what you want it to say? Moreover, the rental agreement *cannot* include certain provisions, *must* include certain provisions and disclosures to be enforceable in a court of law, and *should* include certain other provisions, so that your rights are adequately protected.
        - Be sure you have enough insurance.
        - Discuss asset protection with your lawyer.

    b. Review/create your rental agreement (*See* Chapter 2, Section D).

        See Checklist 2

    c. Prepare/assemble your other forms (*See* Chapter 2, Section C).

        See Appendix B

    d. Ensure you have complied with all business and legal requirements.

        See Checklist 3

    e. Get Tenants (*See* Chapter 3).

        See Checklist 4

CHECKLIST NUMBER 2

Review your rental agreement.

a. What must be in your rental agreement

- Disclosure of manager and owner or owner's agent.
- Deliver a signed copy of the written rental agreement to the tenant(s).
- The written rental agreement must be complete.
- The purpose of all non-refundable fees must be stated in writing.
- Rental agreements over 1-year must be written.
- Give the tenant notice that the Act is available free.
- Give the tenant a move-in inspection form.
- Give the tenant notice that s/he may be present during the move-out inspection.
- Give the tenant a pool safety notice.
- Give the tenant notice about lead-based paint.

b. What should be in your rental agreement

- The rental agreement should be written.
- The written rental agreement should be comprehensive.
- The rental agreement should provide for abandonment.
- The rental agreement should provide for payment of expenses incurred to bring legal action.
- The rental agreement should provide for payment of "other expenses" incurred by the landlord.
-The rental agreement should provide for the Tenant's maintenance obligations.
- The rental agreement should provide for regular inspections.
- The rental agreement should address "reasonable" modifications and alterations.
- The rental agreement should provide how partial payments are applied to amounts due.
- The rental agreement should provide for a reasonable late fee.
- The rental agreement should provide for rental tax increases.
- The rental agreement should include a liquidated damages provision.
- The rental agreement should include waiver of jury trial.

CHECKLIST NUMBER 2 (continued)

Review your rental agreement (continued)

c. What cannot be in your rental agreement

- The landlord cannot require the tenant to:
    - waive the tenant's rights;
    - agree to pay attorneys' fees; or
    - agree to limit the landlord's liability.
- The landlord cannot collect a security deposit
  equal to more than one and one-half month's rent.
- The landlord cannot include provisions that are contrary to the Act.

CHECKLIST NUMBER 3

<u>"Quick Start" for new landlords and "Checklist" for existing landlords</u>.

Okay, you have just bought a rental property and want to know all the various things you must do and legal "hoops" you must jump through in order to operate your rental business properly and legally. Or, you already have rentals and you want to verify that you have done everything correctly. Below, in outline form, is a list of items that every new and existing landlord must (and should) do and/or consider.

a. Licensing (i.e., business license; real estate license, if applicable).

b. Sales tax license (i.e., state, county, city).

c. Income tax - Discuss impact of rental property ownership with your accountant (i.e., passive loss rules, "active participation" in management, advantages and dis-advantages of owning property in corporate name, etc.).

d. Insurance
   - Property insurance
   - Rental replacement insurance
   - Workmen's Compensation (for employees)
   - Liability insurance

e. Compliance with local laws
   - Does "For Rent" sign comply with local sign ordinance?
   - Compliance with pool barrier laws (pool cover or fenced pool).
   - City code inspection
   - Fire marshal inspection
   - Parking -   Number of required spaces, restrictions on types of vehicles that may be parked on the property, liability for abandoned vehicles, local law regarding towing of vehicles from the rental property.

f. Set-up/revise procedures for new tenants, evictions, and rental unit preparation.

g. Written and published list of minimum acceptable tenant information (*see* Chapter 3, Section E(2)) and occupancy standard (*see* Chapter 3, Section E(1)(a)).

CHECKLIST NUMBER 4

Getting Tenants

a. Follow the General Guidelines for Doing Business.
- Be honest
- Be straightforward
- Keep it simple
- Be businesslike
- Be authoritative
- Stay up-to-date
- Err Conservatively

b. Prepare unit for new tenant.
- Curb appeal
- Interior appearance

c. Attract applicants -- Advertising.
- Free Advertising (or nearly free)
- Sign
- Appearance of property
- Present tenants
- Word of mouth
- Paid Advertising
- Newspaper
- Bulletin boards
- Specialized rental magazines
- Real estate brokers/agents
- Nondiscriminatory advertising.

d. Show the prospective tenant the unit.
- Property disclosure (i.e., pools, lead-paint, Superfund, etc)

e. Have the tenant fill out the application.
- The first application
- Ask questions, listen to the answers.
- Review the application while the applicant is still there and make sure the application is complete.
- The second application
- Select the best tenant; reject all others.
- Do not discriminate

f. Term of tenancy.

APPENDIX B

<u>FORMS</u>

FORM 1 - *See* Chapter 3, Section D(1) and D(2) regarding use of this form.

TENANT APPLICATION

HOW DID YOU HEAR ABOUT THIS RENTAL UNIT / COMPLEX?	
☐ Sign ■ Other Tenant ☐ Billboard ☐ Newspaper ☐ Friend ☐ Magazine ☐ Other:	

Do you wish to have a pet (of any type) on/in the rental property? ☐ Yes (type:) ■ No	Have you ever been evicted (as either a commercial or residential tenant)? ☐ Yes ■ No
Have you ever filed Bankruptcy? ☐ Yes ■ No If yes, when? What Chapter?	Have you ever been convicted of a crime (other than minor traffic)? ☐ Yes ■ No
How many vehicles do you wish to park on the Rental Property? *2*	Do you presently have a telephone at home? ■ Yes ☐ No Phone Number: *555-3333*
Taking into account all your other expenses, can you afford the rent on this unit? ■ Yes ☐ No	When do you plan on moving in? *In 30 days.*
How long do you anticipate staying? *12 months*	How is your credit? ■ Good ☐ Fair ☐ Ooops

Name: *Terry Tenant*	Name: *Tina Tenant*
Address: *(If less than 5 years, continue on back of form)* *222 North Oak Street, Anytown, AZ*	
Current Landlord's Name: *Bob Jones*	
Address: *(If less than 5 years, continue on back of form)* *112 North Oak Street, Anytown, AZ*	
Phone No.: *555-3333*	Present Rent: *$450.00*
How Long There: *2 years*	May I Call for Reference? ■ Yes ☐ No
Why are you Moving? *Job Transfer*	
Current Employer: *OMNI Products, Inc.*	Work Phone Number: *555-4444*
Address: *505 West Ash Street, Anytown, AZ*	
Supervisor's Name: *Sarah Supervisor*	
Phone No.: *555-4444*	Gross Monthly Income: *$2,000.00*
How Long There: *5 years*	May I Call for Reference? ■ Yes ☐ No

REFERENCES: (minimum two)		
Name: *Fran Friend*	How Known: (friend, boss, etc.) *Friend*	Phone No.: *555-5555*
Name: *Barry Boss*	How Known: (friend, boss, etc.) *Boss*	Phone No.: *555-6666*
Name: *Tom Tenant*	How Known: (friend, boss, etc.) *Your tenant/a friend*	Phone No.: *555-7777*

Applicants declare that the foregoing information is true and complete. Providing false information on the Application is grounds for termination. Applicants authorize Landlord to obtain information regarding credit history, confidential information and criminal record from any source and/or anyone listed on this form. Landlord charges and collects herewith a nonrefundable application fee; this fee is used to defray the administrative expense of processing and screening applications.

Signature: *Terry Tenant*	Signature: *Tina Tenant*

(You may wish to publish your minimum acceptable tenant criteria on the back of this form; *see* **page 116)**

TENANT APPLICATION

HOW DID YOU HEAR ABOUT THIS RENTAL UNIT / COMPLEX?

☐ Sign ☐ Other Tenant ☐ Billboard ☐ Newspaper ☐ Friend
☐ Magazine ☐ Other:

Do you wish to have a pet (of any type) on/in the rental property? ☐ Yes (type:) ☐ No	Have you ever been evicted (as either a commercial or residential tenant)? ☐ Yes ☐ No
Have you ever filed Bankruptcy? ☐ Yes ☐ No If yes, when? What Chapter?	Have you ever been convicted of a crime (other than minor traffic)? ☐ Yes ☐ No
How many vehicles do you wish to park on the Rental Property?	Do you presently have a telephone at home? ☐ Yes ☐ No Phone Number:
Taking into account all your other expenses, can you afford the rent on this unit? ☐ Yes ☐ No	When do you plan on moving in?
How long do you anticipate staying?	How is your credit? ☐ Good ☐ Fair ☐ Ooops
Name:	Name:
Address: *(If less than 5 years, continue on back of form)*	
Current Landlord's Name:	
Address: *(If less than 5 years, continue on back of form)*	
Phone No.:	Present Rent: $
How Long There:	May I Call for Reference? ☐ Yes ☐ No
Why are you Moving?	
Current Employer:	Work Phone Number:
Address:	
Supervisor's Name:	
Phone No.:	Gross Monthly Income: $
How Long There:	May I Call for Reference? ☐ Yes ☐ No

REFERENCES: (minimum two)

Name:	How Known: (friend, boss, etc.) Phone No.:
Name:	How Known: (friend, boss, etc.) Phone No.:
Name:	How Known: (friend, boss, etc.) Phone No.:

Applicants declare that the foregoing information is true and complete. Providing false information on the Application is grounds for termination. Applicants authorize Landlord to obtain information regarding credit history, confidential information and criminal record from any source and/or anyone listed on this form. Landlord charges and collects herewith a nonrefundable application fee; this fee is used to defray the administrative expense of processing and screening applications.

Signature:	Signature:

FORM 2 - *See* Chapter 3, Section D(3) regarding use of this form.

TENANT INFORMATION SHEET

Property Address: *123 N. Oak Street, Anytown, Arizona*	Home Phone No.: *555-2222* Work Phone No.: *555-1111*

TENANT INFORMATION
(To be completed by each Adult Occupant)

Name: *Terry Tenant*	
Place of Birth: *Tucson, Arizona*	Date of Birth: *June 1, 1950*
Social Security No.: *555-11-2222*	Driver's License No.: *555-22-9999*
Parents' Names: *Dick & Jane Tenant*	
Address: *111 North Elm Street, Anytown, AZ*	
Person to Notify in Case of Emergency: *Fran Friend*	
Address: *222 North 1st Avenue, Phoenix*	Phone No.: *555-5555*
Children: *Tanya Tenant*	Age: *2*
Tony Tenant	Age: *7*
Have you ever filed Bankruptcy? ■ No □ Yes	When: Under what Chapters?
Have you ever been evicted? ■ No □ Yes	When:
Do you wish to have a pet? □ No ■ Yes	Type and Weight: *fish (1 ounce)*
Have you ever been convicted of a crime (other than minor traffic)? ■ No □ Yes	How many vehicles do you wish to park on the Rental Property? *2*
Will you park any commercial vehicles on the property? ■ No □ Yes	Do you presently have a telephone at home? *No* Number:
Taking into account all your other expenses, can you afford the rent on this unit? □ No ■ Yes	When do you plan to move in? *ASAP*
How long do you anticipate staying? *2 years*	How is your credit? ■ Good □ Fair □ Ooops

BANK INFORMATION

Where do you bank? *Wells Fargo Bank*	Branch: *Main*
Checking Account No.: *01-2222*	Savings Account No.: *02-1111*
Other Account No.: *IRA - 03-4444*	Other Account No.:

VEHICLE INFORMATION
(list information on each vehicle)

Make: *Nissan*	Model: *Sentra*	Year: *1990*	License No.: *XYZ-111*
Lienholder: *Bank One*	Balance Owed: *$6,000.00*		Monthly Payment: *$149.00*
Make: *Chevrolet*	Model: *Camero*	Year: *1982*	License No.: *XYZ-222*
Lienholder: *None*	Balance Owed: *-0-*		Monthly Payment:

TENANT INFORMATION SHEET

Property Address:	Home Phone No.: Work Phone No.:

TENANT INFORMATION
(To be completed by each Adult Occupant)

Name:	
Place of Birth:	Date of Birth:
Social Security No.:	Driver's License No.:
Parents' Names:	
Address:	
Person to Notify in Case of Emergency:	
Address:	Phone No.:
Children:	Age:
	Age:
	Age:

Have you ever filed Bankruptcy?	☐ No ☐ Yes	When:	Under what Chapters?
Have you ever been evicted?	☐ No ☐ Yes	When:	
Do you wish to have a pet?	☐ No ☐ Yes	Type and Weight:	
Have you ever been convicted of a crime (other than minor traffic)?		How many vehicles do you wish to park on the Rental Property?	
Will you park any commercial vehicles on the property?		Do you presently have a telephone at home? Number:	
Taking into account all your other expenses, can you afford the rent on this unit?	☐ No ☐ Yes	When do you plan to move in?	
How long do you anticipate staying?		How is your credit? ☐ Good ☐ Fair ☐ Ooops	

BANK INFORMATION

Where do you bank?	Branch:
Checking Account No.:	Savings Account No.:
Other Account No.:	Other Account No.:

VEHICLE INFORMATION
(list information on each vehicle)

Make:	Model:	Year:	License No.:
Lienholder:	Balance Owed:		Monthly Payment:
Make:	Model:	Year:	License No.:
Lienholder:	Balance Owed:		Monthly Payment:
Make:	Model:	Year:	License No.:
Lienholder:	Balance Owed:		Monthly Payment:

FORM 3 - *See* Chapter 2, Section E(3) regarding use of this form. You are now required by A.R.S. § 33-1321(C) to provide the tenant with "a move-in form for specifying any existing damage to the dwelling unit" at or before the time the tenant moves in. *See also* Form 3A, following Form 3.

PROPERTY INSPECTION CHECKLIST

The premises located at: 111 North Maple Street, #2, Phoenix, Arizona, are clean, safe, in good repair and without defects, with only the following exceptions noted:

Exterior: *__Bedroom window cracked, south side of building needs paint (existing paint is peeling).__*
_____
(i.e., condition of the exterior structure, etc.)

Living room* : *__Hole in carpet (burn mark); stain on carpet, near door.__*
_____

Family room* : *__Hole in south hall; outlet cover missing.__*
_____

Kitchen: *__Cabinet above stove scratched; oven dented near bottom; faucet drips; 1 piece of floor tile broken.__*
_____
(i.e., appliances, cabinets, walls, floor, ceiling, etc.)

Laundry room** : *__None.__*
_____

Hall: *__None.__*
_____

Hall bathroom** : *__Towel rack bent; light cover missing; bathtub porcelain chipped.__*
_____

Bedroom 1* : *__Door marred; hole in carpet, near window; drapes torn.__*
_____

Bedroom 2* : *__Light fixture doesn't work.__*
_____

Master Bedroom** : *__Carpet stain near closet; hole in wall behind door.__*
_____

When completed and signed, this form will be attached to your Rental Agreement. Costs to repair defects not noted on this checklist are the tenant(s)'s responsibility and will be deducted from the security deposit if not repaired prior to vacating the premises. **MAKE A THOROUGH INSPECTION OF THE PREMISES & NOTE ALL DEFECTS!**

*Terry Tenant*_____   *Larry Landlord*_____
       (Tenants)   (Landlord/Owner)
   * i.e., floor, carpet, walls, ceilings, doors, hardware, windows.   ** i.e., fixtures, walls, ceilings, floor, outlets, door, windows.

PROPERTY INSPECTION CHECKLIST

The premises located at: _____, _____, Arizona,
are clean, safe, in good repair and without defects, with only the following exceptions noted:

Exterior:

_____

_____

(i.e., condition of the exterior structure, etc.)

Living Room*:

_____

_____

Family Room*:

_____

_____

Kitchen:

_____

_____

(i.e., appliances, cabinets, walls, floor, ceiling, etc.)

Laundry Room**: _____

_____

Hall: _____

_____

Hall Bathroom**: _____

_____

Bedroom 1*: _____

_____

Bedroom 2*: _____

_____

Master Bedroom**: _____

_____

(For additional rooms, continue on back of form)

When completed and signed, this form will be attached to your Rental Agreement. Costs to repair defects not noted on this checklist are the tenant(s)'s responsibility and will be deducted from the security deposit if not repaired prior to vacating the premises. If you fail to complete and return this form, the landlord will presume that no defects exist. **MAKE A THOROUGH INSPECTION OF THE PREMISES & NOTE ALL DEFECTS!**

Date _____   Date _____

_____   _____

_____   _____

            (Tenants)   (Landlord/Owner)

* i.e., floor, carpet, walls, ceilings, doors, hardware, windows. ** i.e., fixtures, walls, ceilings, floor, outlets, door, windows.

CHECKLIST FOR WALK-THROUGH INSPECTION
LISTA DE INSPECCIOŃ

Tenant Name/*Nombre de Inquilino*:_____

Dwelling Address/*Dirección*:_____

Note the condition of each area and document any needed repairs.
Nota la condición de cada cuarto y de cada reparación.

ROOM/*Cuarto*	COMMENTS/*Comentarios* MOVE-IN DATE: *Fecha de Posesión:*	COMMENTS/*Comentarios* MOVE-OUT DATE: *Fecha de Mudanza:*
Kitchen (Cocina)		
Stove/Oven (*Estufa/Horno*)		
Refrigerator (*Nevera*)		
Sink (*Fregadero)*)		
Cabinets (*Gabinete*)		
Light Fixtures (*Luces*)		
Floor (*Piso*)		
Walls/Ceiling (*Pared/Techo*)		
Living Rooms (Sala)		
Carpeting (*Alfombra*)		
Walls/Ceiling (*Pared/Techo*)		
Curtains or Blinds (*Cortinas*)		
Windows/Screen (*Ventanas*)		
Bedroom #1 (Recámara #1)		
Carpeting (*Alfombra*)		
Walls/Ceiling (*Pared/Techo*)		
Curtains or Blinds (*Cortinas*)		
Windows/Screen (*Ventanas*)		
Light Fixtures (*Luces*)		
Closet (*Armario de Ropaje*)		
Bedroom #2 (Recámara #2)		
Carpeting (*Alfombra*)		
Walls/Ceiling (*Pared/Techo*)		
Curtains or Blinds (*Cortinas*)		
Windows/Screen (*Ventanas*)		
Light Fixtures (*Luces*)		
Closet (*Armario de Ropaje*)		

ROOM/*CUARTO*	COMMENTS/*Comentarios* MOVE-IN DATE: *Fecha de Posesión:*	COMMENTS/*Comentarios* MOVE-OUT DATE: *Fecha de Mudanza:*
Bathroom #1 (Baño #1)		
Tub/Shower (*Bañadera/ducha*)		
Floor (*Piso*)		
Sink (*Lavamanos*)		
Medicine Cabinet (*Botiquin*)		
Toilet (*Taza de Baño*)		
Walls/Ceiling (Pared/*Techo*)		
Bathroom #2 (Baño #2)		
Tub/Shower (*Bañadera/ducha*)		
Floor (*Piso*)		
Sink (*Lavamanos*)		
Medicine Cabinet (*Botiquin*)		
Toilet (*Taza de Baño*)		
Walls/Ceiling (*Pared/Techo*)		
Other (Otro)		
Electrical Outlets (*Enchufes Electrónicos*)		
Plumbing (*Fontanería*)		
Vents (*Abertura de Ventilación*)		
Thermostat (*Termóstato*)		
Smoke Alarm (*Alarma de Humo*)		
Water Heater (*Calenton de agua*)		
Cooler or A/C (*Acondicionado de Aire*)		
Heater (*Calefacción*)		
Doors (*Puertas*)		

Other Comments/*Otro Comentarios*: _____
_____
_____
_____
_____

NOTICE

_____

_____

_____

Notice to Tenant,   Date: _____

    Your Rental Agreement specifies that rent is due on the _____ day of the month. Late charges will be assessed and collected when rent is submitted after the _____ day of the month. Frequent late payment of rent may be grounds for termination of your Rental Agreement.

    The purpose of this letter is to bring this matter to your attention. You should take immediate action to ensure you are in compliance with the payment requirements of the Rental Agreement. If you are encountering temporary financial problems, etc., please come by the office and discuss your situation with me. You are a valued tenant; I will do what I can to help.

                                          _____

                                          _____

                                          _____

                                          _____

Instructions: Fill-in the blank lines in paragraph one, according to the terms of your rental agreement. Sign your name on the first of the four blank lines at the bottom of the form; print your name below your signature. Write your business name, if any (i.e., ABC Apartments), on the next line, followed by the address and telephone number. This is NOT a 5-Day Notice to Pay or Quit and it is not used to begin the eviction process; this is merely a "friendly" reminder to the tenant to pay rent on time. To begin the eviction process, you must serve a 5-Day Notice to Pay or Quit (Form 9).

FORM 4 ↑

FORM 5 - _See_ page 41 regarding use of this form →

Instructions: Fill-in the first three blank lines according to the facts of your situation. In the last paragraph, write in the date that the tenant must pay the balance that is due. Have the tenant sign and date the form. Sign your name on the first of the four blank lines at the bottom of the form; print your name below your signature. Write your business name, if any (i.e., ABC Apartments), on the next line, followed by the address and telephone number.

AGREEMENT TO TENDER AND ACCEPT PARTIAL RENT PAYMENT

_____
_____
_____

Notice to Tenant,   Date: _____

The amount of $_____ is presently due and delinquent. Your partial payment of $_____ is hereby accepted by Landlord, leaving a balance of $_____ remaining due. Acceptance hereof and your continued tenancy is conditioned upon the following:

a.   By accepting this partial payment the Landlord **does not** waive any legal rights, including, but not limited to, the right to collect the total amount due under the lease, including late charges and interest, and the right to bring an action for possession of the leased premises. If payment is accepted after entry of Judgment, unless otherwise provided herein, landlord may obtain and have served/executed a Writ of Restitution five calendar days after entry of Judgment.

b.   Acceptance of the partial payment does not effect a waiver (express or implied) of the "Time of the Essence" provision of your Rental Agreement. Partial payments shall be applied as follows: first, to legal fees and court costs, then to accrued interest on any amounts owed to the landlord, then to late fees, then to amounts owed for damages to the property, then to any other amounts owed by the tenant to the landlord, then to unpaid past due rent, and finally to prepaid rent.

c.   Upon default hereof by tenant, Landlord may proceed with legal action to recover past rent, damages, possession of the leased premises or any other relief permissible by law or under the rental agreement.

d.   If previously served with a "Notice to Pay or Quit," acceptance by the Landlord of this partial rent payment WILL NOT restart the time running for compliance and, pursuant to A.R.S. § 33-1371(B), no additional notice under A.R.S. § 33-1368(B) shall be required.

e.   Other: _____
_____

Your signature below indicates that you understand and voluntarily agree to remit full payment of the remaining outstanding balance, plus accrued charges, in the amount specified above, no later than:_____.

_____   _____
(signature of tenant)   (Date)

_____
_____
_____
_____

NOTICE OF ☐ COMPLAINT ☐ VIOLATION

Notice to Tenant,   Date: _____

☐   Complaints have been made against you for:

_____

_____

_____

_____

☐   You are violating the following term(s) in your Rental Agreement:

_____

_____

_____

You must take action to remedy this/these problem(s) immediately! Your Rental Agreement will be terminated and a lawsuit filed to evict you if you fail to comply.

_____

_____

_____

_____

← FORM 6 - *See* page 63 regarding use of this form. This form is NOT used to begin eviction (use Forms 10 and 11 to begin eviction); it is used to bring complaints/violations to the tenant's attention. Complete the blank lines according to the facts of your situation. Sign your name on the first of the four blank lines at the bottom of the form; print your name below your signature. Write your business name, if any (i.e., ABC Apartments), on the next line, followed by the address and telephone number.

FORM 7 - *See* Page 64 regarding use of this form. This form is specifically drafted for use in Phoenix; similar forms, which comply with local law, may be used.

↓

PARKING VIOLATION

YOUR VEHICLE IS PARKED ON PRIVATE PROPERTY WITHOUT EXPRESS AUTHORIZATION.

UNAUTHORIZED USE of this PRIVATE PROPERTY subjects your vehicle to IMPOUNDMENT at your expense, including TOWING and STORAGE FEES. Phoenix City Code provides that no person shall park a vehicle on private property without the express consent of the owner of such property.

VIOLATION OF SECTION 36-144 IS PUNISHABLE BY A FINE OF UP TO $250.
See PHOENIX, ARIZ., CITY CODE ART. XI, § 36-144(I) (1992).

WARNING: VEHICLE MAY BE TOWED ON <u>NEXT VIOLATION</u>!!

DATE:_____ LICENSE #_____ VEHICLE_____

FORM 8 - *See* pages 154 and 239 regarding use of this form.

→

NOTICE OF IMMEDIATE TERMINATION
OF RENTAL AGREEMENT
FOR MATERIAL AND IRREPARABLE BREACH

_____

_____

_____

Notice to Tenant,   Date: _____

    You are in violation of your Rental Agreement and/or the Arizona Residential Landlord and Tenant Act. The specific act(s) constituting the violation(s) is/are:

☐ Illegal discharge of a weapon   ☐ Prostitution as defined in § 13-3211

☐ Criminal street gang activity as prescribed in § 13-105   ☐ Infliction of bodily harm

☐ Activity as prohibited in § 13-2308 (organized crime)   ☐ Assault as prohibited in § 13-1203

☐ Threatening or intimidating as prohibited in §13-1202

☐ Unlawful manufacturing, selling, using, storing, keeping or giving of a controlled substance as defined in §13-3451

☐ A breach of the lease agreement that otherwise jeopardizes the health, safety and welfare of the landlord, the landlord's agent or another tenant or involving imminent or actual serious property damage; specifically:_____

☐ Other:_____

    You are hereby notified, pursuant to A.R.S. § 33-1368(A), that the above constitutes a _material and irreparable breach_.

        Your Rental Agreement is hereby terminated.

        You are instructed to vacate immediately.

    Concurrently herewith, a lawsuit has been filed against you to evict you and recover possession of the premises, pursuant to A.R.S. § 33-1377.

_____

_____

_____

_____

This notice delivered this date _____ via:

☐ Certified mail

☐ Regular first class mail

☐ Hand delivered

                      Acknowledgment of hand delivery and receipt hereof:

_____

               (signature of tenant)   (date)

FORM 9 - *See* Chapter 2, Section E(7) regarding use of this form. Note: you may want to add or attach the FDPCA notice (*see* Chapter 2, Section E(11)).

FIVE-DAY NOTICE TO PAY OR QUIT

Terry Tenant
123 North Oak Street
Phoenix, Arizona 85999

Notice to Tenant,   Date: *July 2, 1998*

      Pursuant to Arizona Revised Statutes, Title 33, Chapter 10, Section 33-1368(B), you are hereby tendered five-days written notice to remit all due, but as yet unpaid, rent and other amounts owing, in the amount of: *$545.00* (calculated through *July 2, 1998*). The stated amount is calculated as follows:

      $*500.00*_____ Rent for *July 1998*

      $*20.00*_____ Late charges (*$20 on 2nd, plus 1% per day thereafter*)

      $*25.00*_____ Fee for preparing and serving Five-Day Notice.

      $*545.00*_____ Total

The stated "Total" is exclusive of future accruing costs. Additional charges accrue after the date specified above at the daily rate of *$5.00 (1%)*.

      In the event full payment is not tendered within five days after receipt of this notice, your right to possess and occupy the premises will be terminated and an eviction action filed against you to recover possession of the premises, rent, late fees, and any other amounts due under the rental agreement or available by law, including attorney's fees and court costs; you will remain financially responsible for all rent and other charges under the rental agreement until the end of the rental agreement term, subject to the landlord's duty to mitigate damages. Full payment within the five-day period will reinstate the rental agreement. Assuming this notice is delivered on the date specified above, **THE FIFTH DAY FALLS ON: *July 7, 1998*.**

      Alternatively, you may vacate the premises on or before the fifth day. Vacating the premises, however, will not relieve you from liability for the outstanding balance. In the event you have any questions, please contact me.

                     Larry Landlord
                  Larry Landlord (602) 555-1111
                  ABC Apartments
                  123 N. Main Street, Anytown, Arizona 85000

This notice delivered this date *July 2, 1998*_____ via:

☐ Certified mail

☐ Regular first class mail

■ Hand delivered   Acknowledgment of hand delivery and receipt hereof:

               *Terry Tenant*_____ *July 2, 1998*_____

               (signature of tenant)   (date)

FIVE-DAY NOTICE TO PAY OR QUIT

_____

_____

_____

Notice to Tenant,   Date: _____

     Pursuant to Arizona Revised Statutes, Title 33, Chapter 10, Section 33-1368(B), you are hereby tendered five-days written notice to remit all due, but as yet unpaid, rent and other amounts owing, in the amount of: $_____ (calculated through _____). The stated amount is calculated as follows:

    $_____ Rent for _____

    $_____ Rent for _____

    $_____ Late charges (_____)

    $_____ Fee for preparing and serving Five-Day Notice.

    $_____ Other _____

    $_____ Other _____

    $_____ Total

The stated "Total" is exclusive of future accruing costs. Additional charges accrue after the date specified above at the daily rate of $_____.

    In the event full payment is not tendered within five days after receipt of this notice, your right to possess and occupy the premises will be terminated and an eviction action filed against you to recover possession of the premises, rent, late fees, and any other amounts due under the rental agreement or available by law, including attorney's fees and court costs; you will remain financially responsible for all rent and other charges under the rental agreement until the end of the rental agreement term, subject to the landlord's duty to mitigate damages. Full payment within the five-day period will reinstate the rental agreement. Assuming this notice is delivered on the date specified above, **THE FIFTH DAY FALLS ON:**_____.

    Alternatively, you may vacate the premises on or before the fifth day. Vacating the premises, however, will not relieve you from liability for the outstanding balance. In the event you have any questions, please contact me.

_____

_____

_____

_____

This notice delivered this date _____ via:

☐ Certified mail
☐ Regular first class mail
☐ Hand delivered

                            Acknowledgment of hand delivery and receipt hereof:

_____

(signature of tenant)   (date)

FORM 10 - *See* Chapter 5, Section B(3)(b) regarding use of this form.

FIVE-DAY NOTICE OF TERMINATION
NONCOMPLIANCE AFFECTING HEALTH AND SAFETY

Terry Tenant
123 North Oak Street
Phoenix, Arizona 85999

Notice to Tenant,   Date: *July 2, 1998*

You are in violation of your Rental Agreement and/or the Arizona Residential Landlord and Tenant Act and A.R.S. § 33-1341. The specific acts constituting the violation are:

1 - Failure to repair sliding glass door, broken by tenant.

2 - Failure to have trash removed from premises.

3 - Storing gasoline in unsafe containers.

You are hereby notified, pursuant to A.R.S. § 33-1368(A), that this ***noncompliance*** with A.R.S. § 33-1341 (tenant to maintain dwelling unit) ***materially affects health and safety*** and that your right to possess and occupy the premises will terminate upon a date not less than **five (5) days** after receipt of this notice if this noncompliance is not remedied.

Provided this notice is received on the date specified above, your Rental Agreement will terminate on_____*July 7, 1998*_____ if the noncompliance is not remedied.
        (5 calendar days from receipt of notice)

_____*Larry Landlord*_____

_____**Larry Landlord (602) 555-1111**_____

_____**ABC Apartments**_____

_____**123 N. Main Street, Anytown, Arizona 85000****

This notice delivered this date **July 2, 1998**_____ via:

☐ Certified mail

☐ Regular first class mail

■ Hand delivered

Acknowledgment of hand delivery and receipt hereof:

_____*Terry Tenant*_____   _____*July 2, 1998*_____
        (signature of tenant)   (date)

FIVE-DAY NOTICE OF TERMINATION
NONCOMPLIANCE AFFECTING HEALTH AND SAFETY

_____

_____

_____

Notice to Tenant,   Date: _____

      You are in violation of your Rental Agreement and/or the Arizona Residential Landlord and Tenant Act and A.R.S. § 33-1341. The specific acts constituting the violation are:

_____

_____

_____

_____

_____

_____

      You are hereby notified, pursuant to A.R.S. § 33-1368(A), that this *noncompliance* with A.R.S. § 33-1341 (tenant to maintain dwelling unit) *materially affects health and safety* and that your right to possess and occupy the premises will terminate upon a date not less than **five (5) days** after receipt of this notice if this noncompliance is not remedied.

Provided this notice is received on the date specified above, your Rental Agreement will terminate on _____ if the noncompliance is not remedied.
        (5 calendar days from receipt of notice)

_____

_____

_____

_____

This notice delivered this date _____ via:
☐ Certified mail
☐ Regular first class mail
☐ Hand delivered

      Acknowledgment of hand delivery and receipt hereof:

_____
     (signature of tenant)   (date)

FORM 11 - *See* Chapter 5, Section B(3)(a) regarding use of this form.

TEN-DAY NOTICE OF TERMINATION
FOR MATERIAL NONCOMPLIANCE

Terry Tenant
123 North Oak Street
Phoenix, Arizona 85999

Notice to Tenant,   Date: *July 2, 1998*

     You are in violation of your Rental Agreement and/or the Arizona Residential Landlord and Tenant Act. The specific acts constituting the violation are:

1 - Failure to repair damage caused by guest to interior door.

2 - Failure to comply with landlord's rules and regulations; specifically multiple parking violations and parking a commercial vehicle on the premises.

     You are hereby notified, pursuant to A.R.S. § 33-1368(A), that the above constitutes a *material noncompliance* and that your right to possess and occupy the premises will terminate upon a date not less than **ten (10) days** after receipt of this notice if this noncompliance is not remedied.

Provided this notice is received on the date specified above, your Rental Agreement will terminate on_____*July 12, 1998*_____ if the noncompliance is not remedied.

          (10 calendar days from receipt of notice)

                              Larry Landlord
                         Larry Landlord (602) 555-1111
                         ABC Apartments
                         123 N. Main Street, Anytown, Arizona 85000

This notice delivered this date *July 2, 1998*_____ via:
☐ Certified mail
☐ Regular first class mail
■ Hand delivered

          Acknowledgment of hand delivery and receipt hereof:

          Terry Tenant   *July 2, 1998*
          (signature of tenant)   (date)

TEN-DAY NOTICE OF TERMINATION
FOR MATERIAL NONCOMPLIANCE

_____

_____

_____

Notice to Tenant,   Date: _____

     You are in violation of your Rental Agreement and/or the Arizona Residential Landlord and Tenant Act. The specific acts constituting the violation are:

_____

_____

_____

_____

_____

     You are hereby notified, pursuant to A.R.S. § 33-1368(A), that the above constitutes a _**material noncompliance**_ and that your right to possess and occupy the premises will terminate upon a date not less than **ten (10) days** after receipt of this notice if this noncompliance is not remedied.

Provided this notice is received on the date specified above, your Rental Agreement will terminate on _____ if the noncompliance is not remedied.
                (10 calendar days from receipt of notice)

                                                  _____

                                                  _____

                                                  _____

                                                  _____

This notice delivered this date _____ via:
☐ Certified mail
☐ Regular first class mail
☐ Hand delivered

                                    Acknowledgment of hand delivery and receipt hereof:

                                    _____

                                     (signature of tenant)   (date)

FORM 12 - This is a multi-purpose form. You may use it to:

      (1) terminate a month-to-month tenancy, which may be terminated at any time for any reason or for no reason;

      (2) give notice to a tenant, whose rental agreement term is soon due to expire, that you will not be renewing his/her rental agreement, which you may issue for any reason or for no reason; and

      (3) give a ten day notice of termination to a tenant who has committed a second noncompliance (material or affecting health and safety) during the term of the lease of the same or similar nature.

See Chapter 4, Section B(1)(a) regarding use of this form to terminate a month-to-month tenancy. *See* Chapter 5, Section B(3)(e) regarding use of this form to terminate tenancy because of second noncompliance anytime during the term of the lease (including extensions or renewals) of the same or similar nature.

$\longrightarrow$

NOTICE OF TERMINATION OF RENTAL AGREEMENT

_____

_____

_____

Notice to Tenant,   Date: _____

☐ **Termination of month-to-month tenancy.** Pursuant to A.R.S. § 33-1375, you are hereby notified that the landlord has elected to terminate your month-to-month tenancy. Your tenancy will terminate on _____. If you remain in possession beyond this date, your conduct will be deemed willful and you will be considered a "holdover tenant" for purposes of assessing "holdover rent" and/or recovering damages pursuant to A.R.S. § 33-1375(C).

☐ **Notice of nonrenewal.** The term of your present rental agreement is due to expire on _____. You are hereby notified that your tenancy will not be renewed and that you must vacate on or before the expiration date. If you remain in possession beyond this date, your conduct will be deemed willful and you will be considered a "holdover tenant" for purposes of assessing "holdover rent" and/or recovering damages pursuant to A.R.S. § 33-1375(C).

☐ **Ten day notice to terminate for repeated noncompliance.** You were previously notified of a noncompliance on _____. A second noncompliance of the same or similar nature has occurred during the term of the lease and after the previous remedy of the prior noncompliance. Specifically, _____

_____.
(describe noncompliance)

You are hereby notified, pursuant to A.R.S. § 33-1368(A), your right to possess and occupy the premises has been terminated and a lawsuit will be filed to evict you from the premises ten (10) days (or more) after receipt of this notice, unless you vacate the premises within ten days after receiving this notice.

_____

_____

_____

_____

This notice delivered this date _____ via:
☐ Certified mail
☐ Regular first class mail
☐ Hand delivered

Acknowledgment of hand delivery and receipt hereof:

_____

(signature of tenant)   (date)

FORM 13 - *See* Chapter 5, Section A(1) regarding use of this form The landlord is now required to give the tenant upon move-in a written notice, pursuant to A.R.S. § 33-1321(C), that the tenant may be present during the move-out inspection. Giving the tenant this form at the commencement of the tenancy satisfies this requirement. It also reminds them of the notice requirements when the tenant fills out the form.

$\rightarrow$

TENANT'S NOTICE OF TERMINATION

_____
_____
_____

Notice to Landlord,   Date: _____

     I hereby submit my written notice to terminate tenancy. I will vacate the property located at: _____ on _____ .
(rental property address)   (date)

     I understand that I must give at least thirty (30) days' notice and that the thirtieth day of the notice must fall on or before the last day of the present rental period. I understand that **TENANCY CANNOT BE TERMINATED IN THE MIDDLE OF THE RENTAL PERIOD.** Example: Today is April 15 and I wish to terminate tenancy. Notice must be given on or before the last day of the present rental period; the present rental period is April 1 through April 30; therefore, notice must be given on or before April 30, and tenancy will terminate as of May 31.

     I understand that return of any refundable deposits is conditional upon giving adequate notice to terminate and compliance with the other provisions of the Rental Agreement. I understand that any refundable deposits will be mailed within fourteen (14) business days hereof or the date I/we vacate the unit, whichever occurs last. The check for the deposit(s) will be mailed to the address listed below, or, if none provided, to my last known address, less any amounts outstanding for past due rent, charges for cleaning in excess of my cleaning deposit, repairs, any amounts owed by tenant(s) to the landlord, and any other amounts specified in the rental agreement or allowed by law. As previously agreed in the Rental Agreement, I will allow landlord access to the unit to show prospective tenants.

     I understand that I may be present during the move-out inspection. ☐ Please consider this my request to be notified of the date and time of the move-out inspection.

_____   _____
_____   _____

(print names)   (tenants' signatures)

FORWARDING ADDRESS:

_____
_____

FORM 14 - *See* Chapter 2, Section E(6) regarding use of this form. The bottom portion of the form is intended for the landlord's use; this portion of the form **SHOULD NOT be included on the copy of the form sent to the tenants.** The blank form on the next page has been designed so that the shaded area may be printed on the back of the form or on a separate sheet, so that the shaded area is not inadvertently sent to the tenant.

DISPOSITION OF DEPOSITS

In accordance with the Arizona Residential Landlord and Tenant Act, specifically, A.R.S. § 33-1321, the following discloses the disposition of your deposit(s):

DEPOSITS

Nonrefundable deposits:

Cleaning deposit (Nonrefundable)	$ 0.00
Redecorating deposit (Nonrefundable)	$ 100.00
Other _____	$ 0.00
Total:	$ 100.00
Amount refundable:	$ 0.00

Refundable deposits:

Cleaning deposit (Refundable)	$ 75.00
Redecorating deposit (Refundable)	$ 0.00
Security deposit (Refundable)	$ 300.00
Total:	$ 375.00

DEDUCTIONS

Unpaid rent	$	0.00
Late charges	$	0.00
Damages_____	$	65.00
Other _*Replace missing bathroom fixture*_	$	40.00
TOTAL DEDUCTIONS	$	105.00
AMOUNT OF REFUNDABLE DEPOSITS:	$	270.00

■ Refund Due to Tenant   ☐ Balance Due to Landlord; Payment immediately due.

Larry Landlord

_____

This notice delivered this date _*June 5, 1998*_ via:

Larry Landlord (602) 555-1111

ABC Apartments

☐ Certified mail

123 N. Main Street, Anytown, Arizona 85000

■ Regular first class mail

☐ Hand delivered   Acknowledgment of hand delivery and receipt hereof:

N/A

_____
(signature of tenant)   (date)

Notes for landlord: **(Reverse side of Form)**

Refund check #_*1001*_ issued on _*June 5, 1998*_, for $_*270.00*_

Check made payable to: _*Terry and Tina Tenant*_

(should be made payable to all tenants on rental agreement, unless otherwise authorized)

Date tenant vacated the unit and returned keys: _*May 31, 1998*_

Date tenant requested (orally or in writing) return of deposit: _*June 2, 1998*_

Date tenancy terminated: _*May 31, 1998*_

A.R.S. § 33-1321(C) provides that refund must be sent to tenant within fourteen business days after termination of the tenancy and delivery of possession and demand by the tenant.

DISPOSITION OF DEPOSITS

_____

_____

_____

Notice to Tenant,   Date: _____

      In accordance with the Arizona Residential Landlord and Tenant Act, specifically, A.R.S. § 33-1321, the following discloses the disposition of your deposit(s):

DEPOSITS

Nonrefundable deposits:

    Cleaning deposit (Nonrefundable) $_____

    Redecorating deposit (Nonrefundable) $_____

    Other _____ $_____

                                            Total: $_____

                            Amount refundable: $___0.00___

Refundable deposits:

    Security deposit (Refundable) $_____

    Cleaning deposit (Refundable) $_____

    Redecorating deposit (Refundable) $_____

    Other _____ $_____

                                            Total: $_____

DEDUCTIONS

    Unpaid rent $_____

    Late charges $_____

    Damages_____ $_____

    Other_____ $_____

    Other_____ $_____

    Other_____ $_____

    Other_____ $_____

                TOTAL DEDUCTIONS $_____

                AMOUNT OF REFUNDABLE DEPOSITS: $_____

☐ Refund Due to Tenant   ☐ Balance Due to Landlord; Payment immediately due.

                             _____

                             _____

                             _____

                             _____

This notice delivered this date _____ via:

☐ Certified mail

☐ Regular first class mail

☐ Hand delivered

                      Acknowledgment of hand delivery and receipt hereof:

                   _____

                     (signature of tenant)   (date)

(Back side of Disposition of Deposits)
(Do not include this portion of the form on the copy sent to the Tenant)

Notes for landlord:

Refund check #_____ issued on_____ for $_____

Check made payable to: _____
(should be made payable to all tenants on rental agreement, unless otherwise authorized)

Date tenant vacated the unit and returned keys:_____

Date tenancy terminated: _____

Date tenant requested (orally or in writing) return of deposit: _____
(A.R.S. § 33-1321(C) provides that refund must be sent to tenant within fourteen business days after termination of the tenancy and delivery of possession and demand by the tenant.)

→

FORM 15 - *See* Chapter 6, Section B, and page 204, regarding use of this form. This letter informs the tenant that the Sheriff or constable will forcibly remove them from the Premises if they do not vacate by the fifth calendar days. Most tenants prefer to avoid this process. In addition, you are required by statute, A.R.S. § 12-1598.03(2), to serve upon the tenant a written demand for payment of the Judgment before you garnish the tenant's wages; this form satisfies that requirement.

POST-JUDGMENT NOTICE TO TENANTS

_____

_____

_____

Notice to Tenant,   Date: _____

      Judgment has been entered against you in the forcible/special detainer action previously filed against you. Your right to occupy the leased premises was thereby terminated by a court of law and you must vacate.

      In the event you have not voluntarily vacated the leased premises by the fifth calendar day after entry of Judgment, the Court will issue the Landlord a Writ of Restitution. The Writ of Restitution is a Court Order that instructs the Sheriff or Constable to execute the Writ and forcibly remove you and your personal property from the leased premises (this will occur whether or not you are home at the time the Sheriff/Constable arrives).

      The fifth calendar day after entry of Judgment is _____.
You will not receive any further notice to vacate.

      In addition, demand is hereby made for full and immediate payment of the Judgment. Alternatively, you may agree to pay the nonexempt portion of your wages until the Judgment is satisfied. In the event full payment is not received or you have not agreed to pay the nonexempt portion of your wages within ten days after receipt hereof and, thereafter, continue to pay the nonexempt portion of your wages until the Judgment is satisfied, then the landlord will exhaust all remedies under the law to involuntarily collect the Judgment, including a Writ of Garnishment served upon your employer(s).

_____

_____

_____

_____

This notice delivered this date _____ via:
☐ Certified mail
☐ Regular first class mail
☐ Hand delivered

         Acknowledgment of hand delivery and receipt hereof:

_____

      (signature of tenant)   (date)

$\longrightarrow$

FORM 16 - *See* page 249 regarding use of this form. If the tenant leaves personal property behind, you will also need Forms 17 and 18.

FORM 17 and 18 - SALE OF PERSONAL PROPERTY (next two pages after Form 16) - *see* pages 251 to 254 regarding use of these forms.

$\longrightarrow$ $\longrightarrow$

NOTICE OF ABANDONMENT

_____

_____

_____

Notice to Tenant,   Date: _____

☐   **Personal Property Present**. You have been absent from the leased premises, without notice to the landlord, for at least seven days _and_ rent is outstanding and unpaid for at least ten days. There is no reasonable evidence that you are occupying the leased premises, except for the presence of some personal property within the leased premises. Consequently, pursuant to Arizona Revised Statutes, Title 33, Chapter 10, Section 33-1370, you are hereby tendered written notice that the landlord deems the leased premises to be "abandoned," as that term is defined by A.R.S. § 33-1370(H).

☐   **No Personal Property Present**. You have been absent from the leased premises, without notice to the landlord, for at least five days _and_ rent is outstanding and unpaid for at least five days, and none of your personal property remains within the leased premises. Consequently, pursuant to Arizona Revised Statutes, Title 33, Chapter 10, Section 33-1370, you are hereby tendered written notice that the landlord deems the leased premises to be "abandoned," as that term is defined by A.R.S. § 33-1370(H).

Unless you contact the landlord, the landlord shall enter and retake possession of the leased premises five days after this notice has been: (1) posted on the door to the leased premises or some other conspicuous spot and (2) mailed via certified mail, return receipt requested, to your last known address _and_ any alternate addresses known to the landlord. Any personal property remaining on or in the leased premises shall be handled in accordance with A.R.S. § 33-1370. To prevent loss of possession of the leased premises, contact:

_____ at _____ on or before _____.
     (Name)   (phone #)   (5 business days after posting and mailing)

_____

_____

_____

_____

This notice delivered this date _____ via:
☐ Certified mail
☐ Regular first class mail
☐ Hand delivered

                           Acknowledgment of hand delivery and receipt hereof:

             _____
                 (signature of tenant)   (date)

NOTICE OF SALE OF PERSONAL PROPERTY
(TEN DAY NOTICE)

_____

_____

_____

Notice to Tenant,   Date: _____

      You have vacated the Premises (described below), either by abandonment or by eviction, and you have forgotten or abandoned various items of personal property, which remain on the Premises. The landlord has held these items for the period of time required by law (i.e., 10 days after abandonment; 21 days after eviction). You are hereby notified, pursuant to A.R.S. § 33-1023(A), that you have ten (10) days within which to pay all moving and storage expenses incurred by the landlord on your behalf to move and store your personal property. Thereafter, if you do not provide the landlord with written notification of your intent to reclaim your property and, within five days thereafter, remit payment of the moving and storage costs and reclaim your personal property, the personal property will be sold at public auction and the proceeds applied to the amount due (below) and any other amounts allowed by law to be collected by the landlord.

Property Address:

_____

Moving & Storage fees: $_____

_____

_____

_____

_____

This notice delivered this date _____ via:
☐ Certified mail
☐ Regular first class mail
☐ Hand delivered

Acknowledgment of hand delivery and receipt hereof:

_____
    (signature of tenant)   (date)

NOTICE OF SALE OF PERSONAL PROPERTY
(FIVE DAY NOTICE)

_____

_____

_____

Notice to Tenant,   Date: _____

      You are hereby notified, pursuant to A.R.S. § 33-1023(A), that your personal property will be sold at public auction. The public auction will be conducted at _____, on _____, at _____ AM/PM.

                (location)   (date)   (time)

_____

_____

_____

_____

This notice delivered this date _____ via:

☐ Certified mail
☐ Regular first class mail
☐ Hand delivered

Acknowledgment of hand delivery and receipt hereof:

_____

    (signature of tenant)   (date)

Form 19 - *See* page 102 regarding use of this form.

→

Form 20 - Pool Safety Notice (2 pages, following Form 19). *See* page 27 regarding the use of this form.

→ →

LEASE GUARANTY

For valuable consideration, the undersigned hereby jointly and severally, unconditionally and irrevocably, guarantee, warrant and assure to Landlord, without limitation, and as and for their own obligation, the full payment of all sums due by Tenant under this Rental Agreement, including any extensions, amendments or modifications made after the execution hereof, including: Rent, Late Fees, Returned Check Fees, Notice Fees, Drive-by Fees, attorneys' fees, court costs, sums due to Landlord for damages caused to the Premises by Tenant and/or their guests, and any other sums owed by Tenant to Landlord by law, under the Rental Agreement, or otherwise. Guarantor(s) acknowledge and agree that this obligation is separate and independent of that of Tenant and that Landlord may proceed against Tenant, Guarantor(s), or both, at Landlord's option. Guarantor(s) acknowledge and agree that this obligation shall continue until Guarantor(s) is released by Landlord in writing (an oral release shall not be effective). Further, Guarantor(s) hereby unconditionally and irrevocably covenant, until released, to indemnify, defend, exonerate and hold harmless Landlord for any loss, damage or cost of any kind or nature whatsoever, including attorneys' fees, litigation expenses and court costs resulting from any breach or failure of performance on the part of Tenant with respect to any of Tenant's obligations. Guarantor(s) agree that notice of any default delivered to the Tenant shall be deemed notice to Guarantor(s) and hereby waive separate notice to Guarantor(s).

GUARANTOR(S)

_____	_____	_____
Signature	Print Name	Date
_____	_____	_____
Signature	Print Name	Date
_____	_____	_____
Signature	Print Name	Date

AN IMPORTANT NOTICE ABOUT POOL SAFETY*

Drowning is a serious threat to young children in Arizona. Young children also suffer from a high number of near drownings that may lead to permanent, severe disability. Most of these incidents occur in the child's own backyard swimming pool. These tragedies must be stopped. To that end, the Arizona Legislature has passed a law requiring that new occupants of dwellings with pools, and persons having a pool installed, receive this safety message about steps to prevent drownings and the legal responsibilities of pool ownership.

State of Arizona law requires a barrier between the house and pool.**

This law applies to homes with both a child under 6 years of and a pool built after June 1, 1991. This law aims to impede children's access to their own pools. Likewise, all pools must have a barrier to keep out uninvited neighborhood children.

Unless a local code provides otherwise***, **the barrier must:**

- **Entirely enclose the pool area.**
- **Be at least 5 feet high,** measured on the outside of the barrier.
- **Not have openings, handholds or footholds** that can be used to climb the barrier. Wire mesh or chain link fences shall have a maximum mesh size of 1 3/4 inches measured horizontally.
- **Have no openings through which a sphere 4 inches in diameter can pass.** Horizontal components of any barrier shall be spaced not less than 45 inches apart measured vertically or shall be placed on the pool side of the barrier which shall have no opening greater than 1 3/4 inches measured horizontally.
- **Be at least 20 inches from the water's edge.**
- **Prevent direct access from the house to the pool.**

Gates must be self-closing and self-latching with the latch located at least 54 inches above the ground or on the pool side with a release mechanism at least 5 inches below the top of the gate and no opening greater than 1/2 inch within 24 inches of the release mechanism or be secured by a padlock or similar device which requires a key, electronic opener or integral combination which can have the latch at any height. **Gates must open outward from the pool.**

If a wall of the home forms part of the barrier, one of the following must be used:

- A barrier at least 4 feet high between the home and the pool which otherwise meets all of the requirements for a barrier set forth above.
- A motorized, safety pool cover which does not require manual operation other than the use of a key switch which meets the American Society of Testing and Materials (ASTM) emergency standard 13-89 (now ASTM #F 1346-91).
- Self-latching devices on all doors with direct access to the pool. Such latches shall meet the requirements for latches on self-closing gates set forth above.
- Emergency escape or rescue windows from sleeping rooms with access to the pool shall be equipped with a latching device not less than 54 inches above the floor. All other openable dwelling unit or guest room windows with similar access shall be equipped with a screwed-in-place wire mesh screen, or a keyed lock that prevents opening the window more than 4 inches, or a latching device located not less than 54 inches above the floor.

An above-ground swimming pool shall have non-climbable exterior sides which are a minimum height of 4 feet. Any access ladder or steps shall be removable without tools and secured in an inaccessible position with a latching device not less than 54 inches above the ground when the pool is not in use.

---

*   Approved pursuant to Arizona Revised Statutes § 36-1681 and A.A.C. R9-3-101.

**   "Pool" means an in-ground or above-ground swimming pool or other contained body of water 18 or more inches in depth, wider than 8 feet, and intended for swimming.

*** Phoenix, Peoria, Tucson, and some other cities and unincorporated areas of Maricopa, Pima, and Pinal counties have different pool barrier requirements- Check with your city and county governments to see if they have adopted different pool barrier requirements.

Supervision is the key to prevent drownings.

Never leave children unsupervised in the pool or inside the pool area -- **not even for a second!**

Inform guests to your home of the importance of closely watching children around water. At parties, make sure someone is always watching the children around the pool.

Don't count on barriers to keep children from reaching the pool. **No barrier is foolproof.** Barriers only slow a child's access to the pool.

In case of an emergency: act immediately -

1 - <u>Shout</u> for help.
2 - <u>Pull</u> the child out of the water.
3 - <u>Take</u> the child to the phone and <u>dial 911</u> (or the local emergency number) for help-
4 - <u>Check</u> airway and breathing. If needed, start CPR immediately. CPR can save lives, and prevent serious injury.

Other smart tips to protect children around water:

DON'T:
- Don't keep toys, tricycles or other playthings in the pool area. Also, remove items that a child could use to climb over the barrier.
- Don't be distracted by phone calls, doorbells, or chores while children are in the pool. Your full attention should be on the children.
- Don't rely on swimming lessons or "floaties" to protect your children.
- Don't prop gates open.

DO:
- Attend a CPR class. All family members and babysitters should know CPR. For the nearest class, contact your local fire department.
- Post 911 (or the local emergency number) on all phones.
- Learn water rescue. Keep lifesaving equipment mounted near the pool, especially if you can't swim.
- Lock passageways (such as pet doors) leading to the pool.
- Inspect latches and gates regularly; keep them in working order.
- Set a good example. Insist on safety around the pool.

☐ ADHS-DDP-OCDE; S7 AUG 1992 ☐

Historical Note
Emergency rule adopted effective June 16, 1992, pursuant to A.R.S. § 41-1026, valid for only 90 days (Supp. 92-2). Emergency expired.
Adopted effective October 22, 1992 (Supp. 92-4).

Form 21 - *See* pages 28 to 31 regarding use of this form. This is the format provided by EPA and HUD for rental housing.

→

Disclosure of Information on Lead-Based Paint and Lead-Based Paint Hazards

Lead Warning Statement
Housing built before 1978 may contain lead-based paint. Lead from paint, paint chips, and dust can pose health hazards if not taken care of properly. Lead exposure is especially harmful to young children and pregnant women. Before renting pre-1978 housing, landlords must disclose the presence of known lead-based paint and lead-based paint hazards in the dwelling. Tenants must also receive a Federally approved pamphlet on lead poisoning prevention.

Lessor's Disclosure (initial)

_____ (a)   Presence of lead-based paint or lead-based paint hazards (check one below):

☐   Known lead-based paint and/or lead-based paint hazards are present in the housing (explain).

_____

_____

☐   Lessor has no knowledge of lead-based paint and/or lead-based paint hazards in the housing.

_____ (b)   Records and reports available to the lessor (check one below):

☐   Lessor has provided the lessee with all available records and reports pertaining to lead-based paint and/or lead-based paint hazards in the housing (list documents below).

_____

_____

☐   Lessor has no reports or records pertaining to lead-based paint and/or lead-based paint hazards in the housing.

Lessee's Acknowledgment (initial)

_____ (c)   Lessee has received copies of all information listed above.
_____ (d)   Lessee has received the pamphlet *Protect Your Family from Lead in Your Home.*

Agent's Acknowledgment (initial)

_____ (e)   Agent has informed the lessor of the lessor's obligations under 42 U.S.C. 4582(d) and is aware of his/her responsibility to ensure compliance.

Certification of Accuracy
The following parties have reviewed the information above and certify, to the best of their knowledge, that the information provided by the signatory is true and accurate.

_____ Lessor	Date	_____ Lessor	Date
_____ Lessee	Date	_____ Lessee	Date
_____ Agent	Date	_____ Agent	Date

PAMPHLET: "Protect Your Family From Lead in Your Home"   →

If your rental unit contains lead-based paint or lead-based paint hazards, you are required to provide prospective tenants with a pamphlet from the United States Environmental Protection Agency, entitled "Protect Your Family From Lead in Your Home." This pamphlet, "Protect Your Family From Lead in Your Home," is reproduced in its entirely on the next sixteen pages. You may copy these pages directly out of this book (the page numbers and Appendix markings of this book have been omitted so that they will not appear on your copy) and distribute to your prospective tenants, thereby satisfying this requirement. The pamphlet, as reproduced here, is in the proper order and complete -- do not alter in any way before distributing to your prospective tenants.

Alternatively, you may purchase copies of the pamphlet from the U.S. Government Printing Office; telephone number: (202) 512-1800 ($26.00 for 50 copies, document #055-000-00507-9 for English version, document #055-000-00537-1 for Spanish version).

You must also have the tenant complete a lead-based paint disclosure form (*see* Form 21, immediately prior). This is the format provided by EPA and HUD and will satisfy the legal requirements.[1]

See pages 28 to 31 regarding use of the pamphlet and form. *See also* "EPA/HUD Fact Sheet, EPA and HUD Move to Protect Children from Lead-Based Paint Poisoning; Disclosure of Lead-Based Paint Hazards in Housing," EPA-747-F-96-002, March 1996 (reprinted on pages 30 and 31).

---

[1] *See* 24 CFR Part 35; 40 CFR Part 745 (1996).

Protect Your Family From Lead In Your Home

EPA United States Environmental Protection Agency

United States Consumer Product Safety Commission

United States Department of Housing and Urban Development

U.S. EPA Washington DC 20460
U.S. CPSC Washington DC 20207
U.S. HUD Washington DC 20410

EPA747-K-94-001
May 1995

Are You Planning To Buy, Rent, or Renovate a Home Built Before 1978?

Many houses and apartments built before 1978 have paint that contains lead (called lead-based paint). Lead from paint, chips, and dust can pose serious health hazards if not taken care of properly.

By 1996, federal law will require that individuals receive certain information before renting, buying, or renovating pre-1978 housing:

LANDLORDS will have to disclose known information on lead-based paint hazards before leases take effect. Leases will include a federal form about lead-based paint.

SELLERS will have to disclose known information on lead-based paint hazards before selling a house. Sales contracts will include a federal form about lead-based paint in the building. Buyers will have up to 10 days to check for lead hazards.

RENOVATORS will have to give you this pamphlet before starting work.

IF YOU WANT MORE INFORMATION on these requirements, call the National Lead Information Clearinghouse at **1-800-424-LEAD**.

This document is in the public domain. It may be reproduced by an individual or organization without permission. Information provided in this booklet is based upon current scientific and technical understanding of the issues presented and is reflective of the jurisdictional boundaries established by the statutes governing the co-authoring agencies. Following the advice given will not necessarily provide complete protection in all situations or against all health hazards that can be caused by lead exposure.

IMPORTANT!

Lead From Paint, Dust, and Soil Can Be Dangerous If Not Managed Properly

FACT: Lead exposure can harm young children and babies even before they are born.

FACT: Even children that seem healthy can have high levels of lead in their bodies.

FACT: People can get lead in their bodies by breathing or swallowing lead dust, or by eating soil or paint chips with lead in them.

FACT: People have many options for reducing lead hazards. In most cases, lead-based paint that is in good condition is not a hazard.

FACT: Removing lead-based paint improperly can increase the danger to your family.

If you think your home might have lead hazards, read this pamphlet to learn some simple steps to protect your family.

Lead Gets in the Body in Many Ways

1 out of every 11 children in the United States has dangerous levels of lead in the bloodstream.

Even children who appear healthy can have dangerous levels of lead.

People can get lead in their body if they:

◆ Put their hands or other objects covered with lead dust in their mouths.

◆ Eat paint chips or soil that contain lead.

◆ Breathe in lead dust (especially during renovations that disturb painted surfaces).

Lead is even more dangerous to children than adults because:

◆ Babies and young children often put their hands and other objects in their mouths. These objects can have lead dust on them.

◆ Children's growing bodies absorb more lead.

◆ Children's brains and nervous systems are more sensitive to the damaging effects of lead.

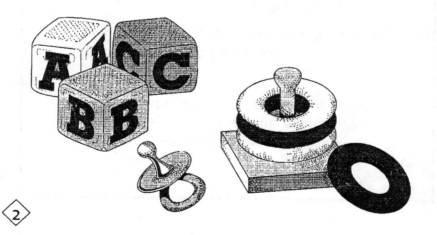

Lead's Effects

If not detected early, children with lead in their bodies can suffer from:

◆ Damage to the brain and nervous system

◆ Behavior and learning problems (such as hyperactivity)

◆ Slowed growth

◆ Hearing problems

◆ Headaches

Lead is also harmful to adults. Adults can suffer from:

◆ Difficulties during pregnancy

◆ Other reproductive problems (in both men and women)

◆ High blood pressure

◆ Digestive problems

◆ Nerve disorders

◆ Memory and concentration problems

◆ Muscle and joint pain

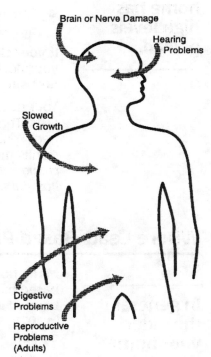

Brain or Nerve Damage

Hearing Problems

Slowed Growth

Digestive Problems

Reproductive Problems (Adults)

Lead affects the body in many ways.

③

Checking Your Family for Lead

Get your children tested if you think your home has high levels of lead.

A simple blood test can detect high levels of lead. Blood tests are important for:

◆ Children who are 6 months to 1 year old (6 months if you live in an older home with cracking or peeling paint).

◆ Family members that you think might have high levels of lead.

If your child is older than 1 year, talk to your doctor about whether your child needs testing.

Your doctor or health center can do blood tests. They are inexpensive and sometimes free. Your doctor will explain what the test results mean. *Treatment can range from changes in your diet to medication or a hospital stay.*

Where Lead-Based Paint Is Found

In general, the older your home, the more likely it has lead-based paint.

Many homes built before 1978 have lead-based paint. The federal government banned lead-based paint from housing in 1978. Some states stopped its use even earlier.

Lead can be found:

◆ In homes in the city, country, or suburbs.

◆ In apartments, single-family homes, and both private and public housing.

◆ Inside *and* outside of the house.

◆ In soil around a home. (Soil can pick up lead from exterior paint, or other sources such as past use of leaded gas in cars).

Where Lead Is Likely To Be a Hazard

Lead-based paint that is in good condition is usually not a hazard.

Peeling, chipping, chalking, or cracking lead-based paint is a hazard and needs immediate attention.

Lead-based paint may also be a hazard when found on surfaces that children can chew or that get a lot of wear-and-tear. These areas include:

◆ Windows and window sills.

◆ Doors and door frames.

◆ Stairs, railings, and banisters.

◆ Porches and fences.

Lead dust can form when lead-based paint is dry scraped, dry sanded, or heated. Dust also forms when painted surfaces bump or rub together. Lead chips and dust can get on surfaces and objects that people touch. Settled lead dust can reenter the air when people vacuum, sweep, or walk through it.

Lead in soil can be a hazard when children play in bare soil or when people bring soil into the house on their shoes. Call your state agency (see page 12) to find out about soil testing for lead.

Lead from paint chips, which you can see, and lead dust, which you can't always see, can both be serious hazards.

⟨5⟩

Checking Your Home for Lead

Just knowing that a home has lead-based paint may not tell you if there is a hazard.

You can get your home checked for lead hazards in one of two ways, or both:

◆ A paint **inspection** tells you the lead content of every painted surface in your home. It won't tell you whether the paint is a hazard or how you should deal with it.

◆ A **risk assessment** tells you if there are any sources of serious lead exposure (such as peeling paint and lead dust). It also tells you what actions to take to address these hazards.

Have qualified professionals do the work. *The federal government is writing standards for inspectors and risk assessors. Some states might already have standards in place.* Call your state agency for help with locating qualified professionals in your area (see page 12).

Trained professionals use a range of methods when checking your home, including:

◆ Visual inspection of paint condition and location.

◆ Lab tests of paint samples.

◆ Surface dust tests.

◆ A portable x-ray fluorescence machine.

Home test kits for lead are available, but recent studies suggest that they are not always accurate. Consumers should not rely on these tests before doing renovations or to assure safety.

What You Can Do Now To Protect Your Family

If you suspect that your house has lead hazards, you can take some immediate steps to reduce your family's risk:

- ◆ **If you rent, notify your landlord of peeling or chipping paint.**

- ◆ **Clean up paint chips immediately.**

- ◆ **Clean floors, window frames, window sills, and other surfaces weekly.** Use a mop or sponge with warm water and a general all-purpose cleaner or a cleaner made specifically for lead. REMEMBER: NEVER MIX AMMONIA AND BLEACH PRODUCTS TOGETHER SINCE THEY CAN FORM A DANGEROUS GAS.

- ◆ **Thoroughly rinse sponges and mop heads after cleaning dirty or dusty areas.**

- ◆ **Wash children's hands often, especially before they eat and before nap time and bed time.**

- ◆ **Keep play areas clean.** Wash bottles, pacifiers, toys, and stuffed animals regularly.

- ◆ **Keep children from chewing window sills or other painted surfaces.**

- ◆ **Clean or remove shoes before entering your home to avoid tracking in lead from soil.**

- ◆ **Make sure children eat nutritious, low-fat meals high in iron and calcium,** such as spinach and low-fat dairy products. Children with good diets absorb less lead.

7

How To Significantly Reduce Lead Hazards

Removing lead improperly can increase the hazard to your family by spreading even more lead dust around the house.

Always use a professional who is trained to remove lead hazards safely.

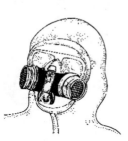

In addition to day-to-day cleaning and good nutrition:

◆ You can **temporarily** reduce lead hazards by taking actions such as repairing damaged painted surfaces and planting grass to cover soil with high lead levels. These actions (called "interim controls") are not permanent solutions and will need ongoing attention.

◆ To **permanently** remove lead hazards, you must hire a lead "abatement" contractor. Abatement (or permanent hazard elimination) methods include removing, sealing, or enclosing lead-based paint with special materials. Just painting over the hazard with regular paint is not enough.

Always hire a person with special training for correcting lead problems—someone who knows how to do this work safely and has the proper equipment to clean up thoroughly. If possible, hire a certified lead abatement contractor. Certified contractors will employ qualified workers and follow strict safety rules as set by their state or by the federal government.

Call your state agency (see page 12) for help with locating qualified contractors in your area and to see if financial assistance is available.

8

Remodeling or Renovating a Home With Lead-Based Paint

Take precautions before you begin remodeling or renovations that disturb painted surfaces (such as scraping off paint or tearing out walls):

◆ **Have the area tested for lead-based paint.**

◆ **Do not use a dry scraper, belt-sander, propane torch, or heat gun** to remove lead-based paint. These actions create large amounts of lead dust and fumes. Lead dust can remain in your home long after the work is done.

◆ **Temporarily move your family** (especially children and pregnant women) out of the apartment or house until the work is done and the area is properly cleaned. If you can't move your family, at least completely seal off the work area.

◆ **Follow other safety measures to reduce lead hazards.** You can find out about other safety measures by calling 1-800-424-LEAD. Ask for the brochure "Reducing Lead Hazards When Remodeling Your Home." This brochure explains what to do before, during, and after renovations.

If you have already completed renovations or remodeling that could have released lead-based paint or dust, get your young children tested and follow the steps outlined on page 7 of this brochure.

If not conducted properly, certain types of renovations can release lead from paint and dust into the air.

Other Sources of Lead

While paint, dust, and soil are the most common lead hazards, other lead sources also exist.

◆ **Drinking water.** Your home might have plumbing with lead or lead solder. Call your local health department or water supplier to find out about testing your water. You cannot see, smell, or taste lead, and boiling your water will not get rid of lead. If you think your plumbing might have lead in it:

  • Use only cold water for drinking and cooking.

  • Run water for 15 to 30 seconds before drinking it, especially if you have not used your water for a few hours.

◆ **The job.** If you work with lead, you could bring it home on your hands or clothes. Shower and change clothes before coming home. Launder your clothes separately from the rest of your family's.

◆ Old painted **toys** and **furniture.**

◆ Food and liquids stored in **lead crystal** or **lead-glazed pottery or porcelain.**

◆ **Lead smelters** or other industries that release lead into the air.

◆ **Hobbies** that use lead, such as making pottery or stained glass, or refinishing furniture.

◆ **Folk remedies** that contain lead, such as "greta" and "azarcon" used to treat an upset stomach.

For More Information

The National Lead Information Center

Call **1-800-LEAD-FYI** to learn how to protect children from lead poisoning.

For other information on lead hazards, call the center's clearinghouse at **1-800-424-LEAD.** For the hearing impaired, call, **TDD 1-800-526-5456**. (FAX: **202-659-1192,** Internet: **EHC@CAIS.COM**).

EPA's Safe Drinking Water Hotline

Call **1-800-426-4791** for information about lead in drinking water.

Consumer Product Safety Commission Hotline

To request information on lead in consumer products, or to report an unsafe consumer product or a product-related injury call **1-800-638-2772**. (Internet: info@cpsc.gov). For the hearing impaired, call **1-800-638-8270**.

Local Sources of Information

State Health and Environmental Agencies

Some cities and states have their own rules for lead-based paint activities. Check with your state agency (listed below) to see if state or local laws apply to you. Most state agencies can also provide information on finding a lead abatement firm in your area, and on possible sources of financial aid for reducing lead hazards.

State/Region	Phone Number		
Alabama	(205) 242-5661	Missouri	(314) 526-4911
Alaska	(907) 465-5152	Montana	(406) 444-3671
Arkansas	(501) 661-2534	Nebraska	(402) 471-2451
Arizona	(602) 542-7307	Nevada	(702) 687-6615
California	(510) 450-2424	New Hampshire	(603) 271-4507
Colorado	(303) 692-3012	New Jersey	(609) 633-2043
Connecticut	(203) 566-5808	New Mexico	(505) 841-8024
Wash. DC	(202) 727-9850	New York	(800) 458-1158
Delaware	(302) 739-4735	North Carolina	(919) 715-3293
Florida	(904) 488-3385	North Dakota	(701) 328-5188
Georgia	(404) 657-6514	Ohio	(614) 466-1450
Hawaii	(808) 832-5860	Oklahoma	(405) 271-5220
Idaho	(208) 332-5544	Oregon	(503) 248-5240
Illinois	(800) 545-2200	Pennsylvania	(717) 782-2884
Indiana	(317) 382-6662	Rhode Island	(401) 277-3424
Iowa	(800) 972-2026	South Carolina	(803) 935-7945
Kansas	(913) 296-0189	South Dakota	(605) 773-3153
Kentucky	(502) 564-2154	Tennessee	(615) 741-5683
Louisiana	(504) 765-0219	Texas	(512) 834-6600
Massachusetts	(800) 532-9571	Utah	(801) 536-4000
Maryland	(410) 631-3859	Vermont	(802) 863-7231
Maine	(207) 287-4311	Virginia	(800) 523-4019
Michigan	(517) 335-8885	Washington	(206) 753-2556
Minnisota	(612) 627-5498	West Virginia	(304) 558-2981
Mississippi	(601) 960-7463	Wisconsin	(608) 266-5885
		Wyoming	(307) 777-7391

EPA Regional Offices

Your Regional EPA office can provide further information regarding regulations and lead protection programs.

EPA Regional Offices

Region 1 (Connecticut, Massachusetts, Maine, New Hampshire, Rhode Island, Vermont)
John F. Kennedy Federal Building
One Congress Street
Boston, MA 02203
(617) 565-3420

Region 2 (New Jersey, New York, Puerto Rico, Virgin Islands)
Building 5
2890 Woodbridge Avenue
Edison, NJ 08837-3679
(908) 321-6671

Region 3 (Delaware, Washington DC, Maryland, Pennsylvania, Virginia, West Virginia)
841 Chestnut Building
Philadelphia, PA 19107
(215) 597-9800

Region 4 (Alabama, Florida, Georgia, Kentucky, Mississippi, North Carolina, South Carolina, Tennessee)
345 Courtland Street, NE
Atlanta, GA 30365
(404) 347-4727

Region 5 (Illinois, Indiana, Michigan, Minnesota, Ohio, Wisconsin)
77 West Jackson Boulevard
Chicago, IL 60604-3590
(312) 886-6003

Region 6 (Arkansas, Louisiana, New Mexico, Oklahoma, Texas)
First Interstate Bank Tower
1445 Ross Avenue, 12th Floor, Suite 1200
Dallas, TX 75202-2733
(214) 665-7244

Region 7 (Iowa, Kansas, Missouri, Nebraska)
726 Minnesota Avenue
Kansas City, KS 66101
(913) 551-7020

Region 8 (Colorado, Montana, North Dakota, South Dakota, Utah, Wyoming)
999 18th Street, Suite 500
Denver, CO 80202-2405
(303) 293-1603

Region 9 (Arizona, California, Hawaii, Nevada)
75 Hawthorne Street
San Francisco, CA 94105
(415) 744-1124

Region 10 (Idaho, Oregon, Washington, Alaska)
1200 Sixth Avenue
Seattle, WA 98101
(206) 553-1200

CPSC Regional Offices

Eastern Regional Center
6 World Trade Center
Vesey Street, Room 350
New York, NY 10048
(212) 466-1612

Central Regional Center
230 South Dearborn Street
Room 2944
Chicago, IL 60604-1601
(312) 353-8260

Western Regional Center
600 Harrison Street, Room 245
San Francisco, CA 94107
(415) 744-2966

Simple Steps To Protect Your Family From Lead Hazards

If you think your home has high levels of lead:

◆ Get your young children tested for lead, even if they seem healthy.

◆ Wash children's hands, bottles, pacifiers, and toys often.

◆ Make sure children eat healthy, low-fat foods.

◆ Get your home checked for lead hazards.

◆ Regularly clean floors, window sills, and other surfaces.

◆ Wipe soil off shoes before entering house.

◆ Talk to your landlord about fixing surfaces with peeling or chipping paint.

◆ Take precautions to avoid exposure to lead dust when remodeling or renovating (call 1-800-424-LEAD for guidelines).

◆ Don't use a belt-sander, propane torch, dry scraper, or dry sandpaper on painted surfaces that may contain lead.

◆ Don't try to remove lead-based paint yourself.

APPENDIX C

<u>STATUTES</u>

- ARIZONA RESIDENTIAL LANDLORD AND TENANT ACT

- LANDLORD AND TENANT STATUTES

- FORCIBLE ENTRY AND DETAINER STATUTES

- ABATEMENT OF CRIME PROPERTY

Legislative changes/amendments to these statutes (above) are enacted from time-to-time. Generally, the changes take effect in the Summer following the legislative session. The following statutes are accurate as of August 1998. If this is not the latest version of the statutes, you may obtain the latest version free of charge from the Arizona Secretary of State. You may also read and download all Arizona statutes, including the above-referenced landlord and tenant statutes, from the Arizona Legislature's Web Site -- **http://www.azleg.state.az.us/**.

ARIZONA RESIDENTIAL LANDLORD AND TENANT ACT
ARIZONA REVISED STATUTES, TITLE 33, CHAPTER 10
(effective July 13, 1995; updated as of August 1998)

ARTICLE 1. GENERAL PROVISIONS

§ 33-1301. Short title
This chapter shall be known and may be cited as the Arizona Residential Landlord and Tenant Act.

§ 33-1302. Purposes
Underlying purposes and policies of this chapter are:

1. To simplify, clarify, modernize and revise the law governing the rental of dwelling units and the rights and obligations of landlord and tenant.

2. To encourage landlord and tenant to maintain and improve the quality of housing.

§ 33-1303. Supplementary principles of law applicable
Unless displaced by the provisions of this chapter, the principles of law and equity, including the law relating to capacity to contract, mutuality of obligations, principal and agent, real property, public health, safety and fire prevention, estoppel, fraud, misrepresentation, duress, coercion, mistake, bankruptcy or other validating or invalidating cause supplement its provisions.

§ 33-1304. Applicability of chapter
This chapter shall apply to the rental of dwelling units. Any conflict between the provisions of chapter 3 and chapter 7 of this title with the provisions of this chapter shall be governed by the provisions of this chapter.

§ 33-1305. Administration of remedies; enforcement
A. The remedies provided by this chapter shall be so administered that the aggrieved party may recover appropriate damages. The aggrieved party has a duty to mitigate damages.

B. Any right or obligation declared by this chapter is enforceable by action unless the provision declaring it specifies a different and limited effect.

§ 33-1306. Settlement of disputed claim or right
A claim or right arising under this chapter or on a rental agreement, if disputed in good faith, may be settled by agreement.

§ 33-1307. Territorial application
This chapter applies to, regulates, and determines rights, obligations and remedies under a rental agreement, wherever made, for a dwelling unit located within this state.

§ 33-1308. Exclusions from application of chapter
Unless created to avoid the application of this chapter, the following arrangements are not covered by this chapter:

1. Residence at an institution, public or private, if incidental to detention or the provision of medical, educational, counseling or religious services.

2. Occupancy under a contract of sale of a dwelling unit or the property of which it is a part, if the occupant is the purchaser or a person who succeeds to his interest.

3. Occupancy by a member of a fraternal or social organization in the portion of a structure operated for the benefit of the organization.

4. Transient occupancy in a hotel, motel or recreational lodging.

5. Occupancy by an employee of a landlord as a manager or custodian whose right to occupancy is conditional upon employment in and about the premises.

6. Occupancy by an owner of a condominium unit or a holder of a proprietary lease in a cooperative.

7. Occupancy in or operation of public housing as authorized, provided, or conducted under or pursuant to title 36, chapter 12,[1] or under or pursuant to any federal law or regulation.

[1] Section 36-1001 *et seq.*

§ 33-1309. Jurisdiction and service of process
A. The appropriate court of this state may exercise jurisdiction over any landlord with respect to any conduct in this state governed by this chapter or with respect to any claim arising from a transaction subject to this chapter. In addition to any other method provided by rule or by statute, personal jurisdiction over a landlord may be acquired in a civil action or proceeding instituted in the appropriate court by the service of process in the manner provided by this section.

B. If a landlord is not a resident of this state or is a corporation not authorized to do business in this state and engages in any conduct in this state governed by this chapter, or engages in a transaction subject to this chapter, he may designate an agent upon whom service of process may be made in this state. The agent shall be a resident of this state or a corporation authorized to do business in this state. The designation shall be in writing and filed with the secretary of state. If no designation is made and filed or if process cannot be served in this state upon the designated agent, process may be served upon the secretary of state, but the plaintiff or petitioner shall forthwith mail a copy of the process and pleading by registered or certified mail to the defendant or respondent at his last reasonably ascertained address. In the event there is no last reasonably ascertainable address and if the defendant or respondent has not complied with section 33-1322, subsections A and B, then service upon the secretary of state shall be sufficient service of process without the mailing of copies to the defendant or respondent. Service of process shall be deemed complete and the time shall begin to run for the purposes of this section at the time of service upon the secretary of state. The defendant shall appear and answer within thirty days after completion thereof in the manner and under the same penalty as if he had been personally served with the summons. An affidavit of compliance with this section shall be filed with the clerk of the court on or before the return day of the process, if any, or within any further time the court allows. Where applicable, the affidavit shall contain a statement that defendant or respondent has not complied with section 33-1322, subsections A and B.

§ 33-1310. General definitions
Subject to additional definitions contained in subsequent articles of this chapter which apply to specific articles thereof, and unless the context otherwise requires, in this chapter:

1. "Action" includes recoupment, counterclaim, setoff, suit in equity and any other proceeding in which rights are determined, including an action for possession.

2. "Building and housing codes" include any law, ordinance or governmental regulation concerning fitness for habitation, or the construction, maintenance, operation, occupancy, use or appearance of any premises, or dwelling unit.

3. "Delivery of Possession" means returning dwelling unit keys to the landlord and vacating the premises.

4. "Dwelling unit" means a structure or the part of a structure that is used as a home, residence, or sleeping place by one person who maintains a household or by two or more persons who maintain a common household. "Dwelling unit" excludes real property used to accommodate a mobile home, unless the mobile home is rented or leased by the landlord.

5. "Good faith" means honesty in fact in the conduct or transaction concerned.

6. "Landlord" means the owner, lessor or sublessor of the dwelling unit or the building of which it is a part, and it also means a manager of the premises who fails to disclose as required by section 33-1322.

7. "Organization" includes a corporation, government, governmental subdivision or agency, business trust, estate, trust, partnership or association, two or more persons having a joint or common interest and any other legal or commercial entity which is a landlord, owner, manager or constructive agent pursuant to section 33-1322.

8. "Owner" means one or more persons, jointly or severally, in whom is vested all or part of the legal title to property or all or part of the beneficial ownership and a right to present use and enjoyment of the premises. The term includes a mortgagee in possession.

9. "Person" means an individual or organization.

10. "Premises" means a dwelling unit and the structure of which it is a part and existing facilities and appurtenances therein, including furniture and utilities where applicable, and grounds, areas and existing facilities held out for the use of tenants generally or whose use is promised to the tenant.

11. "Rent" means payments to be made to the landlord in full consideration for the rented premises.

12. "Rental agreement" means all agreements, written, oral or implied by law, and valid rules and regulations adopted under section 33-1342 embodying the terms and conditions concerning the use and occupancy of a dwelling unit and premises.

13. "Roomer" means a person occupying a dwelling unit that lacks a major bathroom or kitchen facility, in a structure where one or more major facilities are used in common by occupants of the dwelling unit and other dwelling units. Major facility in the case of a bathroom means toilet, or either a bath or shower, and in the case of a kitchen means refrigerator, stove or sink.

14. "Security" means money or property given to assure payment or performance under a rental agreement. "Security" does not include a reasonable charge for redecorating or cleaning.

15. "Single family residence" means a structure maintained and used as a single dwelling unit. Notwithstanding that a dwelling unit shares one or more walls with another dwelling unit, it is a single family residence if it has direct access to a street or thoroughfare and shares neither heating facilities, hot water equipment nor any other essential facility or service with any other dwelling unit.

16. "Tenant" means a person entitled under a rental agreement to occupy a dwelling unit to the exclusion of others.

17. "Term of the lease" means the initial term or any renewal or extension of the written rental agreement currently in effect not including any wrongful holdover period.

§ 33-1311. Obligation of good faith

Every duty under this chapter and every act which must be performed as a condition precedent to the exercise of a right or remedy under this chapter imposes an obligation of good faith in its performance or enforcement.

§ 33-1312. Unconscionability

A. If the court, as a matter of law, finds either of the following:

1. A rental agreement or any provision thereof was unconscionable when made, the court may refuse to enforce the agreement, enforce the remainder of the agreement without the unconscionable provision, or limit the application of any unconscionable provision to avoid an unconscionable result.

2. A settlement in which a party waives or agrees to forego a claim or right under this chapter or under a rental agreement was unconscionable at the time it was made, the court may refuse to enforce the settlement, enforce the remainder of the settlement without the unconscionable provision, or limit the application of any unconscionable provision to avoid any unconscionable result.

B. If unconscionability is put into issue by a party or by the court upon its own motion the parties shall be afforded a reasonable opportunity to present evidence as to the setting, purpose and effect of the rental agreement or settlement to aid the court in making the determination.

§ 33-1313. Notice

A. A person has notice of a fact if he has actual knowledge of it, has received a notice or notification of it or from all the facts and circumstances known to him at the time in question he has reason to know that it exists. A person "knows" or "has knowledge" of a fact if he has actual knowledge of it.

B. A person "notifies" or "gives" a notice or notification to another by taking steps reasonably calculated to inform the other in ordinary course whether or not the other actually comes to know of it. A person "receives" a notice or notification when it comes to his attention, or in the case of the landlord, it is delivered in hand or mailed by registered or certified mail to the place of business of the landlord through which the rental agreement was made or at any place held out by him as the place for receipt of the communication or delivered to any individual who is designated as an agent by section 33-1322 or, in the case of the tenant, it is delivered in hand to the tenant or mailed by registered or certified mail to him at the place held out by him as the place for receipt of the communication or, in the absence of such designation, to his last known place of residence. If notice is mailed by registered or certified mail, the tenant or landlord is deemed to have received such notice on the date the notice is actually received by him or five days after the date the notice is mailed, whichever occurs first.

C. "Notice," knowledge or a notice or notification received by an organization is effective for a particular transaction from the time it is brought to the attention of the individual conducting the transaction and in any event from the time it would have been brought to his attention if the organization had exercised reasonable diligence.

§ 33-1314. Terms and conditions of rental agreement

A. The landlord and tenant may include in a rental agreement terms and conditions not prohibited by this chapter or any other rule of law including rent, term of the agreement and other provisions governing the rights and obligations of the parties.

B. In the absence of a rental agreement, the tenant shall pay as rent the fair rental value for the use and occupancy of the dwelling unit.

C. Rent shall be payable without demand or notice at the time and place agreed upon by the parties. Unless otherwise agreed, rent is payable at the dwelling unit and periodic rent is payable at the beginning of any term of one month or less and otherwise in equal monthly installments at the beginning of each month. Unless otherwise agreed, rent shall be uniformly apportionable from day-to-day.

D. Unless the rental agreement fixes a definite term, the tenancy shall be week-to-week in case of a roomer who pays weekly rent, and in all other cases month-to-month.

E. If a municipality that levies a transaction privilege tax on residential rent changes the percentage of that tax, the landlord on thirty day written notice to the tenant may adjust the amount of rent due to equal the difference caused by new percentage amount of tax. The adjustment to rent shall not occur before the date upon which the new tax is effective. In order for a landlord to adjust rent pursuant to this subsection, the landlord's right to adjust rent pursuant to this subsection shall be disclosed in the rental agreement.

§ 33-1315. Prohibited provisions in rental agreements

A. A rental agreement shall not provide that the tenant does any of the following:

1. Agrees to waive or to forego rights or remedies under this chapter.

2. Agrees to pay the landlord's attorney's fees, except an agreement in writing may provide that attorney's fees may be awarded to the prevailing party in the event of court action and except that a prevailing party in a contested forcible detainer action is eligible to be awarded attorney fees pursuant to section 12-341.01 regardless of whether the rental agreement provides for such an award.

3. Agrees to the exculpation or limitation of any liability of the landlord arising under law or to indemnify the landlord for that liability or the costs connected therewith.

B. A provision prohibited by subsection A of this section included in a rental agreement is unenforceable. If a landlord deliberately uses a rental agreement containing provisions known by him to be prohibited, the tenant may recover actual damages sustained by him and not more than two months' periodic rent.

§ 33-1316. Separation of rents and obligations to maintain property forbidden

A rental agreement, assignment, conveyance, trust deed or security instrument may not permit the receipt of rent free of the obligation to comply with section 33-1324, subsection A.

§ 33-1317. Discrimination by landlord or lessor against tenant with children prohibited; classification; exceptions; civil remedy

A. A person who knowingly refuses to rent to any other person a place to be used for a dwelling for the reason that the other person has a child or children, or who advertises in connection with the rental a restriction against children, either by the display of a sign, placard or written or printed notice, or by publication thereof in a newspaper of general circulation, is guilty of a petty offense.

B. No person shall rent or lease his property to another in violation of a valid restrictive covenant against the sale of such property to persons who have a child or children living with them.

C. No person shall rent or lease his property to persons who have a child or children living with them when his property meets the definition of housing for older persons in section 41-1491.04.

D. A person who knowingly rents or leases his property in violation of the provisions of subsection B or C of this section is guilty of a petty offense.

E. A person whose rights under this section have been violated may bring a civil action against a person who violates this section for all the following:

1. Injunctive or declaratory relief to correct the violation.

2. Actual damages sustained by the tenant or prospective tenant.

3. A civil penalty of three times the monthly rent of the housing accommodation involved in the violation if the violation is determined to be intentional.

4. Court costs and reasonable attorney fees.

F. Nothing in this section shall prohibit a person from refusing to rent a dwelling by reason of reasonable occupancy standards established by the owner or the owner's agent which apply to persons of all ages, and which have been adopted and published before the event in issue. An occupancy limitation of two persons per bedroom residing in a dwelling unit shall be presumed reasonable for this state and all political subdivisions of this state.

G. Subsection B of this section applies only to dwellings occupied or intended to be occupied by no more than four families living independently of each other and in which the owner maintains and occupies one of the living quarters as the owner's residence.

ARTICLE 2. LANDLORD OBLIGATIONS

§ 33-1321. Security deposits

A. A landlord shall not demand or receive security, however denominated, including, but not limited to, prepaid rent in an amount or value in excess of one and one-half month's rent. This subsection does not prohibit a tenant from voluntarily paying more than one and one-half month's rent in advance.

B. The purpose of all nonrefundable fees or deposits shall be stated in writing by the landlord. Any fee or deposit not designated as nonrefundable shall be refundable.

C. With respect to tenants who first occupy the premises or enter into a new written rental agreement after January 1, 1996, upon move-in a landlord shall furnish the tenant with a signed copy of the lease, a move-in form for specifying any existing damages to the dwelling unit and written notification to the tenant that the tenant may be present at the move-out inspection. Upon request by the tenant, the landlord shall notify the tenant when the landlord's move-out inspection will occur. If the tenant is being evicted for a material and irreparable breach and the landlord has reasonable cause to fear violence or intimidation on the part of the tenant, the landlord has no obligation to conduct a joint move-out inspection with the tenant.

D. Upon termination of the tenancy, property or money held by the landlord as prepaid rent and security may be applied to the payment of all rent, and subject to a landlord's duty to mitigate, all charges as specified in the signed lease agreement, or as provided in this chapter, including the amount of damages which the landlord has suffered by reason of the tenant's noncompliance with section 33-1341. Within fourteen days, excluding Saturdays, Sundays or other legal holidays, after termination of the tenancy and delivery of possession and demand by the tenant the landlord shall provide the tenant an itemized list of all deductions together with the amount due and payable to the tenant, if any. Unless other arrangements are made in writing by the tenant, the landlord shall mail, by regular mail, to the tenant's last known place of residence.

E. If the landlord fails to comply with subsection D of this section the tenant may recover the property and money due the tenant together with damages in an amount equal to twice the amount wrongfully withheld.

F. This section does not preclude the landlord or tenant from recovering other damages to which the landlord or tenant may be entitled under this chapter.

G. The holder of the landlord's interest in the premises at the time of the termination of the tenancy is bound by this section.

§ 33-1322. Disclosure and tender of written rental agreement

A. The landlord or any person authorized to enter into a rental agreement on his behalf shall disclose to the tenant in writing at or before the commencement of the tenancy the name and address of each of the following:

1. The person authorized to manage the premises.

2. An owner of the premises or a person authorized to act for and on behalf of the owner for the purpose of service of process and for the purpose of receiving and receipting for notices and demands.

B. At or before the commencement of the tenancy, the landlord shall inform the tenant in writing that a free copy of the Arizona Residential Landlord and Tenant Act is available through the Arizona Secretary of State's Office.

C. The information required to be furnished by this section shall be kept current and refurnished to tenant upon tenant's request. This section extends to and is enforceable against any successor landlord, owner or manager.

D. A person who fails to comply with subsections A and B becomes an agent of each person who is a landlord for the following purposes:

1. Service of process and receiving and receipting for notices and demands.

2. Performing the obligations of the landlord under this chapter and under the rental agreement and expending or making available for the purpose all rent collected from the premises.

E. If there is a written rental agreement, the landlord must tender and deliver a signed copy of the rental agreement to the tenant and the tenant must sign and deliver to the landlord one fully executed copy of such rental agreement within a reasonable time after the agreement is executed. A written rental agreement shall have all blank spaces completed. Noncompliance with this subsection shall be deemed a material noncompliance by the landlord or the tenant, as the case may be, of the rental agreement.

§ 33-1323. Landlord to supply possession of dwelling unit

At the commencement of the term the landlord shall deliver possession of the premises to the tenant in compliance with the rental agreement and section 33-1324. The landlord may bring an action for possession against any person wrongfully in possession and may recover the damages provided in section 33-1375, subsection C.

§ 33-1324. Landlord to maintain fit premises

A. The landlord shall:

1. Comply with the requirements of applicable building codes materially affecting health and safety.

2. Make all repairs and do whatever is necessary to put and keep the premises in a fit and habitable condition.

3. Keep all common areas of the premises in a clean and safe condition.

4. Maintain in good and safe working order and condition all electrical, plumbing, sanitary, heating, ventilating, air--conditioning and other facilities and appliances, including elevators, supplied or required to be supplied by him.

5. Provide and maintain appropriate receptacles and conveniences for the removal of ashes, garbage, rubbish and other waste incidental to the occupancy of the dwelling unit and arrange for their removal.

6. Supply running water and reasonable amounts of hot water at all times, reasonable heat and reasonable air--conditioning or cooling where such units are installed and offered, when required by seasonal weather conditions, except where the building that includes the dwelling unit is not required by law to be equipped for that purpose or the dwelling unit is so constructed that heat, air-conditioning, cooling or hot water is generated by an installation within the exclusive control of the tenant and supplied by a direct public utility connection.

B. If the duty imposed by subsection A, paragraph 1 of this section is greater than any duty imposed by any other paragraph of this section, the landlord's duty shall be determined by reference to that paragraph.

C. The landlord and tenant of a single family residence may agree in writing, supported by adequate consideration, that the tenant perform the landlord's duties specified in subsection A, paragraphs 5 and 6 of this section, and also specified repairs, maintenance tasks, alterations and remodeling, but only if the transaction is entered into in good faith, not for the purpose of evading the obligations of the landlord and the work is not necessary to cure noncompliance with subsection A, paragraphs 1 and 2 of this section.

D. The landlord and tenant of any dwelling unit other than a single family residence may agree that the tenant is to perform specified repairs, maintenance tasks, alterations or remodeling only if:

1. The agreement of the parties is entered into in good faith and not for the purpose of evading the obligations of the landlord and is set forth in a separate writing signed by the parties and supported by adequate consideration.

2. The work is not necessary to cure noncompliance with subsection A, paragraphs 1 and 2 of this section.

3. The agreement does not diminish or affect the obligation of the landlord to other tenants in the premises.

E. If the landlord purchases utility services from a public service corporation for distribution through a system owned or operated by the landlord and imposes separately stated utility or similar charges on the tenants, the aggregate amount of the separately stated charges shall not exceed the actual cost paid by the landlord to the public service corporation for the utility services. The tenant is not required to pay any other separately stated charges for provision of the utility services. This shall not prohibit a mobile home park landlord from charging residents of dwellings rented from the landlord within the mobile home park for utilities in accordance with section 33-1413.01.

§ 33-1325. Limitation of liability

A. Unless otherwise agreed, a landlord, who conveys premises that include a dwelling unit subject to a rental agreement in a good faith sale to a bona fide purchaser, is relieved of liability under the rental agreement and this chapter as to events occurring subsequent to written notice to the tenant of the conveyance. He remains liable to the tenant for any property and money to which the tenant is entitled under section 33-1321.

B. Unless otherwise agreed, a manager of premises that include a dwelling unit is relieved of liability under the rental agreement and this chapter as to events occurring after written notice to the tenant of the termination of his management.

§ 33-1329. Regulation of rents; authority

A. Notwithstanding any other provisions of law to the contrary the state legislature determines that the imposition of rent control on private residential housing units by cities, including charter cities, and towns is of statewide concern. Therefore, the power to control rents on private residential property is preempted by the state. Cities, including charter cities, or towns shall not have the power to control rents.

B. The provisions of subsection A shall not apply to residential property which is owned, financed, insured or subsidized by any state agency, or by any city, including charter city, or town.

ARTICLE 3. TENANT OBLIGATIONS

§ 33-1341. Tenant to maintain dwelling unit

The tenant shall:

1. Comply with all obligations primarily imposed upon tenants by applicable provisions of building codes materially affecting health and safety.

2. Keep that part of the premises that he occupies and uses as clean and safe as the condition of the premises permit.

3. Dispose from his dwelling unit all ashes, rubbish, garbage and other waste in a clean and safe manner.

4. Keep all plumbing fixtures in the dwelling unit or used by the tenant as clean as their condition permits.

5. Use in a reasonable manner all electrical, plumbing, sanitary, heating, ventilating, air-conditioning and other facilities and appliances including elevators in the premises.

6. Not deliberately or negligently destroy, deface, damage, impair or remove any part of the premises or knowingly permit any person to do so.

7. Conduct himself and require other persons on the premises with his consent to conduct themselves in a manner that will not disturb his neighbors' peaceful enjoyment of the premises.

§ 33-1342. Rules and regulations

A. A landlord, from time to time, may adopt rules or regulations, however described, concerning the tenant's use and occupancy of the premises. Such rules or regulations are enforceable against the tenant only if:

1. Their purpose is to promote the convenience, safety or welfare of the tenants in the premises, preserve the landlord's property from abusive use or make a fair distribution of services and facilities held out for the tenants generally.

2. They are reasonably related to the purpose for which adopted.

3. They apply to all tenants in the premises in a fair manner.

4. They are sufficiently explicit in prohibition, direction or limitation of the tenant's conduct to fairly inform the tenant of what the tenant must or must not do to comply.

5. They are not for the purpose of evading the obligations of the landlord.

6. The tenant has notice of them at the time the tenant enters into the rental agreement.

B. A rule or regulation adopted after the tenant enters into the rental agreement is enforceable against the tenant if a thirty day notice of its adoption is given to the tenant and it does not constitute a substantial modification of the tenant's rental agreement.

C. If state, county, municipal or other governmental bodies adopt new ordinances, rules or other legal provisions affecting existing rental agreements, the landlord may make immediate amendments to lease agreements to bring them into compliance with the law. The landlord shall give a tenant written notice that the tenant's lease agreement has been amended, and the notice shall provide a brief description of the amendment and the effective date.

§ 33-1343. Access

A. The tenant shall not unreasonably withhold consent to the landlord to enter into the dwelling unit in order to inspect the premises, make necessary or agreed repairs, decorations, alterations or improvements, supply necessary or agreed services or exhibit the dwelling unit to prospective or actual purchasers, mortgagees, tenants, workmen or contractors.

B. The landlord may enter the dwelling unit without consent of the tenant in case of emergency.

C. The landlord shall not abuse the right to access or use it to harass the tenant. Except in case of emergency or if it is impracticable to do so, the landlord shall give the tenant at least two days' notice of his intent to enter and enter only at reasonable times.

D. The landlord has no other right of access except by court order and as permitted by § 33-1369 and § 33-1370, or if the tenant has abandoned or surrendered the premises.

§ 33-1344. Tenant to use and occupy as a dwelling unit

Unless otherwise agreed, the tenant shall occupy his dwelling unit only as a dwelling unit.

ARTICLE 4. REMEDIES

§ 33-1361. Noncompliance by the landlord

A. Except as provided in this chapter, if there is a material noncompliance by the landlord with the rental agreement, including a material falsification of the written information provided to the tenant, the tenant may deliver a written notice to the landlord specifying the acts and omissions constituting the breach and that the rental agreement will terminate upon a date not less than ten days after receipt of the notice if the breach is not remedied in ten days. If there is a noncompliance by the landlord with section 33-1324 materially affecting health and safety, the tenant may deliver a written notice to the landlord specifying the acts and omissions constituting the breach and that the rental

agreement will terminate upon a date not less than five days after receipt of the notice if the breach is not remedied in five days. For the purposes of this section, material falsification shall include availability of the unit, except when a holdover tenant is in illegal possession or in violation of the rental agreement, the condition of the premises and any current services as represented by the landlord in writing as well as any written representation, as well as any representation regarding future services and any future changes regarding the condition of the premises, the provision of utility services and the designation of the party responsible for the payment of utility services. The rental agreement shall terminate and the dwelling unit shall be vacated as provided in the notice subject to the following:

1. If the breach is remediable by repairs or the payment of damages or otherwise and the landlord adequately remedies the breach prior to the date specified in the notice, the rental agreement will not terminate.

2. The tenant may not terminate for a condition caused by the deliberate or negligent act or omission of the tenant, a member of the tenant's family or other person on the premises with the tenant's consent.

B. Except as provided in this chapter, the tenant may recover damages and obtain injunctive relief for any noncompliance by the landlord with the rental agreement or section 33-1324.

C. The remedy provided in subsection B of this section is in addition to any right of the tenant arising under subsection A of this section.

D. If the rental agreement is terminated, the landlord shall return all security recoverable by the tenant under section 33-1321.

§ 33-1362. Failure to deliver possession

A. If the landlord fails to deliver physical possession of the dwelling unit to the tenant as provided in section 33-1323, rent abates until possession is delivered and the tenant may do either of the following:

1. Upon at least five days' written notice to the landlord terminate the rental agreement and upon termination the landlord shall return all prepaid rent and security.

2. Demand performance of the rental agreement by the landlord and, if the tenant elects, maintain an action for possession of the dwelling unit against the landlord or any person wrongfully in possession and recover the damages sustained by him.

B. If the landlord fails to deliver constructive possession to the tenant because of noncompliance with section 33-1324, rent shall not abate. Tenant may proceed with the remedies provided for in section 33-1361.

C. If a person's failure to deliver possession is willful and not in good faith, an aggrieved person may recover from that person an amount not more than two months' periodic rent or twice the actual damages sustained by him, whichever is greater.

§ 33-1363. Self-help for minor defects

A. If the landlord fails to comply with section 33-1324, and the reasonable cost of compliance is less than three hundred dollars, or an amount equal to one-half of the monthly rent, whichever amount is greater, the tenant may recover damages for the breach under section 33-1361, subsection B, or may notify the landlord of the tenant's intention to correct the condition at the landlord's expense. After being notified by the tenant in writing, if the landlord fails to comply within ten days or as promptly thereafter as conditions require in case of emergency, the tenant may cause the work to be done by a licensed contractor and, after submitting to the landlord an itemized statement and a waiver of lien, deduct from his rent the actual and reasonable cost of the work, not exceeding the amount specified in this subsection.

B. A tenant may not repair at the landlord's expense if the condition was caused by the deliberate or negligent act or omission of the tenant, a member of the tenant's family or other person on the premises with the tenant's consent.

§ 33-1364. Wrongful failure to supply heat, air conditioning, cooling, water, hot water or essential services

A. If contrary to the rental agreement or section 33-1324 the landlord deliberately or negligently fails to supply running water, gas or electrical service, or both if applicable, and reasonable amounts of hot water or heat, air-conditioning or cooling, where such units are installed and offered, or essential services, the tenant may give reasonable notice to the landlord specifying the breach and may do one of the following:

1. Procure reasonable amounts of hot water, running water, heat and essential services during the period of the landlord's noncompliance and deduct their actual reasonable cost from the rent. If the landlord has failed to provide any of the utility services specified in this section due to nonpayment of the landlord's utility bill for the premises, and if there is no separate utility meter for each tenant in the premises such that the tenant could avoid a utility shut-off by arranging to have services transferred to the tenant's name, the tenant may either individually or collectively with other tenants arrange with the utility company to pay the utility bill after written notice to the landlord of the tenant's intent to do so. With the utility company's approval the tenant or tenants may pay the landlord's delinquent utility bill and deduct from any rent owed to the landlord the actual cost of the payment the tenant made to restore utility services. The tenant or tenants may continue to make such payments to the utility company until the landlord has provided adequate assurances to the tenant that the above utility services will be maintained.

2. Recover damages based upon the diminution in the fair rental value of the dwelling unit.

3. Procure reasonable substitute housing during the period of the landlord's noncompliance, in which case the tenant is excused from paying rent for the period of the landlord's noncompliance. In the event the periodic cost of such substitute housing exceeds the amount of the periodic rent, upon delivery by tenant of proof of payment for such substitute housing, tenant may recover from landlord such excess costs up to an amount not to exceed twenty-five per cent of the periodic rent which has been excused pursuant to this paragraph.

B. A landlord shall provide all utilities and services specified in the lease agreement.

C. A landlord shall not terminate utility services as specified in subsection A of this section which are provided to the tenant as part of the rental agreement, except as necessary to make needed repairs or as provided in section 33-1368. Subsequent to the execution of the rental agreement, a landlord may not transfer the responsibility for payment of such utility services to the tenant without the tenant's written consent.

D. If a landlord is in violation of subsection C of this section, the tenant may recover damages, costs and reasonable attorneys fees and obtain injunctive relief. Nothing in this section shall preclude a tenant's right to recover damages as specified in section 33-1367.

E. A lease agreement shall not contain any terms contrary to this section.

F. In addition to the remedy provided in paragraph 3 of subsection A of this section, in the event the landlord's noncompliance is deliberate, the tenant may recover the actual and reasonable cost or fair and reasonable value of the substitute housing not in excess of an amount equal to the periodic rent.

G. If the tenant proceeds under this section, he may not proceed under section 33-1361 or section 33-1363 as to that breach, except as to damages which occur prior to the tenant proceeding under subsection A or B of this section.

H. The rights under this section do not arise until the tenant has given notice to the landlord and such rights do not include the right to repair. Such rights do not arise if the condition was caused by the deliberate or negligent act or omission of the tenant, a member of the tenant's family or other person on the premises with the tenant's consent

§ 33-1365. Landlord's noncompliance as defense to action for possession or rent

A. In an action for possession based upon nonpayment of the rent or in an action for rent where the tenant is in possession, if the landlord is not in compliance with the rental agreement or this chapter, the tenant may counterclaim for any amount which he may recover under the rental agreement or this chapter. In that event after notice and hearing the court from time to time may order the tenant to pay into court all or part of the undisputed rent accrued and all periodic rent thereafter accruing and shall determine the amount due to each party. The party to whom a net amount is owed shall be paid first from the money paid into court and the balance, if any, by the other party. However, if no rent remains due after application of this section, or if the tenant is adjudged to have acted in good faith and satisfies a judgment for rent entered for the landlord, judgment shall be entered for the tenant in the action for possession.

B. In an action for rent where the tenant is not in possession, the tenant may counterclaim as provided in subsection A but the tenant is not required to pay any rent into court.

§ 33-1366. Fire or casualty damage

A. If the dwelling unit or premises are damaged or destroyed by fire or casualty to an extent that enjoyment of the dwelling unit is substantially impaired, the tenant may do either of the following:

1. Immediately vacate the premises and notify the landlord in writing within fourteen days thereafter of his intention to terminate the rental agreement, in which case the rental agreement terminates as of the date of vacating.

2. If continued occupancy is lawful, vacate any part of the dwelling unit rendered unusable by the fire or casualty, in which case the tenant's liability for rent is reduced in proportion to the diminution in the fair rental value of the dwelling unit.

B. If the rental agreement is terminated the landlord shall return all security recoverable under section 33-1321. Accounting for rent in the event of termination or apportionment is to occur as of the date the tenant vacates all or part of the dwelling unit.

§ 33-1367. Tenant's remedies for landlord's unlawful ouster, exclusion or diminution of services

If the landlord unlawfully removes or excludes the tenant from the premises or wilfully diminishes services to the tenant by interrupting or causing the interruption of electric, gas, water or other essential service to the tenant, the tenant may recover possession or terminate the rental agreement and, in either case, recover an amount not more than two months' periodic rent or twice the actual damages sustained by him, whichever is greater. If the rental agreement is terminated the landlord shall return all security recoverable under section 33-1321.

§ 33-1368. Noncompliance with rental agreement by tenant; failure to pay rent; utility discontinuation

A. Except as provided in this chapter, if there is a material noncompliance by the tenant with the rental agreement, including material falsification of the information provided on the rental application, the landlord may deliver a written notice to the tenant specifying the acts and omissions constituting the breach and that the rental agreement will terminate upon a date not less than ten days after receipt of the notice if the breach is not remedied in ten days. For the purposes of this section, material falsification shall include the following untrue or misleading information about the:

1. Number of occupants in the dwelling unit, pets, income of prospective tenant, social security number and current employment listed on the application or lease agreement.

2. Criminal records, prior eviction record, current criminal activity. Material falsification of information in paragraph 2 of this subsection is not curable under this section. If there is a noncompliance by the tenant with Section 33-1341 materially affecting health and safety, the landlord may deliver a written notice to the tenant specifying the acts and omissions constituting the breach and that the rental agreement will terminate upon a date not less than five days after receipt of the notice if the breach is not remedied in five days. However, if the breach is remediable by repair or the payment of damages or otherwise, and the tenant adequately remedies the breach prior to the date specified in the notice, the rental agreement will not terminate. If there is an additional act of these types of noncompliance of the same or similar nature during the term of the lease after the previous remedy of noncompliance, the landlord may institute a special detainer action pursuant to section 33-1377 ten days after delivery of a written notice advising the tenant that a second noncompliance of the same or similar nature has occurred. If there is a breach that is both material and irreparable and that occurs on the premises, including but not limited to an illegal discharge of a weapon, prostitution as defined in section 13-3211, criminal street gang activity as prescribed in section 13-105, activity as prohibited in section 13-2308, the unlawful manufacturing, selling, using, storing, keeping or giving of a controlled substance as defined in section 13-3451, infliction of bodily harm, threatening or intimidating as prohibited in section 13-1202, assault as prohibited in section 13-1203 or a breach of the lease agreement that otherwise jeopardizes the health, safety and welfare of the landlord, the landlord's agent or another tenant or involving imminent or actual serious property damage, the landlord may deliver a written notice for immediate termination of the rental agreement and shall proceed under section 33-1377.

B.   A tenant may not withhold rent for any reason not authorized by this chapter. If rent is unpaid when due and the tenant fails to pay rent within five days after written notice by the landlord of nonpayment and the landlord's intention to terminate the rental agreement if the rent is not paid within that period of time, the landlord may terminate the rental agreement by filing a special detainer action pursuant to section 33-1377. Prior to the filing of a special detainer action the rental agreement shall be reinstated if the tenant tenders all past due and unpaid periodic rent and a reasonable late fee set forth in a written rental agreement. After a special detainer action is filed the rental agreement is reinstated only if the tenant pays all past due rent, reasonable late fees set forth in a written rental agreement, attorney fees and court costs. After a judgment has been entered in a special detainer action in favor of the landlord, any reinstatement of the rental agreement is solely in the discretion of the landlord.

C.   The landlord may recover all reasonable damages, resulting from noncompliance by the tenant with the rental agreement or section 33-1341 or occupancy of the dwelling unit, court costs, reasonable attorney fees and all quantifiable damage caused by the tenant to the premises.

D.   The landlord may discontinue utility services provided by the landlord on the day following the day that a writ of restitution or execution is executed pursuant to section 12-1181. Disconnection shall be performed only by a person authorized by the utility whose service is being discontinued. Nothing in this section shall supersede standard tariff and operational procedures that apply to any public service corporation, municipal corporation or special districts providing utility services in this state.

E.   The landlord shall hold the tenant's personal property for a period of twenty-one days beginning on the first day after a writ of restitution or writ of execution is executed as prescribed in section 12-1181. The landlord shall use reasonable care in moving and holding the tenant's property and may store the tenant's property in an unoccupied dwelling unit owned by the landlord, the unoccupied dwelling unit formerly occupied by the tenant or off the premises if an unoccupied dwelling unit is not available. If the tenant's former dwelling unit is used to store the property, the landlord may change the locks on that unit at the landlord's discretion. The landlord shall prepare an inventory and promptly notify the tenant of the location and cost of storage of the personal property by sending a notice by certified mail, return receipt requested, addressed to the tenant's last known address and to any of the tenant's alternative addresses known to the landlord. To reclaim the personal property, the tenant shall pay the landlord only for the cost of removal and storage for the time the property is held by the landlord. Within five days after a written offer by the tenant to pay these charges the landlord must surrender possession of the personal property in the landlord's possession to the tenant upon the tenant's tender of payment. If the landlord fails to surrender possession of the personal property to the tenant, the tenant may recover the possessions or an amount equal to the damages determined by the court if the landlord has destroyed or disposed of the possessions before the twenty-one days specified in this section or after the tenant's offer to pay. The tenant shall pay all removal and storage costs accrued through the fifth day after the tenant's offer to pay is received by the landlord or the date of delivery or surrender of the property, whichever is sooner. Payment by the tenant relieves the landlord of any further responsibility for the tenant's possessions.

F.   A tenant does not have any right of access to that property until all payments specified in subsection E of this section have been made in full, except that the tenant may obtain clothing and the tools, apparatus and books of a trade or profession and identification or financial documents including all those related to the tenant's immigration status, employment status, public assistance or medical care. If the landlord holds the property for the twenty-one day period and the tenant does not make a reasonable effort to recover it, the landlord, upon the expiration of twenty-one days as provided in this subsection, may administer the personal property as provided in section 33-1370, subsection E. The landlord shall hold personal property after a writ of restitution or writ of execution is executed for not more than twenty-one days after such an execution. Nothing in this subsection shall preclude the landlord and tenant from making an agreement providing that the landlord will hold the personal property for a period longer than twenty-one days.

G.   For the purposes of this chapter, the tenant shall be held responsible for the actions of the tenant's guests that violate the lease agreement or rules or regulations of the landlord if the tenant could reasonably be expected to be aware that such actions might occur and did not attempt to prevent those actions to the best of the tenant's ability.

H.   For purposes of this section, "days" means calendar days.

§ 33-1369. Failure to maintain

If there is noncompliance by the tenant with section 33-1341 materially affecting health and safety that can be remedied by repair, replacement of a damaged item or cleaning and the tenant fails to comply as promptly as conditions require in case of emergency or within fourteen days after written notice by the landlord specifying the breach and requesting that the tenant remedy it within that period of time, the landlord may enter the dwelling unit and cause the work to be done in a workmanlike manner and submit an itemized bill for the actual and reasonable cost or the fair and reasonable value thereof as rent on the next date when periodic rent is due, or if the rental agreement has terminated, for immediate payment.

§ 33-1370. Abandonment; notice; remedies; personal property; definition

A. If a dwelling unit is abandoned after the time prescribed in subsection H of this section, the landlord shall send the tenant a notice of abandonment by certified mail, return receipt requested, addressed to the tenant's last known address and to any of the tenant's alternate addresses known to the landlord. The landlord shall also post a notice of abandonment on the door to the dwelling unit or any other conspicuous place on the property for five days.

B. Five days after notice of abandonment has been both posted and mailed, the landlord may retake the dwelling unit and rerent the dwelling unit at a fair rental value if no personal property remains in the dwelling unit. After the landlord retakes the dwelling unit, money held by the landlord as a security deposit is forfeited and shall be applied to the payment of any accrued rent and other reasonable costs incurred by the landlord by reason of the tenant's abandonment.

C. If the tenant abandons the dwelling unit, the landlord shall make reasonable efforts to rent it at a fair rental. If the landlord rents the dwelling unit for a term beginning prior to the expiration of the rental agreement, it is deemed to be terminated as of the date the new tenancy begins. If the landlord fails to use reasonable efforts to rent the dwelling unit at a fair rental or if the landlord accepts the abandonment as a surrender, the rental agreement is deemed to be terminated by the landlord as of the date the landlord has notice of the abandonment. If the tenancy is from month to month or week to week, the term of the rental agreement for this purpose shall be deemed to be a month or a week, as the case may be.

D. After the landlord has retaken possession of the dwelling unit, the landlord may store the tenant's personal possessions in the unoccupied dwelling unit that was abandoned by the tenant, in any other available unit or any storage space owned by the landlord or off the premises if a dwelling unit or storage space is not available. The landlord shall notify the tenant of the location of the personal property in the same manner prescribed in subsection A of this section.

E. The landlord shall hold the tenant's personal property for a period of ten days after the landlord's declaration of abandonment. The landlord shall use reasonable care in holding the tenant's personal property. If the landlord holds the property for this period and the tenant makes no reasonable effort to recover it, the landlord may sell the property, retain the proceeds and apply them toward the tenant's outstanding rent or other costs which are covered in the lease agreement or otherwise provided for in title 33, chapter 10 or title 12, chapter 8 and have been incurred by the landlord due to the tenant's abandonment. Any excess proceeds shall be mailed to the tenant at the tenant's last known address. A tenant does not have any right of access to that property until the actual removal and storage costs have been paid in full, except that the tenant may obtain clothing and the tools, apparatus and books of a trade or profession and any identification or financial documents, including all those related to the tenant's immigration status, employment status, public assistance or medical care. If provided by a written rental agreement, the landlord may destroy or otherwise dispose of some or all of the property if the landlord reasonably determines that the value of the property is so low that the cost of moving, storage and conducting a public sale exceeds the amount that would be realized from the sale.

F. For a period of twelve months after the sale the landlord shall:

1. Keep adequate records of the outstanding and unpaid rent and the sale of the tenant's personal property.

2. Hold any excess proceeds which have been returned as undeliverable for the benefit of the tenant.

G. If the tenant notifies the landlord in writing on or before the date the landlord sells or otherwise disposes of the personal property that the tenant intends to remove the personal property from the dwelling unit or the place of safekeeping, the tenant has five days to reclaim the personal property. To reclaim the personal property the tenant must only pay the landlord for the cost of removal and storage for the period the tenant's personal property remained in the landlord's safekeeping.

H. In this section "abandonment" means either the absence of the tenant from the dwelling unit, without notice to the landlord for at least seven days, if rent for the dwelling unit is outstanding and unpaid for ten days and there is no reasonable evidence other than the presence of the tenant's personal property that the tenant is occupying the residence or the absence of the tenant for at least five days, if the rent for the dwelling unit is outstanding and unpaid for five days and none of the tenant's personal property is in the dwelling unit.

§ 33-1371. Acceptance of partial payments.

A. A landlord is not required to accept a partial payment of rent or other charges. A landlord accepting a partial payment of rent or other charges retains the right to proceed against a tenant only if the tenant agrees in a contemporaneous writing to the terms and conditions of the partial payment with regard to the continuation of the tenancy. The written agreement shall contain a date on which the balance of the rent is due. The landlord may proceed against a tenant in breach of this agreement or any other breach of the original rental agreement as provided in article 4 of this chapter and in title 12, chapter 8. If the landlord has provided the tenant with a notice of failure to pay rent as specified in section 33-1368, subsection B prior to the completion of the agreement for partial payment, no additional notice under section 33-1368, subsection B is required in case of a breach of the partial payment agreement.

B. Acceptance of rent, or any portion thereof, with knowledge of a default by tenant or acceptance of performance by the tenant that varied from the terms of the rental agreement or rules or regulations subsequently adopted by the landlord constitutes a waiver of the right to terminate the rental agreement for that breach, except as specified in subsection A of this section.

§ 33-1372. Landlord liens; distraint for rent

A. A lien or security interest on behalf of the landlord in the tenant's household goods is not enforceable unless perfected before the effective date of this chapter.

B. Distraint for rent is abolished.

§ 33-1373. Remedy after termination

If the rental agreement is terminated, the landlord may have a claim for possession and for rent and a separate claim for actual damages for breach of the rental agreement.

§ 33-1374. Recovery of possession limited

A landlord may not recover or take possession of the dwelling unit by action or otherwise, including forcible removal of the tenant or his possessions, willful diminution of services to the tenant by interrupting or causing the interruption of electric, gas, water or other essential service to the tenant, except in case of abandonment, surrender or as permitted in this chapter.

§ 33-1375. Periodic tenancy; hold-over remedies

A. The landlord or the tenant may terminate a week-to-week tenancy by a written notice given to the other at least ten days prior to the termination date specified in the notice.

B. The landlord or the tenant may terminate a month-to-month tenancy by a written notice given to the other at least thirty days prior to the periodic rental date specified in the notice.

C. If the tenant remains in possession without the landlord's consent after expiration of the term of the rental agreement or its termination, the landlord may bring an action for possession and if the tenant's holdover is willful and not in good faith the landlord, in addition, may recover an amount equal to not more than two months' periodic rent or twice the actual damages sustained by the landlord, whichever is greater. If the landlord consents in writing to the tenant's continued occupancy, section 33-1314, subsection D applies.

§ 33-1376. Landlord and tenant remedies for abuse of access

A. If the tenant refuses to allow lawful access, the landlord may obtain injunctive relief to compel access, or terminate the rental agreement. In either case, the landlord may recover actual damages.

B. If the landlord makes an unlawful entry or a lawful entry in an unreasonable manner or makes repeated demands for entry otherwise lawful but which have the effect of unreasonably harassing the tenant, the tenant may obtain injunctive relief to prevent the recurrence of the conduct or terminate the rental agreement. In either case, the tenant may recover actual damages not less than an amount equal to one month's rent.

§ 33-1377. Special detainer actions; service; trial postponement

A. Special detainer actions shall be instituted for remedies prescribed in section 33-1368. Except as provided in this section, the procedure and appeal rights prescribed in title 12, chapter 8, article 4[1] apply to special detainer actions.

[1] Section 12-1171 *et seq.*

B. The summons shall be issued on the day the complaint is filed and shall command the person against whom the complaint is made to appear and answer the complaint at the time and place named which shall be not more than six nor less than three days from the date of the summons. The tenant is deemed to have received the summons three days after the summons is mailed if personal service is attempted and within one day of issuance of the summons a copy of the summons is conspicuously posted on the main entrance of the tenant's residence and on the same day the summons is sent by certified mail, return receipt requested, to the tenant's last known address. The summons in a special detainer action shall be served at least two days before the return day and the return day made on the day assigned for trial. Service of process in this manner shall be deemed the equivalent of having served the tenant in person for the purposes of awarding a money judgment for all rent, damages, costs and attorney fees due.

C. For good cause shown supported by an affidavit, the trial may be postponed for not more than three days in a justice court or five days in the superior court.

D. In addition to determining the right to actual possession, the court may assess damages, attorney fees and costs as prescribed by law.

E. If a complaint is filed alleging a material and irreparable breach pursuant to section 33-1368, subsection A, the summons shall be issued as provided in subsection B of this section, except that the trial date and return date shall be set no later than the third day following the filing of the complaint. If after the hearing the court finds that the material and irreparable breach did occur by a preponderance of the evidence, the court shall order restitution in favor of the plaintiff not less than twelve nor more than twenty-four hours later.

F. If the defendant is found guilty, the court shall give judgment for the plaintiff for restitution of the premises, for late charges stated in the rental agreement, for costs and, at the plaintiff's option, for all rent found to be due and unpaid through the periodic rental period provided for in the rental agreement as described in section 33-1314, subsection C and shall grant a writ of restitution.

G. If the defendant is found not guilty, judgment shall be given for the defendant against the plaintiff for costs, and if it appears that the plaintiff has acquired possession of the premises since commencement of the action, a writ of restitution shall issue in favor of the defendant.

ARTICLE 5. RETALIATORY ACTION

§ 33-1381. Retaliatory conduct prohibited

A. Except as provided in this section, a landlord may not retaliate by increasing rent or decreasing services or by bringing or threatening to bring an action for possession after any of the following:

1. The tenant has complained to a governmental agency charged with responsibility for enforcement of a building or housing code of a violation applicable to the premises materially affecting health and safety.

2. The tenant has complained to the landlord of a violation under section 33-1324.

3. The tenant has organized or become a member of a tenants' union or similar organization.

4. The tenant has complained to a governmental agency charged with the responsibility for enforcement of the wage-price stabilization act.

B. If the landlord acts in violation of subsection A of this section, the tenant is entitled to the remedies provided in section 33-1367 and has a defense in action against him for possession. In an action by or against the tenant, evidence of a complaint within six months prior to the alleged act of retaliation creates a presumption that the landlord's conduct was in retaliation. The presumption does not arise if the tenant made the complaint after notice of termination of the rental agreement. "Presumption", in this subsection, means that the trier of fact must find the existence of the fact presumed unless and until evidence is introduced which would support a finding of its nonexistence.

C. Notwithstanding subsections A and B of this section, a landlord may bring an action for possession if either of the following occurs:

1. The violation of the applicable building or housing code was caused primarily by lack of reasonable care by the tenant or other person in his household or upon the premises with his consent.

2. The tenant is in default in rent.

The maintenance of the action does not release the landlord from liability under section 33-1361, subsection B.

LANDLORD AND TENANT
ARIZONA REVISED STATUTES, TITLE 33, CHAPTER 3
(Updated as of August 1998)

NOTE: These statutes generally do not apply to the rental of dwelling units (i.e., residential housing), *see* A.R.S. §§ 33-381, 33-1304, and 33-1308.

ARTICLE 1.   OBLIGATIONS AND LIABILITIES OF LANDLORD

§ 33-301. Posting of lien law and rates by innkeepers

Every keeper of a hotel, inn, boarding, lodging or apartment house, or auto camp, shall post in a conspicuous place in the office or public room, and in every bedroom of the establishment, a printed copy of §§ 33-951 and 33-952, with a printed statement of charges by the day, week or month for meals, lodging or other items furnished.

§ 33-302. Maintenance of fireproof safe by innkeeper for deposit of valuables by guests; limitations on liability of innkeeper for loss of property of guests

A. An innkeeper who maintains a fireproof safe and gives notice by posting in a conspicuous place in the office or in the room of each guest that money, jewelry, documents and other articles of small size and unusual value may be deposited in the safe, is not liable for loss of or injury to any such article not deposited in the safe, which is not the result of his own act.

B. An innkeeper may refuse to receive for deposit from a guest articles exceeding a total value of five hundred dollars, and unless otherwise agreed to in writing shall not be liable in an amount in excess of five hundred dollars for loss of or damage to property deposited by a guest in such safe unless the loss or damage is the result of the fault or negligence of the innkeeper.

C. The innkeeper shall not be liable for loss of or damage to merchandise samples or merchandise for sale displayed by a guest unless the guest gives prior written notice to the innkeeper of having and displaying the merchandise or merchandise samples, and the innkeeper acknowledges receipt of such notice, but in no event shall liability for such loss or damage exceed five hundred dollars unless it results from the fault or negligence of the innkeeper.

D. The liability of an innkeeper to a guest shall be limited to one hundred dollars for property delivered to the innkeeper to be kept in a storeroom or baggage room and to seventy-five dollars for property deposited in a parcel or checkroom.

E. For the purpose of this section the term "inn" includes hotel, boarding house, lodging house, apartment house, motel and auto camp.

§ 33-303. Discrimination by landlord or lessor against tenant with children prohibited; penalty; exceptions

A. A person who knowingly refuses to rent to any other person a place to be used for a dwelling for the reason that the other person has a child or children, or who advertises in connection with the rental a restriction against children, either by the display of a sign, placard, written or printed notice, or by publication thereof in a newspaper of general circulation, is guilty of a petty offense.

B. No person shall rent or lease his property to another in violation of a valid restrictive covenant against the sale of such property to persons who have a child or children living with them nor shall a person rent or lease his property to persons who have a child or children living with them when his property lies within a subdivision which is presently designed, advertised and used as an exclusive adult subdivision. A person who knowingly rents or leases his property in violation of the provisions of this subsection is guilty of a petty offense.

§ 33-304. Statement for rent constituting property tax

Beginning from and after December 31, 1980, the owner or lessor of property leased or rented solely for residential purposes shall upon request furnish to the tenants of such property a written statement of the percentage of rental payments that are attributable to property tax as prescribed by section 43-1060.

ARTICLE 2. OBLIGATIONS AND LIABILITIES OF TENANT

§ 33-321. Maintenance of premises

A tenant shall exercise diligence to maintain the premises in as good condition as when he took possession, ordinary wear and tear excepted.

§ 33-322. Damages to premises; classification

Removal or intentional and material alteration or damage of any part of a building, the furnishings thereof, or any permanent fixture, by or at the instance of the tenant, without written permission of the landlord or his agent, is a class 2 misdemeanor.

§ 33-323. Liability of person in possession of land for rent due thereon

Every person in possession of land out of which rent is due is liable for the amount or proportion of rent due from the lands in his possession, although it is only a part of the land originally demised, without depriving the landlord of other legal remedies for recovery of rent.

§ 33-324. Denial of landlord's title by lessee in possession prohibited

When a person enters into possession of real property under a lease, he may not, while in possession, deny the title of his landlord in an action brought upon the lease by the landlord or a person claiming under him.

ARTICLE 3. TERMINATION OF TENANCIES

§ 33-341. Termination of tenancies

A. A tenancy from year to year terminates at the end of each year unless written permission is given to remain for a longer period. The permission shall specify the time the tenant may remain, and upon termination of such time the tenancy expires.

B. A lease from month to month may be terminated by the landlord giving at least ten days notice thereof. In case of nonpayment of rent notice is not required.

C. A tenant from month to month shall give ten days notice, and a tenant on a semimonthly basis shall give five days notice, of his intention to terminate possession of the premises. Failure to give the notice renders the tenant liable for the rent for the ensuing ten days.

D. When a tenancy is for a certain period under verbal or written agreement, and the time expires, the tenant shall surrender possession. Notice to quit or demand of possession is not then necessary.

E. A tenant who holds possession of property against the will of the landlord, except as provided in this section, shall not be considered a tenant at sufferance or at will.

§ 33-342. Effect of lessee holding over

When a lessee holds over and retains possession after expiration of the term of the lease without express contract with the owner, the holding over shall not operate to renew the lease for the term of the former lease, but thereafter the tenancy is from month to month.

§ 33-343. Premises rendered untenantable without fault of lessee; nonliability of tenant for rent; right to quit premises

The lessee of a building which, without fault or neglect on the part of the lessee, is destroyed or so injured by the elements or any other cause as to be untenantable or unfit for occupancy, is not liable thereafter to pay rent to the lessor or owner unless expressly provided by written agreement, and the lessee may thereupon quit and surrender possession of the premises.

ARTICLE 4. REMEDIES OF LANDLORD

33-361. Violation of lease by tenant; right of landlord to re-enter; summary action for recovery of premises; appeal; lien for unpaid rent; enforcement

A. When a tenant neglects or refuses to pay rent when due and in arrears for five days, or when tenant violates any provision of the lease, the landlord or person to whom the rent is due, or his agent, may re-enter and take possession, or, without formal demand or re-entry, commence an action for recovery of possession of the premises.

B. The action shall be commenced, conducted and governed as provided for actions for forcible entry or detainer, and shall be tried not less than five nor more than thirty days after its commencement.

C. If judgment is given for the plaintiff, the defendant, in order to perfect an appeal, shall file a bond with the court in an amount fixed and approved by the court payable to the clerk of the superior court, conditioned that appellant will prosecute the appeal to effect and will pay the rental value of the premises pending the appeal and all damages, costs, and rent adjudged against him.

D. If the tenant refuses or fails to pay rent owing and due, the landlord shall have a lien upon and may seize as much personal property of the tenant located on the premises and not exempted by law as is necessary to secure payment of the rent. If the rent is not paid and satisfied within sixty days after seizure as provided for in this section, the landlord may sell the seized personal property in the manner provided by section 33-1023.

E. When premises are sublet or the lease assigned, the landlord shall have a like lien against the sublessee or assignee as he has against the tenant and may enforce it in the same manner.

§ 33-362. Landlord's lien for rent

A. The landlord shall have a lien on all property of his tenant not exempt by law, placed upon or used on the leased premises, until the rent is paid. The lien shall not secure the payment of rent accruing after the death or bankruptcy of the lessee, or after an assignment for the benefit of the lessee's creditors.

B. The landlord may seize for rent any personal property of his tenant found on the premises, but the property of any other person, although found on the premises, shall not be liable therefor. If the tenant fails to allow the landlord to take possession of such property, the landlord may reduce the property to possession by an action to recover possession, and may hold or sell the property for the payment of the rent.

C. The landlord shall have a lien for rent upon crops grown or growing upon the leased premises, whether the rent is payable in money, articles of property or products of the premises, and also for the faithful performance of the terms of the lease, and the lien shall continue for a period of six months after expiration of the term of the lease.

D. When premises are sublet, or when the lease is assigned, the landlord shall have the same lien against the sublessee or assignee as he has against the tenant and may enforce the lien in like manner.

ARTICLE 5. APPLICABILITY OF CHAPTER

§ 33-381. Limitation

This chapter shall apply to all landlord-tenant relationships except for landlord-tenant relationships arising out of the rental of dwelling units which shall be governed by chapter 10 or 11[1] of this title.

[1] Section 33-1301 *et seq.* or 33-1401 *et seq.*

SPECIAL ACTIONS AND PROCEEDINGS RELATING TO PROPERTY
ARIZONA REVISED STATUTES, TITLE 12, CHAPTER 8
(Updated as of August 1998)

§ 12-1171. Acts which constitute forcible entry or detainer

A person is guilty of forcible entry and detainer, or of forcible detainer, as the case may be, if he:

1. Makes an entry into any lands, tenements or other real property, except in cases where entry is given by law.

2. Makes such an entry by force.

3. Wilfully and without force holds over any lands, tenements or other real property after termination of the time for which such lands, tenements or other real property were let to him or to the person under whom he claims, after demand made in writing for the possession thereof by the person entitled to such possession.

§ 12-1172. Definition of forcible entry

A "forcible entry," or an entry where entry is not given by law within the meaning of this article, is:

1. An entry without the consent of the person having the actual possession.

2. As to a landlord, an entry upon the possession of his tenant at will or by sufferance, whether with or without the tenant's consent.

§ 12-1173. Definition of forcible detainer; substitution of parties

There is a forcible detainer if:

1. A tenant at will or by sufferance or a tenant from month to month or a lesser period whose tenancy has been terminated retains possession after his tenancy has been terminated or after he receives written demand of possession by the landlord.

2. The tenant of a person who has made a forcible entry refuses for five days after written demand to give possession to the person upon whose possession the forcible entry was made.

3. A person who has made a forcible entry upon the possession of one who acquired such pos-session by forcible entry refuses for five days after written demand to give possession to the person upon whose possession the first forcible entry was made.

4. A person who has made a forcible entry upon the possession of a tenant for a term refuses to deliver possession to the landlord for five days after written demand, after the term expires. If the term expires while a writ of forcible entry applied for by the tenant is pending, the landlord may, at his own cost and for his own benefit, prosecute it in the name of the tenant.

§ 12-1173.01. Additional definition of forcible detainer

A. In addition to other persons enumerated in this article, a person in any of the following cases who retains possession of any land, tenements or other real property after he received written demand of possession may be removed through an action for forcible detainer filed with the clerk of the superior court in accordance with this article:

1. If the property has been sold through the foreclosure of a mortgage, deed of trust or contract for conveyance of real property pursuant to title 33, chapter 6, article 2.[1]

2. If the property has been sold through a trustee's sale under a deed of trust pursuant to title 33, chapter 6.1.[2]

3. If the property has been forfeited through a contract for conveyance of real property pursuant to title 33, chapter 6, article 3.[3]

4. If the property has been sold by virtue of an execution and the title has been duly transferred.

5. If the property has been sold by the owner and the title has been duly transferred.

B. The remedies provided by this section do not affect the rights of persons in possession under a lease or other possessory right which is superior to the interest sold, forfeited or executed upon.

C. The remedies provided by this section are in addition to and do not preclude any other remedy granted by law.

[1] Section 33-721 et seq.   [2] Section 33-801 et seq.
[3] Section 33-741 et seq.

§ 12-1174. Immateriality of time possession obtained by tenant

It is not material whether a tenant received possession from his landlord or became his tenant after obtaining possession.

§ 12-1175. Complaint and answer; service and return

A. When a party aggrieved files a complaint of forcible entry or forcible detainer, in writing and under oath, with the clerk of the superior court or a justice of the peace, summons shall issue no later than the next judicial day.

B. The complaint shall contain a description of the premises of which possession is claimed in sufficient detail to identify them and shall also state the facts which entitle the plaintiff to possession and authorize the action.

C. The summons shall be served at least two days before the return day, and return made thereof on the day assigned for trial.

§ 12-1176. Demand for jury; trial procedure

A. The clerk or justice of the peace shall at the time of issuing the summons, if requested by the plaintiff, issue a venire to the sheriff or constable of the county commanding him to summon a jury of eight persons, if the proceeding is in the superior court, and six persons, if in the justice court, qualified jurors of the county, to appear on the day set for trial to serve as jurors in the action. The venire shall be served and returned on the day assigned for trial. The trial date shall be no more than five judicial days after the aggrieved party files the complaint.

B. If the plaintiff does not request a jury, the defendant may do so when he appears, and the jury shall be summoned in the manner set forth in subsection A.

C. If any jurors fail to attend, or are excused after being challenged, the jury shall be completed by causing other qualified jurors to be summoned immediately.

D. The action shall be docketed and tried as other civil actions.

§ 12-1177. Trial and issue; postponement of trial

A. On the trial of an action of forcible entry or forcible detainer, the only issue shall be the right of actual possession and the merits of title shall not be inquired into.

B. If a jury is demanded, it shall return a verdict of guilty or not guilty of the charge as stated in the complaint. If a jury is not demanded the action shall be tried by the court.

C. For good cause shown, supported by affidavit, the trial may be postponed for a time not to exceed three calendar days in a justice court or ten calendar days in a superior court.

§ 12-1178. Judgment; writ of restitution; limitation on issuance

A. If the defendant is found guilty, the court shall give judgment for the plaintiff for restitution of the premises, for all charges stated in the rental agreement and for costs and, at the plaintiff's option, for all rent found to be due and unpaid through the periodic rental period, as described in section 33-1314, subsection C, as provided for in the rental agreement, and shall grant a writ of restitution. If the defendant's social security number is contained on the complaint at the time of judgment, the person designated by the judge to prepare the judgment shall ensure that defendant's social security number is contained on the judgment.

B. If the defendant is found not guilty, judgment shall be given for the defendant against the plaintiff for costs, and if it appears that the plaintiff has acquired possession of the premises since commencement of the action, a writ of restitution shall issue in favor of the defendant.

C. No writ of restitution shall issue until the expiration of five calendar days after the rendition of judgment. The writ of restitution shall be enforced as promptly and expeditiously as possible. The issuance or enforcement of a writ of restitution shall not be suspended, delayed, or otherwise affected by the filing of a motion to set aside or vacate the judgment or similar motion unless a judge finds good cause.

§ 12-1179. Appeal to superior court; notice; bond

A. Either party may appeal from a justice court to the superior court in the county in which the judgment is given by giving notice as in other civil actions within five calendar days after rendition of the judgment pursuant to this section. The appeal shall be filed in accordance with this section, and the time to appeal shall not be extended or otherwise affected by the filing of a motion to set aside or vacate the judgment or similar motion.

B. A party seeking to appeal a judgment shall file with the notice of appeal a bond for costs on appeal, which shall be in an amount set by the justice of the peace sufficient to cover the costs on appeal. The bond shall be payable to the clerk of the superior court. If a party is unable to file a bond for costs on appeal, the party shall file with the justice court a notice of appeal along with an affidavit stating that he is unable to give bond for costs on appeal and the reasons therefor. Within five court days after the filing of the affidavit, any other party may file, in the justice court, objections to the affidavit. The justice of the peace shall hold a hearing on the affidavit and objections within five court days thereafter. If the justice court sustains the objections, the appellant shall file, within five court days thereafter, a bond for costs on appeal as provided for in this section or in such lesser amount as ordered by the justice court.

C. A party seeking to appeal a judgment may stay the execution of either the judgment for possession or any judgment for money damages by filing a supersedeas bond. The justice court shall hold a hearing on the motion within five court days after the parties advise the justice court of their failure to stipulate on the amount of the bond. The stay is effective when the supersedeas bond or bonds are filed.

D. The party seeking to stay the execution of the judgment for possession shall file a supersedeas bond in the amount of rent accruing from the date of the judgment until the next periodic rental date, together with costs and attorney's fees, if any. The tenant shall pay to the clerk of the superior court, on or before each periodic rental due date during the pendency of the appeal, the amount of rent due under the terms of the lease or rental agreement. Such amounts shall be made payable by the superior court to the owner, landlord or agent as they accrue to satisfy the amount of periodic rent due under the lease or rental agreement. In all cases where the rent due under the terms of the lease or rental agreement is paid through the office of the clerk of the superior court as set forth in this subsection, the order of the court may include a one-time handling fee in the amount of ten dollars to be paid by the party seeking to stay the execution of the judgment for possession. In no event shall the amounts paid per month exceed the amount of monthly rent charged by the owner for the premises. Where habitability as provided for in sections 33-1324 and 33-1364 has been raised as an affirmative defense by the tenant to the nonpayment of rent or when the tenant has filed a counterclaim asserting a habitability issue, the superior court will retain all money paid under this subsection pending a final judgment.

E. If during the pendency of the appeal the party seeking to stay the execution of the judgment for possession fails to pay the rent on the periodic rental due date, the party in whose favor a judgment for possession was issued may move the superior court to lift the stay of execution of the judgment for possession. The superior court shall hear the motion to lift the stay of the execution of the judgment for possession and release accrued monies, if any, within five court days from the failure of the party to pay the periodic rent due under the terms of the lease or rental agreement. If the judgment appealed from involves a finding of a material and irreparable breach pursuant to section 33-1368 or section 33-1476, subsection D, paragraph 3 the superior court shall treat it as an emergency matter and conduct a hearing on a motion to lift the stay of execution of the writ of restitution within three days. If the third day is a Saturday, Sunday or other legal holiday, the hearing shall be heard on the next day thereafter.

F. The party seeking to stay the execution of the judgment for money damages shall file a supersedeas bond in the amount of the judgment, together with costs and attorney's fees, if any. The amount of the bond shall be fixed by the court and payable to the clerk of the superior court.

§ 12-1180. Stay of proceedings on judgment; record on appeal

When the appeal bond is filed and approved, the justice of the peace shall stay further proceedings on the judgment and immediately prepare a transcript of all entries on his docket in the action and transmit it, together with all the original papers, to the clerk of the superior court of the county in which the trial was had.

§ 12-1181. Trial and judgment on appeal; writ of restitution

A. On trial of the action in the superior court, appellee, if out of possession and the right of possession is adjudged to him, shall be entitled to damages for withholding possession of the premises during pendency of the appeal and the court shall also render judgment in favor of appellee and against appellant and the sureties on his bond for damages proved and costs.

B. The writ of restitution or execution shall be issued by the clerk of the superior court and shall be executed by the sheriff or constable as in other actions.

§ 12-1182. Appeal to supreme court; stay and bond
A. In a forcible entry or forcible detainer action originally commenced in the superior court, an appeal may be taken to the supreme court as in other civil actions.

B. The appeal, if taken by the party in possession of the premises, shall not stay execution of the judgment unless the superior court so orders, and appellant shall file a bond in an amount fixed and approved by the court, conditioned that appellant will prosecute the appeal to effect and will pay the rental value of the premises pending the appeal and all damages, costs, and rent adjudged against him by the superior court or the supreme court.

§ 12-1183. Proceedings no bar to certain actions
The proceedings under a forcible entry or forcible detainer shall not bar an action for trespass, damages, waste, rent or mesne profits.

SPECIAL ACTIONS AND PROCEEDINGS IN WHICH THE STATE IS A PARTY
ARIZONA REVISED STATUTES, TITLE 12, CHAPTER 7
(Updated as of August 1998)

ARTICLE 12. ABATEMENT OF CRIME PROPERTY

---

§ 12-991. Nuisance; commercial buildings used for crime; action to abate and prevent
A. The use of a commercial building or place regularly used in the commission of a crime is a nuisance and the criminal activity causing the nuisance shall be enjoined, abated and prevented and damages may be recovered.

B. If there is reason to believe that a nuisance as described in subsection A exists, the attorney general, the county attorney, the city attorney or a resident of a county or city who is affected by the nuisance may bring an action in superior court to abate and prevent the criminal activity, except that:

1. The court shall not assess a civil penalty against any person unless that person knew of the unlawful acts.

2. The court shall not enter an order of closure.

3. The injunction shall be necessary to protect the health and safety of the public or to prevent further criminal activity.

4. The order shall not affect the owner's interest in the building or place used for the criminal activity.

§ 12-991.01. Nuisance; residential property used for crime; action to abate and prevent; notice
A. The use of a residential property regularly used in the commission of a crime is a nuisance and the criminal activity causing the nuisance shall be enjoined, abated and prevented and damages and expenses may be recovered.

B. If there is reason to believe that a nuisance as described in subsection A exists, the attorney general, the county attorney, the city attorney or a resident of a county or city who is affected by the nuisance may bring an action in superior court against the owner, occupant or tenant of the affected residential property to abate and prevent the criminal activity under the following requirements and conditions:

1. A civil penalty under this section shall not exceed two thousand five hundred dollars and the court shall not assess a civil penalty against any person unless that person knew of the unlawful acts.

2. The court shall not enter an order of closure.

3. The injunction shall be necessary to protect the health and safety of the public or to prevent further criminal activity.

4. The order shall not affect the owner's interest in the residential property used for the criminal activity unless the owner:

(a) Is a defendant in the action,

(b) Knew of the criminal activity, and

(c) Failed to take substantial actions legally available to abate the nuisance.

5. If the owner knew of the criminal activity and failed to take substantial actions legally available to abate the nuisance, the order may assess the owner for the cost of abating the nuisance. The assessment is a lien against the owner's interest in the residential property upon recording with the county recorder in the county where the property is located. A city or town may bring an action to enforce the lien in superior court in the county in which the residential property is located at any time after the lien is recorded.

C. For purposes of this section, an owner is considered to know of the nuisance if the owner has received notice of multiple docketed responses or criminal offenses occurring on the residential property. A law enforcement agency, a municipal attorney, a county attorney, the attorney general or a person who is at least twenty-one years of age may serve the notice for purposes of this subsection, either personally or by certified mail, to the owner at the owner's last known address or at the address to which a tax bill for the residential property was last mailed or the owner's agent at the agent's last known address. The notice shall be printed in at least twelve point type in the following form:

Notice

This is formal notice that your property at (insert address) has had (insert number of) arrests or number of docketed responses for alleged criminal activity and is considered a nuisance under [A.R.S. § 12-991.01]. A copy of the police reports is attached.

You must immediately take substantial actions that are legally available to you to abate the nuisance from your property. If you fail to do so, a restraining order to abate and prevent continuing or recurring criminal activity will be pursued.

Ultimately, if you fail to cooperate to abate the nuisance, the authorities will abate the nuisance and their costs will be a lien on your property.

§ 12-992. Commercial property nuisances; temporary restraining order; notice; hearing

A. If the existence of a nuisance on commercial property as described in § 12-991 is shown in the action to the satisfaction of the court either by verified complaint or affidavit, the court shall enter a temporary restraining order to abate and prevent continuance or recurrence of the criminal activity. The complaint shall be verified unless it is filed by the attorney general or a county or city attorney.

B. Notice of the entry of a restraining order, copies of the restraining order and the complaint and notice of an opportunity for a hearing shall be served on the defendant named in the action. Service shall be made pursuant to the Arizona rules of civil procedure.

C. A person who is directed to abate criminal activity pursuant to a temporary restraining order issued pursuant to subsection A of this section may request a hearing within ten days after receiving the notice. A verified answer to the complaint shall be filed with the request for a hearing. If a hearing is requested, notice of the request shall be served on the plaintiff. The temporary restraining order remains in effect until the hearing is completed.

D. If at the hearing the court determines that reasonable grounds exist to believe that a nuisance, as described in § 12-991, subsection A, exists, the court shall issue a permanent injunction abating the criminal activity and may issue any other order that is reasonably necessary to abate the criminal activity, including damages. If the court determines that reasonable grounds do not exist to believe that a nuisance exists, the court shall dismiss the action and terminate the temporary restraining order.

E. A hearing on an action under this section shall be set within thirty days after the request is filed or after a verified answer to the complaint is filed if a temporary restraining order has not been issued. Before the hearing, the court may order any discovery that the court considers to be reasonably necessary and appropriate.

F. If a hearing is not requested, the court shall issue a permanent injunction abating the criminal activity.

§ 12-992.01. Residential property nuisances; temporary restraining order; notice; hearing

A. If the existence of a nuisance on residential property as described in § 12-991.01 is shown in the action to the satisfaction of the court either by verified complaint or affidavit, the court shall enter a temporary restraining order to abate and prevent continuance or recurrence of the criminal activity. The complaint shall be verified unless it is filed by the attorney general or a county or city attorney.

B. Notice of the entry of a restraining order, copies of the restraining order and the complaint and notice of an opportunity for a hearing shall be served on the defendant named in the action. Service shall be made pursuant to the Arizona rules of civil procedure.

C. A person who is directed to abate criminal activity pursuant to a temporary restraining order issued pursuant to subsection A of this section may request a hearing within ten days after receiving the notice, shall file a verified answer to the complaint with the request for a hearing and shall serve notice of the request on the plaintiff. The temporary restraining order remains in effect until the hearing is completed.

D. If at the hearing the court determines that reasonable grounds:

1. Exist to believe that a nuisance described in § 12-991.01, subsection A, exists, the court:

(a) Shall issue a permanent injunction abating the criminal activity.

(b) May issue any other order that is reasonably necessary to abate the criminal activity, including damages.

2. Do not exist to believe that a nuisance exists, the court shall dismiss the action and terminate the temporary restraining order.

E. A hearing on an action under this section shall be set within thirty days after the request is filed or after a verified answer to the complaint is filed if a temporary restraining order has not been issued. Before the hearing, the court may order any discovery that the court considers to be reasonably necessary and appropriate.

F. If the court determines at the hearing that reasonable grounds exist to believe that a nuisance as described in § 12-991.01 exists or on default of an answer to the complaint, the court:

1. Shall issue a final judgment, including a permanent injunction abating the criminal activity.

2. May issue any other order that is reasonably necessary to abate the criminal activity, including orders:

(a) To pay damages.

(b) To enhance the lighting on the property.

(c) To award expenses that were incurred in abating the nuisance, including:

(i) The costs of investigation and enforcing the restraining order.

(ii) Reasonable attorney fees.

(iii) A civil penalty of not more than two thousand five hundred dollars.

G. If the defendant is the landlord and the nuisance is created by the tenant, and the landlord unsuccessfully attempts a forcible entry and detainer action, the court may terminate the restraining order and dismiss the complaint.

§ 12-993. Precedence of action; reputation of place as evidence; dismissal; costs

A. An action that is described in § 12-991 or 12-991.01 and that is filed has precedence in the trial courts over all actions except juvenile proceedings, criminal proceedings, election contests and hearings on injunctions.

B. In the action, evidence of the general reputation of the building or place is admissible for the purpose of proving the existence of the nuisance.

C. If the action is brought by a citizen and the court finds that there was no reasonable basis for bringing the action, the court may assess costs and reasonable attorney fees against the citizen. If the court determines that reasonable grounds do exist and issues a final judgment in favor of the plaintiff, the court may assess costs and reasonable attorney fees against the defendant.

§ 12-994. Violation; classification

In addition to or in lieu of any other power that the court possesses to enforce a temporary restraining order, an injunction or any other order, a person who violates or disobeys a temporary restraining order, an injunction or any other order issued by the court pursuant to this article is guilty of a class 6 felony.

APPENDIX D

COURTS

APACHE COUNTY			
City/Town	Precinct	Street Address & Phone #	Mailing Address
Wide Ruins Sanders Chambers St. Michaels Ganado Ft. Defiance Houck Lupton Window Rock	Puerco	P.O. Box 336 Sanders, AZ 86512 (502) 688-2954 Justice Court and Small Claims Court	Same
Round Valley Eagar Greer Alpine Nutrioso McNary Vernon Springerville	Round Valley	130 N. South Mountain Ave. Springerville, AZ 85938 (502) 333-4613 Justice Court and Small Claims Court	P.O. Box 1356 Springerville AZ 85938
St. Johns Concho	St. Johns	70 West 3rd South St. Johns, AZ 85936 (502) 337-4364, Ext. 271 Justice Court and Small Claims Court	P.O. Box 308 St. Johns, AZ 85936
Teec Nos Pos Dennehotso Lukachukai	Teec Nos Pos	U.S. 191, M.P. 73 Chinle, AZ 86503 (502) 674-5922 Justice Court and Small Claims Court	P.O. Box 888 Chinle, AZ 86503

COCHISE COUNTY			
City/Town	Precinct	Street Address & Phone #	Mailing Address
Bisbee Tombstone	No. 1	207 N. Judd Bisbee, AZ 85603 (502) 432-9540 Justice Court and Small Claims Court	207 N. Judd Bisbee, AZ 85603
Douglas	No. 2	661 "G" Avenue Douglas, AZ 85607 (502) 364-3561 Justice Court and Small Claims Court	Same
Benson St. David Pomerene	No. 3	500 South Highway 80 Benson, AZ 85602 (502) 586-2247 Justice Court and Small Claims Court	P.O. Box 2167 Benson, AZ 85602
Willcox	No. 4	450 South Haskell Willcox, AZ 85643 (502) 384-2105 Justice Court and Small Claims Court	Same
Bowie San Simon	No. 6	201 North Central Avenue Bowie, AZ 85605 (502) 847-2303 Justice Court and Small Claims Court	P.O. Box 317 Bowie, AZ 85605

COCONINO COUNTY			
City/Town	Precinct	Street Address & Phone #	Mailing Address
Flagstaff Sedona	Flagstaff	Flagstaff Justice Court 100 East Birch Avenue Flagstaff, AZ 86001 (502) 779-6806 Justice Court and Small Claims Court	Same
Fredonia	Fredonia	100 North Main Fredonia, AZ 86022-0559 (502) 643-7472 Justice Court and Small Claims Court	P.O. Box 559 Fredonia, AZ 86022
Page	Page	547 Vista Avenue Page, AZ 86040 (502) 645-8871 Justice Court and Small Claims Court	P.O. Box 1565 Page, AZ 86040
Williams Parks Supai Grand Canyon	Williams	117 West Route 66 Suite 180 Williams, AZ 86046 (502) 635-2691 Justice Court and Small Claims Court	Same

GILA COUNTY			
City/Town	Precinct	Street Address & Phone #	Mailing Address
Globe Roosevelt Young	Globe	Globe Justice Court 1400 East Ash Street Globe, AZ 85501 (502) 425-3231, Ext. 320 Justice Court and Small Claims Court	Same
Hayden- Winkelman Christmas Dripping Springs	Hayden- Winkelman	Highway 177 Winkelman, AZ 85292 (502) 356-7638 Justice Court and Small Claims Court	P.O. Box 680 Winkelman, AZ 85292
Miami Claypool Central Heights	Miami	506 Sullivan Street Miami, AZ 85539 (502) 473-4461 Justice Court and Small Claims Court	Same
Payson Gisela Tonto Basin	Payson	714 South Beeline Highway Suite 103 Payson, AZ 85541 (502) 474-5267 Justice Court and Small Claims Court	Same
Pine Strawberry Whispering Pines	Pine	304 Hard Scrabble Pine, AZ 85544 (502) 476-3525 Justice Court and Small Claims Court	P.O. Box 2169 Pine, AZ 85544

GRAHAM COUNTY			
City/Town	Precinct	Street Address & Phone #	Mailing Address
Safford Solomon Thatcher Central Bonita	No. 1	800 W. Main St. Safford, AZ 85546 (502) 428-1210 Justice Court and Small Claims Court	Same
Pima Klondyke Ft. Thomas	No. 2	136 West Center Pima, AZ 85543 (502) 485-2771 Justice Court and Small Claims Court	P.O. Box 1159 Pima, AZ 85543

GREENLEE COUNTY			
City/Town	Precinct	Street Address & Phone #	Mailing Address
Clifton	Clifton/ Morenci-No. 1	5th & Leonard Clifton, AZ 85533 (502) 865-4312 Justice Court and Small Claims Court	P.O. Box 517 Clifton, AZ 85533
Duncan	Duncan-No. 2	Fairground Rd., Bldg. #2 Duncan, AZ 85534 (502) 359-2536 Justice Court and Small Claims Court	P.O. Box 208 Duncan, AZ 85534

LA PAZ COUNTY			
City/Town	Precinct	Street Address & Phone #	Mailing Address
Quartzsite	No. 4	730 W. Cowell Quartzsite, AZ 85346 (502) 927-6313 Justice Court and Small Claims Court	P.O. Box 580 Quartzsite, AZ 85346
Salome	No. 5	310 Salome Rd. Salome, AZ 85348 (502) 859-3871 Justice Court and Small Claims Court	P.O. Box 661 Salome, AZ 85348
Parker	No. 6	1105 Arizona Avenue Parker, AZ 85344 (502) 669-2504 Justice Court and Small Claims Court	Same

MARICOPA COUNTY			
City/Town	Precinct	Street Address & Phone #	Mailing Address
Buckeye	Buckeye	100 North Apache Suite "C" Buckeye, AZ 85326 (602) 506-8118 Justice / Small Claims	Same
Chandler	Chandler	2051 West Warner Road, Suite 20 Chandler, AZ 85224 (602) 963-6691 Justice / Small Claims	Same
East Mesa	East Mesa	4811 East Julep Suite 128 Mesa, AZ 85205 (602) 985-0188 Justice / Small Claims	Same
West Mesa	West Mesa	2050 West University Mesa, AZ 85201 (602) 964-2958 Justice Court	Same
North Mesa South Mesa Gilbert	North Mesa South Mesa	1837 South Mesa Drive Suite B103 Mesa, AZ 85210 (602) 926-3051 Justice Court	Same
North Mesa	North Mesa	1837 S. Mesa Drive, Suite A201 Mesa, AZ 85210 (602) 926-9731 Justice Court	Same
Central Phoenix	Central Phoenix	1 West Madison Phoenix, AZ 85003 (602) 506-1168 Justice / Small Claims	Same

East Phoenix	No. 1	1 West Madison Suite 1 Phoenix, AZ 85003 (602) 506-3577 Justice Court and Small Claims Court	Same
East Phoenix	No. 2	4109 North 12th Street Phoenix, AZ 85014 (602) 266-3725 Justice Court and Small Claims Court	Same
Phoenix	Northwest Phoenix	11601 North 19th Avenue Phoenix, AZ 85029 (602) 506-3968 Justice Court and Small Claims Court	Same
Phoenix	Northeast Phoenix	10255 North 32nd Street Phoenix, AZ 85028 (602) 506-3731 Justice Court and Small Claims Court	Same
Phoenix	South Phoenix	217 East Olympic Phoenix, AZ 85040 (602) 243-0318 Justice Court and Small Claims Court	Same
Phoenix	West Phoenix	527 West McDowell Phoenix, AZ 85003 (602) 256-0292 Justice Court and Small Claims Court	Same

Phoenix	Maryvale	4622 West Indian School Road, D10 Phoenix, AZ 85031 (602) 506-2970 Justice Court and Small Claims Court	Same
Gila Bend	Gila Bend	209 East Pima Gila Bend, AZ 85337 (520) 683-2651 or (602) 506-1589 Justice Court and Small Claims Court	P.O. Box 648 Gila Bend, AZ 85337
Glendale	Glendale	6830 North 57th Drive Glendale, AZ 85301 (602) 939-9477 or (602) 506-3402 Justice Court	Same
Peoria	Peoria	7420 West Cactus Peoria, AZ 85381 (602) 979-3234 Justice Court	Same
Scottsdale	Scottsdale	3700 North 75th Street Scottsdale, AZ 85251 (602) 947-7569 Justice Court and Small Claims Court	Same
Tempe	Tempe	1845 East Broadway #8 Tempe, AZ 85282 (602) 967-8856 Justice Court and Small Claims Court	Same

Tolleson	Tolleson	9550 West Van Buren Suite 6 Tolleson, AZ 85353 (602) 936-1440 Justice Court	Same
Wickenburg	Wickenburg	155 North Tegner Wickenburg, AZ 85390 (520) 684-2401 or (602) 506-1554 Justice Court and Small Claims Court	P.O. Box Z Wickenburg, AZ 85358

MOHAVE COUNTY			
City/Town	Precinct	Street Address & Phone #	Mailing Address
Bullhead City	Bullhead City	2225 Trane Rd. Bullhead City, AZ 86442 (520) 758-0709 Justice Court and Small Claims Court	Same
Moccasin	Moccasin	123 South Main Moccasin, AZ 86022 (520) 643-7104 Justice Court and Small Claims Court	H.C. 65, Box 90 Moccasin, AZ 86022
Kingman	Kingman	401 Spring St. Kingman, AZ 86402 (520) 753-0710 Justice Court and Small Claims Court	P.O. Box 29 Kingman, AZ 86402
Lake Havasu City	Lake Havasu City	2001 College Dr. Lake Havasu City, AZ 86403 (520) 453-0705 Justice Court and Small Claims Court	Same

NAVAJO COUNTY			
City/Town	Precinct	Street Address & Phone #	Mailing Address
Holbrook Indian Wells Keams Canyon Pinon Woodruff Joseph City Kayenta	No. 1	Navajo County Governmental Center 100 E. Carter Dr. Holbrook, AZ 86025 (520) 524-4228 Justice Court and Small Claims Court	P.O. Box 668 Holbrook, AZ 86025
Winslow Oraibi Polacca Tees To Toreva	No. 2	605 East 3rd Street Winslow, AZ 86047 (520) 289-6840 Justice Court and Small Claims Court	P.O. Box 808 Winslow, AZ 86047
Snowflake Taylor Heber Overgaard	No. 3	73 West 1st South Snowflake, AZ 85937 (520) 536-4141 Justice Court and Small Claims Court	Same
Show Low Cibecue Clay Springs Linden Pinedale	No. 5	561 East Deuce of Clubs Show Low, AZ 85901 (520) 537-2213 Justice Court and Small Claims Court	P.O. Box 3085 Showlow, AZ 85902
Lakeside Pinetop Whiteriver	No. 7	1360 North Niels Hansen Lane Lakeside, AZ 85929 (520) 368-6200 Justice Court and Small Claims Court	P.O. Box 2020 Lakeside, AZ 85929

PIMA COUNTY			
City/Town	Precinct	Street Address & Phone #	Mailing Address
Tucson	Nos. 1, 2, 4, 5, and 6	115 North Church Ave. Tucson, AZ 85701 (520) 882-0044 Justice Court and Small Claims Court	Same
Ajo	No. 3	111 La Mina Ajo, AZ 85321 (520) 387-7684 Justice Court and Small Claims Court	Same

PINAL COUNTY			
City/Town	Precinct	Street Address & Phone #	Mailing Address
Florence Coolidge	No. 1	94 W. Butte Florence, AZ 85232 (520) 868-6578 Justice Court and Small Claims Court	P.O. Box 1818 Florence, AZ 85232
Casa Grande Sacaton	No. 2	820 East Cottonwood Lane Building B Casa Grande, AZ 85222 (520) 836-5471 Justice Court and Small Claims Court	Same

Eloy Red Rock Picacho	No. 3	801 North Main Street Eloy, AZ 85231 (520) 466-9221 Justice Court and Small Claims Court	P.O. Box 586 Eloy, AZ 85231
Mammoth	No. 4	Kino Street & Catalina Mammoth, AZ 85618 (520) 487-2262 Justice Court and Small Claims Court	P.O. Box 117 Mammoth, AZ 85618
Oracle	No. 5	1470 Justice Drive Oracle, AZ 85623 (520) 896-9250 Justice Court	OMSR Oracle, AZ 85623
Superior Kearney	No. 6	60 East Main Superior, AZ 85273 (520) 689-5871 Justice Court and Small Claims Court	Same
Apache Junction Queen Creek Queen Valley	No. 7	575 North Idaho Road Apache Junction, AZ 85219 (602) 982-2921 Justice Court and Small Claims Court	Same
Maricopa Stanfield	No. 8	44625 West Garvey Rd. Maricopa, AZ 85239 (520) 568-2451 Justice Court and Small Claims Court	P.O. Box 201 Maricopa, AZ 85239

SANTA CRUZ COUNTY			
City/Town	Precinct	Street Address & Phone #	Mailing Address
Nogales	No. 1	2150 North Congress Nogales, AZ 85628 (520) 761-7853 Justice Court and Small Claims Court	P.O. Box 1150 Nogales, AZ 85628
Patagonia Sonoita East Santa Cruz	No. 2	3147 St. Rt. 83, #104 Sonoita, AZ 85637 (520) 455-5796 Justice Court and Small Claims Court	P.O. Box 100 Patagonia, AZ 85624

YAVAPAI COUNTY			
City/Town	Precinct	Street Address & Phone #	Mailing Address
Bagdad Hillside	Bagdad	100 Main Street Bagdad, AZ 86321 (520) 633-2141 Justice Court and Small Claims Court	P.O. Box 243 Bagdad, AZ 86321
Beaver Creek Childs Cornville Irving Lake Montezuma Page Springs Village of Oak Creek	Camp Verde	3505 West Highway 260, Suite 101 Camp Verde, AZ 86322 (520) 567-3353 Justice Court and Small Claims Court	Same
Congress Rincon Yarnell	Yarnell	22591 Lookaway Yarnell, AZ 85362 (520) 427-3318 Justice Court and Small Claims Court	P.O. Box 65 Yarnell, AZ 85362

Black Canyon City Bumble Bee Canyon City Castle Canyon Mesa Castle Hot Springs Cleator Crown King Dewey Humble	Mayer	12840 Central Mayer, AZ 86333 (520) 632-7342 Justice Court and Small Claims Court	P.O. Box 245 Mayer, AZ 86333
Hillside Kirkland Chono Valley Camp Wood Groom Creek Walnut Grove Wagoner	Prescott	Yavapai County Courthouse Room 112 Prescott, AZ 86301 (520) 771-3300 Justice Court and Small Claims Court	Same
Seligman Ashfork	Seligman	200 Floyd St. Seligman, AZ 86337 (520) 422-3281 Justice Court and Small Claims Court	P.O. Box 56 Seligman, AZ 86337

YUMA COUNTY			
City/Town	Precinct	Street Address & Phone #	Mailing Address
Gadsen Somerton	No. 2	350 West Main Somerton, AZ 85350 (520) 627-2722 Justice Court and Small Claims Court	P.O. Box 458 Somerton, AZ 85350
Roll Wellton Tacna Mohawk Aztec Hyder	No. 3	10260 Dome Street Wellton, AZ 85356 (520) 785-3321 Justice Court and Small Claims Court	P.O. Box 384 Wellton, AZ 85356

GLOSSARY

A, B

Abandonment - As defined in the Act, "means either the absence of the tenant from the dwelling unit, without notice to the landlord for at least seven days, if rent for the dwelling unit is outstanding and unpaid for ten days and there is no reasonable evidence other than the presence of the tenant's personal property that the tenant is occupying the residence or the absence of the tenant for at least five days, if the rent for the dwelling unit is outstanding and unpaid for five days and none of the tenant's personal property is in the dwelling unit." *See* A.R.S. § 33-1370(H) (West Supp. 1998).

Act - Refers to the Arizona Residential Landlord and Tenant Act. The Act is contained in Chapter 10 of Title 33 of the Arizona Revised Statutes, A.R.S. §§ 33-1301 to -1381 (West 1990 & Supp. 1998).

Action - As defined in the Act, "includes recoupment, counterclaim, setoff, suit in equity and any other proceeding in which rights are determined, including an action for possession." *See* A.R.S. § 33-1310(1) (West Supp. 1998).

Adequate notice - Should be defined in the rental agreement or, if not addressed in the rental agreement, is defined by statute. In short, it is the amount of notice required (by the rental agreement or statute) necessary to be given by a party before certain action is taken (i.e., increase in rent, vacating rental unit, terminating the rental agreement). *See, e.g.,* A.R.S. § 33-1375 (West Supp. 1998).

Answer - A pleading filed by a defendant in response to a complaint or by cross-defendant in response to a cross-claim.

Arizona Reports - A legal publication containing written opinions of Arizona courts.

A.R.S. § ##-#### - Refers to Arizona Revised Statutes Annotated, which is properly cited as: ARIZ. REV. STAT. ANN. § ##-#### (West 1990 & Supp. 1998), but for brevity is cited herein as A.R.S. § ##-####, where "##-####" is the specific statute title and section number.

Asset protection - A plan or strategy that shields some, most or all of your assets from liability. Asset protection is briefly discussed in Chapter 1, Section C and Chapter 2, Section B.

Asset search - A search of public records and records that are not readily available to the public, for the purpose of discovering the location and/or extent of assets and holdings of a person or entity. An asset search is typically ordered from some type of investigative service; the cost ranges from $50 to $250 (more if you want to expand the search to include other counties and/or states).

Building and housing codes - As defined in the Act, "include any law, ordinance or governmental regulation concerning fitness for habitation, or the construction, maintenance, operation, occupancy, use or appearance of any premises, or dwelling unit." *See* A.R.S. § 33-1310(2) (West Supp. 1998).

C

Case - A general term for an action, cause, suit, or controversy at law or in equity. A judicial proceeding for the determination of a controversy between parties, wherein rights are enforced or protected, or wrongs are prevented or redressed.

Citations - Reference to legal authorities and precedents, such as constitutions, statutes, reported cases and treatises. Used in arguments to courts, in legal text-books, law review articles, legal briefs, or the like, to establish or fortify the proposition(s) advanced.

Cite - *See* Citation.

Cleaning deposit - Money belonging to the tenant and held by the landlord to pay for cleaning of the rental unit in the event the tenant does not leave it clean when the tenant vacates the unit at the end of the tenancy.

Complaint - A pleading filed by a plaintiff to initiate a lawsuit (i.e., the document filed by the landlord to initiate a Special Detainer action). *See Answer* for related reference.

Counterclaim - A pleading filed by a defendant against the plaintiff, asserting a cause of action against the plaintiff that may or may not be related to the factual situation giving rise to the plaintiff's cause of action against the defendant. The counterclaim is filed with the answer.

D

Deposits - *See Security*, *cleaning deposit*, or *redecorating deposit*.

Distraint for rent - Seizure; the act of distraining or making a distress. Normally referring to a landlord seizing the property of a tenant for failure of the tenant to pay rent when due. Distraint for rent is not permitted for residential property subject to the Act.

Dwelling unit - As defined in the Act, "means a structure or the part of a structure that is used as a home, residence, or sleeping place by one person who maintains a household or by two or more persons who maintain a common household. `Dwelling unit' excludes real property used to accommodate a mobile home, unless the mobile home is rented or leased by the landlord." *See* A.R.S. § 33-1310(4) (West Supp. 1998).

E

Et seq. - An abbreviation for *et sequentes* or *et sequentia*; means, "and the following." Thus a reference to A.R.S. § 33-1301, *et seq.*, means Section 33-1301 and the following sections.

Eviction - Dispossession by process of law; the act of depriving a person of the possession of land or rental property which he has held or leased. *See Special Detainer action*.

Exclusions
- As used in A.R.S. § 33-1308, means particular circumstances under which the rental of residential rental property is <u>not</u> subject to the Act.

- As used in connection with an insurance policy, refers to certain conditions or circumstances that are not covered by the policy.

Execution - *See Writ of Execution*.

F, G, H

Familial Status -
The federal law definition is: "Familial status" mans one or more individuals (who have not attained the age of 18 years) being domiciled with - (1) a parent or another person having legal custody of such individuals or individuals; or (2) the designee of such parent or other person having such custody, with the written permission of such parent or other person. The protections afforded against discrimination on the basis of familial status shall apply to any person who is pregnant or is in the process of securing legal custody of any individual who has not attained the age of 18 years. 42 U.S.C.A. § 3602 (West 1995).

The state law definition is: In this article, a discriminatory act is committed because of familial status if the act is committed because the person who is the subject of discrimination is: (1) Pregnant, (2) Domiciled with an individual younger than eighteen years of age in regard to whom the person either: (a) Is the parent or legal custodian, (b) Has the written permission of the parent or legal custodian for domicile with that person, (3) In the process of obtaining legal custody of an individual younger than eighteen years of age. A.R.S. § 41-1491.01 (West 1992).

Five-Day Notice to Pay or Quit - Written notice given by the landlord to the tenant, pursuant to A.R.S. § 33-1368(B), informing the tenant that if s/he does not pay rent that is due within five days, the landlord may terminate the rental agreement and file a Special Detainer action. *See* A.R.S. § 33-1368(A); *see also* Appendix B, Form 9.

Forcible detainer - Properly called a Special Detainer action when used in connection with an eviction from residential real property. *See Special Detainer action*.

Garnishment - *See Writ of Garnishment*.

Good faith - As defined in the Act, "means honesty in fact" in the conduct or transaction concerned. *See* A.R.S. § 33-1310(5) (West Supp. 1998).

Homestead - A legal mechanism, creating an artificial estate in land, devised to protect the possession and enjoyment of the owner of the land against the claims of his/her creditors by exempting the property from execution and forced sale, so long as the property is occupied as a home. The Arizona homestead exemption is now automatic and no filing is required. *See* A.R.S. 33-1101.

Housing codes - Building and housing codes, as defined in the Act, "include any law, ordinance or governmental regulation concerning fitness for habitation, or the construction, maintenance, operation, occupancy, use or appearance of any premises, or dwelling unit." *See* A.R.S. § 33-1310(2) (West Supp. 1998).

I, J, K

Judgment - The official and authentic decision of a court of justice upon the respective rights and claims of the parties to an action or suit therein litigated and submitted to its determination.

Judgment creditor - One who has obtained a money judgment against his debtor (or defendant), under which he may enforce execution.

L

Landlord - As defined in the Act, "means the owner, lessor or sublessor of the dwelling unit or the building of which it is a part, and it also means a manager of the premises who fails to disclose as required by § 33-1322." *See* A.R.S. § 33-1310(6) (West Supp. 1998).

Lease - Any agreement that gives rise to a relationship of landlord and tenant (in the case of real property). *See rental agreement*.

Litigation - A lawsuit; legal action, including all proceedings therein. A contest in a court of law for the purpose of enforcing a right or seeking a remedy.

M, N

Noncompliance - As used in the Act, refers to a failure of the landlord or the tenant to comply with the terms and conditions of the rental agreement, rules and regulations, and/or the Act. *See* A.R.S. §§ 33-1361, -1368 (West 1990 & Supp. 1998).

Nonrefundable fee or charge - A fee paid by a tenant to the landlord, normally at the commencement of the tenancy, that both parties understand will be retained by the landlord at the end of the tenancy. Pursuant to A.R.S. § 33- 1321(B), nonrefundable cleaning and redecorating fees or charges <u>must</u> be stated in writing and the purpose thereof disclosed.

Notice
  - See Five-Day Notice to Pay or Quit.
  - See Five-Day Notice of Termination of Rental Agreement for Noncompliance with Rental Agreement Materially Affecting Health and Safety.
  - See Ten-Day Notice of Termination of Rental Agreement for Material Noncompliance with Rental Agreement.

Notice of Complaint/Violation - Written notice given by landlord to tenant to inform tenant of: (1) complaints against the tenant by other tenants, neighbors, etc. and/or (2) violation of some term or condition of the rental agreement or rules and regulations. This notice may form the basis for subsequent eviction if the problem reoccurs. *See* A.R.S. § 33-1368(A); *see also* Appendix B, Form 6.

Notice of Immediate Termination of Rental Agreement for Material and Irreparable Breach - Written notice given by landlord to tenant, pursuant to A.R.S. § 33-1368(A), to immediately terminate a tenant's rental agreement if a breach occurs that is both material and irreparable, such as a discharge of a weapon on the premises or infliction of bodily harm on the landlord, his agent or another tenant or involving imminent serious property damage. *See* Appendix B, Form 8.

Notice Reinstating Time of the Essence - Written notice given by landlord to tenant to inform the tenant that, although the landlord may have waived certain violations and noncompliance in the past, the landlord will require strict compliance with the terms and conditions of the rental agreement and/or the rules and regulations.

Notice to Terminate Tenancy - Written notice given by tenant or landlord to inform the other party that s/he wishes to terminate his/her tenancy. *See* Appendix B, Forms 12 and 13.

O

Opinion - When used in connection with a judge's decision in a case, means the written opinion of the judge outlining the facts and law pertinent to the case and (normally) the judge's reason(s) for deciding the case the way s/he did.

Organization - As defined in the Act, "includes a corporation, government, governmental subdivision or agency, business trust, estate, trust, partnership or association, two or more persons having a joint or common interest and any other legal or commercial entity which is a landlord, owner, manager or constructive agent pursuant to § 33-1322." *See* A.R.S. § 33-1310(7) (West Supp. 1998).

Owner - As defined in the Act, "means one or more persons, jointly or severally, in whom is vested all or part of the legal title to property or all or part of the beneficial ownership and a right to present use and enjoyment of the premises. The term includes a mortgagee in possession." *See* A.R.S. § 33-1310(8) (West Supp. 1998).

P

Pacific Reporter, Second Series - A legal publication that contains written opinions of courts from Alaska, Arizona, California, Colorado, Hawaii, Idaho, Kansas, Montana, Nevada, New Mexico, Oklahoma, Oregon, Utah, Washington and Wyoming.

Pay or Quit - See Seven-Day Notice to Pay or Quit.

Person - As defined in the Act, "means an individual or organization." *See* A.R.S. § 33-1310(9) (West Supp. 1998).

Personal Jurisdiction - The power of a court over the person of a defendant (*in personam* jurisdiction), in contrast to the jurisdiction of a court over a defendant's property or his interest therein (*in rem* jurisdiction).

Post and Mail - A form of service of process, when other forms of service are unavailing, consisting of displaying the documents in a prominent place (i.e., upon the door) and mailing a copy of the notice or pleading (i.e., a Summons and Complaint) to the tenant's last known address, by certified mail, return receipt requested. *See, e.g.,* A.R.S. § 33-1377(B) (West Supp. 1998).

Posting - See Post and Mail.

Precedent - An adjudged case or decision of a court, considered as furnishing an example or authority for an identical or similar case afterwards arising or a similar question of law. A rule of law established for the first time by a court for a particular type of case and thereafter referred to in deciding similar cases.

Pre-empted - Pre-emption is a doctrine adopted by the United States Supreme Court holding that certain matters are of such a national, as opposed to local, character that federal laws Pre-empt or take precedence over state laws. As such, a state may not pass a law that is inconsistent with a federal law. As applied to landlord/tenant law, federal laws addressing Section 8 housing and Indian Reservations pre-empt the Act.

Premises - As defined in the Act, "means a dwelling unit and the structure of which it is a part and existing facilities and appurtenances therein, including furniture and utilities where applicable, and grounds, areas and existing facilities held out for the use of tenants generally or whose use is promised to the tenant." *See* A.R.S. § 33-1310(10) (West Supp. 1998).

Process server - One authorized by the court to deliver *service of process*.

Promulgated - To publish or proclaim formally (i.e., a law, decree of court, etc.) or to put into operation.

Public housing - Is more specifically defined in Chapter 12 of Title 36 of the Arizona Revised Statutes Annotated, A.R.S. §§ 36-1401 to -1501 (West 1993 & Supp. 1998), but generally refers to housing that is owned and operated by the government for low income families.

Q, R

Redecorating fee - Money paid by the tenant to the landlord at the commencement of the tenancy (or thereafter) to pay for redecorating of the rental unit (i.e., new paint, new carpet, new drapes, etc.) at the end of the tenancy, to prepare the unit for occupancy by the next tenant.

Rent - As defined in the Act, "means payments to be made to the landlord in full consideration for the rented premises." *See* A.R.S. § 33-1310(11) (West Supp. 1998).

Rental agreement - As defined in the Act, "means all agreements, written, oral or implied by law, and valid rules and regulations adopted under § 33-1342 embodying the terms and conditions concerning the use and occupancy of a dwelling unit and premises." *See* A.R.S. § 33-1310(12) (West Supp. 1998).

Roomer - As defined in the Act, "means a person occupying a dwelling unit that lacks a major bathroom or kitchen facility, in a structure where one or more major facilities are used in common by occupants of the dwelling unit and other dwelling units. Major facility in the case of a bathroom means toilet, or either a bath or shower, and in the case of a kitchen means refrigerator, stove or sink." *See* A.R.S. § 33-1310(13) (West Supp. 1998).

Rules and regulations - Guidelines established by the landlord that govern the use and occupancy of the leased premises. *See* A.R.S. § 33-1342 (West Supp. 1998).

S, T

Section 8 Housing - The federal housing assistance program that provides rent subsidies for low income families. *See* Tax Exemption of Obligations of Public Housing Agencies and Related Amendments, 24 C.F.R. §§ 811.101 to -.110 (1997).

Security - As defined in the Act, "means money or property given to assure payment or performance under a rental agreement. "Security" does not include a reasonable charge for redecorating or cleaning." *See* A.R.S. § 33-1310(14) (West Supp. 1998). Generally means money or property held by the landlord as security for unpaid rent or damages to the rental unit.

Security deposit - *See Security*.

Service of Process - Delivery of summons, complaint, writ, etc.; signifies delivery to or leaving them with the party to whom or with whom they ought to be delivered or left. The mode of delivery (i.e., personal service, service by mail, service by publication, etc.) may be prescribed by statute or by rule of procedure.

Seven-Day Notice to Pay or Quit - Written notice given by the landlord to the tenant, pursuant to A.R.S. § 33-1368(B), informing the tenant that if s/he does not pay rent that is due within seven days, the landlord may terminate the rental agreement and file a Special Detainer action. Replaced in July 1995 by a Five-Day Notice to Pay or Quit. *See* Appendix B, Form 9.

Single family residence - As defined in the Act, "means a structure maintained and used as a single dwelling unit. Notwithstanding that a dwelling unit shares one or more walls with another dwelling unit, it is a single family residence if it has direct access to a street or thoroughfare and shares neither heating facilities, hot water equipment nor any other essential facility or service with any other dwelling unit." *See* A.R.S. § 33-1310(15) (West Supp. 1998).

Special Detainer action - Legal process, brought pursuant to A.R.S. § 33-1377, to evict a tenant from residential rental property.

Statute - An act of the legislature declaring, commanding or prohibiting something; a particular law enacted and established by the will of the legislative department of government.

Summons - Document used to commence a civil action and requiring person named to appear and answer allegations in a pleading (i.e., a Complaint).

Tenant - As defined in the Act, "means a person entitled under a rental agreement to occupy a dwelling unit to the exclusion of others." *See* A.R.S. § 33-1310(16) (West Supp. 1998).

Term of Lease - As defined in the Act, "means the initial term or any renewal or extension of the written rental agreement currently in effect not including any wrongful holdover period." *See* A.R.S. § 33-1310(17) (West Supp. 1998).

U, V, W, X, Y, Z

With prejudice - As applied to a judgment of dismissal, means that the dismissal has the same conclusive effect as does an adjudication of the case on the merits; the action cannot be refiled against the same adversary, based on the same facts.

Writ of Execution - An order of the court empowering the Sheriff to seize property of a judgment debtor to satisfy a money judgment.

Writ of Garnishment - An order of the court whereby a person's property, money or credits, that are in the possession or control of another party, are applied to payment of a debt to a judgment creditor.

Writ of Restitution - When used herein, refers to an order of the court, after judgment is entered in the landlord's favor in a Special Detainer action, restoring the right to possess residential real property to the landlord.

1 - 14

5-Day Notice of Termination of Rental Agreement for Noncompliance with Rental Agreement Materially Affecting Health and Safety - Written notice given by the landlord to the tenant, pursuant to A.R.S. § 33-1368(A), informing the tenant that there is a noncompliance with the rental agreement that material affects health and safety and that if not remedied by the tenant within five days of the notice, the rental agreement will terminate in five days. *See* Appendix B, Form 10.

5-Day Notice to Pay or Quit - Written notice given by the landlord to the tenant, pursuant to A.R.S. § 33-1368(B), informing the tenant that if s/he does not pay rent that is due within five days, the landlord may terminate the rental agreement and file a Special Detainer action. *See* Appendix B, Form 9.

7-Day Notice to Pay or Quit - Written notice given by the landlord to the tenant, pursuant to A.R.S. § 33-1368(B), informing the tenant that if s/he does not pay rent that is due within seven days, the landlord may terminate the rental agreement and file a Special Detainer action. **Replaced in July 1995 by a Five-Day Notice to Pay or Quit.** *See* Appendix B, Form 9.

10-Day Notice of Termination of Rental Agreement for Noncompliance with Rental Agreement Materially Affecting Health and Safety - Written notice given by the landlord to the tenant, pursuant to A.R.S. § 33-1368(A), informing the tenant that there is a noncompliance with the rental agreement

that material affects health and safety and that if not remedied by the tenant within five days of the notice, the rental agreement will terminate in ten days. **Replaced in July 1995 by a 5-Day Notice.** *See* Appendix B, Form 10.

10-Day Notice of Termination of Rental Agreement for Material Noncompliance with Rental Agreement - Written notice given by the landlord to the tenant, pursuant to A.R.S. § 33-1368(A), informing the tenant that there is a material noncompliance with the rental agreement and that if not remedied by the tenant within ten days of the notice, the rental agreement will terminate in ten days. *See* Appendix B, Form 11.

14-Day Notice of Termination of Rental Agreement for Material Noncompliance with Rental Agreement - Written notice given by the landlord to the tenant, pursuant to A.R.S. § 33-1368(A), informing the tenant that there is a material noncompliance with the rental agreement and that if not remedied by the tenant within ten days of the notice, the rental agreement will terminate in fourteen days. **Replaced in July 1995 by a 10-Day Notice.** *See* Appendix B, Form 11.

INDEX

- Words that appear in *highlighted text* (i.e., bold and italics) in the main section of the <u>Arizona Landlord's Deskbook</u> are found in this Index, followed by a list of pages where the term may be found.

- A page number followed by - **Q** - indicates that the term appears in the Quick Reference Section (pages 215 to 225).

- A page number followed by - **P** - indicates that the term appears in the Procedures Section (pages 225 to 255).

- A page number followed by - **Form** - indicates the location of a form that pertains to that term.

A B

G H I

Garnishment - *See* Writ of Garnishment.

Getting Tenants - *See* Chapter 5.

Inspection form - *See* Forms.

J K L M

N

O P

Q R

U V W X Y Z

1 - 14

NOTES

NOTES

NOTES

NOTES

ARIZONA RULES OF COURT

Published by West Group, available through Consumer Law Books Publishing House.

Includes:

- **Arizona Rules of Civil Procedure**
- **Arizona Rules of Criminal Procedure**
- **Arizona Rules of Evidence**
- **Arizona Rules of Civil Appellate Procedure**
- Arizona Rules of Procedure for Special Actions
- Arizona Rules of the Supreme Court
- **Uniform Rules of Practice of the Superior Court of Arizona**
- Rules of Practice for the Arizona Tax Court
- **Local Rules of Practice for the Superior Courts (all counties)**
- Uniform Rules of Procedure for Arbitration
- Uniform Rules of Practice for Medical Malpractice Cases
- Superior Court Rules of Appellate Procedure - Civil
- Superior Court Rules of Appellate Procedure - Criminal
- Rules of Procedure for Enforcement of Tribal Court Involuntary Commitment Orders
- Rules of Procedure for Judicial Review of Administrative Decisions
- Rules of Procedure for Juvenile Court
- **Rules of Procedure in Traffic Cases**
- **Rules of Procedure in Civil Traffic Violation Cases**
- Local Rules of Practice and Procedure - City Court - City of Phoenix
- Local Rules of Practice and Procedure - City Court - City of Tucson
- Rules of Procedure for the Commission on Judicial Conduct
- **Arizona Child Support Guidelines**
  - and more.

Only $49.95

(includes sales tax, shipping and handling)

To order your copy today, call the Consumer Law Books Publishing House Order Line:

1-800-229-7686

REGISTRATION FORM

If you purchased this book by calling the <u>Arizona Landlord's Deskbook</u> Order Desk or by mail from Consumer Law Books Publishing House, then you are **already registered** to receive notice when the laws change and the <u>Arizona Landlord's Deskbook</u> is updated in accordance therewith.

If you purchased this book at a bookstore or by any means other than stated above, then you are **not registered** and will not receive notice when the laws change and the <u>Arizona Landlord's Deskbook</u> is updated in accordance therewith **unless** you register. If you wish to be registered, simply complete the form below (or a copy of the form below) and mail it to the publisher.

REGISTRATION FORM

NAME	_____
ADDRESS	_____
	_____
	_____

Phone # _____

<u>Point of Purchase</u>:

☐ Bookstore (name of store) _____
☐ Mail order
☐ Other _____

Mail to: Consumer Law Books Publishing House
Post Office Box 16146
Phoenix, Arizona 85011-6146

ORDER DESK

To order additional copies of the <u>Arizona Landlord's Deskbook</u>, call:

1-800-229-7686